Global Crises and the Crisis of Global Leadership

This groundbreaking collection on global leadership features innovative and critical perspectives by scholars from international relations, political economy, medicine, law and philosophy, from North and South. The book's novel theorization of global leadership is situated historically within the classics of modern political theory and sociology, relating it to the crisis of global capitalism today. Contributors reflect on the multiple political, economic, social, ecological and ethical crises that constitute our current global predicament. The book suggests that there is an overarching condition of global organic crisis, which shapes the political and organizational responses of the dominant global leadership and of various subaltern forces. Contributors argue that meaningfully addressing the challenges of the global crisis will require far more effective, inclusive and legitimate forms of global leadership and global governance than those that have characterized the neoliberal era.

STEPHEN GILL is Distinguished Research Professor of Political Science, York University, Toronto, and a former Distinguished Scholar in International Political Economy of the International Studies Association. His publications include *The Global Political Economy* (with David Law, 1988), *American Hegemony and the Trilateral Commission* (Cambridge University Press 1991), *Gramsci, Historical Materialism and International Relations* (editor, Cambridge University Press 1993), *Power, Production and Social Reproduction* (with Isabella Bakker, 2003) and *Power and Resistance in the New World Order* (2003; second edition 2008).

Global Crises and the Crisis of Global Leadership

Edited by

Stephen Gill

CAMBRIDGE UNIVERSITY PRESS
Cambridge, New York, Melbourne, Madrid, Cape Town,
Singapore, São Paulo, Delhi, Tokyo, Mexico City

Cambridge University Press
The Edinburgh Building, Cambridge CB2 8RU, UK

Published in the United States of America by
Cambridge University Press, New York

www.cambridge.org
Information on this title: www.cambridge.org/9781107674967

First published 2012

Printed in the United Kingdom at the University Press, Cambridge

A catalogue record for this publication is available from the British Library

Library of Congress Cataloging-in-Publication Data

Global crises and the crisis of global leadership / edited by Stephen Gill.
   p. cm.
  ISBN 978-1-107-01478-7 (hbk.)– ISBN 978-1-107-67496-7 (pbk.)
  1. Political leadership. 2. Leadership. 3. Financial crises–History–
21st century. 4. Crises–History–21st century. I. Gill, Stephen, 1950-
  JC330.3.G56 2011
  352.23'6–dc23

                                  2011019262

ISBN 978-1-107-01478-7 Hardback
ISBN 978-1-107-67496-7 Paperback

To leaders of all parties and movements

Contents

Contributors

UPENDRA BAXI is Emeritus Professor of Law in Development, University of Warwick, and Emeritus Professor of Law, University of Delhi (1973–96), where he was also its Vice Chancellor (1990–94). He also served as Vice Chancellor, University of South Gujarat, Surat (1982–5); Honorary Director (Research), the Indian Law Institute (1985–8); and President of the Indian Society of International Law (1992–5). His recent publications include *The Future of Human Rights* (2008), *Human Rights in a Posthuman World: Critical Essays* (2007) and *The Right to Human Rights Education: Critical Essays* (2007).

SOLOMON (SOLLY) BENATAR is Emeritus Professor of Medicine, University of Cape Town, and currently Professor, Dalla Lana School of Public Health, University of Toronto. He is a founder member of the South African Academy of Science, and an elected Foreign Member of the United States National Academy of Science's Institute of Medicine and of the American Academy of Arts and Sciences. His publications include over 270 articles on respiratory diseases, academic freedom, health care services, medical ethics, human rights and global health. His most recent work is edited with Gillian Brock, *Global Health and Global Health Ethics* (Cambridge University Press 2011).

A. CLAIRE CUTLER is Professor of International Relations and International Law in the Political Science Department at the University of Victoria, Canada. Her publications include *Private Power and Global Authority: Transnational Merchant Law in the Global Political Economy* (Cambridge University Press 2003) and *Private Authority and International Affairs* (1999).

TIM DI MUZIO is a Postdoctoral Research Fellow at the Centre of Excellence in Global Governance Research, University of Helsinki, investigating questions connected to the future of the global political economy and the social reproduction of a globalized market civilization largely premised upon cheap fossil fuels. He has recently published articles in *Global Governance* and *New Political Economy*.

HILAL ELVER is Research Professor in Global and International Studies at the University of California, Santa Barbara, and former professor at the University of Ankara Law School. She was founding legal adviser to the Turkish government's Ministry of Environment and General Director of Women's Status in the Prime Minister's Office. Her publications include *Peaceful Uses of International Rivers: A Case of Euphrates and Tigris Rivers Basin* (2002), *Human Rights: Critical Concepts in Political Science* (co-editor with Richard Falk and Lisa Hajjar; five volumes, 2008) and a recently completed book manuscript, *Secularism and Religious Freedom in Constitutional Democracies*.

RICHARD A. FALK is Albert G. Milbank Professor Emeritus of International Law and Politics at Princeton University and, since 2002, Visiting Distinguished Research Professor in Global and International Studies at the University of California, Santa Barbara. The author of some fifty books, his recent works include *The Costs of War: International Law, the UN, and World Order after Iraq* (2008) and *Achieving Human Rights* (2009). He is Board Chair of the Nuclear Age Peace Foundation and, since 2008, Special Rapporteur for Occupied Palestinian Territories for the United Nations Human Rights Council.

STEPHEN GILL is Distinguished Research Professor of Political Science, York University, Toronto, and a former Distinguished Scholar in International Political Economy of the International Studies Association. His publications include *The Global Political Economy* (with David Law, 1988), *American Hegemony and the Trilateral Commission* (Cambridge University Press 1991), *Gramsci, Historical Materialism and International Relations* (editor, Cambridge University Press 1993), *Power, Production and Social Reproduction* (with Isabella Bakker, 2003) and *Power and Resistance in the New World Order* (2003; second edition 2008). Website: www.stephengill. com.

ADAM HARMES is Associate Professor in Political Science at the University of Western Ontario, Canada. He is the author of *Unseen Power: How Mutual Funds Threaten the Political and Economic Wealth of Nations* (2001) and *The Return of the State: Protestors, Power-Brokers and the New Global Compromise* (2004). He has also published essays in *New Left Review* and *Review of International Political Economy*.

MUSTAPHA KAMAL PASHA is Professor and Chair of the Department of Politics and International Relations at the University of Aberdeen,

United Kingdom. Previously, he taught at the School of International Service, American University, in Washington, DC (1993–2005). He is the author of *Colonial Political Economy* (1998) and co-author of *Out from Underdevelopment Revisited: Changing Global Structures and the Remaking of the Third World* (1997). He also co-edited *Protecting Human Security in a Post-9/11 World* (2007) and *International Relations and the New Inequality* (2002).

NICOLA SHORT is Associate Professor of Political Science, York University, Toronto. A former editor of *Millennium*, she is the author of *The International Politics of Post-Conflict Reconstruction in Guatemala* (2007). She has been a visiting scholar at the Centre for Global Political Economy at the University of Sussex, United Kingdom, and holds her PhD in International Relations from the London School of Economics.

INGAR SOLTY is Politics Editor of *Das Argument*, and co-founder and Board member of the North-Atlantic Left Dialogue (NALD), an annual summit of left intellectuals organized by the Rosa Luxemburg Foundation and funded by the German Foreign Office. He is the author of *Das Obama-Projekt* (2008) and co-author of *Der neue Imperialismus* (2004) and articles in *Capital and Class, Socialism and Democracy, Das Argument, Z* and other periodicals.

TEIVO TEIVAINEN is Professor of World Politics at the University of Helsinki as well as Director of the Program on Democracy and Global Transformation at the San Marcos University in Lima, Peru. He is a founding member of the International Council of the World Social Forum. His main publications include *A Possible World: Democratic Transformation of Global Institutions* (with Heikki Patomäki, 2004), *Pedagogía del poder mundial: Relaciones internacionales y lecciones del desarrollo en América Latina* (2003) and *Enter Economism, Exit Politics: Experts, Economic Policy and the Damage to Democracy* (2002).

Acronyms

CEO	chief executive officer
CGI	Clinton Global Initiative
CDSs	credit default swaps
CDOs	collateralized debt obligations
EU	European Union
G8	Group of Eight (heads of state)
G20	Group of Twenty (finance ministers and central bankers)
GATS	General Agreement on Trade in Services
GDP	gross domestic product
ICC	International Criminal Court
ICESCR	International Covenant on Economic, Social and Cultural Rights (United Nations)
ICJ	International Court of Justice
ICSID	International Center for the Settlement of Investment Disputes (World Bank)
ICWE	International Conference on Water and the Environment (1972)
ICZ	Islamic cultural zone
IFG	International Forum on Globalization
IFI	international financial institution
ILO	International Labour Organization
IMF	International Monetary Fund
IPCC	Intergovernmental Panel on Climate Change
ISDA	International Swaps and Derivatives Association
MAD	mutual assured destruction
MAS	Movement Toward Socialism (Bolivia)
ppm	parts per million (e.g. greenhouse gas concentrations)
NAFTA	North American Free Trade Agreement

OECD	Organisation for Economic Co-operation and Development
R2P	Responsibility to Protect
REN21	Renewable Energy Policy Network for the 21st Century
SAPs	Structural Adjustment Programs (supervised by the World Bank)
SEA	Single European Act
START	[Third US–Russian] Strategic Arms Reduction Treaty
TRIPS	Trade-Related aspects of International Property Rights (WTO agreement)
TUC	Trades Union Congress (UK)
UDHR	Universal Declaration of Human Rights
UN	United Nations
UNCED	UN Conference on Environment and Development (Rio de Janeiro, 1992)
UNDP	United Nations Development Programme
UNEP	United Nations Environmental Programme
UNFCCC	United Nations Framework Convention on Climate Change
UNHCHR	United Nations High Commissioner for Human Rights
UNICEF	United Nations Children's Fund
UNWFP	United Nations World Food Programme
WHO	World Health Organization
WSF	World Social Forum
WTO	World Trade Organization
WWC	World Water Council

Acknowledgements

This volume was created as part of a collective effort involving the reflections of the scholars of different generations who inaugurated the Helsinki Symposium at the Collegium for Advanced Studies of the University of Helsinki in early May 2010. The goal of the Symposium was to look beyond the necessary and important but nevertheless narrow focus on the global financial meltdown of 2007–10 that has preoccupied so many, to reflect on much deeper, more structural issues that affect our civilizations in the emerging world order. The contributors are drawn from the ranks of critical theorists from both the global North and the global South. The several disciplines that they reflect constitute some of the key fields of knowledge necessary for conceptualizing and understanding the intersecting global crises from the vantage point of both dominant and subaltern forces as they struggle over the making of our collective future. The contributors wrote their initial papers in the winter of 2009/10 and shared their ideas with each other and with members of the Collegium at the Helsinki Symposium. The volume is therefore global in its forms of knowledge, in its object of analysis and in regard to the geographical, cultural and intellectual backgrounds of its contributors. As noted, the discussions took place in Finland, a very globally oriented Nordic nation that also stands at the crossroads between East and West.

This was all made possible by the generosity and support of a number of organizations: as noted, the Collegium for Advanced Studies, University of Helsinki; the Jane and Aatos Erkko Foundation, Finland; the Canadian Social Science and Humanities Research Council; the Office of the Rector, University of Helsinki; the Centre of Excellence in Global Governance Research, University of Helsinki; the Finnish Institute of International Affairs; the Centre of Excellence in Research on European Law, University of Helsinki; the Faculty of Law, University of Helsinki; and the Department of Political Science and the Faculty of Arts, York University, Toronto.

Of course, it is not just organizations that support academic research; those who lead them often make all the difference. The fact that I was able to take up the Jane and Aatos Erkko Chair in the Study of

Contemporary Society at the Helsinki Collegium for Advanced Studies was made possible by the support of the former Vice President and Provost of York University, Sheila Embleton (now Distinguished Research Professor and herself a specialist on Finnish – and, indeed, many other languages), by the political theorist Professor George Comninel (Chair of the Department of Political Science, York University) and Robert Drummond (Professor of Political Science, York University), who supported me as the much-valued Dean of the Faculty of Arts as well as a warm colleague who has always sought to realize the potential of others.

Of my colleagues in Finland, my very warmest thanks go to Professor Juha Sihvola, who, when he was Director of the Helsinki Collegium, graciously invited me to spend what was a very enjoyable and productive year in Finland. When I got there I was also welcomed and kindly supported by Professor Sami Pihlström, a gifted philosopher who succeeded Juha as Director of the Collegium. I also express my sincere gratitude to his very fine colleague, Maria Soukkio, whose tremendous organizational skills – and good grace – were indispensable throughout my stay. I also warmly thank the following administrative members of the Collegium for their help and support: Kaisa Apell, Dr Kustaa Multamäki (now of the Academy of Finland), Tuomas Tammilehto, Aarno Villa (for his technical wizardry) and the two fine Collegium research assistants who worked with me throughout on this and related projects – Kirsi L. Reyes and Taavi Sundell. I consider myself to be very lucky indeed to have worked with such able, gifted and well-organized colleagues.

For their intellectual contribution, I am also particularly grateful to three Fellows of the Helsinki Collegium who acted as commentators at the Helsinki Symposium: Sara Heinämaa, Academy Research Fellow and Professor of Theoretical Philosophy, Uppsala University, Sweden; James Mittelman, Distinguished Visiting Fellow and University Professor of International Affairs, American University, Washington, DC; and Andreas Bieler, Research Fellow and Professor of Political Economy, University of Nottingham, United Kingdom.

I am very grateful to other colleagues and friends from Finland and overseas who helped with my work there: Otto Bruun, Giuseppe Caruso, Ruurik Holm, Nikolay Koposov, Elias Krohn, Liisa Laakso, Mikko I. Lahtinen, Aki Petteri Lehtinen, Maria Manner, Kaarlo Metsäranta, Petri Minkkinen, Tapio Ollikainen, Heikki Patomäki, Antti Ronkainen, Mika Rönkkö, Mikko Sauli, Marja Saviaro, Heikki Taimio, Teija H. Tiilikainen, Laura Tuominen, Raimo Väyrynen, Gereon Wolters and – last but not least – the film-maker Gustavo Consuegra, who made videos of conversations and events organized by the Collegium. These can be viewed on www.uni-utopia.net. In addition, the following gifted young intellectuals from York University made invaluable contributions to the construction of this volume: Karl Dahlquist, Paul Foley, Julian Germann, Hironori (Nori) Onuki and – not least – Adrienne Roberts, who produced a first-class synopsis of the Symposium discussions.

I am also indebted to three anonymous peer reviewers for insightful comments on the manuscript, and especially to John Haslam, Josephine Lane and Rosina Di Marzo at Cambridge University Press for excellent editorial work and support. I am particularly grateful for the added polish given to this book by Mike Richardson's first-class copy-editing work. I also thank Peter Scarth for the fine painting that underlies the cover image, and Greg Scarth for transforming it so successfully into its current design.

Last, I acknowledge and thank Isabella Bakker, Visiting Fellow of the Helsinki Collegium, Trudeau Fellow and Professor of Political Science at York University. She helped me to conceptualize and plan this volume and made numerous insightful comments on the manuscript as it was being developed. She co-chaired, co-hosted and helped to organize the May Symposium, including graciously hosting a fine reception and party following the debates that was greatly enjoyed by all involved. While I am responsible for this book's shortcomings, all the contributors and its readers should recognize that many of its strengths are due to her leadership, intellect, inspiration and theoretical imagination. Indeed, it is appropriate that these acknowledgements should contain at least one of her views on the question of leadership, as reflected in the following exchange from her favourite movie, *Chinatown* (1974):

JAKE GITTES: Why are you doing it? How much better can you eat? What could you buy that you can't already afford?
NOAH CROSS: The future, Mr Gittes! The future.

Stephen Gill

Introduction: global crises and the crisis of global leadership

Stephen Gill

The subject of this book is global *crises* and the crisis of global leadership. Its title refers to crises, in the plural, because – despite the incessant and important focus on the financial and economic crisis that has preoccupied much of the world over the past three years – in the current global conjuncture the world faces a diversity of intersecting, but none-theless ontologically distinct, crises. These are located not only within political economy but also in ethics, law, society, culture and ecology – and they all call into question the prevailing models of global development and governance. Nevertheless, although these intersecting crises are distinct, most of the authors in this collection connect them with some of the contradictions associated with the current neoliberal phase of global capitalism. Taken together, these crises may be said to combine in what I call a *global organic crisis*.

The term 'global leadership' is initially used in this volume in the *singular*, since there is an identifiable, neoliberal nexus of ideas, institutions and interests that dominates global political and civil society – one that is associated with the most powerful states and corporations. This nexus involves a form of leadership and expertise intended to sustain and enlarge capitalist market society and its associated principles of governance; in particular, it claims to provide effective mechanisms of stabilization and the ability to master crises – a claim of competence that is challenged in this book. Moreover, although neoliberal crisis management is preoccupied with economic stabilization, it has generally made minimal effort to address the fundamental crises of livelihood and social reproduction (the way in which production is connected to the wider social conditions within which it operates) that afflict a majority of the world's population, such as the global health, food, energy and ecological crises. Moreover, in responding to crises, neoliberal political leaders have frequently sought to make 'unholy' alliances with

I am particularly grateful to Isabella Bakker for comments and to Julian Germann for research assistance in connection with this chapter.

1

authoritarian and dictatorial forces, particularly in much of the Third World; in both North and South they have also sought to maintain a condition of depoliticization and political apathy. The goal has been to channel and incorporate forms of resistance and contain fundamental political contestation as to the nature and purposes of rule. Whether this strategy can continue is an open question.

Indeed, in several parts of the world, this neoliberal governing formula of authoritarianism and/or controlled electoral democracy/depoliticization is coming under increasing, popular, grassroots pressure. It is not just in Latin America that this is happening, where, in Venezuela and Bolivia, 'twenty-first-century' socialism has produced a substantial shift towards a new political order, consolidating progressive, more democratic constitutional forms as well as new regional economic and security alliances outside US control. In early 2011 a wave of Arab revolt, originating in Tunisia, spread throughout the Middle East. It encompassed not only the epicentre of Arab civilization, in Egypt, but also moved quickly to Algeria, Morocco, Libya, Yemen and Bahrain. It was met initially with repression in some contexts, particularly brutal in Libya, provoking civil war and panic in the oil markets. In Tunisia and Egypt, peaceful protests – with protesters, apparently, behaving en masse as a form of revolutionary collective leadership – quickly forced the resignation of their long-standing military dictators. Demands were made for a new political order, with more democracy, redistribution and meaningful rights. The protests were motivated by a variety of grievances but originated in outrage concerning the way that authoritarian and dictatorial leaders had, particularly since the early 1990s, orchestrated policies directed by the International Monetary Fund (IMF) of neoliberal restructuring, including privatization, to plunder the state and the economy for themselves and for their business allies – while the majority suffered poverty, mass unemployment, and soaring food prices as well as repression and a denial of basic rights and dignity. This state of affairs was widely perceived as being orchestrated by the strategic interests of the United States and Israel with Arab leaders as its subordinates, despite widespread popular opposition to Israeli policies, particularly in Palestine. The regional uprisings drew on a broad swathe of spontaneous and organized *secular* forces in ways that put to rest the Orientalist myth that inheres in the 'clash of civilizations' hypothesis – specifically, that Muslim masses can be mobilized only through religion (see Chapter 8, by Mustapha Pasha). The uprisings also refute 'the claim of American-sponsored dictators that they are the great bulwark against a rising tide of "Islamo-fascism" (a word of American coinage) that is sweeping the Arab lands. What are in fact sweeping across the Arab world today are the good old values of the French Revolution' (Ahmad 2011).[1] What these revolutionary changes share is their secular, democratic form and a repudiation of years of imperialism and neoliberal restructuring. In the Arab world they herald, particularly given the novel ways in which they combine spontaneous and organized forces in a mass collective leadership, 'the autumn of the patriarchs' (Ahmad 2011). These forms seem to be consistent with an emergent 'postmodern prince' (see Chapter 13).

By contrast, neoliberal leadership operates from the 'top down' to underpin 'market civilization' and its governing discourse of 'disciplinary neoliberalism' (Gill 1995a). Such leadership – which operates systematically to favour affluent strata of the population – seeks to stabilize dominant power structures and strategies of rule, albeit with some marginal modifications under crisis conditions in ways that do not fundamentally challenge the dominant modes of accumulation and power. This formula is what we can expect to guide the powerful Egyptian army in the aftermath of President Mubarak's resignation, taking its political guidance from the United States and Israel. Whether this moment signals not only the probable end of patriarchal leadership but, more acutely, the end of disciplinary neoliberalism in the Arab world is a more open question. Neoliberalism can go with authoritarian, technocratic or, indeed, limited electoral forms of leadership and indirect democracy. Strategic cooperation between Israel, Egypt and the United States guarantees Israeli domination of the region; Egypt offers the Pentagon a crucial military platform and privileged access to the Suez Canal, and so the United States will seek to maintain its strategic assets in Egypt. The United States may 'allow a controlled democratizing process ... and hope that the elections held under this umbrella will be won mainly by the liberal, IMF-oriented elite' – the very outcome, Aijaz Ahmad (2011) notes, that many of the protesters have hoped for. Progressive forces seeking an authentic revolution may therefore come to be co-opted and constrained in a 'passive revolution', to use Antonio Gramsci's phrase (Hoare and Nowell-Smith 1971).

This global situation helps form some of the backdrop to the considerations of this volume. Indeed, one of the key features of disciplinary neoliberalism since its emergence in the 1970s is how, until now, its crises of accumulation (e.g. debt and financial crises) have also provided opportunities for dominant forces to extend and deepen neoliberalism

---

[1] Aijaz Ahmad (2011) cites a report by the Carnegie Endowment for International Peace of February 2010 that there were over 3,000 protests by Egyptian workers between 2004 and 2010 – a level of organized collective action that dwarfs the 2011 political protests 'in both scale and consequence'.

as a geopolitical project, as I noted in the early 1990s (Gill 1990; see also Panitch, Albo and Chibber 2011). In the present conjuncture, dominant forces in the global North have taken advantage of the crisis of accumulation to deepen and extend disciplinary neoliberalism – a strategy facilitated by the general absence of significant, organized forces of opposition. As has been noted, this is less obviously the case in the global South, where the global crisis of accumulation coincides with a crisis of authoritarian rule, perhaps opening up new possibilities for progressive forces to press for new forms of governance.

A crisis of neoliberalism?

In this context, a number of influential commentators have been arguing recently that the global crisis of accumulation is also a fundamental crisis of neoliberalism. This argument is also widespread in the popular and academic literature. Communist philosopher Slavoj Žižek (2009), for example, argues that neoliberalism actually 'died twice': as a 'political doctrine' after 9/11 (the attacks on the United States on 11 September 2001 that resulted in the destruction of the World Trade Center and part of the Pentagon), and as a 'utopian economic project' after the financial meltdown of 2007. Indeed, variants of the Žižek hypothesis concerning the 'end' of neoliberalism have become the conventional wisdom across various disciplines and theoretical standpoints; for example, Nobel Prizewinners in economics Joseph Stiglitz (2010) and Paul Krugman (2009a) see the economic crisis as provoking the end of neoliberalism and market fundamentalism. Nevertheless, the majority of the works produced on the recent global crisis of accumulation, including those by Stiglitz and Krugman, ultimately seek to stabilize and reproduce the principal aspects of the existing capitalist order, albeit with improved financial and prudential regulation and some redistribution (for macro-economic as well as political reasons).

Krugman, Stiglitz and Žižek all, in their different ways (I believe), tend to misread our present global situation. They also beg the question: what is neoliberalism and how do we define it? Moreover, how do we know when it has ended? Indeed, most economists treat neoliberalism as if it is simply an economic doctrine and set of policy formulas; Žižek seems to treat it as a form of ideology underpinned by relations of violence, and separates its 'political' and 'economic' dimensions, whereas the two are, in reality, combined.

By contrast, the contributors to this volume see neoliberalism as more complex: not only as a set of doctrines and ideologies but also, and simultaneously, as a set of social forces deeply connected to and inscribed in the restructuring of global political and civil society – and, indeed, connected to the reconstitution of the self in ways that frame what is deemed politically and economically possible. Put differently, disciplinary neoliberalism fosters and consolidates a possessively individualist, marketized 'common sense' that militates against solidarity and social justice; however, it is a normative project, one that is contested yet still dominant (rather than hegemonic). Moreover, it is worth remembering that not only has disciplinary neoliberalism as a set of institutions and policy frameworks been advanced through the imposition of policy frameworks in the context of crises of accumulation but also, in the terminology used by the World Bank, it has been 'locked in' by the proliferation of new liberal constitutions or major constitutional revisions since the 1980s (involving perhaps eighty nations in all), as well as by the many liberalizing trade and investment agreements such as the World Trade Organization (WTO) and North American Free Trade Agreement (NAFTA) and, not least, by a key feature of the past three decades: the adoption of constitutionally guaranteed arrangements for macroeconomic policies such as the creation of independent central banks and balanced budget laws. I call the sum of these arrangements the *new constitutionalism*. They are intended to shape economic reforms and policies in a neoliberal direction, and to make alternative development models to market civilization, such as communism or even forms of state capitalism, much more difficult to bring about. New constitutional frameworks and laws are very difficult – though not impossible – to change (Gill 1992, 1998a, 1998b).

Nevertheless, the prestige of the neoliberal globalizing elites and political leaders has been called significantly into question as a result of the financial meltdown and its negative economic and social repercussions. What seems to be missing from many of the prevailing policy debates – reflecting the narrowly materialist and possessive individualism that pervades neoliberal political consciousness – are a large number of the crucial issues that were marginalized from consideration during the financial meltdown, such as transformations in health, energy supplies, the challenges of climate change, and issues of livelihood (associated, for example, with the provisioning of freshwater and the apparently inexorable rise in global food prices). In sum, at issue is how basic conditions of existence are increasingly mediated by the world capitalist market system and under neoliberal governance arrangements.

This volume is alive to such concerns. It also takes seriously the possibilities for the emergence of alternative forms of global leadership. Nonetheless, at the time of writing it remains the case that, despite the fact that the crisis of accumulation has been deep and relatively extensive, it has not provoked a corresponding crisis of legitimacy for neoliberal governance in the global North, where its impact has arguably been greatest. Nor, indeed, has it in much of the global South, although Latin America provides a number of important progressive exceptions to this generalization. Furthermore, evidence from the most recent conclave of the world's plutocrats and political and corporate leaders in Davos, at the 2011 annual meeting of the World Economic Forum, suggests that, although the leaders of the globalizing élites assume they have weathered the political storms caused by the economic and financial meltdown, they remain concerned about questions of 'global security', by which they mean the security of capital and their worldwide investments, particularly in light of the 2011 uprisings in Egypt and elsewhere in the Arab world. This indicates that the global situation may be in flux.

This book therefore interrogates these moments of crisis and leadership. It explores some of the national and global ideologies, practices and associated forms of power, authority and legitimacy and how they connect to different conceptions and forms of leadership, including that of experts (epistemic communities), politicians, plutocrats, supreme courts and other justices, and, not least, the organic intellectuals of both ruling elements and subaltern forces as they struggle to define concepts that can justify and direct the exercise of authority and the actual or potential direction of national and global society. Specifically at issue is how these forms of leadership may – or may not – perceive, understand or respond to a range of crises (economic, social and ecological) that pose deep threats to aspects of life and livelihood on the planet – that is, to the combined challenge of an emerging *global organic crisis* (Gill 1995a, 2003a, 2008, 2010).

Nonetheless, some might query whether there really is, actually or potentially, a 'global' organic crisis, since many parts of the world, such as India and China, have continued to grow and develop; indeed, Craig Murphy has noted that many parts of the global South have had a 'good crisis', insofar as many of the reforms that they implemented in response to the Asian financial and economic crisis of 1997–8 have made their financial structures and patterns of economic development more internally robust and better insulated from external financial shocks originating in New York, London or Tokyo (Murphy 2010). Murphy's point is well made. It is of course important to emphasize the geographical and social unevenness of both the experience and impacts of financial and economic crises across the global social and geopolitical hierarchy.

However, this is only part of the story. It is also important to reflect critically on the nature and quality of existing development patterns, particularly those that serve to generalize the dominant model of market civilization – a development model that is wasteful, energy-intensive, consumerist, ecologically myopic and premised on catering mainly to the affluent. Moreover, the development of China and India is far from the happy story some seem to paint – a point that the Chinese leadership seems to have recently acknowledged by prioritizing redistribution and social welfare in its next five-year plan, not least to deal with growing social and ecological contradictions and widespread political unrest. For example, every day in China there are enormous numbers of localized protests concerning living conditions and corruption. Illustrating the displacement of livelihoods and the crisis of social reproduction that characterizes the present phase of primitive accumulation in China, the government estimates that 58 million 'left-behind children' (almost 20 per cent of all children in China and about a half of the children living in the countryside) now live with their grandparents or in foster centres, because their parents have left to earn income in the factories and cities (Hille 2011):

Mao sent millions of parents into labour camps and their children to the countryside; he forced families to abandon the stoves in their homes and to use communal kitchens and dorms. Even so, Mao failed, ultimately, to destroy the family as the basic cell of Chinese society. Today, what the dictator was unable to accomplish with force is being realized instead by the lure of money.

Meanwhile, in India, we see mass suicides of farmers as a debt crisis envelops their lives; elsewhere in the country perhaps as many as 800 million poor people have been hardly touched by the changes. Most live in the shadow of 'shining India'. The global situation is therefore replete with deep contradictions. On the one hand, few would deny that material conditions are improving for many Chinese and Indians, and that this should continue to be the case. On the other hand, if the market civilization model of capitalist development not only continues in the wealthier countries but also becomes more generalized in India, China and other large developing countries such as Brazil (notwithstanding President Lula's redistributive policies), and also assuming that the US rulers sustain their policies and military capabilities along similar lines to now in order to defend and extend that model, I hypothesize that the global organic crisis will intensify. Its effects will be felt in ways that will be uneven geographically, unequal politically and socially and materially hierarchical. Put differently, the organic crisis may also be globalizing across regions and societies at varying speeds, and it will probably be differentiated in its effects on life chances and basic conditions of existence, generating diverse political effects within and across jurisdictions and throughout the social and political spectrum. Politically, and perhaps paradoxically, at this moment the global organic crisis has *not* been manifested as a crisis of legitimacy in the global North (although less so in many parts of the global South). However, the question is: will this situation persist – and, indeed, can the current neoliberal frameworks of global leadership retain legitimacy and credibility while developing a constructive and meaningful set of policies to address it? If not, what are the prospects for alternative concepts of global leadership and frameworks of rule?

Questions and issues addressed

This issue – which centres on the relations between rulers and ruled and on the purposes of political power – helps to frame many of the contributions in this book, since it points the way for a rethinking of some of the questions of crisis, leadership, democracy, justice and sustainability in the emerging world order.

In this context, the objective of this volume is twofold: to be both analytical and normative. These objectives – the 'is' and the 'ought' of politics – are interconnected. Indeed, Gramsci (Hoare and Nowell-Smith 1971: 144) once observed in 'The modern prince' that, in the field of political science, what is most 'primordial' and 'real' in political life is often ignored, notably the basic question of what constitutes the relations between leaders and led, and how this distinction is socially and politically constructed and reproduced – indeed, whether the purpose of leadership is either to maintain or, ultimately, to abolish this very distinction in order to create new forms of global social and political relations.

To give focus to this volume, contributors were asked to address a common set of issues, listed below. Each of these issues relates to one or other of two central and interrelated questions. (1) Leadership of what, for whom and with what purpose? (2) Crises of what, for whom and with what repercussions?

Contributors were asked, therefore, to focus on some of the following issues.

(1) What do global crises tell us about the nature of political representation and the legitimacy and efficacy of national, regional and global institutions in situations of crisis?
(2) What is the relation between consent and coercion, and between force and persuasion, in the theory and practice of global leadership?
(3) How is local and global consent or acquiescence to neoliberal governance developed and sustained in situations of crisis? What is the role in this regard of the institutions of global governance (such as the G8 and G20), the media or leadership by experts?

(4) How do modes of governance premised upon the primacy of the world market relate to local and global provisions for human rights, welfare, health, livelihood, human security and human development, in North and South?

(5) What do current patterns of global development imply for the carrying capacity of the planet?

(6) What is the relation between global crises and the processes of what Karl Marx called original accumulation and dispossession? How do these relate to basic issues of livelihood, health, sustainability and the integrity of the biosphere?

(7) How are crises and patterns of global leadership mediated by ideology, religion, myth and patterns of identity? How, for example, does Orientalism mediate the relations between the leadership, politics and ethics of Islamic communities and those of the 'West'?

(8) Why, despite the depth and scale of contemporary crises, particularly those associated with finance and capital accumulation since 2007, is the prevailing response still, at the time of writing, defined by the dominant neoliberal narratives, institutions, actors and expert communities? Why has this deep crisis of global capitalism not provoked a deep crisis of legitimacy, a crisis in dominant forms of rule or a turning point in global leadership? How far can we expect this to continue to be the case?

(9) What, therefore, are other forms of global leadership – reactionary or progressive – that can be imagined and anticipated as we look towards the foreseeable future?

Lineages and concepts

The considerations that motivate this book can be read as a new research agenda on the perennial and often imperial theme of leadership in world affairs and, specifically, how that leadership has addressed – and may address – global crises. Of course, in ancient civilizations, much of this related to the strategies of kings and rulers, in the form of guidance from philosophers and diplomatic advisers.[2]

---

[2] 'During the end of the fourth century and the beginning of the fifth century BC in China, Confucius and Mencius wrote essays on the proper behaviour of leaders. Aristotle, in his *Politics*, describes the characteristics of the kings and kingship in ancient Greece (fourth century BC). In eleventh-century Iran, Unsuru'l-Ma'ali wrote *Qabus-Nameh* and Nezam Mulk Tussi wrote *Siyassat Nameh*, advising kings on effective governance.' Julian Germann, 'Global leadership', unpublished aide-mémoire prepared for the Helsinki Symposium, May 2010.

A number of works began to shift the focus of these considerations away from the inter-dynastic power struggles of their times and focused, respectively, on the material and historical conditions of leadership, and on ways to rethink the relationship between leaders and led in and across different social formations. Ibn Khaldun of Tunis provided observations and guidance on the material conditions of the rise and fall of civilizations and questions of political rule in the Maghreb in the fourteenth century (Abd al-Rahman ibn and Issawi 1950; Pasha 1997). In Renaissance Italy, Niccolò Machiavelli drew on the exemplars of history and myth as a guide to virtuous and effective leadership, embodied in the form of the ideal *condottiere* (Machiavelli 1975 [1513]).[3] *The Prince* was intended not only to help guide the most powerful dynastic houses of Italy in their statecraft but also to show the way forward to the possibilities for Italian unification – under conditions of imperial domination whereby the affairs of the peninsula were subordinated externally by the integral power of Spain and France. However, *The Prince* was a critical work, also intended to provide instruction on the ethics and practice of political leadership to the common people in the piazza. As Gramsci (Hoare and Nowell-Smith 1971: 126) put it, 'In the conclusion, Machiavelli merges with the people, becomes the people,' noting that the epilogue of *The Prince* is a political manifesto providing both criteria for virtuous forms of rule and an instruction manual, explaining to those 'not in the know' exactly how rulers actually rule. In turn, Gramsci provided his own meditation on ethical and moral leadership, and the role and organization of national and global political parties, which he saw as a necessary precursor to the winning of governmental power – the communist party was the 'modern prince'. From this reading, then, political leadership involves the relations between leaders and led, and leaders provide not only political organization and judgement but also ethical and moral qualities that are concerned with the nature and future direction of society.

However, despite this lineage, the concept and basis of *global* leadership and its relationship to crises continues to be inadequately understood and poorly theorized in the social sciences. There are, of course, some very notable exceptions, such as the work of the late Franz Neumann (1942), E. H. Carr (1946) and Giovanni Arrighi (1982). Nonetheless, much of the modern literature has not advanced further than the 'great man' approach, despite the fact that the best of that

---

[3] See the Glossary for an explanation of terms such as 'condottiere'.

literature contains important reflections on history and the making of world orders (such as Acheson 1969).[4] However, the majority of such work is more narrowly focused and principally concerned to provide 'advice to the prince' as to how to rule his subjects – and those of other countries – albeit in an era in which US global power is perceived as being in crisis (Brzezinski 2004, 2008). A large proportion of this literature is preoccupied with seeking to ensure that US power or imperialism remains the leading force in world affairs – a perspective that assumes the superiority of both US liberal democracy and the forms of neoliberal capitalism it seeks to extend globally (see, for example, Halperin *et al.* 2007). This perspective thus endorses a set of imperial practices premised on inequality that deny the freedom and potential of others. Put differently, it endorses a hypocritical form of global leadership that actively negates the central moral claim of liberal democracy: that it provides the optimum political and economic conditions for all human beings to actualize their potential.

Much of the remaining international relations literature on global leadership is either narrowly concerned with such formation of political elites or the shifting patterns of power politics (e.g. the current preoccupation with potential shifts of leadership towards the Asia-Pacific powers). In addition, this literature has an instrumentalist and utilitarian rather than an ethical-political frame of reference. Much of this literature assumes that the stability of the existing order is the most important political good, and that the principal role of leadership is associated with sustaining order and managing crises. A key example of this is the neorealist theory of hegemonic stability (Kindleberger 1973). It generally argues that, particularly in situations of global economic crisis, a dominant (hegemonic) power must have both the capability and the will to lead and must enforce economic openness and the liberal rules that govern the world economic order, or else a crisis may result in its collapse. From this perspective, many of the problems of the Great Depression of the 1930s are attributed to the fact that the United States had the capability to lead but did not do so; it failed to act as lender of last resort or to manage the interbank payment system when the financial system came under pressure – in significant contrast with the early twenty-first century, when stimulus

---

[4] This 'great man' heritage is present in much of the specialized literature on global leadership forums such as the G8/G20 summits. Akin to diplomatic history, this literature tends to approach leadership as a chronicle of personalities, events and negotiations (see Bayne 2000, 2005, and Hodges 1999).

measures inspired by the thinking of John Maynard Keynes have been clearly and massively in evidence.[5]

A rival set of Marxist theorizations of global leadership draws upon Vladimir Lenin's concept of inter-imperial rivalry between capitalist states – a rivalry assumed to intensify in situations of global economic crisis, caused principally by the over-accumulation of capital and/or under-consumption. Others draw on Karl Kautsky's concept of 'ultra-imperialism', and argue that cooperation may be possible involving a *temporary* truce between otherwise hostile capitalist entities (on both, see Callinicos 2009). An intermediate position in these debates is that the cohesion of capitalist states after 1945 is due to the 'super-imperialism' of the United States – in effect, a Marxist variant of the theory of hegemonic stability that sees the United States as the guarantor of global capitalism. It sees global cooperation as a product of American super-imperialism and 'empire' (Gowan 1999, 2010; Panitch and Konings 2008). Similarly, it sees the roots of the present crisis in US-led neoliberalism and Wall Street finance.[6] Other post-Marxist literature elaborates a structural variant of the empire hypothesis that global power inheres in the networks of capitalism with no leadership element per se (see, for example, Hardt and Negri 2001). An influential world systems thesis sees a 'transnational capitalist class' directing the project of globalization (see, for example, Sklair 2000 and Robinson 2004). This more instrumentalist perspective assumes that the said transnational capitalist class – as a kind of executive committee for the global bourgeoisie – has both the unity of purpose and the political capability to overcome two fundamental global crises (Sklair 2001: 6):

The transnational capitalist class is working consciously to resolve two central crises, namely (i) the simultaneous creation of increasing poverty and increasing wealth within and between communities and societies (the class polarisation crisis) and (ii) the unsustainability of the system (the ecological crisis).

---

[5] A modified 'liberal realist' version of this perspective is influential in G8 ruling circles as a result of the Ford Foundation-funded Princeton Project, embraced by the administration of President Obama; one of the leaders of that project, Anne-Marie Slaughter, is a key official in the US Department of State under Hillary Clinton (Ikenberry and Slaughter 2006; Clark 2009). Simultaneously, the Obama administration employed its massive stimulus and bailout programme to avoid another Great Depression.

[6] Referring to 'the present crisis' (in the singular), the editors of *Socialist Register* note in their preface that 'the speculative orgy that neoliberalism unleashed' will be followed by austerity and 'the possibility of long-term stagnation' (Panitch, Albo and Chibber 2011). Similarly, David McNally (2011) argues that, although neoliberal restructuring in the 1970s and subsequently was able to generate economic expansion, the deep recession of 2008–10 is a turning point that will be followed by a 'global slump', an era of shrinking markets, austerity and growing political conflict.

The enormous business literature on global leadership is also concerned with the problems confronting the transnational capitalist class, but sees these principally not as political and ecological challenges (and implicitly questions of legitimacy) but as problems of efficient corporate management or administration, decision-making and processes, and cultural and political sensitivity to local conditions. The litmus test of leadership is the level of profit in global markets. Oddly enough, relatively neglected in the management literature – as well as in much of the literature just reviewed – are the many important global forums that help to shape the strategic perspectives of capital and the state. Examples include the World Business Council on Sustainable Development and the scenario planning used by corporations and government agencies (e.g. by Shell, whose methods have been used by the CIA) not only to influence policy but also to anticipate political challenges to economic and cultural globalization. Organizations such as the World Economic Forum, the Trilateral Commission and the new Clinton Global Initiative (CGI) bring together dominant globalizing élites from government, corporations, universities, political parties, media, entertainment, the sciences and the arts to forge a consensus and to initiate strategic concepts of global leadership. What seems to be missing from these initiatives is precisely what Sklair (2000) claims was being attempted over a decade ago: comprehensive *evidence* of well-resourced, broad-based and serious efforts to deal with ever-widening global inequality, the systematic undermining and dispossession of livelihoods and growing threats to the integrity of the biosphere. The fact that this evidence is not forthcoming is perhaps not surprising if one reflects on the realities of the existing state of relations between rulers and ruled on a world scale. Why should international capitalists worry about growing global inequality and class polarization, or, indeed, the future of the planet, if there are no powerful political forces that force them to do so? Perhaps a more convincing hypothesis is that, far from creating a coherent redistributive and ecologically sustainable structure of globalization presided over by a transnational capitalist class, the opposite is true. What is gradually emerging is a more and more unequal and increasingly hierarchical global political and civil society directed by dominant social forces associated with disciplinary neoliberalism that seek to extend market civilization on a world scale, in ways that will further class polarization and the ecological crisis alike.

Finally, several of the perspectives just reviewed fail to account for the fact that, despite international conflicts and rivalries, in contrast to the Long Depression of the late nineteenth century, and the world economic crisis of the 1930s, ever since the 1970s economic crises seem to have produced greater, more institutionalized and geopolitic-ally extensive cooperation among capitalist states, in ways that cannot be simply reduced to US power or 'empire', on the one hand, or to the instrumentalities of an executive committee of the transnational capitalist class, on the other. We need to take account of the changing structures of world order and the reorganization of the global political economy, which has progressively produced a more globally inte-grated, albeit crisis-prone, and increasingly global capitalism. Only with a clearer ontology of world order can we more adequately begin to theorize patterns of cooperation and conflict associated with global crises (for analyses of this question, see Cox 1987, Gill 1990 and van der Pijl 1984, 1998).

Global leadership and the making of history

Global leadership is therefore a part of a global dialectic that serves to constitute the making of history. To understand this process, our theori-zations must proceed historically. One way to think about this is to conceptualize the relations between leaders and led, both within and across states, as depending upon and being shaped by the formation, perspectives, leadership and organization of *historical blocs* of social forces, including their ethical and political perspectives. A historical bloc forms the basis for political rule in a particular form of state, since it encompasses the leading forces that operate within political and civil society. It entails a combination of ideas, institutions and material potentials that shape the direction of state and civil society both within and across different jurisdictional boundaries.

Global leadership therefore has to be based in the historical blocs that have substantial anchorage in the forces of political and civil society across a range of jurisdictions. Indeed, it must involve analytical, peda-gogical, ethical and political qualities: leaders must not only seek to define what is unique and specific about the current conjuncture in their communications with those they lead and organize, but they must also find ways to justify a course of action and mobilize resources to act effectively on it. There is, therefore, an ethical and moral dimension to leadership that this volume takes seriously, both as an object of analysis and as a normative commitment. Here realistic analysis of the current forms and patterns of global leadership relative to the crises in world order is combined simultaneously with an endeavour to imagine and explore prospects for new kinds of global leadership that might be collective, progressive, democratic, tolerant and consistent with eco-logical and social sustainability.

The contributors see a basic responsibility of critical intellectuals as the need to explain the nature of our global predicament and to offer alternative paradigms of progress and leadership. There is also a belief that a vast collective effort is needed to help shift world development away from continuation of its currently destructive logic, and, indeed, to avert more reactionary solutions based on authoritarianism, neo-fascism and right-wing populism. The situation is acute, as it would appear that key aspects of the old order seem to be no longer sustainable. However, a new order is still in the throes of being born. Nevertheless, in one important respect today's conjuncture is dissimilar to the 1930s, in that, at least in the global North, the left seems to have offered only limited resistance and few credible alternatives to the neoliberal responses to the crisis of accumulation of the past three years.

The present conjuncture therefore has specific features. As such, it forms a somewhat different object of analysis from that of one of my first books on questions of global hegemony and leadership (Gill 1990). Then the focus was on the emerging global order at the end of the Cold War. That moment formed a key turning point at the end of the long postwar crisis of superpower relations, between 1947 and 1991, when the world – in the throes of a long economic expansion – was organized on both East–West and North–South geopolitical axes. This was a world order characterized by two rival hegemonies, each with the capacity to destroy life on the planet (a capacity they retain). The 'end' of the Cold War therefore posed the question of world leadership and the future of world order in an acute way. My study examined the ideology and consciousness of the globalizing élites in an emerging transnational power bloc that was linked to the extension of liberal capitalism – ideology and consciousness were not seen simply as the reflection of material forces. Global leadership, at least in the 'West', involved organic intellectuals drawn from both the 'public' and 'private' sectors, from governments (including the intelligence and military apparatuses) and political and civil societies of the metropolitan capitalist countries of North America, western Europe and Japan, as well as from international organizations such as the North Atlantic Treaty Organization (NATO), the IMF, the World Bank and, to a lesser extent, the United Nations (UN). The strategic goals (grand strategy) of the US-led Western international historical bloc were to promote a liberal world order (capitalist globalization), to marginalize communism or socialism and to oppose economic nationalism.

The 'private' leadership forums within this bloc, such as the Trilateral Commission and its sister organization at Davos, the World

Economic Forum, were, in effect, parts of a prototypical global political party of capital, and they have been designed to do two things: (1) to promote strategic initiatives to shift the balance of global forces and geopolitical alignments in ways beneficial to transnational capitalism; and (2) to 'master' or manage the crises of capitalist development. If these two tasks were performed successfully they would enhance the prestige of leadership and marginalize opposition and alternative frameworks for organizing world order. As noted, these well-organized forces of capital have been able to define responses to crises in ways that have intensified market disciplines and privatization, promoted liberal constitutional frameworks and extended private property rights – albeit at the expense of greater social inequality and growing ecological crises.

Since the late 1970s economic crises have therefore been a means to restructure social, class and geopolitical relations to favour capital, especially finance capital, on a world scale – namely the North–South and East–West geopolitical axes, as well as the social relations between capital and labour. The power of capital has expanded its global reach, membership and institutional frameworks, as with the WTO and NAFTA, the latter created in 1994. Its nexus of power now incorporates countries such as Mexico, India and China, which have become more economically powerful – reflecting the widening poles of capital accumulation. Since the 1990s the leaders of the major capitalist states in the G8 and G20 have based their approaches to governance chiefly on the primacy of the world market and the discrediting of alternative social projects of leadership, rule and governance. This has also been accompanied by a situation of impunity for the political leaders of the United States, which has strengthened its already huge military capability and encircled the globe in a ring of steel to extend and protect its foreign 'assets', not least in terms of the control of foreign oil and minerals, as in Iraq and Afghanistan.

Nevertheless, the recent financial crash (which had previously been deemed impossible by G8 political leaders, central bankers and the vast majority of mainstream economists), and its aftermath of economic emergency involving huge bailouts of banks and efforts to stabilize the macroeconomics of global capitalism, have raised serious questions about the sustainability – and, indeed, the credibility – of neoliberal forms of governance. A key question for this book is therefore: how far is this situation provoking a crisis or a turning point in global leadership? Have we reached a moment, or can we foresee a moment, when this type of global leadership is no longer credible, has lost its prestige and is to be made fully accountable for the way in which its actions and policies have been inconsistent with or inimical to the human rights of its citizens and those of other countries?[7]

Contents and organization of the book

With these observations in mind, this book strives to contribute to a realistic and critical analysis of global power relations and structures, as well as imagining feasible futures, including those governed by alternative practices of leadership to those that have prevailed in the early twenty-first century. In this sense, perhaps the central question that gives focus to the considerations here is encapsulated in this quotation from Gramsci (Hoare and Nowell-Smith 1971: 144):

In the formation of leaders, one premise is fundamental: is it the intention that there should always be rulers and ruled, or is the objective to create the conditions in which this division...of the human race...is no longer necessary?

The book therefore articulates and debates rival concepts, principles and forms of global ethical and political leadership, and links these considerations to the question of new and emerging forms of global political agency and global governance in the early twenty-first century. Put differently, the volume considers whether there is an emerging global ethical crisis or crisis of hegemony that calls out for alternative paradigms of global development and new frameworks of law, constitutionalism and governance.

For purposes of exposition this book is organized into four parts, although many of the contributions overlap and, indeed, go beyond

---

[7] Given the international legal obligations of *all* UN member governments to protect and to fulfil the human rights of their people, including their economic and social rights, it is perhaps significant that it is at this present juncture that the UN has engaged in its first ever Universal Periodic Review of the United States. It involved an assessment of US policies associated with the financial collapse and whether US government responses were consistent with its human rights obligations. The UN review made 228 recommendations, identifying how US policy remains inconsistent with key economic, social and cultural human rights, including commitments to prevent racial, gender and economic discrimination, and rights to education, health, housing, social security and food, particularly those of children, the disabled, migrants, 'persons of enforced disappearance' and indigenous peoples. The review called on the United States to recognize the International Criminal Court, to respect rulings of the International Court of Justice, to abolish the death penalty and to ratify conventions against torture and to close the Guantanamo Bay detention centre. Other recommendations included curbing the United States' eavesdropping activities and arms expenditures, the lifting of the country's unilaterally imposed embargoes and sanctions on other countries, and for the United States to protect freedom of expression, for example of journalists (UN 2011). See also Center for Women's Global Leadership *et al.* 2010.

these divisions. Each chapter has a short summary that outlines its key considerations. The book has an extensive bibliography, an index and a glossary of terms.

Following this introductory chapter, Part I, Concepts of Global Leadership and Dominant Strategies, deals with the conceptualization of global leadership and global crises, and seeks to identify some of the key elements in the prevailing strategies of rule associated with the most powerful forces in the world order today. One element highlighted is how dominant strategies of rule are combined under neoliberalism. Some of the key features of neoliberalism identified in the book include (1) increases in the turnover time of capital and the widening exploitation of human beings and nature; (2) the deeper commoditization of politics and culture; (3) strategies of depoliticization designed to marginalize or discredit political alternatives; (4) practices of global governance that extend the world market and facilitate expanded capital accumulation, some of which are shaped by 'experts' who define concepts and strategies of regulation, claim understandings of crises and provide market-based solutions to global problems; and (5), in this context, neoliberalism involves a tendency towards commoditized, undemocratic and charismatic forms of leadership and an aesthetic of crisis that promotes the market as the most efficient and desirable solution to all problems.

Part II, Changing Material Conditions of Existence and Global Leadership: Energy, Climate Change and Water, deals with changes in some of the most basic material conditions of existence, and explores associated strategies of leadership. The contributions also consider how far and in what ways our prevailing cultural and political forms tend to be premised upon historically unique forms of social reproduction – forms that draw upon ever more energy-intensive patterns of production and destruction (especially military power), consumption and transportation in ways that are simply not sustainable. The governance practices and forms of global leadership associated with these development patterns are related both to the world's over-dependence on fossil fuels and to the extended use of military power. These developments have very negative implications for global climate change, pose menacing threats to communities and the world's food systems, and form part of the ominous trend towards the increasingly privatized governance of the global commons and the means of livelihood (e.g. access to freshwater supplies). Such issues and questions are all scrutinized and critically discussed in Part II.

Parts III and IV address questions of global ethics and global politics, particularly from the vantage point of subaltern forces in world order. The contributors to Part III, Global Leadership Ethics, Crises and

Subaltern Forces, approach these questions from very different ontological perspectives: medicine and global health; the cultural and
political formations of the Islamic world; and how subaltern forces
can harness constitutional and legal systems for emancipation. These
contributions offer alternatives, insights and examples that might
help to produce more progressive forms of politics and a truly global
ethic of responsibility. One example is how humanity might consider
a world order perspective premised not upon seeing the planet as
constituted by a 'clash of civilizations' but upon an open-minded
dialogue between civilizations to develop shared concepts of world
order and humane global governance. Another example concerns
how subaltern forces can redress the way that dominant institutions
deny the fundamental human rights of subordinated peoples – or,
indeed, their right to have rights – and, in so doing, invent new rights
and moments of liberation.

Part IV, Prospects for Alternative Forms of Global Leadership,
explores further some of the other potential forms of global leadership
and the political strategies that might be emerging to deal with global
crises and structural problems. One concerns new patterns of global
democratization that seek to minimize hierarchical forms of political
organization, as in the World Social Forum (WSF); others concern left
and right projects for leadership, such as in the United States and
Germany, where, in the shadow of the global crises, the emergence of
right-wing populism can be discerned – a phenomenon that has surfaced
particularly significantly in the United States. The third chapter in
Part IV explores the prospects for new progressive coalitions to emerge
that would involve cooperation between (non-neoliberal) flanks of liberalism and social democracy. It highlights the potentials associated with
an emerging social democratic multilateralism that would involve, for
example, policy measures such as the harmonization of global taxation
and other forms of regulation, which could produce more equitable
global outcomes. The final chapter re-articulates the concept of global
organic crisis and its implications for dominant strategies and subaltern
forces alike, and seeks to posit future potentials for progressive forces in
the form of a theoretical manifesto. Other alternatives that this book
does not consider in detail are new projects of global governance that
might be associated with the (re-)emergence of India and China on the
global stage. It goes without saying that these are only some of a range of
potential alternatives that might reshape global governance and world
order in coming decades.

In sum, it is increasingly plausible to argue that the modern world
has now reached a kind of crossroads or critical juncture at which

fundamental choices must be confronted in ways that will shape our collective futures. The choices cannot be seen simply as the work of 'great men' or as merely reflecting the geopolitical machinations of particular states as such; rather, they will be shaped by already existing global struggles concerning the making of world order.

Part I

Concepts of Global Leadership and Dominant Strategies

1   Leaders and led in an era of global crises

Stephen Gill

Summary

This chapter introduces different concepts of crisis, tracing them to two distinct roots. The first derives from medical discourse, indicating a turning point in an illness, a moment when a patient either goes on to die or starts to recover. It signifies a moment of emergency or danger, such as the response of leaders following 9/11 or to the global financial crash since 2008 – two states of exception or emergency involving extraordinary measures previously thought to be unlikely if not impossible. These measures are justified by the need to preserve a 'civilization' or a way of life as defined by its political leaders. The second meaning of the word 'crisis' has an eschatological sense, as in the collapse of communist rule in eastern Europe, when Western triumphalism proclaimed the 'end of history', with all possible alternatives to liberal capitalism as a governing strategy seemingly exhausted. Nonetheless, if the deep crisis of global accumulation (and its links to society and ecology) is structural it will necessitate much more radical changes than if it is simply a crisis associated with the business cycle remedied through macroeconomic stabilization by G20 governments. This situation, therefore, opens up opportunities for imagining new and progressive forms of global leadership.

Introduction

I start with five preliminary points of introduction before reviewing in more detail some of the key contributions to this volume.

First, the works by Machiavelli and Gramsci discussed in the Introduction provide an initial basis for a critical interrogation of the nature of global leadership and global crisis. Both were written to demystify relations of power and invoked imagined forms of leadership that might help

I am indebted to Isabella Bakker for comments and suggestions on this chapter.

to give rise to new forms of state and legitimate frameworks of political order. However, both writers founded these imaginaries on a sober and clear-headed realism about their own times, in order to think through more constructive, sustainable and feasible futures that would allow for the development of human potentials.

Second, the realism of our time involves a deep structural crisis of capitalism coupled to forms of global governance that seek to stabilize and legitimate an unjust set of global social relations – despite the fact that, at the time of writing, it is by no means obvious that G8 and G20 leaderships have succeeded in stabilizing capitalism. From a more critical perspective, this is nothing more than a temporary fix involving a rhetoric of 'normalcy' that cannot contain the internal contradictions of capitalist development, not the least of which is the way in which existing patterns of consumption and production, including militarization and waste, seem to be well beyond the carrying capacity of the planet. It is therefore very difficult to imagine a future in which the deeper contradictions of capitalism can be overcome without some fundamental transformations in world order and global society.

Third, this volume approaches such issues from the perspective of critical theory. Critical theory is concerned with the demystification of power and the development of alternative frameworks to expand human potentials and possibilities. Put differently, the notion of critique is not simply what Marx called 'the ruthless criticism of all that exists'. Critique is also a mechanism to generate alternative ways of thinking (Gill 2009). Nevertheless, one of the immediate challenges for critical theory in general, and for what Gramsci called the philosophy of praxis in particular, is the need to overcome the eschatology of the end of history, which implies that no feasible alternatives can credibly be posed to going beyond disciplinary neoliberalism and the ways in which it will condition responses to the global organic crisis.

Fourth, a critical and realistic perspective must also be forward-looking, and seek to imagine more feasible, just and sustainable forms of global leadership and world order. More precisely, one of the key barriers that will need to be overcome for this possibility to be realized lies in the principal form of eschatology today: the dominance of neoliberal discourse, which tends to discount the future as well as the lineages of history by compressing all temporality into an unreflective time of immediacy associated with a single model of society and culture – a monoculture of society and of the mind. This notion of time has become part of the new 'common sense' associated with disciplinary neoliberalism: its ontology is antithetical to the notion of the making of history and tantamount to a denial of human creative agency.

Built deep into neoliberal ontology is the unreflecting acceptance of narrow individualism and the expansion of the commodity form into new areas of life that previously were considered to be inalienable. This connects to the generalized acquiescence in mainstream political discourse and the media to the widening of the privatization of control over basic elements of life, including the main institutions of social reproduction in health, education and care more generally.

Indeed, for many people this immediacy is associated with an intensified exploitation of human beings and the environment alike, yielding a growing sense of social precariousness. What seems to be emerging is a global sense of insecurity and perpetual crisis. This characteristic has typically been associated with the condition of most people in the global South – a condition that now seems to be generalizing to encompass growing parts of the more affluent global North. If the conditions of existence in these two worlds have begun not only to interpenetrate but also to merge, what are the implications of this merger for our conceptions of identity and for the ontology of global crises?

As a consequence, therefore, the fifth point is that what we seem to be facing is a perhaps unprecedented type of structural crisis of capitalism that is simultaneously a crisis of market civilization. It should be contrasted with what most economists, politicians, bankers and media have tended to address particularly since 2007, namely the booms and slumps of the business cycle. This mainstream problématique transforms fundamental political questions involving the allocation of enormous resources into technical questions to be presided over by liberal economic experts, who then propose more efficient forms of regulation and macroeconomic interventions to stabilize and promote capital accumulation and economic growth (such as Shiller 2008 and Wolf 2009; these examples reflect a vast literature).

Some heterodox economists, by contrast, have tended to view the present situation as involving a transition from one form of capitalist social structure of accumulation and regulation to a new form (from Fordism and welfare nationalism to disciplinary neoliberalism and potentially to a new form of capitalism; see, for example, Kotz 2009). More specifically, many radical political economists have seen the financial meltdown on Wall Street as the product of over-accumulation and under-consumption, driven by the increased turnover time of capital, and caused in part by the historical assault on working-class living standards in the post-Fordist conjuncture as trade unions and left-wing political parties were weakened, particularly in the capitalist core countries (Wolff 2009). The latter perspective is reflected in several contributions to a recent special edition of the journal *Historical Materialism* (Ashman 2009; McNally 2009).

Nevertheless, what is often missing even in the radical literature is an acknowledgement that the deep structural crisis of ecology/political economy is quite distinct from *political* crises. The problem of political legitimacy for disciplinary neoliberalism has been met by strategies of depoliticization (see Chapter 2, by Nicola Short): as yet we have not seen any of the regimes governing North American or European polities being toppled. Because of the growth of the structural and direct power of capital, which has been significantly consolidated following the end of the Cold War, this is not an analogous situation to that faced by the Ancien Régime during the French Revolution, despite US president Barack Obama's reported comment to the Wall Street titans that he was all that stood between them and the 'pitchforks'.

Here it is important once again to underline the fact that crises may be unequally and unevenly experienced. For example, many protected workers in Europe benefit from unemployment insurance, welfare payments and other benefits, which have allowed them to maintain their standard of living, avoiding the catastrophic effects that the crisis of the 1930s had on European workers, who experienced mass unemployment.

At the same time, it is probably true to say that organic crisis has been experienced in the Third World ever since the colonial era, and felt even more acutely with the intensification of patterns of what Marx called original or primitive accumulation, resulting in the ongoing dispossession of livelihoods throughout much of the world, in addition to intensifying ecological destruction (De Angelis 2001, 2004, 2007; Harvey 2005; Di Muzio 2007). Nevertheless, many problems once associated with the global South seem now to be migrating to the capitalist core of the world order. For example, what was once the Third World sovereign debt crisis is now becoming ever more a global sovereign debt crisis, encompassing the European Union, and potentially the United States as well, at both federal and local levels, triggered by the financial implosion and the costs to public finances of the huge bailouts of the banks and big corporations.

Perspectives on crisis, leadership and our present predicament

What, then, does the term 'crisis' imply for our analysis of the present conjuncture? And what does it imply for questions of leadership? Of course, there is no unified sense that can cover all uses; the concept of crisis has overlapping meanings – meanings that can be partly traced back to earlier usages. The ontology of the present has historical roots, even when neoliberal mentalities focus upon the immediate and evacuate history into a form of empty time. Nonetheless, we can trace the roots of the concept of crisis back to two different sources, each of which has different implications for political agency.

The first meaning has its origins in medical discourse, and is associated with a turning point in an illness, a critical moment after which a patient is either destined to die or is able to proceed to a recovery. It signifies, particularly in today's world, a moment of emergency or danger: think of the response following 9/11, or, indeed, the responses to the global crisis of accumulation, each of which has given rise to states of exception or emergency, in which extraordinary measures are carried out that had previously been regarded as unlikely or even impossible. These measures are justified by the need to preserve a 'civilization' or a way of life as defined by its political leaders. In the most affluent capitalist powers this way of life is energy-intensive, consumerist, individualist, wasteful, ecologically destructive, unhealthy and ultimately unsustainable, as Chapters 5 to 8 make very clear.

Second, 'crisis' has an eschatological sense. If we think back to the collapse of communist rule in eastern Europe, Western triumphalism proclaimed the 'end of history', with all possible alternatives to liberal capitalism as the governing strategy seemingly exhausted; it was said that now we all lived in Margaret Thatcher's world, in which 'there is no alternative' to the capitalist market system.[1] In a sense, the idea of an end of history acted to define the horizon of the present and the limits to any alternative visions of the future. Politics was to be reduced to what James Buchanan (1991) calls 'ordinary politics', with all the fundamental political and constitutional decisions about alternative paths and forms of development already precluded.

In both senses, therefore, crises have become central to governing strategy. Presented as an appropriate response to the 'emergencies' of the past two decades is the view shared by all mainstream parties, that there is no alternative to disciplinary neoliberal governance of capitalism. 'Ordinary politics' is consistent with support for the extension of market civilization, whether it be in the form of 'green capitalism' or growth in the vast potential consumer markets (the new 'global middle classes') of India and China. Nonetheless, the combination of emergency response and measures framed by the eschatology of the end of

---

[1] See Chapter 10, by Teivo Teivainen, which discusses the World Social Forum and how its slogan 'Another world is possible' was developed precisely to challenge the eschatology of the 'end of history' postulate as offering no political alternatives.

history poses the question if and whether this discourse can permit ruling forces to argue persuasively that the crises can be mastered or stabilized, so that 'normalcy' can be resumed. This issue is debated throughout this book.

Indeed, a key political question is the degree to which social forces can conceive of the links between different moments of crisis, and how they combine to address them through various forms of leadership – an issue taken up in the various contributions, which, in a variety of ways, seek to identify what is distinctive or unique in the present global conjuncture. In the rest of this section I highlight two examples.

With respect to the present conjuncture, Nicola Short in Chapter 2 sees neoliberalism as a response to the crisis of capitalist profitability that emerged in the 1970s. It proceeds, in part, by turning social goods and social services into marketable commodities (creating new markets) and by sustaining and extending existing markets through the introduction of new credit and debt mechanisms. Despite the fact that workers' real wages have either been stagnant or in decline in many countries, especially in the United States, the indebted hyper-consumerism of contemporary capitalism has, thus far, continued. Politically, neoliberalism seeks to obviate a crisis of legitimation via a shift towards 'governance' and through an 'aesthetic of crisis'. The latter presents the market as the most efficient and desirable solution to all problems in a commodity form of politics. Electoral politics is primarily governed by immediacy – in terms of the issues highlighted in television advertising – and television provides the main form of political communication, characterized by sound and video 'bites' in a process determined above all by money. US-trained political consultants and media experts oversee vast and growing electoral expenditures; in other countries, American political operatives often direct the campaigns.

By contrast, Chapter 4, by Tim Di Muzio, takes a long-term vantage point to make sense of what is specific about our present conjuncture. He conceptualizes the history of the global political economy 'as divided into three eras: the pre-fossil-fuel age, the age of fossil fuels and the post-carbon age'. By dividing history in this way, Di Muzio shows how the emergence of global market civilization today is historically specific and 'undergirded by affordable, accessible and abundant fossil fuels'. Citing evidence concerning peak oil (the time, in the near future, when the prevailing scientific consensus is that oil production will peak and then start to decline) and patterns of use, he argues that the consumption of such fuels is not sustainable, as it compounds problems of climate change and poses massive political and social questions concerning a necessary transition to a post-fossil-fuel economy.

This therefore brings us back to the question of leadership, and, indeed, the relations between rulers and ruled on a world scale. Leadership, despite being connected to the immediate mastery of crises, differs fundamentally from some of the other ontological forms, in that it involves communicative relations and social and political power between different elements of a social formation. By contrast, the ontology of the global ecological crisis involves long-term effects, often gradual and cumulative, entailing interaction between human and non-human systems. Human systems of production and consumption, as well as of destruction, have a cumulative impact upon those of the biosphere, sometimes with highly unpredictable feedback effects. This has created a set of conditions and circumstances that leaders are, in a sense, simply presented with. Of course, this does not mean that leaders should act with no regard to the ecological and social consequences of their actions – for example, if they choose to engage in the accelerated introduction of nuclear energy as a means of dealing with global climate change. What may make sense today may not make sense for successor generations when they deal with the repercussions of the need to decommission nuclear power stations, and when they are saddled with the stewardship of our nuclear waste.

Nevertheless, as there may be no direct link between economic crisis and political crisis, a crisis of leadership or authority may have very little to do with a turning point in the relationship between human beings and the biosphere. Indeed, how we understand these questions is often mediated by the discourses and judgments of 'experts' – an issue to which I turn in the following section.

Leadership by experts?

One of the more interesting questions concerning the nature of leadership in global capitalism relates to the role of experts, or epistemic communities that define forms of regulation and governance in key sectors of the global political economy.

Until the financial collapse of 2007, most mainstream macroeconomists and financial economists assumed that the propensity to slump and depression in modern capitalism had been conquered, with the result that macroeconomic planning had become a technical exercise concerned simply with the fine tuning of the business cycle. It was further assumed that the spreading of risk through financial innovations such as derivatives and the self-regulation of financial capitalism introduced over the past three decades had made for a much less risky and more stable system – one that would continue to deliver prosperity.

Indeed, much of the reasoning of this fraternity of economists was underpinned by an almost religious belief in the validity of the so-called 'efficient markets hypothesis'.

Another way to look at this is to see that certain members of these epistemic communities act as organic intellectuals from the vantage point of dominant political and economic interests. Organic intellectuals both articulate the goals and legitimate the actions and institutions of the ruling elements of a given society, seeking to stabilize the basic relations between rulers and ruled, simultaneously marginalizing and incorporating opposition. One function of these organic intellectuals is to depoliticize fundamental questions relating to the nature of capitalism, transforming political debates into technical questions directed at appropriate means rather than at questioning the fundamental ends of the capitalist system; they represent accumulation through the commodity form and markets *as if* it were common sense. In this way, despite the economic slump of 2007–10, and the collapse of the theories meant to explain it, the dominant narratives are still represented as the only credible ways to address economic problems.

It is, of course, important to underline the context. When the financial meltdown occurred credit lines were frozen and banks refused to lend to each other, confidence collapsed and the central banks of the world engaged in a huge financial rescue operation, costing according to some estimates as much as $17 trillion.[2] A particular curiosity of that moment was the way in which the economic experts scrambled to explain the financial collapse, which, according to their theories, was an impossible occurrence. This was then followed by a series of *mea culpas* premised upon the idea that, very soon, they would resume their positions of authority as leading economists, and that normalcy would be restored.

An amusing example concerns a high-level group of private sector economists, bankers and academics convened by the British Academy, following a state visit to the London School of Economics in November 2008 by Queen Elizabeth II. After being taken around the school and shown charts indicating the scale of the financial collapse, the queen asked why it was that, if the collapse was so enormous, nobody had anticipated it, or indeed acted to prevent it. The British Academy decided to write a letter in response to the monarch's question. It concluded: 'Your Majesty, the failure to foresee the timing, extent and severity of the crisis and to head it off, while it had many causes, was principally a failure of the collective imagination of many bright people

---

[2] All dollar amounts in this volume are in US currency unless stated otherwise.

[sic], both in this country and internationally, to understand the risks to the system as a whole.'[3] Paul Krugman (2009b) has noted that those US economists who gave warnings were ignored or marginalized as cranks.

A further example Krugman recounts is instructive. It occurred at a special conference convened in 2005 to honour Alan Greenspan's long tenure as chairman of the US Federal Reserve System. Greenspan, a market guru and follower of the individualist philosopher Ayn Rand, has views close to leading neoliberals such as Friedrich von Hayek and Milton Friedman. Greenspan was a firm believer in the wisdom of financial economics and the providential self-regulating capacity of financial markets. At the special conference a contrarian paper was presented warning that the US financial system was taking on potentially dangerous levels of risk. The paper was mocked as misguided 'by almost all present', including Ben Bernanke, Greenspan's successor at the Fed; Obama's economic czar (and former president of Harvard) Lawrence Summers; and his Treasury secretary, Tim Geithner.

Their views were consistent with the neoliberal conventional wisdom of the time, as expressed by the IMF in its *Global Financial Stability Report* of April 2006, which cited, approvingly, comments by Greenspan that the global financial system was 'far more flexible, efficient, and hence resilient...than existed just a quarter-century ago'. This Panglossian report argued that banks had dispersed and diversified credit risk, and that technical innovations now allowed supervisors and firms to monitor market and credit risks in 'real time' (IMF 2006: 1 2). The IMF's chairman summarizes the key finding of the report thus (ibid.: 132):

[IMF] Directors welcomed the continued resilience of the global financial system, which has been supported by solid global growth, low inflation, abundant liquidity, and flat yield curves. They considered that financial conditions will likely remain benign in the most likely scenario of continued growth, contained inflation, and stable inflationary expectations.

The IMF view, therefore, was that the financial system was 'much more resilient' and far less prone to bank failures and credit problems than it had been for a quarter of a century!

Krugman (2009b; emphasis added) also notes: 'Economics, *as a field*, got in trouble because *economists* were seduced by the vision of a *perfect, frictionless market system*' so that they became 'blind' to the very possibility of 'catastrophic failures in a market economy.' Krugman is referring

---

[3] See www.britac.ac.uk/news/newsrelease-economy.cfm. The open letter to the queen was dated 22 July 2009 (accessed 18 February 2011).

to the hegemony of the efficient markets hypothesis in the thinking of neoliberal economists. Nevertheless, by October 2008 Greenspan finally admitted that he was in a state of 'shocked disbelief', as his 'whole intellectual edifice...collapsed' (Krugman 2009b). However, with respect to financial reforms, Wall Street maintained control over the policy response to the crisis and debates on changes, confining the policy discussion principally to modifications to the existing forms of regulation.

In Chapter 5, Richard Falk also explores the role of an epistemic community of experts, in this case the community of leading scientists, whose virtually unanimous consensus is that global warming is taking place, that it poses immense threats to the future of many communities and to global food supplies and other aspects of livelihood, and that it is mainly a consequence of the energy-intensive processes of production and consumption associated with market civilization. Needless to say, the economists just discussed rarely look at the qualitative components of economic growth associated with market civilization, concentrating instead on abstract financial aggregates.

However, in contrast to the neoliberal economists, the arguments and evidence marshalled by the scientists warning of the problems of climate change have been attacked on a consistent basis by the so-called 'climate change sceptics'. These sceptics, who articulate the interests of many of the world's largest energy corporations and interests, perhaps wilfully, seek to maintain and defend wasteful economic practices. Their stance was encapsulated in the refusal by US president George H. Bush to attend the Rio de Janeiro United Nations Conference on Environment and Development (UNCED) in 1992 with the words 'Our lifestyle is not negotiable'. Many of his successors in the White House have acted in ways consistent with this ecologically myopic perspective.

Accordingly, this poses the question: why are some epistemic communities seen as having the authoritative solutions to key problems, whereas others are attacked as being based upon faulty knowledge systems, and their credibility undermined? Neoliberal experts – lawyers, bond raters and economists working for central banks – are presented as if they are independent of political forces, allowing them to claim impartiality in defining public policy responses to crises.

The ethics and politics of progressive global leadership

A further task of this volume is to address ethical and political questions in relation to basic conditions of existence and to ask how these can be transformed. Some chapters bring into relief different facets of these questions.

Hilal Elver's chapter, Chapter 6, illustrates a shift in global governance and leadership concerning freshwater supplies. At issue is whether water can be considered to be a fundamental human right that should be made available to all on an affordable basis or whether such a basic human necessity – one that underpins all life forms – can be treated as a commodity to be exploited for profit. Governance has gravitated towards a hybrid of public–private mechanisms, heavily shaped by the private water corporations, which stand to make enormous profits from supplying water, as well as by private epistemic communities, which are mainly influenced by the private water companies. This is therefore an area in which we can expect growing contestation; at present only a small proportion of global freshwater supplies is controlled by private market mechanisms.

For Solomon Benatar, in Chapter 7, the various dimensions of ethical, moral and material crisis just noted are symptoms of a world in a state of entropy or degradation – a situation in which perhaps the biggest ethical challenge of our time is the state of world health. To address the challenge of radically improving the health of the vast majority of the planet's population requires transformations in our prevailing modes of thought and knowledge – in short, new paradigms of progress, institutions and values. Of these, the most important values are solidarity and social justice that can challenge the inertia inherent in the present order and better address this global categorical imperative.

Mustapha Pasha, in Chapter 8, sees neoliberalism and Orientalism as inimical to plurality, including the pluralities (and contradictions) of Islam. He therefore argues that progressive global leadership must avoid the fundamental errors of Orientalism, which deny the variety of Islamic concepts of justice, equality, human dignity and fairness as well as its conceptions of world order. Indeed, although as a result of the first ever Islamic revolution, in Iran, 'Islamicists no longer see the establishment of an Islamic political and social order as an impossibility', discourses of reconciliation have emerged from that country. Such discourses, including Mohammad Khatami's call for dialogue among civilizations based upon their renouncing the will to power, help us to imagine a more humane world order – in stark contrast to the 'clash of civilizations' viewpoint, which is in effect a neoconservative hypothesis that implies continuous global confrontation (Huntington 1996). Certain Islamic conceptions of leadership are interesting in terms of the ethical and political frameworks they offer for future norms of global leadership: leadership that involves justice, guardianship, trust and moral responsibility, whereby authority and obedience are understood to be interwoven and circumscribed by ethical principles and by respect for cultural and religious diversity. Such ethical Islamic leadership is premised on limited sovereignty and by constraints on material pursuits, so that each conforms to the sustainability of the human species.

To conclude, what would progressive forms of global leadership look like? To answer this question requires us to use theoretical imagination – the pessimism of the intelligence combined with an optimism of the will – in ways that have just been outlined. My own view is that we need to think ethically, politically and imaginatively in relation to different forms of power and a range of social and ecological constraints – what Fernand Braudel (1981) calls the 'limits of the possible'. Perhaps more fundamentally, progressive political organization and its political imaginary need to be founded in a realistic consideration of how existing human and non-human structures and forms of power either constrain or facilitate the full realization of human capabilities and potentials, as the necessary framework for visualizing new social and political relations – for instance, in rethinking what I have called, with Isabella Bakker, the nature of, and relations between, power, production and social reproduction (Bakker and Gill 2003).

As an example, throughout this volume a distinction is made between 'power over' and 'power to'. Subaltern forces perceive many forms of structural power as power over: as unjust and illegitimate oppression and subordination that need to be transformed by forms of collective action such as those premised on insurgent reason. This would produce a creative form of 'power to' that might result in greater justice, recognition, redress and redistribution for subaltern forces.[4] Upendra Baxi, in Chapter 9, gives examples of how this power has been exercised in collective action through the justice system, in countries such as India, Brazil and South Africa, allowing for the invention and creation of new forms of rights by those previously denied the right to have such rights – thus enlarging the limits of the possible beyond the previous set of political constraints for new democratic forces.

On the other hand, a further distinction that is made in several chapters is that between the direct power and the structural power of capital, which is a power resource for the few and a constraint for the majority in capitalist social formations. The direct power of capital (power over) is the power of employers over workers or of monopolists

---

[4] Feminist notions of leadership – from a variety of backgrounds – also begin with the notion that power has to be reconceptualized as a capacity or ability to transform oneself and others as an alternative to the more masculine notion of 'power over'. Hence, power and leadership are seen as the capacity to produce change or empowerment rather than domination over others. See Fraser 1997 and Hartsock 1983.

over markets; employers can fire workers if they do not comply with their wishes (subject to the strictures of employment law). By contrast, the structural power of capital is indirect and built into the nature of the system of markets within capitalism. Structural power involves the ability of investors to make investment decisions spontaneously and to move capital into and out of particular sectors or jurisdictions, with potentially significant effects on production and distribution, and, indeed, on entire economies. For instance, investors are free to choose to invest depending on their appraisal of the future potential for profits, which in turn depends upon their perception of the business or investment climate. That perception in turn involves an evaluation of government policies, worker militancy, the level of economic activity and a host of other factors. However, if a general perception arises that the investment climate has deteriorated, investors will probably postpone investment decisions, thereby undermining economic growth and causing unemployment to rise.

This is sometimes called an investment strike, and it is a form of negative power built into the structural power of capital. The power of capital is thus inherently undemocratic, and it has to be made more accountable and consistent with broader social purposes that are productive. Nevertheless, the question remains as to how progressive forces can move beyond countervailing power and a negative critique of capital. Bakker and I have hypothesized a growing global contradiction (Bakker and Gill 2003: 27–9). This involves, on the one hand, the extension of the global power of capital and, on the other, the intensified exploitation of human beings and nature that this process involves, in ways that tend to undermine the basic conditions for stable, sustainable and progressive forms of social reproduction for a majority of people on the planet. This contradiction has been hypothesized as a means of trying to direct the attention of political economy away from a narrow focus on the politics of production or on states and markets in order to be able to see the way in which production is connected to the wider social conditions within which it operates – what feminist political economy calls social reproduction (see Glossary).

It is worth emphasizing that social reproduction (which involves not only biological reproduction and nurturing/caring institutions but also the reproduction of the commodity labour power) fundamentally underpins and constitutes structures of production within capitalism; for example, unpaid domestic work subsidizes capital by serving as a means of the general reproduction of the workforce. On the other hand, work can be seen as a potentially creative process that lies outside capital. Labour, by contrast, is a particular aspect of work, which in a capitalist social formation is that part of work time appropriated and controlled by capital in the labour–capital relation. A key goal of progressive politics, therefore, is connected to the idea of liberation and freeing up the time of all workers so that they are equally able to act as engaged citizens.

One of the defining characteristics of our time is not the onset of a leisure society, which was widely discussed as a possibility in the 1960s (in retrospect, this seems to have been a figment of the imagination of science fiction writers), but its virtual opposite: people are working harder and harder across the world. Workers everywhere are increasingly at the mercy of employers, as a result of declining rates of unionization. The unpaid work of caring and nurturing and reproduction of the commodity labour power is increasingly downloaded into households, and principally onto the backs of women.

Accordingly, one key to progressive politics is control over time: to shorten the working day, to lower the retirement age and to institutionalize policies that meaningfully enhance the value of unpaid caring work. A new progressive politics must engage in these key issues of social reproduction and link them to progressive macroeconomic policies, including progressive forms of taxation and a significant redistribution of resources: the opposite of the current macroeconomic 'exit strategies' adopted by most of the G20 that are discussed in Chapter 13. Put differently, when capital penetrates into basic social and human institutions it produces destabilizing consequences for or a general crisis of social reproduction, constituting one of the key contradictions of capitalist development itself.

Progressive forms of leadership need to understand precisely how these mechanisms – the complexity of which is only hinted at above – work and how they operate as aspects of the discipline of capital relative to states, workers and subaltern forces more generally. Moreover, any discussion of disciplinary power and its links to the direct and structural power of capital and to questions of social reproduction needs to be related to relations of inequality and domination so as to allow fully for a critique that enables subaltern forces to understand and confront the power/knowledge regimes of capitalism. Such a critique would highlight how such power does not simply (or even necessarily) include the accumulation of (useful) goods for livelihood. Its principal goal is the accumulation of abstract monetary values that allow control over the behaviour of other human beings; that is, it is an accumulation of power over others.

This perspective is a necessary precursor to a more effective and legitimate regulation of capital at the national and global levels. In this context, new pricing mechanisms and new systems of regulation need to be devised so that production benefits livelihood and underpins human development (Albritton 2009: 199–211).

With respect to questions of leadership, new progressive policies must also therefore be linked to new forms of political organization, in order to construct institutions that allow women and men alike to engage fully in politics and leadership activities. This means a new politics not only of identity, recognition and representation but also one of social reproduction, redistribution, solidarity and social justice. New norms of leadership need to take into account that *all* individuals bear responsibility for the care of the young and the old, the healthy and the sick, and ensure that social institutions are in place so that these needs are fully met.

Indeed, in our discussion at the Helsinki Symposium, Bakker cited recent feminist research on this question related to business and education leaders. One study showed that almost a half of women earning over $100,000 in the United States, such as female executives, have no children. Data for leading women academics at US research universities was consistent with these findings (Cheung and Halpern 2010). The pattern seems to be that men are rewarded for having children whereas women are not. Progressive forms of leadership and political organization must therefore overcome such gender norms and take full account of the organization of people's everyday lives. The concluding chapter of this volume takes up some of these themes.

2 Leadership, neoliberal governance and global economic crisis: a Gramscian analysis

Nicola Short

Summary

This chapter begins with an exegesis of Antonio Gramsci's conception of leadership in order to outline how several of his key concepts and ideas might be relevant for the present historical moment, in terms of understanding both the endurance of neoliberal governance and the intellectual and organizational imperatives for building a viable alternative politics. The chapter seeks to provide the conceptual groundwork for other chapters of this book by outlining, for example, concepts that are invoked and developed in these other chapters that consider our present predicament. These concepts include hegemony and 'common sense'; the political party ('The modern prince'); the role of organic intellectuals; and Gramsci's views on democratic, collective leadership versus charismatic leadership.

Democratic leadership emphasizes the *collective* nature of identifications through a political party, constituted on the basis of pedagogical exchange between leaders and led, so that, ultimately, there is no distinction between the two. By contrast, undemocratic leadership relies on individual *charisma* and never develops an organizational capacity for broader participation. Without ever denying the supreme importance of political organization, Gramsci saw political leadership as a form of radical democracy that encompassed the development of the popular capacity in order to create new forms of state and society – and, by implication, world order. He therefore rejected not only right-wing authoritarianism but also left-wing, élitist or vanguard political tendencies.

Introduction

This chapter seeks to lay some of the conceptual groundwork for other parts of this volume by outlining how Gramsci conceptualized some of his key ideas on hegemony, political parties and organic intellectuals, and specifically his concepts of collective and charismatic leadership. The chapter also offers a preliminary sketch of some of the principal characteristics of the economic and social aspects of the neoliberal historical period. It therefore raises questions concerning the potential for progressive leadership and emancipatory politics under such conditions.

Leadership is in many senses a central problematic in Gramsci's work. He was concerned to explain how left-wing forces failed to translate the political opportunities offered by the economic crisis of the 1930s into lasting social change, in spite of widespread labour organization and activism at the time. With this historical situation in mind, this chapter seeks to highlight how, in contrast to the 1930s, consent or political acquiescence under neoliberal governance is obtained in ways that both resemble and yet differ from those times. In so doing, I seek to signal how we might consider the mechanisms through which neoliberal forces prevail, ideologically and politically, particularly in periods of crisis, and how alternative conceptions and practices of leadership may, under certain conditions, offer more progressive solutions to problems associated with what Stephen Gill, in his chapters in this collection, calls the global organic crisis.

The current crisis follows several decades of intensive neoliberal restructuring, which has involved an intensification of the role of the capitalist market in structuring social life. Restructuring was a response to a crisis of profitability but nevertheless involved policies that have undermined stability and that have resulted in increasingly frequent financial crises. However, although such crises have established new opportunities for accumulation, their political impact has been mitigated by the promotion of a new aesthetic sensibility regarding the role of the market in daily life: the market is now represented as if it has a timeless logic, as a form of myth, of predestination or – as the editor notes in the previous chapter – an eschatology that denies the possibility of fundamental social and political change.

Neoliberal policies have been made possible through not only the restructuring of production and the relations between capital and labour but also by new arrangements that more fully institutionalize the distinction between the 'political' and the 'economic', so as to insulate the latter from accountability to the former. The neoliberal shift has therefore transformed the categories associated with Gramsci's concepts of economism (discussed below) and his analysis of leadership and forms of ideology; for example, neoliberalism turns electoral politics into a commodified arena such that political parties can no longer represent positions outside the logic of market capitalism. Neoliberal media and educational deregulation support this move, such that other institutions of political and civil society increasingly cannot operate independently of market logic.

The transformation of social relations under the neoliberal period has therefore thoroughly reconstructed leadership so that it reflects more closely the undemocratic, charismatic tendencies that Gramsci analysed as posing challenges for democratic forces in the 1930s. In what follows, these three questions – Gramsci's notion of leadership, the socio-economic effects of neoliberalism and their implications for democratic praxis – are taken in turn.

Gramsci's conception of leadership[1]

In this section I outline the way that Gramsci saw questions of agency and political practice as a preface to some of the wider considerations on the multiple forms of leadership and varieties of global crises addressed in this volume. For example, this chapter anticipates the detailed discussion of Gramsci's concepts of hegemony, passive revolution and subaltern political agency contained in this book.

Here my emphasis is more on Gramsci's specific engagement with the agency of leadership rather than the structural logic of class rule, although the two cannot be neatly disaggregated. Nevertheless, for Gramsci, leadership was always a question of political practice, particularly directed at progressive social change (Hoare and Nowell-Smith 1971: 200–1). Moreover, as Michele Fillippini (2009: 219) has noted, in Gramsci's work the word '*direzione*' is nearly always accompanied by an adjective specifying its *particular* context (e.g. 'caste and religious leadership', 'intellectual and moral leadership', 'social and political leadership').[2] In addition, for Gramsci, the problematic was often the

---

[1] A note on texts: this essay relies a great deal on Gramsci (Hoare and Smith 1971), particularly for the essay on 'The modern prince', which appears in *Quaderno del Carcere 30* (1933–4 xii). As a later notebook, this text has not yet been translated in the more comprehensive Columbia University Press series, which has reached *Quaderno 8* to date: Buttigieg (2007) includes *Quaderni 6* to *8*; see also Buttigieg (1991) and (1996).

[2] Hoare and Smith (1971: 55, fn 5) outline the challenge:

There is a real problem in translating the Italian '*dirigere*' and its compounds: *direzione*, *dirigente*, *diretto*, *direttivo*, etc. '*Dirigere*' means to 'direct, lead, rule', when...Gramsci counterposes it to '*dominare*' we translate it 'to lead'. '*Dirigente*' is the present participle of '*dirigere*' – e.g. '*classe dirigente*' is the standard equivalent of 'ruling class' – and as a noun is the normal word for (political) 'leader', where Gramsci uses it...in counterposition to '*dominante*' we have translated it as 'leading'. '*Diretto*' as an adjective means 'direct', as a past participle has been translated to 'led'. [...] '*Direzione*' covers the various meanings of the word 'direction' in English, but is also the normal word for 'leadership', and has usually been translated as such here.

question of collective leadership, its degree of democratic involvement and its level of organization, including its pedagogical capacity in developing the organizational and intellectual resources of its members – a point taken up later in this volume by Teivo Teivainen, in Chapter 10, in his discussion of the (so far inconclusive) debates in the World Social Forum over organizational and political structures and by Ingar Solty, in Chapter 11, which explores neoliberal, progressive and right-wing popular forms of mobilization and organization.

Perhaps the best known of Gramsci's discussions of leadership is 'The modern prince', which appears relatively late in the *Prison Notebooks* (*Quaderno 30*, 1933–4) and seems to incorporate a number of themes of his writings on leadership that also appeared in his earlier works. Anticipating the question of the role of critical theory raised by Gill earlier in this book, Gramsci argued that Machiavelli's project of exposing (and demystifying) the logic of power must have been directed precisely at an audience not of rulers, who would already be privy to such knowledge, but to those 'not in the know' (Hoare and Nowell-Smith 1971: 135). Although Gramsci problematized Machiavelli's conception of politics as a discrete activity, divorced from the socio-economic, he therefore argued that the problematic Machiavelli confronted was the same one that Marx faced in his own time: to demystify the operation of power to make way for more progressive alternatives (ibid.: 136).

One of the themes in Gramsci's discussion of 'The modern prince' was the question of the embodiment of leadership. Gramsci noted that Machiavelli's innovation in *The Prince* is to provide a new aesthetic expression of political ideology and political science in the 'dramatic form of a "myth", which in fact has a protagonist, the *condottiere*'.[3] Appealing to an individual allowed Machiavelli to move beyond the limitations of the previous categories of political ideology or political science, and their (ibid.: 125)

pedantic classifications of principles and criteria for a method of action... Instead, he represented this process in terms of the qualities, characteristics, duties and requirements of a concrete individual. Such a procedure stimulates the artistic imagination of those who have to be convinced, and gives political passions a more concrete form.

The recent *Dizionario Gramsciano* includes entries for '*direzione*', '*dirigenti-diretti*', '*diritti e doveri*', '*diritto*' and '*diritto naturale*' (found throughout the notebooks), as well as '*capo*' (attributed to *Quaderno 6*, section 97, and *Quaderno 5*, section 127) and '*capo carismatico*' (*Quaderno 2*, section 75); see Liguori and Voza (2009: 219–27, 101).

[3] See Glossary.

The Prince does not exist as an individual in any direct historical sense, but as a projection of the Sorelian myth, the political ideology as collective fantasy that works to organize a collective will, not through purely rational political argument but through more aesthetic expression. Thus, despite Machiavelli's elaborate attention to rigorous reasoning, in the final analysis, his linking of a *historically specific* 'people' to the logic of rule in *The Prince* led Gramsci to conclude: 'The entire logical argument now appears as nothing other than auto-reflection on the part of the people – an inner reasoning worked out in the popular consciousness' (ibid.: 125–6).

Gramsci therefore contended that the *modern* prince 'cannot be a real person or concrete individual' but 'can only be an organism, a complex element of society in which a collective will, which has already been recognized and has to some extent asserted itself in action, begins to take concrete form' (ibid.: 129). He argued that the political party plays the role of consolidating a collective will into a more universal expression in the modern era (something that is lacking, for example, in the WSF, as Teivainen notes in Chapter 10). However, this discussion was accompanied by a caveat about individual leadership, to the effect that cases in which 'historical-political actions which are immediate and imminent, characterized by the necessity for lightning speed, can be incarnated mythically by a concrete individual' (ibid.).

Nonetheless, charismatic leadership was the sign of political immaturity, whereby political principles appear to the populace as 'vague and incoherent' and require 'an infallible Pope to interpret' (ibid.: 320). Such movements and parties have the appeal of 'passion' but suffer from fragile foundations for long-term success. In similar conditions involving the absence of proper political organization, a state might step in to lead on behalf of a particular social group. Thus Gramsci developed his conception of 'passive revolution' through an analysis of the role of Piedmont in the Italian Risorgimento. In that case, the state functioned to secure the dominant group's position despite the latter's failure to lead. In situations of passive revolution, 'a State replaces local social groups in leading a struggle of renewal' (ibid.: 105–6; see also Chapter 9, by Upendra Baxi, on the relationship between passive revolution and the variety of forms of subaltern political struggle in the post-colonial world).

Indeed, Gramsci's conception of leadership can perhaps be seen most clearly through his discussion of the role of the political party and its function as an agent of transformation involving philosophical and ideological leadership. Political parties require three elements: a mass base, a principal cohesive element (what might be termed 'practical' leadership) and 'an intermediate element, which articulates the first element with the second and maintains contact between them, not only physically but also morally and intellectually' (ibid.: 152–3). Indeed, some party functions may be conducted through ostensibly 'apolitical' agents, such as the implicit political role of the media (in his day, *The Times* in the United Kingdom or *Corriere della Sera* in Italy) (ibid.: 148–9). Again, it is instructive to compare these elements to the constitution of political parties and ideological apparatuses in the era of disciplinary neoliberalism, in which media concentration has accelerated with increasing control by conservatives and neoliberals. Moreover, Gramsci was writing in an age prior to television and the internet. Gramsci also noted that a part of the 'left' register of his time was the apolitical posture of the anarchist movement, which even in direct (terrorist) action 'presents itself explicitly as purely "educative"' (ibid.: 149).

Furthermore, Gramsci noted that in one-party states (such as those currently coming under increasing popular pressure across the Arab world) the 'party' appears to lose its political character and seems to function in an exclusively technical guise, wherein 'political questions are disguised as cultural ones, and as such become insoluble' (ibid.: 149). Gramsci's discussion of the role of the party in politics therefore touches upon a number of political positions. On the right, he critiqued the fascist pretence of claims to 'individualism' and of being 'anti-party' (ibid.: 146). Such claims are disingenuous, because there is in fact a party structure underlying the formation of such movements and their leaders, though Gramsci conceded that it was difficult even for the analyst to identify and document the plethora of 'molecular' developments contributing to their emergence; thus 'currents of opinion are normally taken as already constituted around a group or dominant personality' (ibid.: 194). It should be noted that, with the urbanization and the mass media of his era, Gramsci saw that such molecular processes had become accelerated (a process that, we might add, is continuing today) (ibid.: 195). On the left, he criticized the anarcho-syndicalist valorization of spontaneity over party leadership for failing to aspire to genuine political power – a position he characterized as being perpetually dependent on existing parties and power arrangements. Gramsci therefore critiqued the 'voluntarism' of both right and left, which celebrates the individual over the collective and is characterized by 'false heroisms and the pseudo-aristocracies' that leave underlying social and political conditions unchanged (ibid.: 202–5). The latter point is useful as a litmus test to assess the degree to which spontaneous protests can lead to structural transformation in countries such as Egypt and Libya in the aftermath of their early 2011 revolts.

Thus, although 'there really do exist rulers and ruled, leaders and led', the more significant question is whether this should remain the case. 'In the formation of leaders, one premise is fundamental: is it the intention that there should always be rulers and ruled, or is the objective to create the conditions in which this division is no longer necessary?' (ibid.: 144). In this context, good leadership promotes organizational development over charismatic appeal (Buttigieg 2007: 83). It also promotes the development of the capacities of parties and movements towards broad democratic participation, such that the leadership cadre might include anyone from within the organization – a criterion that is far from being met in most left parties today. Such strategies should involve the active interaction of 'leaders and led', 'a continual adaptation of the organization to the real movement, a matching of thrusts from below with orders from above, a continuous insertion of elements thrown up from the depths of the rank and file into the solid framework of the leadership apparatus which ensures continuity and the regular accumulation of experience' (Hoare and Nowell-Smith 1971: 188–9).

Gramsci's project therefore navigated the proper balance between two constituencies. On the one hand, parties need to construct capable leaders to ensure their ability potentially to rule: insufficient central leadership might inhibit the translation of local political power to broader scales (ibid.: 192). On the other hand, they must remain democratic, as Gramsci's discussion of 'Spontaneity and conscious leadership', a reflection on the experience of the Factory Council Movement in Turin, attests. Gramsci defended the movement from critiques of 'voluntarism' by arguing that engagement with 'real men [sic], formed in specific historical relations, with specific feelings, outlooks, fragmentary conceptions of the world, etc.' was inherently necessary to any left political project (ibid.: 198).

Most importantly, leadership must be capable of recognizing and productively harnessing popular sentiment, not merely for the sake of positive social change but for guarding against its obverse: right-wing reaction. As Chapter 11, by Ingar Solty, warns, such reaction can become especially pronounced during economic crisis (ibid.: 199):

Neglecting, or worse still despising, so-called 'spontaneous' movements, i.e. failing to give them a conscious leadership or to raise them to a higher plane by inserting them into politics, may often have extremely serious consequences. It is almost always the case that a 'spontaneous' movement of the subaltern classes is accompanied by the right wing of the dominant class, for concomitant reasons. An economic crisis, for instance, engenders on the one hand discontent among the subaltern classes and spontaneous mass movements, and on the other conspiracies among the reactionary groups, who take advantage of the objective weakening of the government in order to attempt *coups d'état.*

Leadership must provide proper political and historical analysis in order to promote the sustainable longevity of a movement's political programme, and in particular to address the challenges presented by the fact that 'mass ideological factors always lag behind mass economic phenomena', and thus 'an appropriate political initiative is always necessary to liberate the economic thrust from the dead weight of traditional policies – i.e. to change the political direction of certain forces which have to be absorbed if a new, homogeneous political-economic historical bloc, without internal contradictions, is to be successfully formed' (ibid.: 168).

As noted earlier, Gramsci's problematic of leadership also addressed the question of *economism* (see also Chapter 10). In a fairly lengthy passage in 'The modern prince', he read economism as the general fallacy of separating the economic from the political (ibid.: 159–68).[4] Liberalism expressed the archetype of economism, since 'it must be made clear that *laissez-faire* too is a form of State "regulation"' (ibid.: 160). Syndicalism was also guilty of such divisions, either through an explicit separation of the political and the economic, or an implicit one in the rejection of seeking state power.[5] However, the fundamental risk of economism emerging from such distortions, for Marxists, was how it leads to distractions from structural analyses of crises, displacing them with narratives of individual profit and conspiracy (e.g. the debates in 2007–10 over excessive bonuses for bankers rather than those that might focus on the contradictions of financial capitalism). In response to complex historical events, 'economism asks the question: "Who profits directly from the initiative under consideration?" and replies with a line of reasoning which is as simplistic as it is fallacious: the ones who profit directly are a certain fraction of the ruling class reducing critical activity to the 'exposure of scandals' (ibid.: 166, 164).

By contrast, Gramsci's conception of leadership was central to his conception of hegemony, and thus to his view of power and politics (ibid.: 57–8):

A social group can, and indeed must, already exercise 'leadership' before winning governmental power (this indeed is one of the principal conditions for the winning of such power); it subsequently becomes dominant when it exercises power, but even if it holds it firmly in its grasp, it must continue to 'lead' as well.

---

[4] See Chapter 10, by Teivo Teivainen, on economistic elements within the World Social Forum and Chapter 11, by Ingar Solty, on the economism of the contemporary left.

[5] This theme is long-standing in Gramsci's work: see for example: 'The conquest of state' and 'Address to the anarchists' (Hoare 1977: 73–8, 185–9).

Hegemony must be continually renewed through the exercise of intellectual and moral leadership, and such leadership requires understanding and appealing to the interests of subordinate groups. There is little in the *Prison Notebooks* on the specifics of 'intellectual and moral leadership', though Gramsci did discuss intellectuals in some detail. Although potentially counter-hegemonic, they more often serve as 'deputies' exercising the subaltern functions of social hegemony and political government for the dominant group, generating 'spontaneous' consent and justifying state coercion (ibid.: 12). Indeed, Gramsci used the term 'intellectual' to mean anyone who actively articulates rationales for the political-social order – a category whose ranks have greatly expanded in the modern era along with the expansion of the capitalist states and their education and media systems. 'The democratic-bureaucratic system has given rise to a great mass of functions which are not all justified by the social necessities of production, though they are justified by the political necessity of the dominant fundamental group' (ibid.: 13).

Nevertheless, for intellectual activity to have any leadership potential it must be compatible with the 'common sense' of the groups to be influenced – 'the conception of the world which is uncritically absorbed by the various social and cultural environments in which the moral individuality of the average man is developed' (ibid.: 419). Only philosophies that engage with common sense can succeed; as Stuart Hall (1996: 431) puts it, 'Formal coherence cannot guarantee [an ideology's] organic historical effectivity. That can only be found when and where philosophical currents enter into, modify and transform the practical, everyday consciousness or popular thought of the masses.'[6]

In sum, Gramsci's discussion of leadership brings our attention to a number of issues. As leadership is always imbued with political considerations, Gramsci placed a great deal of emphasis on the organizational and pedagogical requirements for developing sustainable progressive political movements. An individual may serve to personify the social myth of a political movement, but, for genuinely inclusive, emancipatory projects, the modern prince should be the political party. This tension between the individual and the structural was echoed in the discussion on economism and its risks during economic crises, and in his stress

---

[6] Notions of hegemony and common sense are invoked, in somewhat different ways, in the respective contributions to this collection by Claire Cutler (Chapter 3), Upendra Baxi (Chapter 9), Ingar Solty (Chapter 11) and Stephen Gill (Chapter 13). They all consider, in different ways, the role of organic intellectuals and political action associated with both dominant and subaltern forces.

on the necessity for a proper historical analysis in animating a social myth. In what follows, I draw on such ideas to assess aspects of the neoliberal historical moment.

The context for leadership today: the neoliberal moment

This section considers factors central to a Gramscian analysis of leadership, with reference to the material foundations of the neoliberal order, the role global institutions and experts play in establishing and sustaining them, and their implications for the logics of political power, social order, authority and democratic participation. These issues help to illuminate how neoliberalism maintains itself ideologically in periods of crisis, and what horizons for alternatives this moment might produce.

Neoliberalism is an intellectual, political and economic project: it emphasizes the use of market-based mechanisms to organize economic, political and social affairs, and promotes economic policies designed to lower inflation, deficits and public debt and to create 'macroeconomic stability'. As a theory of political economy, neoliberalism promotes the universalization of the market form, based on the ethico-political positions that markets are a direct expression of human rationality, less discriminatory than political institutions that might be captive to 'special interests', and the most efficient mechanism for organizing social and economic affairs (see Chapter 12, by Adam Harmes, for a reading of its theoretical basis in the work of Friedrich von Hayek and James Buchanan). As a political project, neoliberalism transforms the state and international organizations into institutions governed to the largest extent possible by market logic and responsible for inculcating market mechanisms and rationalities into spheres previously governed by other means. As economic policy, neoliberalism addresses a crisis of capital profitability by expanding and intensifying arenas for accumulation, for example through the commodification of previously 'social' goods and by extending debt structures.

The neoliberal historical moment can be said to have begun in the 1970s, when the concept's theories were adopted in the industrialized countries as the response to the conditions of inflation and unemployment that had emerged in the late 1960s. Neoliberalism was not the only possible solution to such economic conditions, but it became historically effective through strategies of intellectual and moral leadership articulated to the structural power of capital in the core liberal states (Cox 1987: chap. 8; Duménil and Lévy 2004; Gill 1990). Much of the political realization of the neoliberal project was initially associated with 'strong', charismatic, individual leadership, particularly in the Anglophone core countries, the United States led by Ronald Reagan and the United Kingdom led by Margaret Thatcher, though the first neoliberal economic restructuring occurred in Chile under the authoritarian rule of General Augusto Pinochet.

In attempting to insulate market-based decision-making from social forces, neoliberalism places a great emphasis on 'technocratic' expertise (which endorses an apolitical view of economic analysis) and constructs institutions that isolate economic policy from political forces – a point that is explored at length by Claire Cutler in Chapter 3 (see also Harvey 2005: 66). The neoliberal project is therefore also associated with a 'technocratic' turn in leadership, especially in developing countries, where state leaders have increasingly been trained in economics and engineering (Hira 2007), or else they are, like Mubarak and many across the Arab world, still drawn from the ranks of the military. In this way, fundamental political questions are treated as if they can have only a single, technical solution; in this sense neoliberalism also operates, as Stephen Gill notes in Chapter 1, through an eschatological discourse associated with the end of history hypothesis. Thatcher's famous phrase 'There is no alternative' therefore united the first generation of neoliberal leadership, associated with right-wing political parties, and subsequent generations of 'centre-left' or 'third way' neoliberal politicians (Chang and Grabel 2004; Gill and Law 1993; Munck 2003). As Teivo Teivainen notes in Chapter 10, the World Social Forum developed its own famous slogan, 'Another world is possible', precisely in order to create a new form of mobilizing myth that could counter neoliberalism's attempt to foreclose such political possibilities.

One of the reasons for the birth of the WSF, and other related progressive forces opposed to disciplinary neoliberalism, was the fact that the emergence of neoliberalism globally has been associated with significant changes in the international politico-economic order and the consequent restructuring of the economies and societies of many states. In the early 1970s, faced with a deteriorating trade balance, the United States abandoned its position underwriting the Bretton Woods scheme for stabilizing international exchange rates based on the dollar's convertibility to gold at $35 per ounce. Following a further decade of dollar decline, the US Federal Reserve under the chairmanship of Paul Volcker dramatically raised interest rates in 1981 (the 'Volcker shock'), restoring the position of finance domestically and abroad, and provoking the Third World debt crisis. These developments would lead to the reorientation of the IMF, and later the World Bank, towards managing the debt crisis through Structural Adjustment Programs (SAPs) (Bello 2002;

Feinberg 1988). In the 1990s the least institutionalized dimension of the postwar international economic order – the trade and investment regime – developed its organizational frameworks in the creation of the WTO, whose *raison d'être* would be the intensification of trade liberalization in certain economic sectors – particularly services, including media and education – by the reduction of trade and investment barriers (Chorev 2007; McChesney 2001; Warf 2003). Simultaneously, profit levels were restored through wage compression and assaults on organized labour, and cuts to the social wage were made through the reduction of benefits. Production formerly located in the global North moved to the global South as capital pursued lower-waged labour. Finance capital became the dominant site of profitability. As Gérard Duménil and Dominique Lévy (2004) acknowledge and Kees van der Pijl has documented (1984; 1998), this process reflects only the most recent phase of the internationalization of capital associated with finance.[7]

These developments would contribute to a number of regional financial crises and, in 2008, a global financial crisis, subsequently generalized as an economic crisis. Such instability was facilitated, paradoxically, by the emergence of instruments such as derivatives that were initially designed to provide greater certainty for capital in the absence of the more predictable exchange rates previously afforded by the Bretton Woods system (see Chapter 3 for more detail on derivatives). Ultimately, derivatives functioned to facilitate financial speculation (McNally 2009: 58).[8] However, equally importantly, the rise of such financial instruments led to the 'securitization' of working-class, consumer debt (based on mortgages and credit cards), thus incorporating the working classes of the North into the neoliberal regime of accumulation along two lines: through the provision of credit, which was necessary for the maintenance of consumption in the face of wage compression; and through the speculation on the long-term profitability of such debt (McNally 2009: 61).

Politically, neoliberalism also promotes, ideologically, the transformation of traditional state power or 'government' towards arrangements informed by ethico-political claims regarding the market, captured in the

---

[7] Kees van der Pijl (1998) foregrounds the renewed subordination of labour and the restructuring of the profit-distribution process to favour finance in his account of neoliberalism and transnational class formation. This is a much more satisfying account than the arguably more influential discussion provided by William I. Robinson (2004), which deduces a transnational capitalist class from a globalization process that is read as largely technologically driven.

[8] Parallels between the naïve assumptions behind speculative lending underlying the 2008 financial crisis and the Third World debt crisis initiated in the late 1970s seem worthy of note: that real estate would never lose value in guaranteeing mortgage-backed securities and that countries could not go bankrupt.

new preference for the term 'governance' (van der Pijl 1998: 77). The neoliberal domestic policy agenda involves pursuing, typically in the name of 'fiscal responsibility' or economic efficiency, balanced budgets, the reduction of state spending on social programmes and the privatization of state-owned assets and services. The reduction of state spending on social programmes is accompanied by state monitoring of the eligibility and administration of reconstituted programmes designed to inculcate market rationalities, such as those associated with the transformation of 'welfare' to 'workfare' (Abramovitz 2006; Morgen and Masovsky 2003; Weigt 2006). Neoliberalism also therefore involves significant implications for patterns of social reproduction: the privatization of various forms of care repositioned many aspects of social reproduction from the welfare and developmental states to the market and, for those who could not afford to purchase such services, the household (Bakker 2007: 545–6; Elson 1995). The voluntary and non-governmental organization (NGO) sectors may in some cases compensate for the decline of state services for those who cannot afford it (or in many contexts, especially some developing countries, for those who never had access; Kamat 2004). This has meant not only an expansion of commodified caregiving but the emergence of developments designed to protect the privileged from neoliberal socio-economic consequences, such as gated communities and privatized security services (Davis 2006: 115–20; Pow 2009).

Indeed, as Claire Cutler (Chapter 3) and Stephen Gill (Chapter 1) make clear, neoliberalism creates markets for products and services to offset its (anti)social effects as well as securing mechanisms and practices that allow it to define and profit from 'risks' and crises more generally. Thus, Naomi Klein (2008) has documented the emergence of 'disaster capitalism', whereby crises (both natural and man-made) provide the conditions for capital penetration in situations in which social forces had previously resisted, such as the creation of luxury resorts in fishing villages in post-tsunami Sri Lanka, the gentrification of New Orleans in the aftermath of Hurricane Katrina and the reconstruction of the Iraqi state with private capital. Indeed, neoliberalism may be said to contain within it a deeply rooted *aesthetic of crisis*, emerging as it did as a solution to the crisis of the welfare state in the North and the debt crisis of the developmental state in the South.[9] This aesthetic involves an appeal to the market to provide resources that ostensibly could not be mobilized sufficiently in scale or time through public mechanisms, as well as to the

---

[9] By 'aesthetic', I mean 'the whole program of social, psychical and political reconstruction' associated with the bourgeois politics of consent (Eagleton 1988: 327).

logic of ensuring profitability for such private investments. Accordingly, regional currency and financial crises following liberalization policies have been managed in favour of wealthy investors rather than the working classes of the affected countries, even though within neoliberal ideology they are cast as the responsibility of national policy-making failures rather than those of international markets or financial institutions (Chang 2000; Duménil and Lévy 2004).

Although neoliberal rhetoric criticizes state power in favour of the market, in addition to the state's role in monitoring market-oriented government and social restructuring, it also requires the state to establish the institutional and legal foundations for such market mechanisms and to guarantee protections for capital.[10] Gill has called the construction of such institutional and legal frameworks the 'new constitutionalism' (Gill 1992, 1998a, 1998b). In contrast to traditional notions of constitutionalism, which protect the rights of individuals, neoliberal new constitutionalism 'confers privileged rights of citizenship and representation to corporate capital' through the imposition of discipline on public institutions by insulating key aspects of the economy from democratic oversight and strengthening the surveillance mechanisms associated with access to international finance, such as the international financial institutions and private bond-rating agencies (Gill 2003a: 132). This can also be achieved, for example, through 'multi-level governance', the strategic (re)distribution of political authority across jurisdictional levels to ensure that 'market-inhibiting policy competencies' are decentralized to levels of government at which they cannot constrain capital (Harmes 2006; see also his Chapter 12 in this volume). The neoliberal *raison d'état* accepts the world market as 'the ultimate determinant of development', and the role of the state, beyond constructing the appropriate frameworks for private property and the market, involves adopting a strategy for its own competitiveness (Cox 1987: 290).

The neoliberal technocratic turn parallels the rise of charismatic leadership in ways that have sought to redefine intellectual and moral leadership around the questions of governance and democracy, such that they are increasingly defined in non-participatory terms.[11] Across the industrialized countries, voter turnout and party affiliation have

---

[10] Indeed, neoliberalism's general appeal to the courts as a form of dispute resolution reflects a strong upper-class bias (Harvey 2005: 78).

[11] Again, this echoes Stephen Gill's argument about the 'new constitutionalism', in that, as Peter Mair suggests, 'this process of redefinition lies in highlighting the distinction between what has been called "constitutional democracy" and what we might call "popular democracy"' (Mair 2006: 29). Thus, neoliberal public intellectuals such as

decreased in the neoliberal period; there is greater voter volatility across parties and a greater incidence of 'split ticket' voting (Mair 2006). The neoliberal emphasis on governance involves the claim that democracy is best understood in apolitical, non-partisan, 'party-less' terms (Mair 2000: 28). Good governance is to be understood as administration rather than politics, whereby 'objective solutions to social, economic or cultural problems are most likely to be found after you have established a judicious mix of institutional correctness and expert, non-partisan judgments' (ibid.: 32–3). Indeed, politics is understood to be alienating to citizens, and thus, as one of Tony Blair's Cabinet members (Lord Falconer) purportedly argued, the 'depoliticizing of key decision-making is a vital element in bringing power closer to the people' (Mair 2006: 26, fn 25). Neoliberal political leaders identify with the project of governance – technocratic coalitions for ostensibly non-partisan problem-solving – rather than political platforms. As a result, '[Bill] Clinton's famous strategy of "triangulation" in 1996 was presented as a transcendence of the shabby interests of partisan politics in favour of a government of "the people"' (Mair 2000: 32). In many cases, Western political parties have rebranded themselves so that they drop the term 'party' in their names (New Labour replaced the Labour Party, while in Italy neither the Democratici di Sinistra on the left nor Forza Italia on the right uses the term) (ibid.). Thus, neoliberal governance incorporates 'citizen preferences' in commercial terms, established through focus groups and the logic of consumer preferences, to develop marketing strategies for politicians seeking office (Sussman and Galizio 2003: 314). Political commitments, insofar as they exist, are cast as 'contracts' between voters and politicians. Peter Mair cites New Labour, but this certainly echoes the US Republicans' 'Contract with America' (Mair 2000: 33). Voting is relegated to providing post hoc legitimation of the 'political' system.

Although Gramsci was spared the joys of television, today the ever-increasing use of TV advertising for political campaigns in Western democracies – now permitted in the United Kingdom, France, Germany, Italy, Austria and Sweden, in addition to the United States – increases the cost of campaigns, thereby privileging wealthier interests, and affects the discourse of politics, demanding that candidates 'speak the grammar and idiom of television' (Sussman and Galizio 2003: 319–20). All this establishes a greater emphasis on 'personality, "character", and "leadership"', because 'appealing personalities are currency of high denomination in

---

Fareed Zakaria now argue that the Western model (to be emulated) is best understood not in terms of participatory democracy but constitutional liberalism, not 'the mass plebiscite but the impartial judge' (Mair 2006: 30).

media logic' (ibid.: 317). Thus it is that many contemporary analyses of 'leadership' are in fact studies of political media strategies, including tactics to establish a sense of identification with and confidence in the candidate, at the expense of those relationships with the party (Finlayson 2002). The transformation of election laws in continental Europe, for example in France and Italy, which now list individuals rather than parties, also underlines this move. The neoliberal commercial election format is underwritten by international political consultants, predominantly from or trained in the United States, who 'help establish or reinforce enclaves of collaboration between different state elites and bring about a fuller integration of politics and market economics, a standardization of politics and political discourses that emphasize market choices and technocracy as the measure of rational decision making and freedom and the "inefficiencies" of public spending' (Sussman and Galizio 2003: 314). Consultants from US political parties began to work directly on international elections from the mid-1990s onwards in the United Kingdom, Israel, Mexico, Canada, and Russia (ibid.: 321–4). Such consultants have a preference for the more predictable conditions of smaller voter turnout, which thus enhance their credibility (ibid.: 317).

Although it is harder to find scholarly discussions of the specific relationships, deregulation has amplified the role of private media as 'party functionary' in many places. The most conspicuous cases are media moguls who have turned into 'charismatic' politicians, such as Silvio Berlusconi, Thaksin Shinawatra, Sebastian Piñera or Michael Bloomberg. However, the private media have played an increasingly prominent role in partisan politics in the neoliberal period in other contexts, such as the relationship between Tony Blair and Rupert Murdoch (Hinsliff 2006; Vulliamy 2005), or Fox News in the United States (Frau-Meigs 2008). Robert McChesney has documented the incredible concentration of media in the neoliberal period, such that, for example, twenty companies receive 75 per cent of all global advertising revenue, coordinated by five or six companies owning 'super-ad' agencies (McChesney 2001: 7).

In sum, the neoliberal period has extended the logic of market-based decision-making deeper and more extensively across society, transforming the ensemble of social relations, the institutional logics of state and international organizations and the role of political parties and leaders in 'governance'. This transformation has been accomplished in part through an aesthetic of crisis, whereby the market is continuously reasserted as the sole solution to social problems – even those symptoms of neoliberalism itself. The neoliberal reconstruction of electoral politics has created the structural conditions for a new, undemocratic, depoliticized 'common sense' to emerge that is populated by the commodified logic of political leadership across political parties, redefining leadership in the highly undemocratic, charismatic terms that Gramsci cautioned against, and naturalizing the market as beyond the realm of the political entirely.

Conclusion: leadership in the context of neoliberal crisis

The neoliberal preoccupation with leadership (*qua* media communications strategy and televisual charisma) can be read as a symptom of an undemocratic order seeking aesthetic expression in a social myth. In this sense, when Frank Rich characterizes US president Barack Obama – based on eight major books on his leadership released within months of his first year in office – as a Rorschach test, for the range of positions attributed to him by left and right despite the fact that his public statements have remained consistently 'bipartisan [and] moderate', it captures an essential feature of neoliberal leadership: a kind of charisma that can accommodate a very wide breadth of political interpretations (Rich 2010). Indeed, Obama had already written two memoirs before his election, establishing a particularly personal, autobiographical foundation for his remit in public office. It is also telling that the backlash to his leadership equally involved a discourse of a *crisis* of identity: the right-wing anxiety that '[w]e don't really know who Obama is', reflected in the 'birther' movement associated with the emergence of the right-wing populist Tea Party, which made its gains by fostering doubts among the American public as to whether, by birth, Obama is qualified to serve as president (see Chapter 11, by Ingar Solty, on right-wing populism and its links to a complex of social force in Germany and the United States).

The neoliberal period, as in Gramsci's day, has also been characterized by a 'left' divided on the question of the desirability of political power, partly in the guise of postmodernism rather than anarcho-syndicalism (Harvey 2005: 42) and partly for reasons of political organization. In addition, as noted, since the economic crisis hit the North, right-wing populism has become an increasingly visible political force in many industrialized countries. In many senses 'economism' has structured responses to the crisis, particularly at the core in the United States, where narratives of individual/corporate greed and malfeasance are widely reported and accepted, and have translated into efforts to prosecute personal wrongdoing, although consensus on structural measures, even relatively modest regulation, remains much harder to establish (Markon 2010). Indeed, dominant responses to the crisis in the North and in the South through the pressure of the IMF have reproduced neoliberal logics of protecting market profitability over addressing unemployment and reducing government deficits at the expense of social investment (Seabrook 2010; Weisbrot 2010). The internationalization of production, the globalization of market discipline through the restructuring of the state and international institutions, and the appeal to multiscalar 'global governance' to separate more functionally the economic from the political present new challenges to conceptualizing the possibilities for a project of democratic leadership. Furthermore, such neoliberal developments, through the deregulation of media and the internationalization of political services, have transformed party politics, seemingly to evacuate them of their emancipatory potential by institutionalizing organizationally the undemocratic distance between leaders and led. The broader organizational challenges of a new modern prince – or what Gill has called a 'postmodern prince' (see Chapter 13) – require further theorization.

Nevertheless, a few principles can be outlined here. A progressive response must connect the pursuit of political power to a critique of the more pronounced separation of the economic and the political embodied in the new institutional arrangements produced by neoliberalism and new constitutionalism. It should include a strong challenge to the credibility of the market as a social organizing form, and a critique of how capital seeks to expropriate public or social goods – such as healthcare (see Chapter 7, by Solomon Benatar) and public education (one of Gramsci's lifetime concerns) – by turning them into privately owned commodities that can be bought and sold in the marketplace. This challenge can help to generate a new 'common sense' concerning the need for credible links between economic production and socially useful and ecologically sustainable activity. Critical intellectuals – such as the contributors to this book – should exploit the Achilles heels of neoliberalism, such as its aesthetic of crisis, and argue that market fundamentalism is itself a symptom of a crisis of market civilization, and, at a more specific policy level, critique those Keynesian regulatory responses that simply seek to stabilize the rule of the market in social relations. Resubordinating the market to democratic controls will also need to begin with decolonizing party politics from market-governed logics, removing private funding from political campaigns and promoting new regimes of media regulation, and building stronger and more democratic political parties of the non-authoritarian left.

3 Private transnational governance and the crisis of global leadership

A. Claire Cutler

Summary

This chapter explores the centrality of private transnational governance to the crisis of global leadership. It focuses on the role that private transnational lawyers, accountants and expert systems of knowledge play in recasting relationships between leaders and led in the face of global capitalism's deepening crisis. Transnational lawyers and financial experts are analysed as the organic intellectuals and leaders of the nascent global, neoliberal market civilization whose role is to provide the legal expertise and infrastructure for expansive global capitalism. Binding rules facilitate capital expansion by securing investors against existing, new and emergent business risks. Organic intellectuals' success turns upon their ability to legitimate 'expert' rule by successfully characterizing this predominantly private system of governance as public in nature and effect and as 'common sense'. However, the chapter argues that the domain of experts, like that of common sense, is in fact contested, revealing cracks and openings that enable the development of a critical understanding of private transnational governance.

Introduction

This chapter explores the significance of private transnational governance in regulating the global political economy and its centrality to the crisis of global leadership. Transnational governance is a mode of governance that 'structures, guides and controls human and social activities and interactions beyond, across and within national territories' and is 'embedded in and supported by other modes of governance' (Djelic and Sahlin-Andersson 2006: 6). Transnational governance comprises a multiplicity of actors and institutions, including governments, international organizations, transnational business corporations and various private business associations. It is associated generally with the expansion of global capitalism and neoliberal principles that privilege the market as the template of 'good governance' and 'common sense' (Djelic 2006). The particular focus of this chapter is on *private* transnational governance and the central leadership role played by private actors in linking local and global political economies together into complex governance arrangements that serve to discipline national economies and societies according to delocalized and private systems of rule. Corporate and professional actors, such as lawyers, arbitrators, accountants, bankers, insurers and underwriters, as well as systems of private transnational law, assert significant leadership in the global political economy.

However, the significance of private lawmaking is obscured by distinctions between *public* and *private* international law that ascribe political governance roles solely to the former, and not to the latter. Private actors are assumed to operate neutrally and apolitically, as markets putatively function (Cutler 2008a). This makes it difficult to entertain seriously the conceptual or theoretical significance of private sources of lawmaking and dispute settlement, even though they define the *Grundnormen* for global governance. Today private systems of ordering perform crucial roles in managing global capitalism by assisting governing élites in adjusting to the changing terms of competition and risk resulting from global capitalism's ongoing crisis. Indeed, the crisis of leadership is linked to a more general crisis of global capitalism. The former involves a rupture in the relationship between leaders and led, which is linked to the broader crisis of capitalism as an economic system resting upon a certain configuration of public and private spheres. For much of the period since World War II the global political economy was regulated on the basis of the 'compromise of embedded liberalism' (Ruggie 1982), which carved out a protective sphere for securing the public weal in a compromise with expansionary forces of private accumulation. However, that compromise has come undone, and the distinction between public and private goods and purposes that managed the relationships between leaders and led ceases to operate. In practice, the private sphere subverts and absorbs the public sphere to its own ends, as 'crisis management' by private élites becomes part of hegemonic thinking and 'common sense'. Ironically, the mythology of the distinction between spheres continues to operate, rendering obscure the extent to which private purposes now exercise a leadership role (Cutler 1995). However, this leadership role is coming under increasing scrutiny as governments and citizens question the part that economic and financial élites played in precipitating the deepest economic crisis in decades. It is therefore a propitious moment for a re-examination of private transnational governance as a central modality of global capitalism.

This chapter examines corporate and professional actors as the organic intellectuals and leaders of the nascent global, neoliberal market civilization. It addresses their role in providing the legal infrastructure that forms the normative underbelly of and the material conditions for global capitalism, securing neoliberal disciplines through binding national, international and transnational rules and dispute settlement mechanisms that protect against existing, new and emergent business risks. However, as organic intellectuals, their success turns upon their ability to bind together diverse social, economic and political groups by legitimating their activities. This requires the successful characterization of this predominantly private system of governance as efficacious, democratic and universal, effectively obliterating the public/private distinction by recasting *private* interests and outcomes as *public* in nature. The resulting reformulation of public and private spheres raises significant legitimacy concerns about how private transnational leadership defines ethical, political and humane governance, and questions about 'Who gets what?' from private transnational governance. These questions in turn enhance the possibilities of and prospects for challenging the hegemony of private corporate leadership and identifying the necessary conditions for establishing an alternative world order.

The first section provides an empirical overview of private transnational governance, illustrating the pervasiveness of this mode of leadership and linking its purpose to the central – and big – business of 'risk'. The next section critically examines the grounds upon which private transnational governance is legitimated, while the final section assesses the possibilities for alternative modes of global governance and leadership.

Private transnational governance and leadership in the global political economy

The increasing significance of private modes of governance is being recorded in the disciplines of international relations, international business and international law (Cutler, Haufler and Porter 1999; Djelic and Sahlin-Andersson 2006; Graz and Nölke 2008; Hall and Biersteker 2002). A review of the scope of private transnational governance reveals that it takes many forms, involves many different types of actors, sectors, issues and interests that cut across traditional political, economic, cultural, legal, disciplinary and spatial boundaries in complementary and contradictory ways, and results in increasingly complex forms of governance (Grande and Pauly 2005). The governance activities of private actors have been identified in areas of international and transnational economic relations and law, including financial governance and central bank independence (Morgan 2010; Porter 2005), secured financial transactions (Cohen 2007), competition law (Djelic and Kleiner 2006), accounting and auditing practices (Nölke and Perry 2007; Williams 2006), insurance and risk management (Haufler 1997), coordination service firms and bond-rating agencies (Sinclair 2004), the internet and online commerce (Knill and Lehmkuhl 2002), information technologies (Salter 1999), commodity industries and markets (Porter 1999), investor protection and the global investment regime (Schneiderman 2006; Van Harten 2005) and international trade and intellectual property rights (Sell 2003).

In some areas, private actors, including corporations and civil society groups alike, are engaged in governance that traverses sectoral boundaries and issue areas, as in certification schemes that regulate the environmental, labour and human rights activities of industries and producers (Lipschutz and Fogel 2002), including the forestry, organic agriculture, diamond, apparel, fishing, banking and financial industries (Cashore, Auld and Newsom 2003; Clapp and Fuchs 2009; Kantz 2007; McNicol 2006; Meidinger 2006; Schaper 2007).

Private ordering is also dominant today in the corporate social responsibility movement, which engages corporations and private business associations in developing voluntary codes of conduct governing environmental, human rights, labour and corporate governance activities (Cutler 2008b; Haufler 2001). The notion of corporate social responsibility is also extending to matters of international security in formulations of the *security* responsibilities of private security firms (Avant 2005; Wolf, Deitelhoff and Engert 2007). Indeed, there has been increasing concern with the privatization of security and the growing authority of private security firms (Chesterman and Lehnardt 2007; Leander 2005).

Lawyers are articulating conceptions of private transnational law in response to developments that 'break the frames' of the historical unity of law and state and that alter the legal relations between states and supra-state, sub-state and non-state actors involved in transboundary social relations and economic transactions (Teubner 2002). The growing reality of private transnational law is evident in empirical developments associated with the globalization of law and the transnationalization of the legal field (Horn and Schmitthoff 1982; Trubek *et al.* 1994). Recognition of law's increasingly private face characterizes notions of entrepreneurial lawyering (Dezalay and Garth 1996), lawmaking by transnational law firms (Morgan 2006; Quack 2007) and disaggregated sovereignty (Slaughter 2004). In fact, private lawmaking

processes are transforming the fields of both public and private international law, blurring the distinction between the two (Spanogle 1991;
Steinhardt 1991) and creating tensions between national and transnational orders (Cutler 2003).

Conceptions of 'transnational liftoff and juridical touchdown'
(Wai 2001: 29) seek to depict how transnationalized law creates supra-
territorial relations among people by delocalizing and denationalizing
the law (Santos 2002), removing its creation, interpretation and application from the constraints of territorial locations, while then relocaliz-
ing and renationalizing social relations when the laws are enforced
(Cutler 2005). David Schneiderman (2006) analyses the transnational
legality created by the investment rules regime that implicates states in
transnational governance by subordinating them to the demands of
securing and expanding private transnational investment. Similarly, the
emerging global intellectual property regime, though centred on the
public law Agreement on Trade-Related aspects of Intellectual Property
Rights (TRIPS), was initiated by powerful private pharmaceutical,
entertainment and software companies and 'reaches deep into the
domestic regulatory environment of states', subjecting local economic
activities to transnational legal disciplines (Sell 2003: 1). These developments challenge many traditional analytical distinctions, but common to
all of them is the insight that transnational law does not eclipse the
authority of states and national law. Rather, transnational legality recon-
figures the relationships between states and societies by disciplining how
states do business. The transnational is thus not 'located' outside but is
implicated within the national, linking local and global political economies and societies in complex ways (Cutler 2003).

This review illustrates that private transnational governance is recognized as a significant empirical dimension of the contemporary world
order. Moreover, although there are obvious historical antecedents
(Cutler 2003; Cutler, Haufler and Porter 1999), mechanisms of private
ordering have expanded in scope with the globalization of neoliberal
policies of privatization and deregulation and have strengthened their
hold on local political economies and societies. The increasing extent
and intensity of private governance may be seen as the result of particular
historical, material and ideological conditions associated with the current conjuncture. Private transnational governance is a modality of rule
under the new constitutionalism and neoliberal disciplines that lock
states into binding legal arrangements that provide for the free, unre-
stricted movement of goods, services and investment (Gill 2008).

Systems of private and market-based ordering are ideologically
compatible with neoliberalism and flexible production in according

ultimate control to the private sector, corporations and markets, which proponents argue are best able to govern by adjusting to changing terms of global competition and risk (Harvey 2005). Indeed, the deeper purposes of private transnational governance concern the securing of the conditions necessary for the continuing expansion of capitalism, both geographically and substantively, in terms of the expansion of commodifiable interests and property. We know from Marx that continuous expansion has always characterized capitalist development, but it is becoming trickier with the globalization of deregulated markets and accentuated risks, both real and perceived; and it is here, in the identification and management of risk, that lawyers and other professionals, such as accountants, excel.

Indeed, while there is great diversity in the shape that private transnational governance takes in the areas discussed in this chapter, the one unifying factor is the central governance role of the professional and the technical 'expert'. A. Claire Cutler, Virginia Haufler and Tony Porter (1999: 345–8) identify technical knowledge and expertise as important in constituting and legitimating the authority of private actors. They note the 'epistemic authority' of bond raters, maritime transport lawyers and intellectual property lawyers in creating the legal regimes governing these areas. Rodney Bruce Hall and Thomas Biersteker (2002: 14) similarly observe the authority wielded by private actors with expertise. In fact, for Porter (2005: 2), technical expertise is so significant in legitimating private transnational governance that he identifies *technical authority* as analytically and functionally distinct from both *public* authority and *private* authority.

A recent study of experts and private transnational governance (Quack 2010) focuses on a variety of areas. However, the central and contested role of experts emerges most acutely in analyses of the governance of the current financial crisis (Morgan 2010) and the legal regulation of private security firms (Cutler 2010). In both cases, experts engage not only in the management and control of risk but also in the construction of risk as 'risk shapers' (Nitzan and Bichler 2009: 210). That these professionals are in the business of risk management would probably not be disputed, but that they are also engaged in the manufacture of risk and in creating perceptions of ever more risks that need to be secured against challenges belief in professional integrity and neutrality. However, as is argued later, risk management is 'big business'. Professionals construct their livelihoods through the creation of 'universals' (Dezalay and Garth 2010: 116) and 'imaginaries' (Kennedy 2005: 17, 24) that produce consensual world views, to which laypeople defer as 'expert' knowledge.

Many regard experts as creating new modes of governance that are reflexive and adaptable to fast-changing and unpredictable environments (Cooney and Lang 2007). Yves Dezalay and Bryant Garth locate a 'global private justice system' at the 'transnational level', which is best understood as 'a virtual space that provides strategic opportunities for competitive struggles engaged in by *national* actors' (Dezalay and Garth 1996: 3; emphasis in original). Similarly, David Trubek *et al.* (1994: 411) emphasize that legal élites are reconfiguring national legal fields through their transnational lawmaking and interactions. Through the globalization of business law and the influence of 'epistemic communities', being 'loose connections of knowledge-based experts who share certain attitudes and values and substantive knowledge, as well as ways of thinking about how to use that knowledge' (Braithwaite and Drahos 2000: 501), lawyers are celebrated as valuable entrepreneurs for creating transformative legal forms. For example, innovative securities, like derivatives, allow the expansion of capital through the repackaging of debt and are heralded as creative risk management. They enable control over uncertainties in a dynamic global political economy (ibid.: 502). However, this view is contested by others who believe that reliance on the scientific knowledge of experts conceals their very real and unaccountable power (García-Salmones 2009: 167). Moreover, this power is said to recast 'problems of politics as problems of expert knowledge' through a 'managerial-technical' revolution that is sweeping the legal world (Koskenniemi 2007: 8).

Most problematically, analysts tend to conceptualize risk as external to capital and requiring need of management or mitigation in order to secure capital accumulation (Braithwaite and Drahos 2000). What is missing is the recognition that risk is in fact internal to capitalist accumulation: it is *'integral'* in a most elementary way to processes of accumulation (Nitzan and Bichler 2009: 212). Indeed, the manufacture of risk is possibly one of the most dynamic and expansionary characteristics of modern capitalist activity, and thus figures centrally in the works of more critically minded studies. Modern society is a 'risk society' (Beck 2000) and a 'risk culture' (Giddens 1991: 3). However, it is not a 'risk society' because life 'is inherently more risky than it used to be', but because 'the concept of risk becomes fundamental to the way both lay actors and technical specialists organize the social world. Under conditions of modernity, the future is continually drawn into the present through the reflexive organization of knowledge environments', producing a 'colonization of the future' (ibid.: 3–4). In addition, disembedding social relations as expert systems of technical knowledge gives rise to a continuous state of monitoring and profiling for new risks and dangers (ibid.: 19, 111). Moreover, the identification of new risks to be secured against fuels many industries, including those of insurance, credit rating and private security (Krahmann 2008). Arguably, this permanently hard-wires a crisis mentality into the fabric of leadership and governance, normalizing and naturalizing conditions of high risk and crisis and thereby securing unlimited market potential for risk specialists. This is because 'risk society', by its very nature, delivers authority to experts by privileging technical and scientific knowledge (Giddens 1991: 30–1; Cutler 2010). How, though, is expert knowledge legitimated? How are the activities of private corporations, business associations and professionals such as lawyers and accountants rendered as authoritative as those of leaders and governors? I turn now to a critical assessment of the persuasiveness of the various rationales offered in legitimation of private transnational governance.

Who let the fox guard the hen house?

In many ways the notion of private governance turns conventional understanding of constitutionalism and government on its head, by transforming, if not perverting, the very essence of 'government'. As Martti Koskenniemi (2007: 16) observes, 'Constitutionalism, as we know it from the national context, relies on some basic understanding of the common good, and some sense of law as a shared project for a reasonably clearly defined (and often historically informed) objective.' Leadership and governance are concerned with advancing the public good. They are not concerned with advancing private interests, for that would constitute private interest governance and raise profound concerns about democratic legitimacy (Streeck and Schmitter 1985). Proponents of private transnational governance are aware of these concerns and have explored a number of means for addressing potential democratic deficits arising through private modes of leadership. As these means have been thoroughly explored elsewhere (Cutler 2010), this discussion highlights the main rationales advanced in support of the legitimacy of private transnational governance and the central leadership role of experts.

As a starting point, the standard employed to assess the legitimacy of private actors engaged in governance is that of 'democratic' legitimacy, and it draws upon liberal theories of politics and political economy (Bodansky 1999). The idea is that, to be legitimate, private decision-makers must operate according to at least a semblance of democratic criteria. Democratic legitimacy is assessed through the adequacy of participation in decision-making processes and the procedural quality of these processes, in terms of their transparency and deliberative dimensions. The focus is on 'input' and 'throughput' legitimacy (Scharpf 1999, 2009; Wolf 2006), and analysts look for indications that private processes of decision-making involve consultation with the relevant 'stakeholders' and consider the plurality of interests involved in the decision at hand. However, as Daniel Bodansky (1999: 600) observes, 'Principles of procedural fairness – transparency, public access, and so forth – are important, but do not answer the crucial question of who should make decisions and how they should do so.'

Accordingly, legitimacy is also assessed in terms of the end or 'output' of the process and judged according to the effectiveness and efficiency of the process for addressing collective action problems and providing public goods. The result should thus achieve a 'public' end and serve the common weal (Scharpf 2009: 5). Here the specific technical knowledge and professional knowledge of the expert emerge as central legitimating mechanisms, for it is the expert who is regarded as competent to deliver the most efficient and effective solution to a problem. In addition, it is the expert who, through claims to objectivity as a trained specialist, is trusted as best to decide from among competing choices and to determine the 'optimal' result. However, this begs several questions, not the least of which is who decides what is optimal and for whom. Indeed, the authorizing significance of the expert as 'an authority', as distinct from one 'in authority', as in the case of a government official, 'is based on, is possessed by virtue of, demonstrated knowledge, skill, or expertise concerning subject matter or activity' (Flathman 1980: 16–17). The authority of the international commercial lawyer or arbitrator, accountant or banker is regarded as deriving from his or her professional knowledge and expertise in the matter at hand. However, this immediately raises the problem that expert knowledge is also a commodity to be bought and sold, and is subject to supply and demand in a market. Experts may therefore have conflicting roles as private market participants and as interpreters of the public weal.

Such conflict is recognized in the literature on private transnational governance. The neutrality of private security firms has been challenged by many who question the extent to which they can in fact create the demand for their services by identifying ever more risks against which their clients have to be secured (Cutler 2010; Leander 2005; Williams 2006). There is growing recognition of the influence exercised by coordination service firms, such as law firms, insurance companies, management consultancies, credit-rating agencies, stock exchanges and financial clearing houses, which have 'a deep infrastructural impact on the economy' and exercise 'epistemic authority' as they 'spread the basic preconditions for the operations of financialized capitalism' and the disintermediation of finance (Nölke and Perry 2007: 126, 131). In fact, the public repercussions of private transnational governance have been brought to the forefront by recent economic upheavals and the 'legitimation crisis' facing financial markets, which Glenn Morgan (2010: 17) argues constitutes 'a moment of epochal change'. Morgan (2010: 22) analyses the market for credit default swaps (CDSs),[1] a form of derivative central to the financial crisis and developed during a 'cognitive revolution' in the 1990s with the 'development of financial economics as an academic discipline associated with the development of theories of capital market efficiency and risk management'. Morgan (2010: 22) identifies derivatives as 'key areas of innovation central to the expansion of the financial system', and illustrates how they function as a

way of managing risk, as they enable buyers to exchange uncertainties (about interest rates, currency fluctuations, equity process, commodity prices) for certainties. In principle, risks are diversified across the system, migrating to those institutions which have the expertise to calculate them and the capital to hold them and away from those organizations which wish to concentrate on other things than potential instabilities.

At least, this is the theory upon which the private transnational authorities governing the system operated. The International Swaps and Derivatives Association (ISDA) is the private industry association that developed the standard contract utilized in the industry for derivatives and swaps and provides 'a form of transnational private rule-making' (ibid.: 25). ISDA worked with national governments to ensure the enforceability of these contracts under national law, but simultaneously ensured that it had maximum freedom to manage these transactions free from national legal oversight and regulation. This is a perfect example of the 'transnational liftoff and juridical touchdown' discussed earlier.

---

[1] Derivatives are essentially contracts whose value depends upon the price of another underlying asset, index or interest rate (Morgan 2010: 22). CDSs are a form of derivative that differ distinctly from the first derivatives, pioneered in the 1970s for trading on regulated exchanges, in that the former are not traded on regulated exchanges but are traded 'over the counter' (OTC). Such OTCs were developed in the 1980s and are bilateral contracts between two people who decide the price for the product. OTCs are inherently riskier than CDSs traded on exchanges, because defaults are borne by the parties and not by the exchange, as in the case of derivatives traded on an exchange. Accordingly, there is the risk that default by one trader might trigger default by another and system-wide defaults in situations of contracts with multiple counterparties. Morgan (2010: 23) notes that the collapse of Barings Bank and Enron were related to trading in OTC derivatives markets. He also notes that the CDS market grew at the same time as the market for collateralized debt obligations (CDOs), as purchasers of CDOs would purchase CDSs to protect themselves against default and as a speculative investment.

These transactions are regulated by ISDA, a private transnational organization of financial experts, but then enforced through binding systems
of national law.

Despite doubts expressed by officials in Basel about the stability
and sustainability of the system, ISDA was supported in its initiatives
through the dominant 'free market discourse' and the reluctance of
political leaders to interfere with booming financial markets. However,
ISDA got it wrong, as the world learned when the markets collapsed.
Morgan (2010: 30–1) notes that, by 2007, a 'massive market' in swaps
had developed, largely as a result of huge expansion in the American
and British mortgage markets and the repackaging of original loans in
a 'massive game of pass the parcel'. However, when the value of the
mortgage-backed assets declined, the pressure on swaps increased and
credit markets began to seize up, setting off a contagion of collapses
throughout the market. Morgan documents the response of public
and private actors during the crisis of September and October 2008
and shows how, notwithstanding the instabilities inherent in the
system, private actors managed to secure the commitment of massive
public funding to bail them out, while at the same time maintaining
self-regulatory autonomy. Private actors, including ISDA, went on to
re-establish the market, ensuring that CDSs were given priority status
in the bailout and establishing a complex private system and procedure (netting and auctioning) that enabled the settlement of accounts.
Today, 'far from collapsing in line with the collapse of subprime-based
CDOs, CDS business is, in fact, surviving well with notional values
outstanding at the end of 2008 of $41.868 trillion (compared with
$57.894 trillion the previous year)' (Morgan 2010: 35). Private actors
were successful in keeping their system of regulation fundamentally
intact by presenting their private interests as public in nature by
maintaining the belief that these instruments and procedures were
successful in protecting against credit risk and in distributing risk in
the system (ibid.).

The financial crisis highlights the conflicting roles of the financial
expert. Morgan (2010: 36) notes that ISDA is dominated by bankers
'who work on the trading side of business. Dealers have every incentive
to keep the market opaque and bespoke, which boosted margins – and
profits.' ISDA worked hard to reframe the debate as one about risk
management and control. Morgan (ibid.: 39) concludes that

insiders were keen to constrain the debate and to shift it away from the idea of a
general failure of financialized capitalism to a debate about the mechanics of how
to run it. They sought to narrow down issues from broad questions of the
legitimacy of financial markets as a whole to narrower questions, how to keep

the markets going in a way which enabled them to function effectively according to notions derived from financial economics.

Similar conflicts of interest are identified in experts' transnational regulation of secured transactions (Cohen 2007) and investor protection (Van Harten 2005), while rule through experts marginalizes developing countries in environmental regimes (Roht-Arriaza 1995), international trade regimes (Kapoor 2004; Sell 2003; Shaffer 2004) and international investment regimes (Smythe 2003). There is also distrust that the 'goods' supplied by private transnational governance are in fact 'public' goods (Krahmann 2008). Indeed, the field of private business regulation and corporate social responsibility is described by Morten Ougaard (2006: 235) as a 'field of...discursive and material struggle about business practice' in which the interests and power of business are in conflict with more general societal interests. Experts manage this tension and play a central role in neutralizing and naturalizing expert rule through appeals to objectivity and rationality and by framing their goals and purposes as universals. ISDA was able to recover from the biggest financial crisis in decades, virtually intact, because it was successful in characterizing the bailout as a matter of public confidence and concern and in moving the terms of debate from the legitimacy of the system to its prudent management. In so doing the association capitalized on its role as an expert body, while ensuring the continuing viability of financialized capitalism. I turn now to consider whether there might be fractures in the authority wielded by experts that might offer possibilities for contesting private transnational governance.

Pessimism of the intellect and optimism of the will

In light of the terrain of contesting social forces in which experts operate, it is useful to look for guidance to Antonio Gramsci's conception of the nature and role of organic intellectuals. Gramsci regarded political authority as constituted by relations of both consent and coercion. His famous equation 'state = political society + civil society', 'in other words hegemony protected by the armour of coercion' (Hoare and Nowell-Smith 1971: 263), contemplates governance as a combination of relations of coercion, associated with the military and state laws and the voluntary relations of civil society. However, Gramsci believed that the balance between consent and coercion, which he associated with 'hegemony', emerges from the popular support of civil society. In this, 'organic intellectuals' are crucial 'for creating social conformism which is useful to the ruling groups' line of development' (ibid.: 247). Organic intellectuals advance the private interests of the ruling class as societal and common interests, 'bringing about not only a unison of economic and political aims, but also intellectual and moral unity, posing all questions around which the struggle rages not on a corporate but on a "universal" plane, and thus creating a hegemony of the fundamental social group over a series of subordinate groups' (ibid.: 181–8). Although Gramsci believed that all classes produce intellectuals, it is the organic intellectual who is able to achieve the deepest integration of social groups in society by shaping 'intersubjective forms of consciousness in civil society' (Morton 2007: 93).

Beginning from the understanding that capitalism does not automatically reproduce itself but requires supports and structures that assist in maintaining and expanding the social forces that drive private accumulation, we might think of private transnational governance as a legitimating mechanism for transnational capitalism (Cutler 2009). In this regard, experts as 'organic intellectuals' mediate the dialectical relationship between local and global politico-legal orders and economies, refashioning localities according to the logic of private transnational governance, while simultaneously advancing the transnational expansion of capitalism. They are 'located at the intersection' of national and transnational capitalist systems, 'between territorial and globalizing aspects of world order' (Gill 2008: 194), and they function to represent their disciplinary consensus as 'normal', transmitting it through society, consensually, as 'common sense'. David Kennedy (2005: 5) argues that the world of private transnational governance – '[p]rivate ordering, standards bodies, financial institutions and payment systems, tax systems, trade regimes' – is managed by legal experts who 'communicate with one another in common vernaculars' (ibid.: 6), develop 'expert consensus' (ibid.: 13), and 'rule' by determining 'what is "normal" and what is not' (ibid.: 12). Experts 'do not speak the language of interests or ideologies – they speak professional vocabularies of best practices, empirical necessity, good sense of consensus values' (ibid.: 15).

Significantly, they appear to be objective because, through the creation of 'imaginaries', they 'shape how problems are defined and narrow the range of solutions considered' (ibid.: 17). Their professionalism and expertise ostensibly remove contestation from the field. 'They do not have discretion – they are compelled by their expertise. For them to exercise discretion – "deciding in the exception", to coin a phrase – is to overstep the proper bounds of background work... They advise, they interpret, but they do not rule. Theirs are vocabularies of advice, implementation, technique, know-how – useful for limiting and channelling the power of *others*' (ibid.: 15; emphasis in original). At least this is a legitimating rationale, and 'experts sustain their self-image. . .by locating the "political" elsewhere' (ibid.). Private transitional authority is thus about technical management, not governance. Moreover, by framing this self-image in universal terms, experts are able to advance their world view as common sense throughout society. However, it is important to question how complete or hegemonic such self-understandings are and whether there might be openings for contesting transnational governance by experts.

Although Kennedy makes a persuasive case for consensus rule by experts within particular disciplines, the existence of distinct localities suggests that transnational expertise invokes a range of definitions and understandings at any one time. Moreover, it is perhaps the simultaneous condition of a plurality of 'expertises', evidenced in professional vocabularies between experts in different locations, as well as those between experts in diverse disciplines, that functions to produce variances in the politico-economic salience of a particular regulatory norm or regime and the public's consent for them. For example, in the area of credit and bankruptcy law, the private transnational legal regime is modelled on US commercial law and clearly favours secured creditors over borrowers, marginalizing the interests of consumers, unions and other social groups opposed to the laws (Cohen 2007). However, this version of transnational legal expertise makes 'sense' only in jurisdictions in which American commercial law has won ideological hegemony, and might make less 'sense' in places where this incarnation of the legal form is subject to greater contestation. The terrain of transnational legal norms within diverse localities looks a lot like the terrain of common sense itself: contradictory and open for contestation despite its colonization by certain powerful ideas. This is because this form of 'common sense' is precisely that: common opinion as framed by expert opinion makers. It is not 'good sense' as Gramsci conceived of it in terms of understandings accompanying transformative political praxis. Governance through 'good sense' involves self-reflexivity, as well as a conscious recognition of and moral and ethical engagement with contesting social forces (Hoare and Nowell-Smith 1971: 326, 333, 419–20). Conceptions of 'transnational common sense' thus obscure the underlying disagreements and conflicting interests and views about just how local and global political economies and societies should be governed. The challenge is thus not about discovering cracks or openings in private transnational governance but recognizing that the cracks and openings are always already there.

Accordingly, we might begin from the premise that there is emancipatory potential inherent in private transnational governance. Expertise is a commodity, but it is also a practice conditioned by the nexus between dominant knowledge and power structures. As the professional keepers of knowledge, experts are extraordinarily powerful figures, and they are made all the more powerful by the invisibility of their power through the reification of the public/private distinction in international law (Cutler 1997). Contesting expert rule means piercing the veil of universality that obscures a reflexive and transformative understanding of the world. This position rejects the view that the legal form has been irrevocably commodified or that we exist in a condition of 'the hegemony of hegemony' (Day 2005). Rather, it suggests that it is possible to repoliticize the work of experts. However, more is involved than 'identifying the *stakes* of expert action', in terms of who wins and who loses (Kennedy 2005: 21; emphasis in original). Although understanding the political economy of expert rule in terms of 'who gets what' is important, this conception limits the influence of experts to interest articulation and neglects the constitutive role that experts play in generating perceptions of risk and crisis and in creating the material and discursive conditions for contemporary capitalism. It is only by identifying the politics inherent in expert action and thought that we can begin to think about how private transnational governance might be(come) transformative.

Part II

Changing Material Conditions of Existence
and Global Leadership: Energy, Climate
Change and Water

4   The crisis of petro-market civilization: the past as prologue?

Tim Di Muzio

Summary

Current patterns of high-energy intensive development are not sustainable on account of two major challenges that threaten the social reproduction of this civilization: peak oil and global warming. This chapter seeks to probe the dimensions of this looming crisis at the heart of 'petro-market civilization' by foregrounding the links between energy and social reproduction. In doing so, the chapter makes two interrelated arguments. First, I argue not only that the age of fossil fuels is an exceptional one but also that the discovery and use of fossil fuels have been crucial to the deepening and extension of an incipient market civilization. Second, although there is recognition in both mainstream and more marginal circles that a broad-based global social transformation is needed in order to mitigate the probable consequences of global warming and peak oil, effective policy frameworks are not being put in place to deal with the looming crisis on the scale that would be necessary to transition to a post-fossil-fuel economy. The primary reason why this is so, I argue, is because solutions are informed by a neoliberal governmentality that prioritizes economic growth, international market mechanisms and individual responsibility.

Introduction

The collapse of global capitalization and the subsequent bankruptcy and loss of legitimacy of the financial institutions at the centre of the global political economy called for serious reflection on the failure of public and private leadership, the liberalization of financial markets and the need for more stringent regulation of global finance. Although it is well understood by some that financial crises are nothing new to an economic system based on commodity exchange and the accumulation of capital, the overarching policy debate of the moment appears to be focused on two rather short-term questions or concerns (Marx 1978 [1867];

73

Kindelberger 2005). First, there is the question of how best to avoid or contain future crises through some form of greater public oversight and regulation. Then, second, there is the question of how best to stimulate consumer spending and global economic growth. The problem with this narrow focus on the economic and financial crisis is that it misses the far broader and impending crisis of social reproduction at the heart of a fossil-fuel-dependent global market civilization – a crisis of social reproduction that continues to deepen and spread.[1] The looming crisis on the horizon – which is likely to be a far more devastating one – derives from the fact that the current patterns of high-energy intensive develop-ment can no longer continue, as a result of two major challenges that threaten the social reproduction of this civilizational order: peak oil and global warming. Whereas the financial system was bailed out by the public purse of many governments, it is unlikely that a similar bailout will be able to rescue global society from the consequences of fossil-fuel-dependent growth. Rather, both challenges require long-term planning, coordination and investment, not simply a timely injection of funds.

This chapter seeks to probe the dimensions of this looming crisis by foregrounding the links between energy and social reproduction. Rather than view the history of the global political economy as divided into successive hegemonies with distinct regimes of liberal governance, as some scholars do, when we consider the linkages between energy and the reproduction of civilizations it is perhaps more appropriate to conceptu-alize the history of the global political economy as divided into three eras: the pre-fossil-fuel age, the age of fossil fuels and the post-carbon age (Arrighi 1994; Cox 1987). With this in mind, I make two inter-related arguments. First, I argue not just that the age of fossil fuels is an exceptional one but also that the discovery and use of fossil fuels was crucial to the deepening and extension of an incipient market civilization that, at least by the fifteenth century, had started to emerge only in small pockets of the world (Abu-Lughod 1991; Braudel 1982). The emer-gence and social reproduction of a global market civilization has largely been undergirded by affordable, accessible and abundant fossil fuels. Not only is this situation about to go into reverse in this century, but continuing to use fossil fuels as the primary energy source of global growth only compounds the consequences that global climate change will have on the world's communities. What this means is that the

---

[1] It also sidesteps the debate as to whether the rapid escalation of oil prices in 2007 and 2008 could have precipitated what has been called the 'Great Recession'. On this question, see Hamilton (2009).

looming crisis will be a general crisis of social reproduction on a civilizational, rather than economic or financial, scale.

Second, I want to suggest that, although there is recognition in mainstream and more marginal circles alike that a broad-based global social transformation is needed in order to mitigate the likely consequences of global warming and peak oil, effective policy frameworks are not being put in place to deal with the impending crisis on the scale that will be necessary to make the transition to a post-fossil-fuel economy. In other words, the crisis of our petro-market civilization is also a governmental or leadership crisis. While we may be witnessing the rise of what some have called 'green governmentality' or the multi-scalar attempt to take ecological and environmental data into account when making decisions that will affect future generations, the far more entrenched form of leadership is issued from the register of neoliberal governmentality (Castree 2008; Heynen and Robbins 2005; McCarthy and Prudham 2004). In fact, there is considerable evidence to suggest that, in many aspects of policy, neoliberal governmentality has colonized the emergent attempt to govern within the limits of nature by encouraging 'green capitalism' (Hawken, Lovins and Lovins 2008; Wallis 2009). Since neoliberal governmentality prioritizes economic growth, international market mechanisms and individual responsibility as solutions for ecological problems, I argue that this form of leadership will do little to facilitate the transition to a post-carbon world in the timeframe needed to avoid serious repercussions for fossil-fuel-dependent societies.

In order to flesh out these arguments, I have organized this chapter into four sections. In the first I offer a brief genealogy of what I call a petro-market civilization and how the social reproduction of this civilizational order differs from earlier forms of social reproduction during the era before the widespread use of fossil fuels as a primary energy source. In section two I move to explore some of the consequences that this broad-based social transformation has for future generations and their social reproduction. In the third section I provide an outline of the neoliberal governmentality that currently informs political approaches to alternative energy issues. In the final section I conclude with a few remarks on how the past may be prologue to a much larger crisis if proposed solutions and policies continue to be informed by neoliberal governmentality.

A brief genealogy of petro-market civilization

The capture, conversion, storage and use of energy underpin all historical forms of social reproduction (Smil 1994; UNDP 2000). Recent literature employing the concept of social reproduction is varied but, at a general level, it seeks to draw attention to the conditions, contradictions and transformations in material and/or biological life (Bakker 2007; Bakker and Gill 2003). By 'social reproduction' in this chapter, I mean the ways in which any society produces, consumes and reproduces its life and lifestyles, how it conceptualizes and understands these actions and how it defends and/or justifies its particular pattern of historical development. With this definition in mind, I offer a concise genealogy of what I call a petro-market civilization by focusing on how the social reproduction of this civilizational order differs from earlier forms of social reproduction before the age of fossil fuels.

Although the forms of social reproduction and organization in the era before the widespread use of carbon energy differed, they all had three things in common: (1) they were characterized by low-energy-intensive patterns of development relative to our current era; (2) they did not rely on market provisioning for survival, nor did market values permeate everyday life; and (3) they were pervaded by hierarchies of power and privilege in which the exploitation of surplus was direct and extra-economic (Wood 2002). The primary sources of energy during this pre-fossil-fuel age were phytomass (e.g. plants and wood), certain domesticated animals (e.g. oxen), human slavery and some minor uses of wind and water power. Moreover, land was the primary source of wealth, and, although there were merchants engaged in long-distance trade, this trade was primarily confined to the larger coastal cities of an emerging world economy. The world's population was also very low in comparison to the age of fossil fuels, so that even by 1750, when coal was becoming an important source of energy in Britain, the population of the planet was only some 750 million, compared with today's 6.7 billion.[2] Most of this population lived, worked and died in rural environments. In these conditions, most communities remained at a subsistence level of social reproduction. In other words, social reproduction was localized, consisting of social units and kinship networks relying on various overlapping tactics and strategies of self-provisioning such as hunting, gathering and – later – agricultural cultivation and husbandry for survival.

What all this amounts to is that, although there were various forms of social reproduction before the widespread use of carbon energy, transnational market forces did not mediate or arbitrate the everyday lives and lifestyles of the majority of the world's population. The transition to the current global social order in which the allocation of goods, services and

---

[2] See www.vaughns-1-pagers.com/history/world-population-growth.htm (accessed 14 June 2010).

life chances are mediated and arbitrated by transnational market forces and mechanisms occurred first in Britain, but over the centuries it spread to encompass more of the world's population. The origins of this social transformation can be traced to what Marx called 'primitive accumulation', or the series of violent and fraudulent tactics used to expropriate direct producers from their customary access to the means of subsistence (see Marx 1976 [1867], in particular section 8). Dislocated from the land, former producers were transformed into vagabonds, criminals and wage-workers as ownership over the means of subsistence and work became increasingly privatized and sanctified in law (Hay, Thompson and Linebaugh 1975; Perelman 2000).[3] These processes accelerated after the English Glorious Revolution of 1688, when private social forces subordinated the Crown to parliament.

Although there is no global history of primitive accumulation, by the middle of the nineteenth century Marx was able to observe that most of the peasantry in western Europe had been expropriated, resulting in capitalist private property and the norm of accumulation as a primary logic of production and exchange (Marx 1976 [1867]: 931). The only part of the globe where this process was not complete, argued Marx, was in the colonies of the European powers and some parts of the world not under European colonial occupation. However, since Marx's writing these expropriations have occurred with increasing frequency in the periphery of the global political economy, with large swathes of former direct producers or customary holders of land being forced into cities. One glaring indication of this is the rapid rise of urban slums similar in kind to those found in parts of Europe during the transition to capitalism (UN-Habitat 2003).

In these enclosures and expropriations we can also start to identify a new pattern of social reproduction, whereby the majority of the dispossessed were compelled to rely on the market for their subsistence and survival. It is hard to underestimate the uniqueness of this historical transition. Indeed, in excavating the origins of market economy, Karl Polanyi argues that this social transformation was so radical that it resembled 'more the metamorphosis of the caterpillar than any alteration that can be expressed in terms of continuous growth and development' from earlier forms of economy that were embedded in social networks (Polanyi 1957: 42). This led him to note further that 'previously to our time no economy has ever existed that, even in principle, was controlled by markets' (ibid.: 43). Although there were various

---

[3] Attempts to circumvent the market through various tactics such as gleaning, hunting or fishing were increasingly criminalized in the centuries following the series of enclosures.

attempts by political authorities around the world to mitigate, control and/or direct market forces throughout the twentieth century, by the century's end it had become possible for Stephen Gill to characterize the global political economy as a neoliberal market civilization (Gill 1995a). Gill has identified some of the initial features of this market civilization, arguing that the neoliberal market civilization that emerged in the wake of the Cold War was characterized by the increasing polarization of wealth and life chances, a belief that self-actualization could largely be achieved through consumption, and the potential for widespread ecological devastation if notions of development continued to be premised on generating economic growth. He concludes the piece by asking whether a neoliberal market civilization can be called a 'civilization' at all, given that this pattern of social reproduction and political economy not only is unsustainable but that it also demonstrates many morbid symptoms.

These are all important insights, but one crucial aspect of market civilization is not highlighted in Gill's essay: the fact that the emergence and social reproduction of this civilization was and is wholly dependent upon affordable, accessible and abundant fossil fuels. Oil, coal and natural gas have become so central to the global political economy that it is perhaps more appropriate to characterize world society as a petro-market civilization, albeit recognizing that the access and use of carbon energy is highly uneven.

One indication of this is the fact that the oil and gas industry is the second largest sector of the economy in the world by market capitalization, standing at \$3.153 trillion in 2010.[4] If we add the estimated value of state-run oil and gas companies, then this sector is by far the largest in terms of market value, at roughly \$6.729 trillion.[5] What this suggests is that investors and state managers not only realize the centrality of energy for development prospects but also anticipate that these publicly traded and government-run firms will continue to generate earnings by shaping and reshaping a terrain of social reproduction heavily dependent upon fossil fuels. Since the value or capitalization of these firms is contingent on their profitability, it can be concluded that those in charge of and invested in the largest sector of the global economy – the one that virtually undergirds almost every other sector – have no interest whatsoever in

---

[4] 'FT Global 500 by sector', http://media.ft.com/cms/5d78d01a-68b9-11df-96f1-00144feab49a.pdf (accessed 30 June 2011).

[5] The 'FT non-public 150' estimates the value of state-run oil and gas firms in 2005, and I have adjusted the figure here, to account for inflation, to \$3,576 trillion; www.ft.com/cms/s/2/5de6ef96-8b95-11db-a61f-0000779e2340.html (accessed 30 June 2010).

moving swiftly to post-carbon forms of social reproduction. In fact, the interests of 'big oil and gas' and 'King Coal' run in exactly the opposite direction.

A second indication of how central fossil fuels are to the social reproduction of a market civilization comes from considering the fact that 82 per cent of the world's total primary energy supply consists of fossil fuels. Moreover, 68 per cent of global electricity generation is powered by fossil fuels, while the total final consumption of fossil fuels relative to other fuel sources was 67 per cent in 2008 (IEA [International Energy Agency] 2009: 6, 24, 28). Rather than declining, demand for fossil-fuel-based energy is forecast to increase dramatically in the coming decades, while alternative energy sources are estimated to make up only a small fraction of the world's total primary energy supply. In addition, the IEA argues that 'some $22 trillion of investment in supply infrastructure is needed to meet projected global demand' for energy (IEA 2007: 42). In sum, fossil fuels are projected to continue to be central to the social reproduction of a market civilization in the twenty-first century.

Third, the current world food system – how humans obtain energy – is wholly dependent upon cheap fossil fuels at every stage of the supply chain: producing, harvesting, processing, packaging and distribution. One calculation estimates that 'the modern food system consumes roughly ten calories of fossil fuel energy for every calorie of food energy produced' (Heinberg 2005). What this means is that those fortunate enough to purchase a daily diet are essentially 'eating oil', as suggested by one of the first studies to investigate the degree to which the US food system depends upon cheap petroleum (Green 1978; Pfeiffer 2006). Indeed, not only is oil necessary to run the industrial equipment and farm machinery used to produce food, but the fertilizers, herbicides and pesticides made necessary by large-scale industrial farming are all produced with oil or natural gas. In addition to this, most of the world's food travels thousands of miles and is transported by a global fleet of diesel-burning trucks, and in some cases refrigerated cargo jets. Although this system may be profitable for corporate food giants such as Nestlé, Unilever and Monsanto, it places global society in a highly vulnerable position, since the social reproduction of all communities that are not direct producers and consumers of food is heavily dependent on the corporate sourcing and provisioning of food (Barker 2007; Patel 2008).[6]

Finally, many have observed that technological advances in transportation and communication have led to a more globalized world, in which

---

[6] Subsistence farmers, or those who eat only what they grow, constitute the only sector of the population that is outside the global food regime.

space and time have been compressed. However, although the communication infrastructure of the world may not be as energy-intensive as some processes, the current transportation infrastructure of global trade is one of the most energy-demanding.[7] The social transition away from localized economies and incidental market exchanges to a global economy of market compulsion has made the social reproduction of most societies heavily dependent on plentiful and reasonably priced carbon energy. As Vaclav Smil, the eminent scholar of technical advances, has pointed out (2007: 373–4), 'Moving billions of tonnes of fuels, ores, other raw materials and foodstuffs, as well as astonishing varieties of goods, across national borders' is wholly dependent on two primary movers that are 'fast, inexpensive' and allow for 'mass-scale intercontinental travel': diesel engines and gas turbines. For example, there are currently some 90,000 cargo supertankers that travel the world's oceans; all are powered by 'diesel engines as powerful as land-based power stations' using 'the lowest-quality fuel' (Vidal 2009). Should the price of transporting all these goods become unprofitable or too expensive for consumers, continuing this regime of trade would be senseless from a business standpoint.

In sum, both international markets and fossil fuels have become so central to the social reproduction of global society that it is perhaps now banal to suggest that world society is the first and last petro-market civilization. In other words, given that oil, natural gas and coal are non-renewable resources and that there are no known primary energy sources to replace them on the scale necessary to sustain, let alone deepen and extend, this high-energy intensive model of development, we have to consider this civilizational order historically exceptional and transitory. Even the IEA – the institution responsible for advising Organisation for Economic Co-operation and Development (OECD) countries on energy policy – notes in its *World Energy Outlook 2008* that 'global trends in energy supply and consumption are patently unsustainable – environmentally, economically, socially' (IEA 2008: 3).

If the 'age of fossil fuels' and the emergence, spread and deepening of a global market civilization developed together, as I have suggested, then it is reasonable to investigate some of the consequences of a civilizational order whose social reproduction is contingent on what will become a more scarce and more expensive primary energy resource.

---

[7] However, in a recent report Greenpeace has documented how Facebook and Apple are relying on coal-fired energy plants for their data storage facilities; see Henderson 2010.

The consequences of petro-market civilization

The global transformation away from social reproduction heavily dependent on international markets and non-renewable energy poses immense challenges for leadership and communities the world over. Below I provide a sketch of some, but by no means all, of the important consequences that this form of social reproduction has generated.[8] To do so is to begin to recognize, as many already have, the scale of the transformation required of industrialized market society.[9]

The first and perhaps most obvious consequence of the transition to a petro-market civilization was an end to self-provisioning and the immediate and direct contact with nature. This is not to idealize the past or to suggest that earlier forms of social reproduction were in some way superior and need to be returned to. However, it is to suggest that modern survival and lifestyles are now dependent upon having access to goods and services for purchase on the market. One glaring indication of this transition has been the demographic shift away from a world society in which the majority of the population is primarily rural to one that is increasingly urban or suburban and – for over 1 billion people – consists of living in slums.[10] There are many explanations for this ongoing transition, but what it signals is that more and more people are being disconnected from the land and the livelihood it might have provided. What exacerbates our reliance on the market is the fact that a petro-market civilization and the concomitant explosion in global population has contributed to an extensive division of labour and specialized forms of skills and knowledge. Although this extensive division of labour no doubt contributes to global productivity, it also means that very few of the world's population have the knowledge and skills necessary to provide for themselves if markets break down or prices escalate out of control. This is all the more important when it comes to the question of food security, as the recent series of food riots attest (Doyle 2008; UNEP [United Nations Environment Programme] 2009).

A second consequence of a modern market economy heavily dependent on fossil fuel is the fact that centuries of public and private investment have produced built environments that are largely centred on cheap fossil fuels. The dimensions of a built environment created by

---

[8] One important consequence not explored here is the turn towards industrialized mobile warfare during the age of oil, and what some call postmodern war (Latham 2002).

[9] This recognition is widespread, but perhaps the leading organization promoting the transition to a post-carbon society is the Post-Carbon Institute. See www.postcarbon.org.

[10] See Vidal (2010). The UN notes that one-half of the world's population currently resides in cities, with the level projected to increase to over 79 per cent by 2050.

and dependent on fossil fuels are vast: the construction of thousands of miles of roads, docks and ports for intercontinental shipping, suburbanization, the construction of mcmansions and the retrofitting of cities for car culture, the paving over of arable land for shopping malls and car parks, the destruction of or underinvestment in public transit networks and the construction of industrial parks, large-scale machine-cultivated farms, national airports, coal-fired electricity generation stations, gas stations, chemical plants, massive retail and grocery outlets, and vacation resorts are just some examples. What these human-made and machine-facilitated environments may suggest to future anthropologists is that those in control of investment and policy decisions had a very unsustainable and myopic view of the future. Although there are attempts and incentives to create green cities, there is an equal if not greater trend towards suburbanization in many of the world's cities. In the words of UN-Habitat (2010):

> Urban sprawl has a negative impact on infrastructure and the sustainability of cities. In most cases, sprawl translates to an increase in the cost of transport, public infrastructure and of residential and commercial development. Moreover, sprawling metropolitan areas require more energy, metal, concrete and asphalt than do compact cities because homes, offices and utilities are set farther apart. In many places, urban sprawl encourages new developments that cause significant loss of prime farmland. When cities are improperly planned urban sprawl also adds to environmental degradation.

To sum up, transitioning away from the petro-soaked built environments of the last century will be very difficult without long-term public planning and significant capital investment that reverses trends such as suburbanization.

A third consequence of a petro-market civilization is the warming of the planet and ongoing environmental degradation. As the United Nations Development Programme (UNDP) states in its flagship report, anthropogenic global warming is a scientific fact. Carbon-fuelled economic activity, leading to the release of greenhouse gases into the atmosphere, is the chief contributor to the rise in global temperatures. Although some of these gases are naturally present in the atmosphere, humans have contributed massively to the warming of the planet by boosting their atmospheric concentrations, primarily as a result of burning fossil fuels for industry and transport and, to a lesser extent, by cutting down forests (IPCC [Intergovernmental Panel on Climate Change] 2007: 36). Not surprisingly, rich nations and a global consuming class of roughly 1.7 billion people account for a disproportionately large share of global emissions (UNDP 2007; Worldwatch Institute

2004). Although there have been some international attempts at climate cooperation – the Kyoto Protocol and now the non-binding Copenhagen Accord – leading scientists have emphasized that the commitments made so far are not enough to confront the challenges of global warming (see Chapter 5, by Richard Falk). For this reason, both the UNDP and the IPCC have argued that global society must not only seek out ways to reduce greenhouse gas emissions but also find strategies that will assist communities to adapt to unstable weather patterns.

However, the major problem is that, despite mounting popular awareness, world carbon dioxide (CO_2) emissions are projected to increase at least until 2030, and, many believe, beyond (IPCC 2007: 44). The consequences of climate change are potentially dire, though difficult to predict with certainty, since each region of the world will be affected in different ways. For instance, the IPCC argues, with varying degrees of confidence, that many parts of the world will suffer flooding, drought, the loss of biodiversity, coastal erosion, wildfires, the spread of new diseases and a possible reduction in crop productivity should temperatures continue to rise. Moreover, the UNDP has argued that many of these calamities are already ongoing in the poorest countries of the planet, with 'estimates of the numbers of people who will be forced to move as a result of climate change...ranging from 200 million to 1 billion' (UNDP 2009: 45). Some analysts also believe that, as warming continues, new regions will open up for resource exploitation, leading to increasing competition and perhaps militarized disputes for these new resources (Elhefnawy 2008; Klare 2009).

Neoliberal governmentality

Current trends, then, are patently unsustainable. However, the scale of the social transformation needed to move towards a post-carbon pattern of social reproduction is enormous, and demands nothing less than bold global, national and local community participation and leadership. I would like to suggest here that, although civil society organizations and policy-makers recognize the severity of the task, the solutions currently being proposed are issued from neoliberal governmental discourses that may exacerbate the looming crisis of social reproduction. Neoliberal governmentality is a method and strategy of rule that prioritizes the anarchy of private enterprise, economic growth, market mechanisms and individual responsibility over long-term democratic public planning for sustainable forms of social reproduction.

A recent study has suggested how entrenched and widespread neoliberal policies are, while others have elaborated on and refined

Michel Foucault's initial investigation of neoliberal governmentality (Burchell, Gordon and Miller 1991; Saad-Filho and Johnston 2005). My own purpose here is not to assess these interventions but, rather, to offer a brief conceptualization of neoliberal governmentality and then to show how this mode of rule approaches some of the challenges mentioned above. The politico-strategic rationality that animates neoliberal mentalities of rule starts from the notion that human beings are individual rational actors who pursue their interests by making cost–benefit calculations. For neoliberals, it is impossible for public policymakers to know the individual interests of each person, let alone the sum total of these interests. This leads neoliberals to argue that complex societies should be coordinated by price signals in the market, since these are the most effective and efficient conveyors of information. Moreover, as markets are the primary conveyors of information and allocators of goods and services, they should not be limited by spatial or political boundaries, since this would distort information and constrain human possibilities.

In this rendition of human purpose, there can be no shared, collective or planned vision for a political community to achieve other than preparing for market competition. For neoliberals, to do so would be anathema, because it would imply that some individual or group is imposing its own will on everyone else. However, this starting point is not grounded in an empirically verifiable human nature or ontology for neoliberals; it is a norm or state to be achieved by actively creating the productive constraints that will provide the guidelines and rules for shaping human behaviour, so that it increasingly resembles the behaviour of an imagined *Homo economicus* abstracted from natural limits. In other words, neoliberals are not against planning, as they want to arrange liberty artificially so that individuals can compete to pursue their own ends; however, they are against particular forms of planning that would have individuals directed towards some specific end not of their choosing. What this means is that the utopian goal of neoliberal governmentality is a political community of entrepreneurial firms and individuals that should largely govern themselves according to their interests, defined as financial or material gain. In doing so, these activities are presumed to generate economic growth. However, this politico-strategic rationality is not just directed at creating the conditions of existence for calculating individuals. The government itself is supposed to be subjected to the same market criteria or imperatives. Policies are to be assessed and audited based on their ability to foster private enterprise. Government programmes are to be evaluated for their costs and what they return to the political community, and against the possibility that market forces would be better allocators of publicly provided goods and services.

For this reason, some of the main tactics and techniques employed by neoliberal governors include commodification, privatization, deregulation, 'responsibilizing' individuals and creating incentives for firms. What this means in the context of the looming crisis of social reproduction is that market mechanisms and the consumer and investment choices of individuals and firms will be responsible for meeting the challenges of a post-carbon world order (Bernstein 2002; Conca 2000; Levy and Newell 2002; Mansfield 2004). For example, in place of a coordinated government programme designed to prepare populations for the end of a highly energy-intensive consumerist lifestyle and drastically reducing greenhouse gas emissions, individual responsibility is promoted. These include attempts at reducing personal consumption, conserving energy, recycling waste, buying green organic products, retrofitting houses for energy efficiency, promoting the use of reusable shopping bags, green reskilling and encouraging home gardening, just to mention a few initiatives.

At the level of the firm, incentives are currently directed at promoting a corporate-led green capitalism while at the same time continuing to promote the discovery and extraction of fossil fuels for energy use. Policies to encourage green capitalism include mandating greater fuel efficiency and hybrid cars, funding the research and development of carbon-sequestration and green technologies to control pollution and liberalizing energy markets and making them more competitive. A look at some leading energy policies from the United States and the European Union shows that they also include incentives for firms to exploit renewable energy opportunities in solar, wind, biomass, geothermal, hydroelectric and tidal power, with some claims that renewables should make up a certain percentage of the total primary mix by a given date (White House 2010). For instance, on this last point, the European Union's energy policy aims to have 20 per cent of its primary energy come from renewable sources by 2020 (European Commission 2010). Another leading policy response to global warming has been the promotion of cap and trade systems that allow corporations to pollute up to a point and thereafter purchase permits for additional pollution (Bond 2008).

In other words, neoliberals undoubtedly recognize that a form of social reproduction reliant on fossil fuels and ecological degradation poses significant challenges. The question is this: are neoliberal policies that privilege individual responsibility, private enterprise and market mechanisms capable of preparing world society for a post-carbon-dependent social order within a timeframe that avoids serious crises?

Conclusion: neoliberalism will not save us

There are at least four major reasons for doubting whether neoliberal leadership can provide the solutions. First, relying on the individual investment decisions of firms and their investors to move world society rapidly towards a post-carbon future appears misguided given the rate and scale of change required. Consider, for example, what would have to be done just to replace fossil fuels as a primary energy source (Assadourian 2010: 7):

> In order to produce enough [solar] energy over the next 25 years to replace most of what is supplied by fossil fuels, the world would need to build 200 square meters of solar photovoltaic panels every second plus 100 square meters of solar thermal every second plus 24 3-megawatt wind turbines every hour nonstop for the next 25 years.

Obviously, such an intensive post-carbon energy project is currently not under consideration, despite some minor efforts by governments and companies to create incentives for renewable energy endeavours.[11] Moreover, the scale of investment required to move towards a sustainable green economy is enormous and cannot depend on the whims and speculations of investors and banks with short-term profitability horizons. After some initial excitement in green companies in the first decade of the century, the Renewable Energy Policy Network for the 21st Century (REN21) noted that, during the financial crisis of 2008, the market capitalization of green firms collapsed. According to its recent report (REN21 2009: 15), 'Renewable energy companies closed plants, laid off workers, lowered sales forecasts, reduced production, and revised expansion plans for 2009 and beyond.' In other words, although there has been some expansion of green companies, these firms are largely dependent on speculative finance for their growth (Harvey 2010).

The second set of causes for concern involves investors and firms. First, not all so-called renewable energies appear to be either desirable or sustainable. For example, the recent rush to convert land for biofuel crops such as corn and sugarcane has come under considerable scrutiny, with some studies showing that producing such fuels provides little to no net energy, leads to increasing food prices and has the potential to destroy biodiversity as rainforests and other habitats are destroyed to produce the cash crops (Runge and Senauer 2007; Scharlemann and Laurance 2008). Second, it is well known that manufacturers are often

---

[11] Sweden might be the exception (see Vidal 2006).

not required to internalize the costs of their environmental damage. This makes the costs of goods artificially cheaper and could encourage more fossil-fuel-dependent consumption. Furthermore, fossil fuel companies are infamous for funding climate change scepticism and lobbying government officials for business-friendly policies (Newell and Paterson 1998). According to Erik Assadourian (2010), 'Between subsidies and externalities, total support of polluting business interests was pegged at $1.9 trillion in 2001.' A third cause for concern is that modern investors routinely discount the future as a matter of course. This process is called capitalization, and it involves using a 'discount rate to reduce a stream of future earnings to their present value' (Nitzan and Bichler 2009: 183). What this means is that investors have a technology by which to anticipate the future. If they anticipate that peak oil and global warming are facts that will have future consequences for their investments, they will take these events into consideration – however unpredictable the precise consequences may be (Bichler and Nitzan 2010: 7). What this means is that, far from leading a charge towards alternative post-carbon forms of social reproduction, investors can discount the future consequences of fossil fuel development patterns into their present asset values.[12]

Third, neoliberal governmentality does nothing to challenge an economic system premised upon growth and consumption. In fact, most neoliberal policies have the stated objective – and this is true of Keynesian stimulus packages as well – of promoting growth and consumption (Hamilton 2004). Thus, although alternatives may be constructed on the margin of the global economy (e.g. wind and solar farms), so long as global society is organized around a system of production, distribution and consumption based on fossil fuels, the spatial spread of markets and private profit and accumulation, we can expect that little will be done to move society towards a post-carbon future with a different set of post-consumerist values.

A final problem with neoliberal governmentality is its reliance on individual responsibility. In this instance, neoliberal governors rely on individuals to choose green and sustainable lifestyles. However, not only can individuals choose the opposite, but there are also many structural obstacles to overcome that individuals may have very little power to change. For example, not everyone has the ability to afford nutritious organic food, nor do individuals have much of a say in what kinds of food their community will be supplied with by the food industry. In other words, prioritizing individual agency without dealing with structural

---

[12] See Whitehorn and Leggett (2009). They plead with their audience and the government of the United Kingdom to consider the business risks of peak oil.

obstacles is unlikely to affect the real change required to develop a post-carbon form of social reproduction.

There are, of course, no crystal balls to peer into, but if current trends continue we can expect the crisis of what I have called a petro-market civilization to be severe and protracted as societies scramble to adjust to a world of increasing energy prices and energy scarcity. As I hope to have made clear, both the *rate* and the *scale* of the necessary adaptation and social change are greater than what neoliberal policies can hope to accomplish. Although it may seem banal to say so, in the future we will all live differently. Whether new forms of sociality will be socially just, humane and civilized or whether populations descend into competitive forms of barbarism is an open question. Given past human achievements, there are many reasons to be hopeful; but there are also plenty of reasons for trepidation.

5 Global climate change, human security and the future of democracy

Richard A. Falk

Summary

This chapter focuses on climate change, a key part of the global crisis that exemplifies failures of global leadership. It explores the implications of climate change for democracy and human security. The context for the argument is that the current global crisis poses unprecedented challenges because of its severity and multidimensional character, as well as the absence of either an ideological consensus or effective hegemonic management of global policy formulation and implementation. Global history during the last several centuries has been dominated by Eurocentrism, short-term security and political economy challenges, and violent geopolitics that caused devastation and massive suffering but did not undermine fundamental world order structures.

This comparatively simple framework is being increasingly drawn into question. The *real* new world order has substantially eroded Eurocentric dominance of the policy agenda, the emergence of global warming as potential catastrophic threat has underlined the importance of long-range planning and investment, and the intensifying contradictions of neoliberal forms of capitalism appear to be generating a *systemic* crisis of adjustment, although market forces and government leaders are focused on viewing the current deep world recession as *cyclical* and thus to be corrected by restoring normalcy. Even if this cyclical interpretation seems convincing in the period immediately ahead, it will soon have to acknowledge the increasing displacement of neoliberal modes of production and investment by various forms of state capitalism, as epitomized by China. Also problematic in an original manner is the extent to which the economistic preoccupations of leaders with the woes of profit-seeking businesses and financial entities and anguished workers has made it almost impossible to give appropriate parallel attention to the multiple effects of the growing ecological challenges associated with climate change, growing water scarcities and the prospects of peak oil. Beyond this, it is already evident that the most marginal and vulnerable peoples are destined to have their

present ordeals ignored and, in all likelihood, to be subject to disproportionately great harms and burdens in the future.

Introduction

In this chapter the focus is placed on a relatively obscure dimension of the
world crisis, climate change, and in particular its implications for human
security and democracy. The failures of global leadership are especially
vivid here, as the political mandate to heed the scientific consensus is
obstructed by corporate interests eager to sow doubt as to need (hence
the rise of climate scepticism) and by mass publics demanding overriding
attention to immediate forms of distress. There is present a tragic predicament: the climate change challenge will be deferred until its harm is
palpable, undeniable and no longer containable, much less reversible. In
effect, it is too soon at present to mobilize support for an effective
response, but, by the time it will be possible, it will be too late![1]

Climate change and the limits of statism: the Copenhagen moment

The climate change dimension of the global crisis highlights an important
dimension of the embedded crisis of global leadership, which became
painfully manifest at the UN climate change conference held in Copenhagen between 7 and 19 December 2009. Unfortunately, part of the
failure at Copenhagen was the absence of an atmosphere of sufficient
urgency at the intergovernmental level to address a series of issues arising
from the multiple challenges of climate change as understood, on the
whole, both by the scientific community of experts and on the part of civil
society activists present at the conference, who were denied participation
in or even access to the formal negotiating sessions. Tensions were also
raised by two governments, one a low-lying island state and the other
from sub-Saharan Africa, that felt especially threatened by *present* harms
or the prospect of near-term disasters attributable to global warming
(flooding in one case, drought in the other), both seeking special attention for their well-grounded survival fears. Their genuine sense of
urgency proved non-contagious so far as other delegates were concerned.
It was not only that these states were particularly vulnerable but also that,
because of their size, poverty and underdevelopment, they lack the
capabilities and resources to cope with the anticipated harm by self-help

[1] On the difficulties of generating the sense of urgency before it is too late, see the
formulation of 'Giddens' paradox' (Giddens 2009: 2–3).

responses. More significantly, such political actors lacked the political stature and diplomatic experience to have their concerns taken with the seriousness that they certainly deserved from a human security standpoint by the dominant players at Copenhagen.

Of course, part of the complexity of the climate change challenge arises because responses cannot be delinked from the wider global crisis, which has yet to be fully acknowledged in mainstream circles. At present, the crisis managers of leading states are almost exclusively preoccupied with the restoration of a sense of economic normalcy so far as aggregate growth is concerned, given the persistence of the worst set of economic conditions since the Great Depression of the 1930s. From the sort of critical perspective taken here, this wider crisis cannot be convincingly overcome without the transformation of the world economy in a post-capitalist direction that is sensitive to the ethics of human security. If this understanding of the true nature of the crisis is generally correct then the illusion of economic recovery will be only temporarily salvaged through a reliance on the prevailing cosmetic and instrumental efforts of governments to revive the confidence of bankers and consumers. Such an approach to recovery limits its ambitions to the largely uncritical and systemically unhealthy *restoration* of pre-crisis economic normalcy as this is interpreted from a neoliberal perspective, which entails minimal concerns about extended high rates of unemployment and the unfair distribution of the benefits and burdens of economic growth in an era of globalization. Such a crisis response cannot even qualify as reformist in character in the sense of repudiating discredited market practices and overcoming the deregulatory impulses of neoliberal economic managers. Even if these restorative measures appear successful in the short term, they will lead rather soon to recurrent, and probably worsening, crises in the years ahead. In other words, the policy-making world of governmental and intergovernmental entities has not yet been willing or able to diagnose the crisis correctly, and therefore has almost no prospect of devising an enduringly effective response (Gill 2008; Mittelman 2010).

Even radical rejections of neoliberal orientations towards world economic policy on grounds of equity and stability do not go far enough if they do not include a critique of the dominant security paradigm that dangerously overvalues hard power approaches to conflict resolution and grand strategy.[2] The United States, as the hegemonic presiding presence in world affairs, is the extreme instance of overinvestment in hard power

---

[2] An exceptional effort to rethink security given the contemporary reality, with unparalleled sensitivity to normative concerns, has been made by Ken Booth (2007). See also Chapter 7 of this volume, by Solomon Benatar.

capabilities while at the same time refusing to reduce its budgetary and trade deficits, which are producing precarious levels of indebtedness, or to invest heavily in job creation and the protection of low- and middle-income homeowners. In other words, the global crisis at its core involves a toxic blend of neoliberal ideology with a dysfunctional militarism that is linked to a costly effort to maintain a proactive military presence of global scope, contributing to the perception that the United States is not just a dominant and domineering state. It also a new kind of empire, which refuses to limit its activities to formal territorial boundaries but intervenes covertly and overtly on far-flung, often secret, battlefields.[3]

In addition, this failure of leadership in relation to the global crisis cannot be entirely distinguished from the currently dismal prospects for coping with climate change in a timely manner that minimizes harmful impacts on human security and democracy, especially for those societies that are particularly vulnerable to global warming and lack the indigenous capabilities and resources to adapt or significantly mitigate their carbon footprint.[4] The dominance of the policy agenda of governments by more or less immediate concerns poses one kind of obstacle to appropriate leadership on a global scale, while the abstractness, the irresponsible campaign of climate scepticism driven by special interests, and the perceived remoteness of the alleged detrimental consequences for most countries make it seem impossible to mobilize the kind of massive and intense societal pressures to engender the political support for the costly actions that are needed to keep planetary temperatures from rising above catastrophic levels. Such an unreceptive political atmosphere makes it even more unlikely that greenhouse gas concentrations can be reduced to a level that global warming is neutralized, let alone reverses direction, thereby lessening the harms already being inflicted in a variety of settings.[5] There are many indications that the private sector is having mounting success in its effort to discredit and distract those who advocate major action to address the challenge of global warming, including the community of climate scientists. A few years ago there existed what seemed to be a sufficiently robust scientific

---

[3] In a vast literature, one challenging effort to connect the capitalist and militarist features of the American project is that by Ronnie Lipschutz (2009).

[4] Richard Matthew, Jon Barnett, Bryan McDonald and Karen O'Brien (2010) put forward an argument that proposes focusing policy responses on helping societies that are particularly vulnerable and materially disadvantaged.

[5] For an illuminating response to the climate sceptics, see the article by the chairman of the IPCC (and recipient of the Nobel Prize), Rajendra K. Pachauri (2010). Howard Friel (2010) provides a devastating critique of the methods and work of a leading climate sceptic, which seem part of a conscious effort to confuse the public; also helpful is the discussion by Naomi Oreskes and Erik Conway (2010).

consensus on climate change to make significant measures of adjustment a shared political priority for most governments. Sensing this rising tide of concerns, market forces have reacted by using their financial and media leverage to raise serious public doubts about the seriousness of proximate threats of climate change. In such an atmosphere it becomes politically impossible, especially during a period of recession and jobless recovery, to agree measures that will respond prudently to the climate change challenge. For instance, the idea of imposing a sufficiently high carbon tax to achieve reductions from present-day CO_2 levels so as to keep the planet's temperature from rising by more than $1.5°$ Celsius has been virtually abandoned. The advocacy of a carbon tax causes instant consternation in the business world, backed up by well-financed lobbying efforts that are assigned a demolition task.[6]

A further obstacle arises because of the extreme unevenness of the perceived harm. There exist a few important countries, such as Russia and Canada, that may, as territorial entities, actually benefit from global warming, due to rain and warmth shifting northwards; this weakens, even if it does not eliminate, the incentives for these beneficiaries to lend their support to burdensome regulatory arrangements. In a sense, this obstacle reflects the fragmentary organization of world order, which privileges the self-interest of the parts and neglects the shared interests of the whole. If governments were more sensitive to their participation in a globalizing world, and less focused on maximizing their distinct interests as sovereign states, the adaptive capacities of the world would be greatly enhanced. There have been some modest normative moves in this direction, through such developments as the growth of human rights, recourse to humanitarian intervention and support for the norm of 'responsibility to protect' (R2P). However, these moves are ambiguous in intention and effect, on account of their being intertwined with the selective priorities of geopolitics and the predatory habits of neo-liberalism, which are revealed in the post-conflict atmosphere when lucrative contracts are handed out for construction and access to resources and markets.[7]

In the background of any discussion of climate change are structural and ideological problems with the quality of global leadership. The United Nations can supply the auspices for work on climate change

---

[6] So far, cap and trade proposals to allow the market to generate mechanisms that would ensure adequate reductions of greenhouse gas emissions have not proved to be feasible at meaningful levels. However, for a sophisticated argument for cap and trade as the most practical short-term response to the challenge, see Krugman (2010: 34–41, 46–9).

[7] Anne Orford (2003) identifies this scepticism about the normative claims of humanitarianism brilliantly.

that *procedurally* engages the entire statist membership of global society, but it cannot provide *substantive* leadership. The UN has no autonomous capacity to legislate a treaty framework that *distributes* fairly binding rights and duties among states. At the same time, the normal multilateral treaty framework for a negotiated agreement seems dysfunctional in relation to climate change, partly as a result of the highly uneven goals and material conditions of governments and partly reflecting the sheer unwieldy number of concerned states involved.[8] What might seem more suitable from an efficiency standpoint, even if not acceptable from the perspective of procedural legitimacy, would be to entrust the negotiating of rules and obligations to a small group of states that seemed representative of global realities in the early twenty-first century. To some extent, this was what was controversially attempted at Copenhagen, with the United States trying to find agreement between itself and China, India, Brazil and South Africa, and then selling it to the others. This was an innovative leadership cohort with a somewhat surprising composition, excluding Russia, Japan and even the European Union, and suggesting that the new American approach to leadership is tailored to coalition building that varies from one issue area to another. There is also the legitimacy question, in terms of whether the countries selected have the status and influence to be accepted as representatives of the entire community of states and their publics.

At Copenhagen the Obama leadership style was not very successful, although, arguably, the alternatives of confrontation and gridlock, which seemed likely if the agreed intergovernmental format for negotiations among the more than 150 participating governments had been respected, were likely to have been worse. Nevertheless, the idea of the United States overriding the agreed procedures, and picking its partners, generated widespread resentment and produced an unwillingness to go along. There was open hostility to this hijacking of the agenda at the long plenary that closed the Copenhagen meetings, which certainly weakened the impact of the approach favoured by the United States. The majority

---

[8] The closest example of a successful treaty process benefiting from UN auspices is undoubtedly the Law of the Seas Treaty, which was signed in 1982 after a decade of difficult negotiations. As with climate change, states were very differently situated in relation to the oceans, and the negotiations required delicate bargaining and complex compromises. Unlike climate change, accepting a public order framework for the oceans did not impose variable costs on states or raise such difficult questions about the varying degrees of responsibility. Another example of global public order involved an agreement in which states involved in the Antarctic gave up mining rights for the sake of environmental protection, which seemed negotiable because the size of the economic interests at stake was relatively modest.

of governments, along with representatives of the world environmental movement, left Copenhagen angry and discouraged.

The Copenhagen Accord, which the conference as a whole 'took note' of rather than 'accepted' or 'endorsed', seems nothing more than a 'good faith' pledge by governments to come forward, at some later time, and indicate on a voluntary basis what their country is prepared to do to reduce carbon emissions. This outcome contrasts with much more ambitious earlier expectations that Copenhagen would produce a binding international agreement imposing specific obligations on governments to cut their carbon emissions by a specified amount and in accordance with a fixed schedule designed to regulate global warming in a manner that upholds the global public interests of the peoples of the world. A lawmaking outcome of this character had been already prefigured at UNCED in Rio de Janeiro in 1992, the 'Earth Summit', by the adoption of what then appeared as the encouraging UN Framework Convention on Climate Change (UNFCCC). It is deeply disappointing that there appeared to be more resolve on the part of governments to act collectively to regulate global warming back in 1992, when the dangers and harms were far more speculative and less menacing than they are at present. This may reflect in part the relative ease of agreeing to 'resolve' as compared to the political difficulties that arise as soon as costly behavioural constraints are under consideration.

At the same time, it is encouraging that the division at Copenhagen was not along the traditional North–South divide. Instead, the somewhat strange coalition formed by the US initiative, relying on a strong personal effort by President Obama, was impressively responsive to a changed geopolitical landscape. To partner with Brazil, China, India and South Africa to form an informal conference directorate was undoubtedly a new expression of the US approach to global leadership in the *soft power* setting of environmental geopolitics. By not even bothering to include its normal partners in the North, especially the European Union and Japan, the United States was unambiguously making a world order statement. True, this new collective leadership was not successful in mobilizing a global consensus – at least, not at Copenhagen. In the UN follow-up meeting in Cancún, Mexico, in 2010, although the credibility of the process was partially restored, no progress was made towards an agreement on legally binding emissions targets. However, what did emerge was a stronger global consensus to create a Green Climate Fund and to make new arrangements to prevent deforestation, though with no binding agreement on associated funding mechanisms. Nonetheless, US negotiators (as well as those from other large emitters, such as China and the European Union) expressed satisfaction at the prospect that

voluntary targets will come into force to replace the mandatory requirements of the Kyoto Protocol when it expires in 2012 (the United States
signed the protocol but never ratified it, and thus has not been bound by
its requirements).

As a result, the net outcomes at Copenhagen and Cancún were mainly
discouraging, despite some positive features that might produce better
results at future conferences devoted to climate change. It was, on
balance, important for the United States at both conferences to exert
its influence without relying on Western ideological hegemony in an
important global policy-making arena, although it might have been far
more effective, particularly at Copenhagen, if it had been done with
greater diplomatic preparation and not as a last-minute effort to compensate for an underlying disappointment as a result of the refusal of
the United States and China to accept *substantive* constraints. At the
same time, the new constellation of actors that was given a special status
at Copenhagen, and that helped produce the consensus at Cancún,
although arbitrary in some respects, is far more representative of the
distribution of capabilities and identities than is the permanent membership of the Security Council. This implies American backing for a
more globally inclusive reordering of global policy-making – a process
also noted at the nuclear security summit convened by Obama in April
2010 in Washington. However, the downsides also seem more important. Despite the international popularity of Obama, there was apparent
at Copenhagen a lack of the kind of leadership needed to address climate
change substantively. Obama's credibility was also quite low at the time,
as the Copenhagen summit preceded both his domestic victory in health
care and the signing of the third Strategic Arms Reduction Treaty
(START) with Russia. Obama was politically unable to put forward a
meaningful substantive commitment on behalf of the United States, and
this was enough by itself to doom the conference – an impression of
failure only slightly weakened by the tabling of the Copenhagen Accord.

The American substantive failure is notable. It was undoubtedly
due partly to the widespread realization that Obama would have been
unable to persuade Congress or the American public to accept any
climate change arrangement adopted at Copenhagen that was perceived
as burdening the domestic economy or the citizenry. If the United States
had been in a position to set a high standard of self-regulation then
American leadership might have seemed far more credible to the
gathering of countries at Copenhagen, and probably more effective and
legitimate, although it would still have been properly faulted by its geopolitical tactics, which angered many governments and reinforced the
perception of the United States as a domestically democratic hegemon

that acts anti-democratically in global arenas. It should be pointed out that China and India were also unwilling to make substantive commitments at Copenhagen, thus reducing pressure on the United States.

However, what the Copenhagen and Cancún moments convey above all is a leaderless world system when it comes to climate change, even in the minimal sense of acknowledging and agreeing upon measures to address realistically the seriousness of the problem and the urgency of adopting and implementing mandatory standards to reduce the carbon content of the atmosphere as rapidly as possible. Such a goal was treated as too ambitious to affirm clearly. Despite the intention to create new financing mechanisms to assist poorer countries that was agreed at Cancún, to a large extent the Copenhagen and Cancún Accords both amount to little more than an informal undertaking (if that) by governments to make entirely voluntary pledges to cut their CO_2 emissions in ways and amounts of their own determining. This disappointing result does not take account of the absence of any normative filter that would ensure consideration, at least, of effects of alternative regulatory initiatives from the perspective of the human interest. In the formal proceedings there was no representation other than that provided by governments, and very little official mention of the likely impact of global warming on the lives of people as distinct from the effect on sovereign states. To some extent, the 20,000 or so environmental activists voiced these normative concerns, but in the streets rather than in the arenas of decision, and without any pretence or signs of coherence in global civil society.

Efforts to regulate climate change suggest the importance of distinguishing horizons of feasibility, of necessity and of desire. What is *feasible* from the perspective of regulation and adjustment is not nearly sufficient to satisfy climate change requirements as specified by horizons of *necessity*.[9] Meanwhile, from the point of view of horizons of *desire*, there was no representation at Copenhagen in its official proceedings to insist that responses to climate change challenges be treated in the context of constructing a form of *humane global governance* for present and future generations.[10] Another formulation of a response guided by horizons of desire would be merged with horizons of necessity and would argue that no acceptable results can be achieved until peoples and nation states recognize their solidarity with the Earth and each other and act on it.

---

[9] Bill McKibben (2010) and David Orr (2009) both provide helpful overviews that interpret the scientific consensus as suggesting a deepening crisis that has many of the features of an unfolding ecological catastrophe that has yet to be acknowledged as a *present* phenomenon, not something that is to be encountered in the future.

[10] My attempt to depict such a horizon of desire *as a political project* can be found in Falk (1995).

Critics of an intergovernmental approach to climate change go on to say that human solidarity can arise only on the basis of 'shared fundamental ethical principles' with the short-term goal being 'a sustainable global society of low CO_2 emitters' to be attained by 'a tremendous effort' that is 'too important to leave to the politicians' but must also incorporate in organic collaboration 'the business community and citizens' (Borren, Lubbers and Vanenburg 2009). Such a position insists that a radical reconstituting of global politics is required if one is to have any credible prospect of addressing climate change successfully. Even this kind of critical standpoint, normatively grounded though it is, appears to accept without question the neoliberal orientation of economic globalization as the foundation upon which a responsible climate change consensus has to be built. I share the insistence upon a normative grounding but I do not believe that this can take place in a sustainable way without, at a minimum, recourse to global Keynesianism, if not a transition to some type of post-capitalist world economy shaped by considerations of what is beneficial for people, including ecological prudence.

Constructing the normative architecture for climate change

It should be realized that one of the most distinctive features of modernity in the aftermath of the Enlightenment and the Industrial Revolution has been the overcoming of the pre-modern sense of vulnerability to nature, which was closely associated with the origins and practice of religion. The efforts to appease the gods to avoid the havoc that could be caused by such recurrent natural happenings as floods, fires, droughts, volcanoes or earthquakes were a paramount preoccupation. In modernity, the pendulum has shifted to the belief that nature can be subjugated for the sake of human advantage, by the skilful application of reason as mediated through science and technology. What has shattered this confidence in the last several decades has been the growing sense that population growth, rising standards of living, pollution of the air, land and water, and the finite supply of vital natural resources are imperilling the human future. In effect, nature, though seemingly subdued, had been poised to strike back in more threatening ways than seemed the case in the pre-modern world, in which most experience was local and short-lived, not systemic and enduring. Of course, as Jared Diamond has instructed us, throughout human history there have been a series of collapses of societal scope (Diamond 2005). It is the systemic character and planetary scope of these postmodern environmental concerns that is their defining characteristic, posing unprecedented threats, in addition, to the structure of the modern world order, whose problem-solving capabilities were mainly expected to address subsystemic challenges.

The normative architecture for the regulation of climate change is a work in progress that emerges out of the environmental movement that was initiated in the early 1970s, resulting in an initial upsurge of environmentalism followed by a period of complacency and disregard. Environmentalism has now re-emerged in new forms during the first years of the twenty-first century, primarily around the concerns associated with the multiple adverse environmental effects attributable to current and anticipated levels of global warming.[11] In relation to the focus on leadership, it may be useful to compare briefly these two periods in which themes associated with ecological risk achieved a high profile in the world policy process.

In broad terms, the stimulus for the first cycle reflected the impact of transnational civic activism led by inspirational writers, especially Rachel Carson, and environmental NGOs in the North, especially Greenpeace and Friends of the Earth (Carson 1964). It was also responsive to the work of the Club of Rome, especially its publication *The Limits to Growth*, which caused a big global stir when published in 1972 partly because it invoked the authority of a computer-generated model to contend that the world was heading for an irreversible collapse of industrial civilization if it did not make drastic adjustments within a ten-year window (Meadows *et al.* 1972). The impact was a confusing mixture of small constructive steps that involved, in particular, impressive degrees of global consciousness raising that climaxed at the Stockholm UN Conference on the Human Environment in 1972, important increases in governmental awareness throughout the world and some concerted action to regulate activities causing environmental harm, especially limits to the release of substances causing ozone depletion and restrictions on ocean pollution. In the first cycle, considerable attention was devoted to the damaging effects of demographic pressures on the carrying capacity of the Earth; in particular, this concern was related to issues of population increase in Asian and African countries, which were already having difficulty dealing with mass poverty and food shortages for the poor.

The normative orientation of the first cycle was best set forth in the 'Stockholm Declaration' of the UN Conference on the Human

---

[11] My own effort to depict the early or first crisis of ecological urgency can be found in Falk (1972); for a discussion of what I call the second cycle of ecological urgency, see Falk (2009).

Environment, which called for national action and a sense of responsibility in developing conservation and rational management policies protective of the environment while not hampering unduly the right to
development or sovereignty over natural resources (UNEP 1972). The
'Rio Declaration on Environment and Development', adopted twenty
years later in 1992, reflected changes in the normative outlook: the idea
of development was explicitly related to environmental concerns, and
expressed by way of the new mantra of 'sustainable development'; it was
explicitly recognized that the eradication of poverty was connected with
environmental concerns, and that attention should be given to 'the special
situation and needs of developing countries, particularly the least
developed and those most environmentally vulnerable' (principle 6);
endorsement was given to 'the precautionary approach', which was
explained as taking steps to avoid serious and possibly irreversible environmental harm without waiting for 'full scientific certainty' (principle 15);
and special categories – women, youth and indigenous peoples – were
recognized as having special contributions to make with respect to sustainable development (principles 20 to 22; UN 1992). These are documents
of normative aspiration and are not intended to provide specific policy
guidance, much less formulations of positive law. They should be treated
more as moral pieties than as 'soft law' of the sort that has evolved from
the Universal Declaration of Human Rights (UDHR). At the same time,
such documents do reveal a certain willingness on the part of participating
states to articulate a normative vision that indirectly bears on behavioural
and policy responses, and provides authoritative markers for civil society
activists. In this regard, it is notable that there was no attempt made to
draft a 'Copenhagen Declaration', not because it would not have been
potentially clarifying and useful, even if only aspirational, but evidently
because the divergences were too pronounced with respect to values, risks,
responsibilities and burdens to enable agreement on a consensus text.

The first cycle of ecological urgency brought North–South discord
and distrust to the surface. Countries of the global South contended
vigorously that environmental problems were almost totally attributable
to the activities of the industrial North, and that to insist that the
challenge was global amounted to a thinly disguised campaign to inhibit
development prospects in the South, and thus the benefits of modernity,
and eventual prosperity. There was an entirely different backlash in the
North, especially in the private sector, where environmentalism and the
green politics that it nourished were seen as constituting a serious threat
to profitable industrial enterprise and the settled political establishment
of capitalist societies. In response, powerful organs of opinion in and
out of government derided the allegedly doomsday scenarios of the

Club of Rome and elsewhere as hysterical overreactions. In many ways these negative reactions to claims of ecological urgency were effective, as the North became far more sensitive to the development priorities of the South, and to the sense of equity in relation to late developers, and the prophecies of doom came to be disregarded, and even abandoned.

The global political setting of the first cycle was complex, with this mixing of Cold War tensions and capitalist anxieties with the aspirations of the newly independent countries of the South. In the first cycle, after an initial flurry of apocalyptic worries, neither the scientific community nor the established leadership of government endorsed, or had the means to assess persuasively, the extent of the danger. There were important disagreements as to the essence, nature and depth of the environmental challenge, especially an inconclusive argument about whether to worry more about population increases or rising standards of living, which also contributed to the loss of urgency surrounding environmental challenges. On balance, it is possible to conclude that in the first cycle, despite the double backlash, a short-term adaptive response was successfully generated, although, as later developments confirm, a public mood of complacency was unwarranted because of the cumulative adverse effects of a petroleum economy on ecological stability. Many governments and their publics had truly become attentive to the problems of the pollution of cities and rivers, even oceans, and to the importance of stemming population growth. The worst fears associated with industrial collapse were abated, at least temporarily. A low-profile awareness of the global environmental policy agenda was sustained by a certain bureaucratic momentum within the UN system and by the pressures exerted by environmental activists, but the sense of urgency, as embodied in prophecies of doom, was no longer present, and the first cycle came to a whimpering end.

In the second cycle intense fears have returned, clustered around concerns associated with global warming. Unlike the first cycle, the impetus for action has come from a monumental collection of scientific data under seemingly reliable international auspices, as the efforts of the scientists concerned were acknowledged by a Nobel Peace Prize. An epistemic community of qualified observers exists, and it is now warning of irreversible and fundamental harm to the peoples of the world if steps are not taken to reduce carbon emissions so that the combined CO_2 and non-carbon greenhouse gas concentrations in the atmosphere are kept below the upper safety limit of 350 ppm (parts per million). There is some support among experts for a less burdensome goal, which has been adopted by political leaders, of ensuring that the future concentration of greenhouse gases in the atmosphere does not rise above 400 or 450 ppm, which would require a 50 per cent reduction in the volume of current emissions by 2050, although here, again, controversy prevails, with some sources insisting on 50 per cent reductions from the much lower 1990 emission levels (Hansen 2009). The United States has pledged to make reductions by 2020 of 17 per cent of its 2005 levels, which amounts to only 4 per cent of its 1990 levels, and exemplifies the tendency of governments to do far too little to address the challenge, transferring a much larger burden of adjustment to the future.

What is significant from the perspective of this chapter are several features of the second ecological crisis that were not present during the first cycle: (1) an overlapping consensus among qualified scientific observers as to the general nature of global warming and its harmful effects, with strong policy implications for the manner in which carbon emissions should be regulated worldwide (IPCC 2007; Stern 2007); (2) a further societal consensus on the impact of harmful effects, although it is extremely uneven and has weakened in response to the campaign by the sceptics; (3) a greater sense of urgency with respect to regulatory action in countries of the South, especially vulnerable islands and in sub-Saharan Africa, that lack the resources and capabilities to take sufficient adaptive action to minimize actual and expected harm; and (4) an uneven, yet woefully insufficient, *political* consensus by governments on the nature of the response that is called for, with China and the United States, as global leaders, being among the worst laggards.[12] It is these features that contributed to the perceived failure of response at Copenhagen, helping us understand why the leadership of most governments continues to deflect pressures to shape policy in light of the gravity of the threatened harm, which would seem to require stringent and monitoring controls on greenhouse gas emissions. Instead, governments are content to talk of the dangers but to avoid any serious policy follow-through that commits them to future action.

In light of the Copenhagen failure, with respect either to achieving a workable arrangement based on reaching agreement with all governments participating in the process or by way of an approach achieved through reliance on the American-led directorate of five governments, other leadership models are starting to emerge. For instance, the US secretary of energy, Steven Chu, believes that the key to an effective

---

[12] Part of what makes the political consensus so reluctant to respond responsibly to the challenge of climate change is the success of the well-financed campaign conducted by climate sceptics, exhibiting the regressive influence of neoliberal élites, including most of the mainstream media, which have become increasingly corporatized in ownership as well as dependent with respect to advertising revenue. For an important refutation of climate critics, see Pachauri (2010).

response to climate change is by way of an agreed programme by the United States and China that relies primarily on the creativity of the market to provide the necessary technological fixes (Roth 2010). In a sense, what is being proposed is an eco/eco form of bipolarity (economic and ecological), which is dramatically different from the militarist bipolarity that underpinned, while threatening, world order during the Cold War.[13]

It is relevant for the position taken here that such proposed leadership is not explicitly concerned at all with whether any adjustment burden to global warming is equitable between states, attentive to vulnerable and disadvantaged societies and sensitive to the well-being of peoples. Rather, the Chu approach is based on a new type of geopolitical realism: adapted to the global climate change challenge, functionally driven and normatively myopic.

From knowledge to norms to policy to implementation: a lost cause?

At present, the inability to shape a political consensus among the main state actors, combined with the global, somewhat abstract and seemingly remote nature of the climate change challenge, makes it difficult to establish the motivation needed to undertake significant self-imposed restraints at the level of the state. Devising a solution for climate change has been so far treated as similar to ozone depletion, on account of the realization that the worst harmful effects are often geographically distant from and unrelated to the quantum of contribution to the root causes. In addition, with climate change, what counts as contribution is sharply contested, with the earliest industrial actors reluctant to consider past emissions as relevant for the calculation of present levels of responsibility, while late developers insist that the cumulative contributions over the course of history should be integral to the calculation of duties. For this set of reasons, without some series of traumatizing events generating a sense of urgency that can achieve political leverage, it seems frustrating to place strong hopes in a framework of constraint that regulates effectively and sufficiently the root causes of global warming – namely, carbon and related emissions.[14] In contrast, adjusting to ozone depletion seemed far

---

[13] 'Eco/eco' is my shorthand for 'economic/ecological'. The central preoccupation in the Cold War in the West was to contain presumed Soviet expansionism by reliance on a self-proclaimed 'balance of terror', also known by the instructive acronym MAD, for mutual assured destruction. Of course, eco/eco is still at the margins of the prevailing global imaginary, and can be viewed only as a proposal of interest.

[14] I believe a similar conclusion is reached by Matthew et al. (2010).

easier, because the sense of urgency was not contested by ozone sceptics, the adjustment costs were low enough for the main corporate actors to make them cooperative, alternative technology was available and the funds needed to subsidize phasing out ozone-depleting technologies in the South were sufficiently small to be politically acceptable.

My rather pessimistic assessment of prospects for appropriate climate change regulation is based on drawing a distinction between an *objective* sense of urgency, which is reflected in the scientific consensus, and the absence of a *subjective* sense of urgency, reflecting a range of factors ranging from the impact of climate change sceptics to the difficulty of mobilizing cooperative action among unevenly affected and responsible sovereign states. Sometimes, natural disasters on a large, yet local, scale, as in relation to the Asian tsunami of 2004 or the Haiti earthquake of 2010, can generate a strong empathetic response from rich countries not directly affected, but the difference is that the challenge is limited in scope and time, and the level of help is determined voluntarily and without any negative impacts on market forces. In fact, arguably, disasters offer renewal opportunities for ailing capitalist economies, somewhat analogous to cortisone injections (Klein 2008). For states addressing national security concerns, the prospects for mobilizing a strong response are often more a reflection of *subjective* feelings of threat than any *objective* assessment of danger. This is arguably the case in relation to the long-standing confrontation with Iran, and the mobilization of support for the attack on Iraq in 2003 was certainly based on a manipulation of public fears without much respect for the evidence.

Under these conditions, some have argued that it might produce better results if priority were given to addressing the anticipated effects of climate change rather than to emphasizing its root causes. This would mean channelling resources to and assisting with capacity building on behalf of the most geographically vulnerable and economically disadvantaged states. It would mean a major undertaking, such as a Marshall Plan for Global Warming, that would try to help existentially threatened countries cope with anticipated problems, and leave the politics of carbon reduction in the hands of sovereign states for the present. The downside is that such an approach would seem to invite a 'tragedy of the commons' outcome, leading to a catastrophic rise in the average earth temperature over the next several decades (Hardin 1968). As long as there is no agreed framework of obligatory reductions, the free-rider problem and the benefits of unregulated industrial activities would seem to condemn the planet to unsustainable warming trends.

The originality of the global warming *problématique* arises from the tension between what we know and what it is politically feasible to do.

The epistemological consensus establishes a horizon of necessity that extends far beyond the current horizon of feasibility, and so the world finds itself lacking sustainable governance from eco/eco perspectives even without taking into account horizons of desire, and, with that, the realm of ethics and values concerned with equity and the avoidance of human suffering.

A concluding note on horizons of desire

Climate change has been viewed mainly as a challenge of planetary scope that needs to be addressed intergovernmentally. Civil society activism is in the foreground, performing consciousness-raising roles with respect to generating a mood of urgency, while market forces are working to achieve a consciousness lowering that is designed to diminish pressures for regulation, inducing a mood of public reassurance, if not outright complacency. There is some attention devoted to intergovernmental justice with respect to the distribution of statist burdens of adjustment, with richer countries of the North committed to the transfer of funds facilitating adaptive steps aimed at carbon reduction in the South, principally to encourage various forms of technological mitigation. In addition, there is a verbal acknowledgement that some states face near-term crises due to their exposure to rising ocean levels or severe drought, and this may be translated into new forms of economic assistance, including technological transfers and capacity building as the crisis deepens, and catastrophe threatens.

Three clusters of normative concerns are almost absent from the climate change debate at this point. The first is the distribution of adjustment costs *internal* to sovereign states. The experience with 'first cycle' environmental adjustments suggests that the more vulnerable groups and areas not only experience most of the harm but also bear disproportionate burdens – a form of indirect and regressive taxation. This pattern is evident in relation to the disposal of toxic wastes, the location of nuclear energy facilities and the siting of polluting industry. Greater attentiveness to the equitable distribution of these internal adjustment costs would exhibit increased sensitivity to a human security perspective (but see Garvey 2008; Matthew *et al.* 2010). The second cluster of normative concerns relates to the distribution of adjustment costs as between present and future generations, which are also not factored into the climate change discourse in any serious manner. There is an almost total absence of the precautionary wisdom of indigenous peoples, whose moral imagination extended for several (often seven) generations into the future; in contrast, modern society, intoxicated by its confidence in technological progress, seems almost indifferent to the fate of the world as it imposes itself on our grandchildren's generation (Hansen 2009). Finally, there is the impact of worsening climate conditions on the quality of global governance from the perspective of human rights and democracy; in considering past experience, there seems always to have been, from ancient times, a correlation between reliance on authoritarian and repressive governance when a society is faced with scarcities of vital resources or fundamental security threats. The authoritarian justification usually rests on claims of efficiency together with class pressures to ensure the unjust distribution of burdens, entailing special hardships and extra risks for weaker sectors of society.

What is suggested is not only the weakness of geopolitical leadership to provide a solution required for the security of states, but a set of circumstances at the global level that precludes the effective representation of the human interest in the shaping of global policy. This circumstance is complemented by structures of internal and international authority that are heavily weighted in favour of dominant market forces and the well-being of the affluent.[15] To the extent that moral globalization includes protecting the economic and social rights of the poorer segments of present and future societies, the response to climate change confirms the hegemonic and exploitative character of neoliberal globalization as the operative problem-solving framework. Whether this framework is susceptible to being transformed by a transnational and progressive political and civil society is uncertain at present (Gill 2008: 177–269). The best hope for such a transformation is for a robust transnational progressive populism to create a powerful movement from below for ecological justice. In this crucial regard, we need to rethink our images of leadership, relinquishing faith in leadership from above and investing our hopes and dreams in leadership from below – that is, from the sinews of civil society – born as much from anger as from reason.

---

[15] One approach to enhance such representation would be through the establishment of a global parliament or assembly based on the experience of, but not resembling, the European Parliament (for recommendations along these lines, see Falk and Strauss 2001).

6 The emerging global freshwater crisis and the privatization of global leadership

Hilal Elver

Summary

This chapter deals with a key component of global crisis: the nature of, access to and the multifaceted laws and policy perspectives governing the use of global freshwater. Its focus is also on the global leadership strategies and struggles concerning access to a vital resource for human survival. This struggle involves global market forces and civil society movements. It concerns issues of environmental justice and human security. On the one hand, neoliberal free market principles and new constitutional forms of international economic and trade law have led to the treatment of vital resources such as water as saleable 'commodities'. On the other hand, numerous civil society organizations and human rights lawyers argue that access to drinking water should be a fundamental human right. This chapter argues for an approach to water governance that treats water as a fundamental human right rather than simply as a commodity that is best governed by private corporations and market forces.

Introduction: freshwater scarcity

This chapter explores some of the legal, political and economic structures and processes that are shaping leadership strategies for addressing the emerging global freshwater crisis. It discusses international water laws, control over the market for freshwater supply and the various political forces shaping global water policies. It addresses these questions not simply from the viewpoint of the efficient allocation of water as a commodity but, more fundamentally, as a question of access to water from a human rights perspective. This clash of perspectives will shape the future governance of global freshwater supply in coming years.

The World Health Organization (WHO) and the United Nations Children's Fund (UNICEF) estimate that approximately 1 billion people lack access to adequate drinking water while 2.6 billion people lack access to basic sanitation. The majority of these people live in the developing world. Despite some improvements in recent years and the high priority given to improved access to water and sanitation services by various governments, the UN and a range of civil society organizations, it is estimated that, if current trends continue, by 2015 672 million people will still lack access to adequate drinking water and 2.7 billion people will go short of basic sanitation (WHO and UNICEF 2010). Moreover, as many as 5 million people, the majority of whom are children, die annually from preventable water-related diseases. The lack of access to water and sanitation services has particularly negative implications for women and girls, who tend to be responsible for travelling long distances in order to bring water to their homes (ibid.: 29).

While the world population quadrupled in the last century, the amount of freshwater consumed increased many, many times more. This, coupled with the current acceleration of urban growth, is putting massive pressure on our planet's freshwater resources. It is estimated that, by 2030, half the world will be living under severe water stress. This water scarcity will affect countries highly unevenly. For instance, according to a report released by the Asia Society Leadership Group on Water Security in 2009, one of the most affected areas globally will be Asia, where the urban population is likely to increase by 60 per cent by 2025. As the water needs of growing cities worldwide increase, the need to find sustainable urban water solutions has never been more urgent.

Moreover, the availability of freshwater resources is part of the problem of the sustainability of the biosphere, which has already been significantly affected by early signs of global warming (IPCC 2007). Shifting precipitation patterns and the increased melting of mountain glaciers disrupt previous water patterns, upsetting the timing and quantity of flows. Moreover, rising sea levels will exacerbate saltwater intrusion into the lower reaches of many rivers. Stronger storm surges may also inundate low-lying coastal deltas. States may suffer not just chronic pressures, such as decreased freshwater availability, but also acute crises, such as flooding or drought. Both types of threats can impair food production, endanger public health, stress established settlement patterns and jeopardize livelihoods and social well-being. The effects of global warming on water resources will be particularly damaging to countries in the developing world. Farming, fisheries, forestry and other environmentally sensitive sectors represent significant portions of most developing country economies, making them particularly vulnerable to climate impacts. As such, without effective leadership, the crisis of water availability looms increasingly large.

The shifting focus of international water law and practice

Water has traditionally been considered a part of the ecosystem itself and a public good. Its direct relation with human health is one of the major preoccupations of domestic and international law. Because water is such a versatile resource, several specific areas of law, from environmental to human rights and, finally, international economic law (or trade law), regulate – or, at least, claim to regulate – the use and distribution of water.

Historically, water was one of the important areas of international law in relation to oceans, providing 'freedom of the seas' for the dominant naval powers, and governing the navigational use of rivers, especially in continental Europe, where long rivers are shared and heavily used commercially by two or more countries. After a long period of navigational preoccupation, following the Industrial Revolution concerns about the quality of freshwater resources and pollution problems emerged. So too did a number of international lawyers with an interest in legislation related to water. The perspective adopted by these lawyers was generally informed by a respect for state sovereignty over natural resources, though they also sought means to protect water and the environment from pollution.

During this period, legal struggles related to the governance of water tended to revolve around a conflict between the desire for states to retain control over water resources (largely related to a desire to maintain economic competitiveness in post-colonial settings) and international concerns with water and environmental sustainability. In this context, the management of trans-boundary water resources became one of the most contested issues of international law. This context also set the stage for the emergence of inter-state and intra-state water conflicts in many parts of the world, especially in developing countries situated in arid regions where the quantity of water and the development of water resources were major preoccupations. It was during this period that the two areas of international environmental law and laws governing the use of watercourses began to merge. Although this merger has shaped current international legal thinking about water in a more environmentally conscious manner, it has not yet been able to resolve major international river conflicts, nor to establish international principles regarding the sustainable and equitable use of freshwater resources.

In recent years there have been significant changes relating to the regulation of water resources. As noted above, in addition to trans-boundary issues, the most serious immediate challenges in the twenty-first century are the lack of access to safe drinking water and inadequate

sanitation. This preoccupation requires solutions that go beyond traditional international water law principles, which are grounded in state
sovereignty, national self-interest and reciprocity. What is needed is a
new global approach based on normative principles that value environmental protection and human security above the interests of states and
global market forces.

However, this is not what has emerged. Rather, over the past two
decades water has increasingly been governed according to the neoliberal economic principles outlined in the Washington consensus – the
blueprint for global neoliberal economics that tries to resolve all issues
through the logic of market efficiency. Beginning with the Rio 'Earth
Summit' of 1992, water has increasingly been defined as a *tradable
commodity* that is best governed by private market forces. The
commodification of water has been supported by international business
and trade law, with the help of the WTO, the World Bank and the IMF,
which have effectively created a regulatory framework that legally protects the rights of corporations involved in the water sector over and
above those of the majority of the population; indeed, the new forms of
law and regulation correspond to what Stephen Gill (1992; 1998a;
1998b) refers to as the institutions and neoliberal practices of the 'new
constitutionalism'. Examples include the following.

- International trade bodies such as NAFTA and the WTO have declared
  water to be a tradable commodity, classifying it as a 'commercial good',
  a 'service' or an 'investment' (Barlow and Clarke 2003: 97).
- The WTO's General Agreement on Trade in Services (GATS) has the
  potential to constrain the ability of governments to prevent private
  sector involvement in domestic water management (Flecker and
  Clarke 2005: 76).
- The law plays a key role in privatizing water in the lending conditionality imposed by the IMF, the World Bank and other regional and
  international financial institutions (IFIs). Consistent with the principles of the Washington consensus, these institutions have mandated
  that governments, particularly those in the developing world, pass
  legislation enabling the privatization of water and sanitation systems
  in order to receive loans. The World Bank also serves the interests of
  water companies, both through its regular loan programmes to governments and through its private sector arm, the International
  Finance Corporation, which invests in privatization projects and
  makes loans to companies carrying them out.
- Nevertheless, in recent years the World Bank and other IFIs have
  taken a step back from their overwhelming and largely uncritical

endorsement of the privatization of water services. This shift is largely a result of the failure of many private water projects to generate sufficient revenue for investors; the failure of the private sector to deliver much of the new investment and expanded services as promised to governments; and, not least, the significant grass roots opposition that has emerged in response to water privatization.

However, despite the explicit admission by certain divisions of the World Bank (and others) that the privatization of water services may have negative outcomes, particularly for the poorest, a large proportion of new loans continue to promote and/or compel privatization. A year-long study by the International Consortium of Investigative Journalists, a project of the Washington-based Center for Public Integrity, released in February 2003 found that the majority of World Bank loans for water in the previous five years required the conversion of public systems to private as a condition for the transaction. According to one investigative report, between 2004 and 2008 52 per cent of World Bank water services and sanitation projects – seventy-eight projects totalling $5.9 billion – promoted some form of privatization, and 64 per cent of them promoted some form of cost recovery (Food & Water Watch 2009: 16–17). In addition, in many instances public utilities were urged to restructure themselves along commercial lines, 'turning them into more autonomous bodies governed by a corporation board, with shareholders from both the public and private sectors', and to award management contracts to the private sector (ibid.).

Such new 'public–private partnerships' continue to be informed by the belief that the allocation and management of water is best and most efficiently done by the private sector and global market forces. For proponents of economic globalization, the future of the world is inextricably linked to the future of business. Their conception assumes that private investment should act as the primary engine of growth and that the private sector is best suited to manage the looming water crisis. In other words, public leadership relating to the management of water should be transferred to private leadership.

Private governance of water resources has also been justified as the best and most efficient means of promoting conservation and environmental sustainability. For instance, in 2002, during the UN World Summit on Sustainable Development in Johannesburg, privatization was presented to the world community as a magic formula capable of solving water problems around the globe, in developed and developing countries alike. One reason offered for this is based on the idea that, as countries globalize, their increased wealth will enable them to save more patches of nature from the ravages of exploitation. The argument is that privatization will enable governments to protect water resources from depletion over the long term.

A second line of argument – embraced by the IMF and OECD governments – is based on the idea that the market price of water reflects its 'true' value and, therefore, pricing water according to the dictates of the market is the best means of assuring that there is equilibrium between supply and demand. The OECD recently released three reports that argue for the need to increase the price of water in order to promote conservation. According to the OECD secretary-general, Angel Gurría, 'putting a price on water will make us aware of the scarcity and make us take better care of it' (Jowit 2010; see also OECD 2009). Of course, this approach has the potential to increase the cost of water for some of the poorest sectors of the population while doing little to address the highly inequitable distribution of water resources.

A range of powerful social forces have therefore advanced the idea that the best and most efficient means of addressing the global water crisis involves the privatization of the planet's remaining freshwater, including selling exploitation rights to corporations and allowing the global market to decide who gets to drink and use water. Corporations that deliver the services have a strong self-interest in promoting these initiatives as beneficial to the poor.

Although rich countries have the flexibility to implement selectively, shop around and find the most effective solutions for water sanitation and distribution, poor countries are often pushed by the IMF and the World Bank to adapt their constitutional principles and domestic legal orders so as to allow the privatization of public goods and services previously governed by public institutions and to minimize government regulation. Such governments have little freedom to oppose the tide of privatization and new constitutionalism.

However, what are the possible impacts for the poorest water users of a free market approach to natural resources management in developing countries? Despite the importance of both ecological and social aspects of natural resource management, proponents of the market model have surprisingly little to say on the possible ecological and social consequences of using the free market for water services (Galaz 2004). Policy-makers should be aware that the 'water market' would have the greatest negative effect on underprivileged users. In rural areas in particular, weak NGOs, non-existent or marginalized water user associations and slow governmental agencies will not be able to protect underprivileged water users' rights in courts against water management companies in case of conflict (Galaz 2004).

Who controls the water market?

The market for water infrastructure, sanitation and pollution prevention in the developing world is potentially vast. Currently, water systems are controlled publicly in 90 per cent of communities across the world. However, these numbers are changing rapidly. For instance, in 1990 only 50 million people in twelve countries worldwide got their water services from private companies, but by 2002 the number stood at 300 million and was still growing. There are ten major corporations – constituting a global oligopoly of market players – that now deliver freshwater services for profit. Between them, the three biggest – Suez and Vivendi (recently renamed Veolia Environment) of France and RWE AG of Germany – deliver water and wastewater services to customers in over 100 countries, and they are in a race against, or in some instances cooperate with, others such as Bouygues SAUR, Thames Water (owned by RWE) and Bechtel/United Utilities, with the goal of expanding to every corner of the globe.

If privatization continues at the same speed, the top three alone will control over 70 per cent of the water systems in Europe and North America by 2020. Vivendi (Veolia) earned $5 billion in 1992 from water-related revenues; by 2002 its earnings had increased to over $12 billion. RWE, which moved into the world market with its acquisition of Britain's Thames Water, increased its water revenue by a staggering 9,786 per cent between 1992 and 2002. All three firms are among the top 100 corporations in the world and, together, their annual revenues in 2002 were almost $200 billion and were growing at 10 per cent a year – thus far outpacing the economies of many of the countries in which they operate (Global Water Intelligence 2010). The performance of these companies in Europe and the developing world has been well documented: they have earned huge profits and charged higher prices for water; they have also cut off customers who cannot pay, reduced water quality and engaged in bribery and corruption (Snitow, Kaifman and Fox 2007: 114).

There are numerous accounts of the negative impacts of the privatization of water worldwide. Though these cannot be fully detailed here, a few examples should suffice to demonstrate the point. One well-known example is the case of Bolivia, where the famed 'water war' of 2001 emerged as a direct result of a World Bank initiative involving a Bechtel subsidiary, Abengoa Spain. When the price of water tripled after privatization had been introduced, thousands took to the streets of Cochabamba. This led to a violent conflict between the people, who were later termed 'water warriors', and the local government – a conflict that eventually ended with the termination of the private contract. Bechtel later sued the government of Bolivia for millions of dollars under a bilateral investment treaty for losses in future profits (Olivera and Lewis 2004; see also Shultz 2009).

The *Bechtel versus Bolivia* case went before the International Center for the Settlement of Investment Disputes (ICSID), the World Bank's little-known international arbitration tribunal, which holds all its sessions in secret without any public scrutiny or participation. Bechtel demanded $50 million as compensation for loss of profits, from a country with some of the poorest people in the western hemisphere. A wide range of groups joined to demand that the World Bank open up the arbitration process to public scrutiny. Trade union organizations, environmental groups, consumer organizations, research groups and numerous religious organizations from across the world all joined in presenting a petition to participate in the ICSID tribunal hearing the case. For four years after 2000 Bechtel and the subsidiary Aguas de Tunari found their companies and corporate leaders dogged by protest, damaging press coverage and public demands from five continents that they drop the case. The result was the first time that a leading corporation has ever dropped a major international trade case as a direct result of global public pressure, and it sets an important precedent for the politics of future trade cases like this one.[1]

A similar situation has occurred in other South American countries. For instance, in July 2002 Suez terminated its World-Bank-backed thirty-year contract to provide water and sewerage services to the city of Buenos Aires when the financial meltdown of Argentina's economy meant that the company would not be able to maintain its profit margins. During the first eight years of the contract, weak regulatory practices and contract renegotiations that eliminated corporate risk enabled the Suez subsidiary, Aguas Argentinas SA, to earn a 19 per cent profit rate. Water rates, which the company said would be reduced by 27 per cent, actually rose 20 per cent, while a half of its employees were laid off. Aguas Argentinas also reneged on its contractual obligations to build a new sewage treatment plant. As a result, over 95 per cent of the city's sewage is now dumped directly into the river Plate.

In South Africa, water supplies were cut off to over 10 million people between 2002 and 2004, largely because of their inability to pay for the newly privatized service (Bond 2004). This occurred despite a constitutional guarantee of access to water for all, pointing to the

[1] Ibid.

prioritization of economic commitments and international legal and trade agreements – the new constitutionalism – over and above domestic legal and constitutional guarantees. Similar problems have been reported in many parts of the world as private water companies have increased water rates and cut off services to those who cannot pay the bills, while reducing water quality and refusing to make investments for the improvement of infrastructure, such as leaky pipes.

More recently, in the context of the global financial crisis, with the tightening of international and domestic credit markets, many private companies have failed to meet their obligations to invest in water projects. This has shed serious doubt on the future of numerous public–private partnerships, including those related to water and sanitation. Several countries, including South Africa, Australia, the United States and Mexico and a number of countries in the Middle East, have already cancelled a range of such partnerships (Dwivedi 2010).

These processes have generated numerous resistance movements, which, in turn, have led to the termination of some contracts. In other instances, governments have begun to think about how to withdraw from complex agreements that have been signed with corporate giants, usually prepared by international corporate lawyers. However, in spite of growing public opposition, as noted above, the World Bank and various private interests continue to support privatization projects.

Nonetheless, advocates of privatization have become more sophisticated. For instance, water companies now package their business in human-rights- and environment-oriented language and have become involved with various UN agencies and water-related projects. They argue that many governments in developing countries have failed to recognize their citizens' supposed rights to water and that water privatization can therefore go a long way towards 'quenching the thirst of the poor' (Segerfelt 2005: 13). They claim that public water systems in the developing world generally supply politically connected wealthy and middle-class people, whereas the poor are not hooked up to municipal water.[2] They further note that the poor pay more for their water, as they are often forced to purchase water from contractors who drive tankers to poor districts and sell water by the can for highly inflated prices. On average, this water is twelve times more expensive than water from regular water mains. These are, of course, important problems, but the question is whether private sector actors are the ones best suited to deal with them.

---

[2] Segerfelt (2005) cites one study that says that fifteen countries found that, in the poorest quarters of their populations, 80 per cent of the people were not hooked up to water mains.

Who sets global water policy?

The United Nations and its specialized bodies are generally considered to be the major policy-making institutions in relation to social and environmental issues. The 1977 Mar del Plata meeting was the first water policy meeting under the UN flag, and it focused primarily on drinking water and human use. After that, for almost two decades, there was no serious interest in water issues in the UN. Part of the reason for this was related to the competition and rivalries that existed between the more than twenty UN agencies that claimed water as part of their agenda. However, by the early 1990s this gap had been filled by private 'epistemic communities', which gradually became the home of the water companies.

In 1992 two important conferences took place: the International Conference on Water and the Environment (ICWE) in Dublin and the UN Conference on Environment and Development in Rio de Janeiro. These conferences set the stage for a dramatic shift in the global water agenda, as it was here that the UN first defined water as an 'economic good', thus planting the institutional roots for privatization. These conferences also supported a shift in water governance away from state-oriented, fragmented principles and towards more holistic, stake-holder-oriented participatory principles, which introduced a new role for the private sector, NGOs and international organizations in the global governance of water. Instead of a long-standing international diplomatic norm-making process, a top-down process was quietly begun, as a means to shift the governance of water from the global environmental agenda to economic platforms. Despite calls for a more participatory approach, the core message that emerged from these two conferences was that water has an economic value and that it needs to be managed according to economic principles in order to promote sustainable development (Finger and Allouche 2002: 21). Concerns about equity and poverty were completely ignored.

The idea of leadership by private institutions, regional and non-governmental organizations along with all interested governments was articulated in a more sophisticated manner with the establishment of the World Water Council (WWC) in 1996. This organization is financed and supported by the giant water companies, with participation from the World Bank, the United Nations Development Programme, water policy experts, eminent individuals and mainstream environmental NGOs. Every three years the WWC organizes World Water Forums in different parts of the world, to discuss upcoming issues, establish networks among companies and offer various services to governments for effective water management.[3] Ultimately, this forum has taken on the appearance of a UN agency, and it seeks nothing less than to set the future agenda for global water resource management. It supports the view of water as a commodity and advocates a central role for the private sector in the provisioning of water (see, for instance, WWC 2009).

What is emerging in global water policy, therefore, is a new trend: the leadership role played in the 1990s by the UN system has started to decline, and is now being taken over by new institutions such as the World Water Council, the Global Water Partnership and the Stockholm Water Symposium, all of which continue to advocate governing water through the market mechanism as a means of addressing the water crisis. This privatized global water leadership network is interested in norm-making processes that have traditionally belonged to states, inter-state relations and diplomacy. However, sometimes their norm-making process is completely outside the state-oriented processes, which are still largely governed by international law. When necessary, they act together with local or regional bodies rather than federal governments. Their institution building, style and norm-making efforts could be defined 'as fluid as water'. They are interested in the management of water resources and water services in a vertically integrated manner so that they can control water as a profitable commodity.

Set against the powerful private global water network, more radical NGOs have established their own networks in order to create alternative water policies based on human rights and human security. The more recent campaigns on water issues have a different target. They have mobilized citizens against the privatization of water and bulk water sales and aim to remove water from the global trade list of the World Trade Organization. For instance, the World Coalition against Water Privatization is a global umbrella organization that developed a campaign to keep water out of the WTO at its Johannesburg summit. The 'water warriors' go wherever the 'water barons' go, organize alternative forums and wage street demonstrations in cities where the WWC holds its meetings.[4] Basically, they are trying to inform citizens that their valuable public good is about to be sold by their governments or local authorities to the 'water barons', who in turn take some of the warriors' leaders very seriously. Moreover, the barons are aware that the

---

[3] The first such forum was held in Marrakech in 1997, the second in The Hague in 2000, the third in Kyoto in 2003, the fourth in Mexico City in 2006 and the fifth in Istanbul in 2009.

[4] I have borrowed this language from a project of the Center for Public Integrity, the International Consortium of Investigative Journalists (2003).

privatization of water systems under the banner of 'public–private partnerships' does not always work without major problems, and that political will is required in order to protect their profits. For instance, in Mexico City during the third World Water Forum, the protests were so successful that the WWC organizers had to include the NGOs' leaders on their board in order to pacify the movement.

Access to water? Human rights law and environmental law

A component of the present global conjuncture concerns the conflict between different social forces regarding the ways in which water should be governed in the context of the emerging water crisis. The forces of leadership on one side of the struggle include a number of élites, the governments of many of the developed countries, the IFIs and the private sector, which largely supports a neoliberal approach to the governance of water. These social forces promote the privatization of water as the best and most efficient means of encouraging conservation and view the private sector as an essential partner in the delivery of water and sanitation services. This view has been institutionalized and secured through a range of international trade, lending and other legal agreements that compel governments to privatize services and that seek to protect private investments from 'expropriation' or from future government interventions. On the other side are a range of NGOs, civil society organizations and popular movements, which point to the numerous negative consequences of past privatization projects in order to argue that water privatization increases human insecurity and will ultimately do little to address the water crisis. The latter group of social forces has increasingly begun to frame its position in relation to international human rights law – a trend that seems to have the greatest potential to address the water crisis and to remove this essential resource from the hands of the private sector and the dictates of the capitalist market.

International human rights law is the only area of international law that aims directly at distributive, corrective and procedural justice principles. In general, international human rights law promotes and protects the rights of human beings, as well as the factors that impede enforcement and the punishment of human rights violators, or those factors that increase the likelihood that violations will occur. The essential role of human rights law is particularly important to protect individuals and groups that are considered to be the most vulnerable, and it enables redress for those who could not otherwise obtain access to water if market principles were applied.[5] This also means that 'access to water for all' implies that the implementation of this right is a responsibility of states with respect to their own citizens. However, at present, there are no enforceable norms that protect people's access to water as a human right.

Environmental law is also important in the struggle for the human rights to water. For a long time environmental law and human rights law were regarded as having different targets and interests, and were treated separately. However, there are many areas of significant overlap. For example, the rights to safe food and water, to live in a decent and healthy environment and to participate in environmental decision-making all bear upon both human rights law and environmental law. With the growing importance of environmental law, the international community has taken an interest in investigating and anchoring the relationship between the two fields. The integration of these two fields has been evolving since the 1970s, through national constitutions, regional agreements and international treaties. Some countries have already enacted the 'right to access to drinking water' as a constitutional right; the South African constitution is one example.

International environmental law is primarily preoccupied with the protection of natural resources and avoidance of environmental harms, particularly in the context of trans-boundary resources. Therefore, in relation to water, international environmental law first and foremost deals with how to protect trans-boundary water resources from environmental damage and how to promote principles of equitable sharing between the riparian countries. The most important customary law principle of international environmental law, embodied in principle 21 of the 1972 Stockholm Declaration, stipulates that states have 'the sovereign rights to exploit their own resources pursuant to their own environmental policies', as long as they do not thereby 'cause damage to the environment of other states or areas beyond the limits of national jurisdiction'. International environmental law respects state sovereignty and does not purport to regulate a country's internal environmental problems. In many developing countries, therefore, national law may allow an activity even if it is contrary to international law (Elver 2008: 395). However, in recent years human rights scholars and environmental NGOs have introduced human rights principles to establish remedies to environmentally harmful activities associated with trans-boundary water conflicts. These mechanisms are virtually unique in offering venues of

---

[5] As ideas about what is 'vulnerable' change, understandings of human rights adapt to meet emerging claims associated with new forms of vulnerability.

redress for individuals or groups that need to appeal beyond their own governmental institutions if harm is done to them from neighbouring countries. Nevertheless, in the trans-boundary water context, implementing human rights principles is still a highly controversial idea, since it clashes with the principle of state sovereignty.

Nonetheless, there are numerous ways in which a human rights approach to water can be advanced. For instance, even though the 1948 Universal Declaration of Human Rights does not specifically spell out a right to water, article 3 provides the right to life and article 25 recognizes the right to health and grants it a human rights quality. Both these objectives clearly require the availability of a minimum amount of clean water. The declaration is not binding per se as a General Assembly resolution, yet it is considered as *jus cogens* in international law (McCaffrey 1992: 6).[6] Furthermore, implementing such international human rights principles of access to water at the domestic level also gives citizens additional access to the judicial system – if need be, against their own government.

Similar principles are also included by way of article 6 in the International Covenant on Economic, Social and Cultural Rights (ICESCR) of 1966. In addition, the rights enshrined in articles 11 (which recognizes the right of everyone to an adequate standard of living, including sufficient food and shelter) and 12 (which contains the right to physical and mental health) of the ICESCR also presuppose access to drinkable water. Moreover, the 1966 International Covenant on Civil and Political Rights includes the 'right to life' in article 6. The recent trend among human rights scholars is to expand the right to life under this article as much as possible and to argue that states have a duty to actively pursue policies that are designed to ensure the means of survival for every individual and for all people. Although these rights are somewhat abstract and do not precisely guarantee water rights, they offer the space for judges or administrators to interpret them as such.

Other international human rights treaties include explicit references to the right to water. For instance, article 14 (2) of the Convention on the Elimination of All Forms of Discrimination against Women (1979) stipulates that state parties shall ensure women the right to 'enjoy adequate living conditions, particularly in relation to...water supply'. Similarly, article 24 (2) of the Convention on the Rights of the Child (1989) requires state parties to combat disease and malnutrition 'through the provision of adequate nutritious foods and clean drinking water'.

---

[6] A *jus cogens* is a peremptory norm, or a fundamental principle of international law.

As a social and economic right, the right to water does not encompass a right to access water, directly enforceable by each person against the state. However, the right to water requires governments to progressively increase the number of people with safe, affordable and convenient access to drinkable water. Governments also have to ensure non-discriminatory and affordable access to water (Turk and Krajewski 2003). This, then, offers a legal basis from which to critique the privatization of water, given the general failure of private water companies to expand infrastructure adequately and their tendency to raise water prices in ways that increase the burdens felt by the poorest users and, in particular, women.

In sum, despite the fact that the right of access to water is recognized in environmental law documents, that right has been circumscribed and transformed under conditions of neoliberal economic globalization. Principle 1 of the 1972 Stockholm Declaration established the link between human rights and the environment, despite the fact that it is a declaratory document. However, much later, the 1992 Rio Declaration on Environment and Development failed to declare a concrete, operative individual right to a decent environment. Instead, principle 1 of the declaration uses the word 'entitlement', and principle 3 proclaims the 'right to development'. This formulation may be viewed as a regressive step if compared to the clear language of the Stockholm Declaration adopted twenty years beforehand. Furthermore, the United Nations Convention on Watercourses of 1997 did not refer directly to the right to access to freshwater in a human rights context. Rather, article 10 contains an indirect reference through the concept of 'vital human needs', without defining what they are.

Framing water as a human rights issue conflicts directly with much international economic and trade law, which is shaped by the new constitutionalism. It is argued by neoliberals that human rights and the principles of international economic law are mutually reinforcing. Thus, certain proponents of new constitutional economic and trade law have argued that the liberal principle of non-discrimination is functionally equivalent to constitutional guarantees for basic human rights. However, critics have pointed out that this neoliberal approach focuses mainly on traditional market freedoms, such as the right to trade or the right to own and sell property, and it tends to assume that the right to health, food, shelter and water are best protected and guaranteed through the free market. Moreover, the perspective of human rights in the liberal approach focuses only on the protection of traditional human rights against state intervention (a negative concept of human rights) and does not consider human rights enforced through the state (a positive concept of human rights). In contrast, some critics argue that human rights are more than just narrow legal obligations of governments to adopt or avoid particular policies. Rather, they often require considerable political effort by governments to initiate a variety of policy choices.

Indeed, the United Nations High Commissioner for Human Rights (UNHCHR) has explicitly made this point in a report on the liberalization of trade in services and human rights, noting that mere reliance on liberal markets to promote human rights is insufficient from a human rights perspective. 'In this respect, the obligations on states to respect, protect and fulfil human rights include the responsibility to ensure that private entities or individuals, including transnational corporations over which they exercise jurisdiction, do not deprive individuals of their economic, social and cultural rights' (UNHCHR 2002: 10). In other words, in contrast to the liberal constitutional approach, it is argued that market forces cannot be expected to protect human rights and that governments have an obligation to actively ensure their provisioning. The report continues (ibid.: 10–11): 'The adoption of any deliberately retrogressive measure in the liberalization process that reduces the extent to which any human right is protected constitutes a violation of human rights.'

The conflict highlighted by the UNHCHR between human rights and trade regulations is particularly important in relation to water, since the reclassification of water as a commodity and an economic good in trade law has had negative impacts on the human rights of much of the world's population. As such, conflicts may arise between, for instance, a state's obligations and commitments under the GATS and its commitments to UN human rights agreements. The right to water requires government actions aimed at progressively ensuring universal, equal and reliable access to drinkable water; by contrast, the GATS principle of 'progressive liberalization' implies the commercialization or privatization of provision.

Conclusion

The potential conflict between trade liberalization and the regulation of water services as a means to ensure the progressive realization of the right to water opens an important space in which to offer more progressive approaches to dealing with the global water crisis. The progressive realization of basic human rights such as the right to water needs effective and prudent – indeed, very far-sighted – regulation rather than the forms of deregulation and privatization advocated by neoliberals. If the private sector is to be involved in the provisioning of water, there must be effective social and economic regulation and institutions, and these institutions must also be democratically accountable. Neither the GATS nor any other agreements of the World Trade Organization or capacity-building efforts assist countries with the design of such regulatory regimes, because, quite simply, the objective of the WTO-governed trade regime is the liberalization of trade and investment.

Sustainable water management needs to grapple with pervasive mismatches between the national political level, at which key decisions are made: the individual, societal and economic levels, where the actions generating environmental change occur; and the ecosystemic levels, at which the environmental consequences unfold. Addressing these challenges successfully will require effective global leadership that fosters policy-making structures and processes that can fully encompass multiple scales, from the local to the global, while also navigating the disparate perspectives of diverse users situated at levels extending from households and communities to the national, regional and international.

Four major questions remain for future global leadership – questions that require deep introspection and reflection, and that could serve as guidelines for debates on how we might govern this vital aspect of global governance. (1) Should water, a substance vital to life itself, be treated as if it can be solely a commodity that is the object of profit-making? (2) How can we organize a global world order so that basic public services such as clean water, clean air and universal health care can be made available to all people of the planet regardless of their ability to pay? (3) How can we govern that world so that technological innovations become available for the truly sustainable use of natural resources? (4) Finally, how can we distribute responsibility for protecting our planet among the people, treated as equals, in ways that are equally just?

Part III

Global Leadership Ethics, Crises and Subaltern Forces

7 Global leadership, ethics and global health: the search for new paradigms

Solomon R. Benatar

Summary

Global health is arguably the most pressing moral challenge for human security and well-being in the twenty-first century. In seeking solutions to this, I begin by suggesting the need to acknowledge that the world is in a state of entropy. This is reflected in widening disparities in health across the planet (despite major advances in science and medicine and spectacular economic growth), the emergence and spread of many new infectious diseases, climate change and the recently evolving global economic crisis – all of which are already having devastating effects on population health. These trends will continue if we fail to take appropriate action, and they reveal the need for new paradigms of thinking and action that require a shift in the spectrum of our value system from one dominated by a highly individualistic, competitive, scientific, market approach to health and well-being to an orientation that, while retaining the best of these values, is more inclusive of solidarity, cooperation and socio-economic and ecological sustainability considerations. A thrust towards making such progress could be promoted by expanding the discourses on ethics and human rights, and by developing the global state of mind essential for progress in an increasingly interdependent world.

Introduction

It is becoming apparent to some scholars that global health is the most pressing moral challenge for human security and social well-being in the twenty-first century (Benatar 2005). If this is an accurate diagnosis (and I do not intend to provide the evidence or rationale for this here, as there

This chapter draws extensively on the following previous publications, from which more comprehensive sets of references are available: Benatar (1997a), Benatar, Daar and Singer (2003), Benatar (2005) and Benatar, Lister and Thacker (2010). I am grateful to Stephen Gill for comments.

is already a voluminous literature on this topic), then the next step towards seeking solutions is to achieve widespread acceptance of this diagnosis. Only then can we begin to consider and take appropriate action.

However, before taking these next steps, I would like to extend the above diagnosis and suggest that the state of health across the world is only one of many signs that the world is unstable (as a result of several overlapping crises) and, indeed, in a state of entropy. Such entropy, reflected in widening disparities in health across the globe, is also evident in the following five developments: (1) the emergence and spread of many new infectious diseases (for example, many new virus infections, of which HIV is the best known and most devastating); (2) the rise of multi-drug-resistant organisms (tuberculosis, malaria and staphylococcus being amongst the best known); (3) the degradation of the environment and climate change, reflected in the three previous chapters in this collection; (4) the currently evolving global economic crisis, which is addressed in much of this work; and (5) the impaired reproduction of the social caring institutions that promote human well-being – what is called elsewhere in this volume a crisis of social reproduction. Indeed, following Stephen Gill, we might describe the current state of the world as a constellation of 'multiple crises'. It is not unrealistic to assume that these trends will continue if we fail to take appropriate action. Whether or not we can take such action will depend on what we think needs to be done. Lying at the heart of the problem is a set of values associated with a mindset that has brought great (but not endless) progress that we cherish and that has served some of us well over several centuries (while harming others). The adverse effects that this mindset and its values have engendered for others is now turning back to harm those who have benefited from activities designed to serve themselves – as one author has written in relation to the rise and spread of zoonotic diseases (because of closer interactions between animals and humans in the animal farming industry).[1] The chickens have indeed 'come home to roost' (Benatar 2007).

Growing global instability and threats from the widening gulf between the world's 'haves' and 'have-nots', in all societies, call for innovative ways of thinking and acting. Distinctions between domestic and foreign policy have become blurred, and public health, even in the most privileged nations, is obviously more closely linked than ever to health and disease in impoverished countries. The need for coherence between domestic and foreign policy was acknowledged by US president

---

[1] Zoonotic diseases are those of animal origin.

Bill Clinton many years ago when he declared HIV/AIDS a global emergency, and also by subsequent endeavours to foster a global response to this pandemic. The need for leadership in global health has become even more crucial in the face of the excessive focus on a biomedical approach to health, with neglect of the potential of preventing premature deaths and of improving global health by attending to the societal determinants of disease (Birn, Pillay and Holtz 2009).

Acknowledging these destabilizing trends enables us to realize that we need new paradigms of thinking and innovative action if we are to promote and sustain human well-being, health and security for a greater proportion of the world's population through the twenty-first century and beyond. We have the intellectual and the material resources to achieve this goal; however, the big question is whether we have the vision, commitment and political will to do so.

I begin here by briefly reviewing the values that underlie our modern paradigm within which our conceptions of ethics, progress, science and development are embedded. I then go on to suggest that there are several values that we claim to respect but do not pursue adequately, and that need to be re-examined within an expanded discourse on ethics and human rights. Five transformational approaches and some changes to the metaphors by which we live are offered as potential entry points to shifting our paradigm of thinking and action towards one that fosters greater social justice, enhanced human capabilities and more widespread human flourishing.

A critique of some of the values that underpin our current paradigm

The dominant values that shape our understanding of global health in the global North can be caricatured as (hyper-)individualism, respect for human rights as defined by liberal thinking, belief in neoliberal economics, corporate managerialism, a narrow focus on scientific rather than social solutions to health problems and an oversimplified, linear approach to health issues.

I now briefly review these concepts critically. The first is *individualism*. The prominence given to individualism, and the respect for human rights defined as protection from government interference, have become dominant only since the Universal Declaration of Human Rights in 1948. Although the UDHR defines all rights as inalienable and interdependent, within many Western (modern) societies it is the case that self-determination, civil and political rights and economic freedom (a form of hyper-individualism) are generally valued more highly than positive socio-economic rights, including access to health care, despite great support for the latter (see, for example, Chapman 1994 and Teeple 2000). The failure to achieve socio-economic rights is also a function of the lack of effective governance at the national level in terms of compensating for some of the unequal distribution of wealth, income and life chances that is one of the key characteristics of the spread and growth of global capitalism (Bakker and Gill 2003; Benatar 1998; Pogge 2002). The negative effects of such systemic forces on the achievement of human rights, broadly conceived, should be more widely recognized (Benatar and Doyal 2009).

The second concept that needs to be interrogated is that of *economic growth through liberalization*. Although the forces of global capitalism and economic growth have the potential to relieve enormous human misery, they can also inflict more of that same misery when not properly regulated or channelled towards its relief (at global or national levels). The quest by wealthy countries for endless economic growth through the facilitation of international capital mobility and foreign investment flows constrains the ability of many states to adopt (and pay for) alleviating measures, and thus makes their achievement of socio-economic rights all the more difficult (Benatar 1998; Falk 1999; Labonte *et al.* 2004; Pogge 2002; Rowden 2009; Teeple 2000). Unconstrained market freedoms and greed (hyper-individualism) have also fostered pervasive corruption. The citizens of poor nations have been the victims of fraudulent development projects (Perkins 2004; Rist 1997), tax evasion (Brock 2009) and the sale of arms to corrupt leaders, enabling those leaders to accumulate vast wealth and the power to wage wars of ethnic conflict, with devastating social effects (Burrows 2003). Sadly, the arms trade seems to be associated with organized hypocrisy, as arms-trading countries promote their own economic self-interest above the interests of the inhabitants of other countries whose rights-abusing leaders purchase weapons to protect their own corrupt lives. The brain drain is supported by active measures on the part of wealthy countries to recruit professionals from poorer, developing countries, with neither thought for the consequences for those countries that paid for their training, nor any intention to pay reparations for their loss. This speaks volumes about the interests of the wealthy relative to their concern for the lives of poor fellow humans.

The third concept that needs to be subjected to critique is *corporate managerialism*, which has become an adverse force. This is to be found not only in the business sector but also within the context of complex social institutions, such as hospitals and universities, which are being transformed so that they resemble commercial corporations intent on pursuing their financial goals, with less interest in the non-economic aspects of the lives of those they should be serving. These institutional forces often overshadow the ideology of professionalism, weaken ideals and impede rather than facilitate the social and ethical behaviour that could improve local and global health. The general public and civil society are seen (at best) as customers, rather than as the collective owners of the health care system and co-producers of health.

A fourth problematic and restricted concept with respect to global health is the prevailing and dominant view of *scientific progress*. The general belief in new scientific solutions to health problems often results in large-scale investments in projects, often supported by tax incentives for businesses that promote private profit over public goods. Such belief also prioritizes particular types of science and innovation as *the* solutions to global health problems, even though much knowledge that is already available is not used, and there may also be more appropriate, or even complementary, social solutions. Although it would be foolish to deny the absolutely essential progress that has been made through cutting-edge, often biotechnology-based, research, science in itself is not sufficient to achieve improvements in global health; a social perspective is required. The shortcomings of using a narrow spectrum of approaches are illustrated by the well-funded Bill & Melinda Gates Foundation's Grand Challenge Initiatives on global health, which exemplify approaches that fail to take into consideration the social determinants of health and the research required to pursue constructive solutions (Birn 2005). The example of a poor country such as Cuba in achieving major improvements in population health through the application of the primary care approach is sobering (Huisch and Speigel 2008).

A fifth and related problem lies in the way we pursue solutions to health problems through *linear, compartmentalized thinking*. This approach seeks answers to specific problems without taking sufficient cognizance of the fact that these problems are embedded within complex systems in which numerous positive and negative feedbacks can occur in response to changes in one or another area, and with consequent effects that may differ significantly from outcomes envisaged within a linear approach. In this, the prevailing, view, global health is a technical, scientific problem rather than a broader – and more complex – social one. This narrower perspective constrains thinking into compartmentalized silos in ways that inhibit the type of innovative social and moral imagination that is required to inspire the major progress required to improve global health in the twenty-first century. This is the question to which I now turn.

Expanding the discourses on ethics and human rights

Until the 1960s discussions about ethics were confined largely to philo-sophical and theological studies. Advances in technology and medicine, together with an increased concern for individual rights and freedoms, then led to a new bioethics, in which theologians, philosophers, lawyers and other scholars engaged in a public discourse on applied ethics. Initially, this favoured treating biomedical issues at the level of individual health – such as death and dying, reproductive medicine and research ethics. However, since the birth of modern bioethics in the 1960s, the world has changed profoundly, and there is increasing understanding of how interconnected we all are (Singer 2002). Although the bioethics discourse has remained focused chiefly on interpersonal relationships and is rather parochial, especially in North America, new bioethics discourses are emerging in the fields of public health (Dawson and Verweij 2007; Nixon *et al.* 2008) that could enable us to deal rationally with threats to global health as systemic challenges. This invokes a wider view of the determinants of health and the local and global actors that have to engage these issues (WHO 2008). The new bioethics requires us to look beyond the proclamation of individual rights and values to examine the ways they are applied socially and interact in practice. It also challenges us to re-evaluate, redefine and rebalance these values.

Some years ago I, along with Abdallah Daar and Peter Singer, pro-posed that bioethics, an interdisciplinary field initially focused on the ethics of interpersonal relationships, could act as a bridge and a wedge towards improving health globally through expanded educational and public discourses promoting widely shared foundational values (Benatar, Daar and Singer 2003). Given the potential for the human rights approach to improve health care within nations (the work of the Treat-ment Action Campaign in South Africa in achieving widespread access to antiretroviral drugs is a good example), the case continues to be made for a more intense pursuit of a human rights approach to health (Wolff 2011).

Today, in the face of an evolving global financial crisis that strikingly reveals the shortcomings of long-standing and blindly accepted eco-nomic dogma (Gill 2008; Krugman 2009), I believe that there is an even greater need for action on these issues. Serious reflection on the ethical foundations of global health, and extension of the discourse on ethics and human rights towards a more comprehensive approach, could promote the new mindset needed to improve health and well-being globally. Such a mindset – or what is called elsewhere in this volume a new 'common sense' – requires a realization that health, human rights, economic opportunities, good governance, peace and development are all intimately linked within a complex and interdependent world. The challenges we face in the twenty-first century are to explore these links, to understand their implications, to develop political processes that can harness economic growth to human development, to narrow global disparities in health and to promote a geopolitics that favours peaceful coexistence (Benatar, Gill and Bakker 2009).

The values that our societies claim to uphold, but *do not pursue sufficiently actively*, include the following: (1) respect for all human life and human rights, in association with the correlative *responsibilities* that form part of the conceptual logic of human rights language; (2) consideration of *human needs* and *equity*; (3) *freedom from want*, in addition to *freedom to pursue* individual goals; (4) *democracy*, in a fuller and far more developed form than is currently practised; (5) concern for the environment and climate change; and, last but certainly not least, (6) *solidarity*. Although these values arguably serve together as the basis for global health ethics, none can stand alone. However, the most important of these values is *solidarity*. Solidarity can be defined as a set of attitudes coupled with action, involving a determination to work for the common good across the globe in an era when interdependence is greater than ever, and in which progress should be defined as enhancing capabilities and social justice. Without solidarity it is inevitable that we will ignore distant indignities, violations of human rights, inequities, deprivations of freedom, undemocratic regimes and respect for the environment. If a spirit of mutual caring could be developed on the part of those in wealthy and developing countries, constructive change can be seen as being possible. The pursuit of such values in ways that combine meaningful respect for the dignity of all people with a desire to promote the idea of human development beyond that conceived within the narrow, individualistic, 'economic' model of human flourishing could, it is hoped, serve to promote the peaceful and beneficial use of new knowledge and transformative power.

The way forward for global health ethics: five transformational approaches

A global agenda on conceptions of ethics and human rights that is essential for the achievement of rights must extend beyond rhetoric to include greater attention to duties, social justice and interdependence, locally and globally. The discourses and terrain of health, ethics and human rights provide a rich framework within which such an agenda could be developed and promoted across borders and cultures. When the relatively new interdisciplinary field of bioethics is expanded in

scope so as to embrace and amplify the above widely shared foundational values, a valuable contribution can be made to improving global
health by providing space for such discussions to occur. The vision
articulated by Daar, Singer and me, explicated in detail previously and
summarized here, offers a way forward. It involves five transformational
approaches that could lead to a fairer global economy characterized by
greater cooperation and social justice.

Developing a global state of mind

Developing a global state of mind about the world and our place in it is
perhaps the most crucial element in the development of a new ethic for
global health. Achieving this will require an understanding of the world
as an unstable complex system (Benatar 2005; Wallerstein 1999), the
balancing of individual goods and social goods, and the avoidance of
harm to weak or poor nations through economic and other forms of
extreme exploitation that frustrate the achievement of human rights and
well-being. Immanuel Wallerstein has presciently predicted that 'the first
half of the twenty-first century will...be far more difficult, more
unsettling, and yet more open [to change] than anything we have known
in the twentieth century' (Wallerstein 1999: 1). He argues that any
fundamental change towards a substantively rational system would
embrace both democratic and egalitarian principles as intimately and
inseparably linked to each other.

Michael MccGwire also outlines a rationale for new ways of thinking
in a world that has changed radically (MccGwire 2003). He explicates
the context in which the current 'adversarial national security program'
evolved over the past sixty years and has now 'lost its way' (MccGwire
2001). He argues convincingly that a paradigm shift is necessary towards
what he calls a 'cooperative global security program' – because times and
threats have changed – and that progress will be possible only if attitudes
about relationships, diplomacy, power and security can be reshaped. In
addition, the emergence of a multifaceted social movement –
'globalization from below' (in which people at the grass roots around
the world link up to impose their own needs and interests on the process
of globalization) – illustrates additional pathways to constructive change
(Brecher, Costello and Nowell-Smith 2000; see also Chapter 10, by
Teivo Teivainen, and Chapter 13, by Stephen Gill).

Promoting long-term collective self-interest

In arguing that it is both desirable and necessary to develop a global
mindset in health ethics, I suggest that this change need not be based
merely on altruism. Indeed, I further suggest that even the promotion of

long-term self-interest should be understood in a collective rather than an individualistic sense. This is also essential if we acknowledge that lives across the world are inextricably interlinked, particularly in the longer term, by forces that powerfully shape health and well-being.

Striking a balance between optimism and pessimism

Pessimistic and optimistic viewpoints about prospects for achieving widely shared progress through current globalization trends are both valid, from different perspectives. As pessimism can lead to inaction, and unjustified optimism to ineffectiveness, it is necessary to strike an appropriate balance between these two stances. This will require a platform for dialogue among stakeholders, and a space in which people can share different views about globalization. A broad conception of global bioethics and human rights offers a basis for such a space. Moreover, the problem is not one of pro- and anti-globalization sentiments, or of individual freedom versus community solidarity within different languages about politics. Globalization cannot be avoided. It is an integral aspect of a world in which the clock cannot be turned back on advances in technology, communication, production and transport. However, a distinction needs to be made between neoliberal globalization and an alternative potentiality: social-democratic globalization (Sandbrook 2000; see also Chapter 12, by Adam Harmes).

Developing capacity

The Daar, Singer and Benatar vision promoting an ethic for global health also features the development of capacity and a commitment to a broader discourse on ethics, propagated through centres that are regionally and globally networked in growing and supportive North–South partnerships. Others share this vision (Fidler 2009). A recognition of our responsibility to change the world for the better should also require multinational corporations and national governments to appreciate their new roles in enabling the correct choice of direction to build a better future.

Achieving widespread access to public goods

Broadening the access to public goods requires collective action, including financing (to make sure they are produced), and good governance, to ensure their optimum distribution and use (Kaul, Grunberg and Stern 1999). Global public goods involve more than one country or region of the world. The current international system very effectively stimulates the production and consumption of goods that principally benefit the affluent (e.g. the role of the WTO in promoting international trade) but not the production of public goods – such as a safe childhood and education for all children, basic subsistence needs, the realization of access to health care, labour rights and the protection of human rights. If global health ethics could also be combined with political support for more democratic, egalitarian and cosmopolitan approaches to citizenship and common goods, this would offer the space to pursue imaginative agendas for change towards a fairer, more regulated, economic system that could help catalyse crucial improvements in global health.

Shifting paradigms

Braudel's book *A History of Civilizations* (1995) illustrates how our ability to understand history is broadened by an approach that embraces knowledge of a wide range of geographic, social and political factors and their interaction. I suggest that understanding health and disease requires a similarly broad and integrated approach, and that this justifies an attempt to describe briefly here some emerging *streams of global change*. These illustrate the potential for changes in our basic paradigms of progress, and in how we think and speak about issues to influence health and health care at a global level. The paradigm shift required is away from a spectrum of values dominated by a highly individualistic, competitive, scientific market and consumerist approach to health and well-being towards a new orientation that, while retaining the best of these values, is more inclusive of solidarity, cooperation and modest entitlements that are more sustainable.

Before attempting to describe synoptically some streams of global change (as I see these emerging), using catchphrases, sound bites, slogans and metaphors, I would like to acknowledge the limitations of my ability to interpret and describe major trends in the evolution of ideas. What follows reflects (1) my perspective as a physician trained in the Western tradition who has lived mostly in sub-Saharan Africa and who has tried to understand the world intellectually and existentially from both Western and African perspectives; (2) my interpretation of a range of books and articles by distinguished thinkers whose ideas I attempt to encapsulate here with due humility; and (3) my perception that some of these *streams of change* are torrents, whereas others are mere trickles, flowing in various directions, with differing directions and force, in different countries. I appreciate that there are different perceptions of these forces and of how they can be resisted or promoted to facilitate progress.

From laissez-faire capitalism and authoritarian socialism to 'globalization'

Over the past 500 years economic paradigms have evolved from mercantilism through laissez-faire capitalism and socialism to welfare statism and, more recently, to globalization. During the second half of the twentieth century the evolution towards a global economy continued to enrich some people and some nations at the expense of others – to the point of intolerability. Welfarism has been rejected but the effects of its own policies are now threatening the rich core. Problems that threaten capitalism arise from its own dynamics (Heilbroner 1993; Teeple 2000). Neoliberal policies mark the transition between two eras: from a world of national capital and nation states to a world of international capital and supranational organizations. These embody a shift from the expansion of social reforms to the dismantling of reforms and the supersession of national economies. Neoliberal policies constitute the triumph of capital but also accelerate its adverse consequences – a seriously degraded nature, increasing impoverishment of the working class and growing political autocracy with a reduction of legitimacy (Heilbroner 1993; Rowden 2009; Teeple 2000).

In response, there are emerging new paradigms of thought and new forms of resistance. For example, economic forces favouring a continuing intensification of exploitation are being countered by endeavours to discredit and reverse debt perpetuation and to encourage socially and ecologically sound economic policies that are more favourable to sustainable development on a global basis. The new forms of resistance challenging the legitimacy of the highly individualistic form of liberalism and its associated economic order include multiculturalism, feminism, black consciousness, religious fundamentalism and cosmopolitanism (Brock 2009). In describing twenty-first-century capitalism, Robert Heilbroner (1993) suggests that there will be no easy solutions to such profound problems and no linear scheme of progress into the future. He believes that capitalism will continue, as there was no concept of progress before capitalism, only stoicism, resignation and visions of an afterlife as a consolatory fantasy. Because no other social order seems to be within our grasp, he predicts that a spectrum of capitalisms will prevail, with modifications that, he hopes, will include a framework embracing greater human solidarity and social justice. An alternative suggested by Gary Teeple is that a new tyranny may arise, an economic totalitarianism that, in Hayekian terms, will replace political totalitarianism as a new 'road to serfdom' (Teeple 2000).

From rights to 'rights and responsibilities'

The thrust of capitalism as an economic system emphasizing free markets driven by capital accumulation as a political order within the Western political philosophy of liberal individualism constitutes perhaps the most powerful global force. Nonetheless, counterbalancing socialist perspectives have contributed to the formation of welfare states within social democracies and helped to ensure equitable access to health care and welfare in most European and British Commonwealth countries. The New Deal in the United States has been a less effective social equalizer; perhaps because of the limitations of its commitment to human rights as civil and political rights within the highly individualistic US form of liberalism, which has pitted citizens against each other in competition for access to health care and social welfare. However, the erosion of civic society is becoming a cause for concern. The rise to dominance of patient autonomy over physician beneficence reflects the influence of liberal individualism on the physician–patient relationship, but this is clearly not a solution to the problem of improving health at national or global levels. The need for equity in access to health care and for social justice within and between nations is increasingly being recognized (Brock 2009). The rights of individuals are gradually being balanced by a growing focus on responsibilities – of individuals to themselves and to society at large, as well as of societies to their citizens and of powerful nations to the citizens of other countries. Indeed, the failure of the rhetoric of rights language to achieve even basic rights for so many people in the world is leading to a re-emphasis on responsibilities in the quest for greater equity (WHO 2008).

From the anomic self to the 'embedded self'

Since the collapse of communism, the communitarian challenges to narrow interpretations of liberal individualism are becoming a more acceptable force for change, even if only within a broader conception of liberalism (Mulhall and Swift 1992). A central aspect of this debate relates to the conception of the self: the meaning of being an independent, self-determining individual. For strong individualists, the conception of the self emphasizes individual rights, personal liberty and society structured on the basis of the free association of individuals. A contesting view is that of individuals arising from and being shaped by their societies, with their freedom from want and from preventable disease as well as their freedom to choose understood as being embedded in social attachments. Moreover, in such a society rights would be balanced by responsibilities to themselves, to others and to society – including future generations – within a framework of trans-generational solidarity.

From 'might is right' to 'right is might'

The message from the transformation of South Africa from a pariah nation in which apartheid was upheld by military strength ('might is right') towards a democracy based on ethical foundations is that moral visions ('right is might', as illustrated by Nelson Mandela's life) can be effective long-term forces and that we become more powerful as we share rather than compete with each other (Benatar 1997b). Progress towards more egalitarian relationships between men and women is another example of the way in which power-sharing offers greater opportunities for satisfaction and success than oppression and exploitation.

From realism to 'pluralism and solidarity'

The age-old tendency to base relationships between states on 'realism' (power and force) is now being superseded by the need for 'pluralism' (international law), and for a greater degree of 'solidarity' (justice) between all people in a complexly interdependent world. Classical realism (e.g. associated with Thomas Hobbes and Niccolò Machiavelli) was based on the survival of particular states and led to sweeping justification for imperialism. Modern realism (as articulated by E. H. Carr, Reinhold Niebuhr and Hans Morgenthau) claims that it remains prudent to be concerned about national interest rather than universal interest. However, the world is moving away from the Westphalian system towards a form of complex interdependence between nations, as there is wider recognition that there are some liberal values that are good for international society as a whole (e.g. democracy, human rights, welfare and transnational institutions). States thus become willing to obey international law because they believe it is in their interests to conform. Realism and complex interdependence are simple models at the ends of a spectrum, and the real world is somewhere between the two. The evolution of a hybrid world order reflects the tension between the ends of the spectrum. Justice remains elusive, since justice and order are often at odds with each other; but, as an unjust world is also an unstable one, there is an emerging awareness of the need to empathize with sections of humanity that are geographically or culturally distant from us, although this is not yet sufficiently reflected in foreign policies.

From the acceptability of weapons of mass destruction to their 'illegality'

Slavery was regarded as acceptable in many societies for many generations, and it took half a century for the anti-slavery campaign to establish widespread acknowledgement of slavery as immoral and illegal. Likewise, the peace movements in the world today are working towards deeper understandings of those aspects of modern life that are immoral and should become illegal – such as the trade in weapons and in debt (Sidel 1995).

New perspectives on global health care

With such streams of change in mind, health, disease, illness, suffering and health care systems are best understood from a broad perspective that illuminates their social construction in differing ways of life. Like history, health is a house of many mansions. The many powerful social forces that influence human well-being and approaches to health care have intersected and balanced in a variety of ways in different places and at different times. This is evident at the macro level in the wide range of health care systems around the world, even in adjacent countries exposed to similar trajectories of progress within similar value systems. Although economic globalization is intensifying the profit motive in medicine and disempowering patients and doctors through managed care systems, it is also simultaneously promoting a deeper understanding of the need for social justice in the design and delivery of health care (Buchanan 1995). The power of preventive measures, such as improved living conditions, enhanced female literacy and access to primary health care, to improve individual and population health, as achieved in poor regions such as Kerala in India (Birn, Pillay and Holtz 2009) and Cuba (Huisch and Spiegel 2008), has been acknowledged in the detailed WHO report on the social determinants of health (WHO 2008). The amplification of such achievements is now required more widely across the globe.

Recent interest in global health and global health ethics is therefore gratifying (Benatar and Brock 2011), but what can be achieved will be dependent on what strategies or combinations of these are adopted. David Stuckler and Martin McKee (2008) have suggested that there are at least five metaphors that could be applied to global health. Global health *as foreign policy* is driven by political motives with a view to pursuing particular strategic interests and economic growth; *as security*, it is a strategy that seeks to protect local populations against infectious diseases and bioterrorism; *as charity*, global health strategy focuses on 'victims' and addresses issues of poverty and disempowerment; *as investment*, it is focused on those whose improved health could maximize economic growth. By contrast, global health *as public health* is aimed at decreasing the global burden of disease and focuses on those diseases that constitute the largest proportion of this burden. The authors acknowledge that, although there is much overlap in how these are applied, the strategies and policies that will be pursued (by the United States and other powerful nations and groups) depend crucially on which metaphor is dominant.

A new conception of development

Against a backdrop of a narrow focus on growth, markets and security, of persistent health disparities between rich and poor both *between* and *within* countries, and of evidence of flaws in narrow economic conceptions of development, new ideas and models for development are emerging that transcend the North–South dichotomy and go beyond a conception of development as a uniquely economic process. This entails a shift towards a recognition that all countries are to some degree underdeveloped and that what is needed is to *develop sustainability*, rather than sustain current trajectories of development (Bensimon and Benatar 2006). This new paradigm of development jettisons four flawed assumptions lying behind previous approaches: (i) that 'developing' countries' problems are entirely internal; (ii) that 'developed' countries are examples to be globally emulated; (iii) that the role of the rich in promoting development is defined by altruism; and (iv) that the poor lack the potential to improve their own lives significantly. A new paradigm of the *development of sustainability* involves an explicit inclusion of the ethical challenge to develop a system of global economic governance that could narrow disparities in global health. It would be hard to deny that the vast numbers of global poor and their lower life expectancy represent a clear and significant injustice, particularly when this arises from an excessive consumption of global resources, such as climate-damaging fuels or the exploitation associated with unfair trade practices. One way to address these inequities is through greater attention to global distributive justice (Brock 2009; Pogge 2002; Powers and Faden 2006; Royal Danish Ministry for Foreign Affairs 2000). Measures for compensation based on the principles of sustainability and 'Do no harm' would go some way towards countering the developed countries' failed commitment to overseas financial assistance, which (aside from Sweden, Norway, Denmark, the Netherlands and Luxembourg) has never reached even one-half of the target figure of an amount equivalent to 0.7% of national gross domestic product (GDP).

From endless economic growth to 'growth that facilitates equity'

Lying at the heart of all these adverse developmental and global health trends and the potential for their reversal is an understanding of how the global economy is structured, and could be modified. Developing sustainable well-being for many more people globally requires going beyond economic growth to include new ways of achieving economic redistribution. We need to avoid the global trap in which wealthy people progressively care less for the lives of those whom they relegate to living under inhumane conditions while their own lives become more mean-ingless and inhuman to the underprivileged masses. Although economic equality is an impossible goal, a narrowing of the current gap is surely well within our grasp. Fairer trade rules, debt relief, various equitable forms of taxation, such as the Tobin tax on currency trades across borders (which could generate $100 to 300 billion per year), the preven-tion of tax evasion, and environmental taxes are all potential means of facilitating the development of the solidarity required for peaceful coex-istence in a complex world (Gill and Bakker 2011).

Conclusion

In sum, common forces are reshaping health care in all countries. All countries are facing fiscal constraints in health care. Some are con-strained because they are spending too much trying to apply all that can be done for all who need or want whatever is technically available. Others face restrictions because their economies are being eroded under the onslaught of powerful global forces, including Structural Adjustment Programs linked to trade in debt, which is being described as analogous to the slave trade.[2] Another common force is the rising influence of the managerial sciences in health care, with health care bureaucrats often earning more than most highly skilled scientists or medical practitioners. Money, as the bottom line in medicine nowadays, is displacing the ethos of care that was embedded in medical practice over many centuries (Kassirer 1995).

At the same time, science and technology have radically changed the face of death. Life support systems, organ transplantation and chemo-therapy have challenged the idea of life as finite, and of death as inevit-able. The preservation of life in grotesque states of non-cognitive existence has become the norm in some countries, whose citizens appear to be more concerned with preserving life under these conditions for themselves than with the lack of access to health care for millions of their own fellow citizens, to say nothing about the millions of people dying prematurely in other countries through lack of access to even the most basic care. Physician-assisted suicide, active euthanasia, a swing towards primary health care, complementary medicine and traditional healing are among the wide range of different responses to such 'progress'. The limits of medicine are being recognized, and new relationships are being

---

[2] For example: 'World Debt Day was marked by events in countries across the world, from Australia to Zambia – all demanding an end to debt slavery' (*Jubilee Debt Campaign News Archive*, 17 May 2005; www.jubileedebtcampaign.org.uk/World%20Debt%20Day%20marked%20around%20the%20world+667.twl; accessed 11 May 2011).

forged between doctors, patients and society, as we ask what it means to be ill and to seek help from our community and those we empower to provide help.

The range of ways in which social forces have played out, and will continue to do so, is evident in many continents. In North America, the Canadian government's health insurance system is profoundly different from the predominantly private system in the United States. In Europe, the United Kingdom's National Health Service differs from French and German social insurance models and from the Swiss private system. The chaos in health and health care provision in many poor countries reflects the profound impact of colonial, neocolonial and ongoing exploiting forces, recovery from which, if possible, will be painful and prolonged. Recent disputes over reform to health care provision in the United States (the most expensive system in the world, but with the least impressive results on health) illustrate the problem of making paradigm shifts even in the face of potent arguments and visible failings.

However, the impact of global streams of change described above will take time to become widely manifest, because inertia is sustained by the failure to achieve a widespread recognition of the requirement for such change if peaceful progress is to be fostered. Even those who recognize the validity of changing paradigms work knowingly – or sometimes unknowingly - to protect the status quo for their own benefit. Finally, when work does begin on corrective processes, the legacy of the twentieth century (Hobsbawm 1994), like the legacy of apartheid, will take much hard work and time to overcome.

8   Global leadership and the Islamic world: crisis, contention and challenge

Mustapha Kamal Pasha

Summary

Hegemonic, Orientalist frames of capture and understanding present Islamic models of restructuring social and cultural life as pathologies of alterity or as failures on the part of those living in what I call *Islamic cultural zones* (ICZs) to fully absorb modernity and its cognitive attributes.[1] Such 'zones' include large regions that may span more than one nation, as well as areas within particular nations. The term refers to those parts of the world, particularly in urban centres, in which Islamic culture is most prevalent, such as across much of the Middle East and north Africa. In Orientalist discourse, this tends to render specific forms of political contestation that emanate from such Islamic cultural areas over ethics and questions of justice and dignity as mere representations of a 'clash of civilizations' on a world scale. Silenced in received hegemonic narratives is the deeply political nature of struggles over justice within such zones – to redesign political economy, reshape political community and place ethical constraints on market fundamentalism. In essence, these struggles exemplify efforts to re-imagine legitimate governance, responsibility and leadership. To be sure, global leadership provides the wider context of these struggles. This chapter interprets some contemporary political struggles in such zones against the backdrop of Islamic conceptions of justice as a commentary on the global political economy, focusing particularly on the ethico-political assumptions of 'disciplinary neoliberalism'. The principal aim here is twofold: (1) to reinterpret Islamic ethics – encoded in cultural or religious idiom – as *both* a critique of, and an alternative to, the hegemonic settlement under globalizing conditions; and (2) to draw out the implications of the Islamic critique and alternative for re-imagining global leadership.

---

[1] See Glossary for 'alterity'.

144

Introduction

Critiques of 'disciplinary neoliberalism' (Gill 1995a) have assumed heterodox forms. In some cases, they are encoded in the language of environmentalism, indigeneity, authenticity or religious resurgence. In others, they depend on the political language of resistance to globalization. However, in all instances, critiques meld moral and political disquiet. This disquiet is impregnated *in* and *through* political struggles. Critique exemplifies these struggles. The moral tenor residing in critique tends to disguise the contested nature of social existence and its growing incorporation into globalization. In this vein, *local* instantiations of critique are rarely localized; they have the potential to reveal the contours of an increasingly globalized social reality and its discontents (Mittelman 2000).

This chapter explores an Islamic critique of the present global political constellation as a moral discourse with the potential to offer lineaments of future political alternatives to the world order. Specifically, it reinterprets some latent aspects of political Islam, or Islamism – the self-conscious project of *Islamicizing* politics in the areas of Islamic culture – principally as a challenge to the established social and political order in both its local and global manifestations. Departing from the conventional script, in which the proposed vision of Islamicists is captured either as a general negation of modernity (in its manifold permutations), as a 'return' to the past (Lewis 2003) or as mere resistance to globalization (Barber 1996), this intervention is motivated by the intuition that the language deployed by Islamicists masks key elements of the intrinsically moral and political nature of their critique of the status quo – a critique germinated by the emergence of the 'global modern'. Political Islam here is taken as an internally contested phenomenon, one with many tendencies and contradictions. The received emphasis on violence, or calls for the establishment of an 'Islamic state' or umma (Islamic community) by Islamicists, divert attention away from the general disquiet afflicting Islamic social reality – a condition that finds the vast majority of Muslims in situations of dire economic, political and cultural stress, massive social inequality, and subordination to structures of wealth and power, and with a generalized sense of betrayal by all brands of Muslim political and secular intellectual élites. This sense is heightened within the context of the 'global modern' – the 'spatial extension of modernity' and 'the production of an immanent cognitive and social field that has no outside' (Pasha 2010: 177, note 3).

The 'global modern' limits the horizon of political projects, but it also provides resources for realizing heterodox visions. The field it produces offers 'a condition of possibility for both politicization and de-politicization'; more significantly, 'this field shapes both projects of mimicry and escape'. Mimicry takes 'the form of development and modernization'. By contrast, 'projects of escape struggle to articulate cosmopolitan dreams or dystopias' (ibid.: 177). Two key features of the 'global modern' are particularly important here to help appreciate the hidden transcripts of the political vision proposed by Islamicists: an acute awareness of *global* Muslim connectivity across boundaries; and the conviction that human action is necessary to alter the destiny of the Islamic community (Roy 2004). The latter – itself a modern sensibility – rejects an attitude of acquiescence to an assumed unjust social order. Within the frame of the 'global modern', therefore, Islamicists, who themselves are products of its uneven enactment in terms of power hierarchies, have reinterpreted alternative Islamic notions of justice, equality, human dignity and fairness. These alternatives do not derive merely from Islamic exegesis, but from an active, if fairly elastic, interpretation of the religious texts within the context of Western hegemony and its specific articulation in the Islamic cultural zones. The content of these alternatives betrays the imprint of a very heterodox mix of influences, including Islamic eschatology, the West's own internal dissent, captured in critiques of technology, capitalism, secularity and possessive individualism, and Southern discourses in other non-Islamic areas of the ex-colonial world. This heterodox mix gives the discourses of political Islam a modern and global texture; it also obfuscates the ethical substance of the Islamic message. These discourses would not come to be, and especially not in their present form, without the global connectivity produced by flows of capital, people and cultural products and images.

Paradoxically, though, the ethical and moral vision embedded in discourses of political Islam inverts the original message of Islam as a *moral* community in favour of an ideal of a *political* community, enshrined in the idea of an Islamic state. This radical departure shifts the philosophical terrain of Islam away from transcendence towards an immanentist vision. A principal facet of this departure reworks an essentially secular notion of sovereignty into Islam, with the Islamic state, *not* community, emerging as the focal point of initiating projects of change and transformation. The embrace of political power to necessitate social action redefines obligation not as an act of individual responsibility but as a transaction administered by a watchful and heavily intrusive state. With the ascendancy of political power to unprecedented heights of salience within the new cosmological design, political Islam allows Islam's latent ethical impulses to be compromised. Instrumentality replaces ethics. The goal of building an Islamic community is used to rationalize all the means necessary to attain it.

The recent sustained infusion of *piety* into the regions of Islamic culture, in matters as diverse as the nature of dress, public speech, everyday ethics pertaining to visible expressions of devoutness such as mosque attendance, permissive and prohibited exchanges between members of the opposite sex, attitudes towards work and leisure, and relations within the family under the aegis of political Islam, translates into a growing *politicization of civil society*. Making these matters questions of existential import rather than simply personal preferences significantly alters the social ethos of Islamic society. The boundaries of political Islam have now become more extended, especially against the backdrop of a general retrenchment of the post-colonial secular state. Nevertheless, civil society provides political Islam with its most potent vehicle to wage a 'war of position' against 'decadent' social forces, including the state. Cultural divisions within Islamic civil societies provide fortuitous conditions to introduce alternative (Islamic) terms of discourse into social and political communication. These terms of discourse distort the ethical content of an alternative Islamic vision in highly ambivalent and contradictory ways. However, the difficult task is to recover the distinctive features of an Islamic alternative that is increasingly subordinated to the aims of political Islam and its representation in public consciousness.

This chapter is therefore developed in three stages. In the first, the prevailing difficulty of recognizing ethical currents within Islamicist discourses *as legitimate formulations of alternative conceptions of world order* is located more broadly within the cognitive field produced by Orientalism and its variants. This difficulty is also widespread in dominant versions of international relations scholarship, particularly its assumptions regarding sovereignty, identity and political obligation. The second section probes the fiction of a monolithic Islamicist heuristic. Closer scrutiny reveals that considerable heterodoxy marks political and intellectual commitments in various Islamic political discourses. Despite the apparent overlap and synergy, the different discourses allow access to the complexity of political practice *within* Islamism. Although these political discourses – without exception – seek to diagnose the illness afflicting Islamic state and society in local contexts, they propose divergent remedies. To reiterate, no singular *Islamic* critique is readily accessible. There is considerable divergence between and among the discourses under discussion (Moaddel and Talattof 2000).

Nevertheless, there are common threads binding these discourses, including adherence to a single text, remonstrations for justice drawn from Islamic history, the affinity of a common and shared faith, the experience of both triumph and decline in terms of their civilizations and, above all, an Islamic intersubjectivity transcending spatial and cultural barriers. Furthermore, in the context of West-centred globalization, the psychic, emotional and political aspects of perceived Muslim subordination to the West supply abundant resources for producing both the appearance and reality of a transnational Islamic consciousness. However, the important thing to stress is the presence of major fractures and fissures within Islamic society, drawn from a variety of factors including class, gender, ethnicity, sectarian affiliation, region, language and access to cultural capital linked to West-centred globalization. The final part of the chapter draws out some general inferences from the previous discussion concerning the present global crisis and the crisis of global leadership. Needless to say, the examination here of a very complex theme is highly compressed and mostly indicative. Only a detailed and thorough investigation can yield a more nuanced picture.

Perilous orthodoxy

Despite repeated assaults on Orientalist structures of knowledge production and representation (Mitchell 1988; Said 1978), analyses of Islam remain firmly ensconced in binary classifications. The most salient is the tradition–modern divide, used both to distinguish Islam from the West and to capture internal tensions within Islam. In the first instance, the parsimony of this classification guarantees Islam's location outside the modern. 'Hard' Orientalism confers fixity to familiar attributes of tradition, including unchanging cognitive and behavioural features of Islamic society. These pertain to various facets of social and political life, but allow little variation across space and time. The basic aim, it appears, is to grant Islam an alterity unbridgeable from either the West or modernity: *Islam is placed outside time.* 'Soft' Orientalism, pronounced in theories of modernization and development, leaves open the possibility of change and transformation. However, religion and culture continue to reproduce 'obstacles', which can be removed only through secularization, political and societal modernization and, above all, individuation. Such obstacles are assumed to be inherent to the ICZs (Pasha 2009).

The harder and softer versions of Orientalism share common sentiment not only about political Islam but about Islam in general, as a retrograde phenomenon, hostile to modernity. Their major difference lies in their respective characterizations as to whether Islam is or is not a totalizing faith. In the former instance, *all* variants of Islam are *totalizing*, since this monotheistic faith brooks no separation between mosque and state. Right from the time of its origins, the argument suggests, Islam has collapsed social spheres. In the West, these have been highly differentiated since the advent of the Reformation. Having experienced no similar shift in its religious temper, hard Orientalists (Crone 1980; Lewis 2003; Pipes 1983) essentialize Islam, notwithstanding their unrelenting scrutiny of its past. This sentiment is not shared by soft Orientalists (Binder 1988; Tibi 1998; Voll 1982), who display an awareness of differentiated spheres. However, soft Orientalists also succumb to a binary logic in which only two principal possibilities materialize: traditional and modern Islam. Soft Orientalists are also resistant to the notion of temporal coevality between Islam and the West. The 'modern' in Islam is still lagging behind, aspiring to catch up with the West. A significant implication of this characterization is the refusal to recognize the 'global modern' as *the* condition of possibility for Islamic political movements of all kinds. This refusal also extends to the historical fact of the mutual constitution of Islam and the West. Either the idea of Western exceptionalism or that of Islamic exceptionalism (Pasha 2009) ensures that two worlds exist independently of one another. The recognition of mutual constitution, by contrast, can help dispel both essentialism and the prevailing 'common sense' of timeless Western superiority. It can also afford an awareness of the historicity of social orders, whether past or present.

A corollary of Orientalist sentiment relative to Islam is the easy circulation of the nexus between Islam and violence (Venkatraman 2007). This sentiment is pervasive in the global cultural economy – the worldwide circulation of signs and symbols. Often, the self-characterization and acts of certain Islamic groups endorse the nexus between Islam and violence, either in the excesses of anti-Western rhetoric or in indiscriminate terrorism directed against innocent civilians, and now increasingly against fellow Muslims *within* the Islamic cultural zones. More recently, the self-destructive cycle of violence unleashed by the attacks on civilians on 11 September 2001, the 'war on terror' and the invasions of Afghanistan and Iraq have colonized the international public sphere. The intellectual and political aims of different variants of Islam are easily subordinated to a blurred cartography produced by these events, making it virtually impossible to separate resistance to occupation from 'terror'. The heterodox interpretations of the concept of jihad (Bassiouni 2008) are reduced to a single register: that of holy war. Complexity is compromised as the self-evident nature of the nexus between religion and violence serves as a general template to evaluate and assess all forms of Muslim political and social action. However, within the grossly asymmetrical discursive economy of representation, some clues can be found to this query. To the point, the aim of deciphering alternative conceptions of justice or meaningful societal existence is now easily eclipsed by received representations equating *all* of Islam with terror. Receding into the background are deep ethical codes associated with the 'venture' of Islam (Hodgson 1974), specifically positive principles of equality and justice, individual responsibility and obligation, honour, dignity and respect, tolerance and hospitality, balance or harmony in social and political temperament, and decency and humility. On the other hand, negative principles also provide constraints on avarice, self-centredness, political ambition, social exploitation and any discrimination based on ascriptive ties. In this regard, the design of leadership proposed in both scriptural and lay Islamic literature merits attention. The second section of the chapter addresses some key elements of this question.

Similar problems of apprehending Islam ensue in the dominant narratives of international relations. A specific difficulty attending understandings of Islamic discourses on the *international* front, including Islamic meditations on the shape of global leadership, is the existence, as with Orientalism, of established, albeit implicit, frames of capture in international relations. These understandings typically derive from particular conceptions of politics (Beyer 1994), of the separation of religion and politics or of the convergence between faith and political action in Islam. These conceptions reproduce assumptions of a Westphalian settlement instantiated in narratives of sovereignty, citizenship, right and obligation, the centrepiece of which is the evacuation of religion from inter-state relations (Hurd 2007) or the severance of religious rationalities from the logic of (secular) power. Sovereignty, on this view, adopts the life process of immanence, subordinating claims of transcendence in an increasingly disenchanted universe of human agency and its fragilities. Modern citizenship refuses shared commitments to God and state in favour of the latter. Infused with political agency, but also what Adam Smith (1998 [1776]) refers to as that 'certain propensity in human nature' – the 'propensity to truck, barter and exchange' – the modern subject seeks fulfilment on earthly ground. Political obligation takes on the character of singularity, jealously guarding loyalty to sovereign authority against competition from other sources. Alternative notions of ordering social life or locating human purpose within different hierarchical schemes appear unnatural, pre-modern, atavistic or archaic. Above all, the modularity of the Westphalian settlement serves as a template to perceive relations between political communities across space. Viewed as 'anarchy' (Waltz 1979) or 'anarchical society' (Bull 1977), the terrain of the international takes embrace of the logic of sovereignty or the 'standard of civilization' (Gong 1984) as the only viable models for international relations. In order to function as legitimate members of the world community, non-Western states have to conform to these models. Lost in this hegemonic narrative is the deeply religious character of the Westphalian settlement, including the more profound presence of religiosity in seemingly secular social domains in the West. On this alternative reading, the supposed clash between a 'secular' West and Islam requires re-examination.

Most non-Western states do actually participate in a (post-)Westphalian international community. However, their culturally coded concerns, in engagement with the hegemonic structures of the world system, rarely receive the acknowledgement they deserve; *their* understandings and subjectivities, which inform international relations, remain marginal. Clearly, this is not the case with the political élites in the ICZs. Westphalia – either as utopia or reality – presents no problems for them. The real problem is elsewhere: with the multitude, or those without power or representation. Compromised by their own élites, the multitude seek counter-avenues of political articulation. Their alternative mappings of ethics, justice, equality, dignity and fairness remain residual to the hegemonic scheme, in which their 'national' élites willingly participate in order to secure power, wealth, privilege and longevity. Typically, the concerns of the Muslim multitude appear in the guise of grievance or critique of the existing world order. However, embedded in Islamic discourses are not merely a critique of the world but the lineaments of alternative worlds. The religious idiom of these discourses tends to mask the intensity of critique, as it becomes susceptible to dismissal within an economy of secular language.

Alternatives, cast in the language of globalization or cosmopolitanism, provide fruitful avenues for escaping the strictures of Westphalia, but offer no determinate pathways to comprehend the 'return of religion' in world politics. Cosmopolitan impulses take religious sentiment as a latest form of particularism – one that would eventually succumb to the power of universalism embedded in cosmopolitan dream-worlds (Bhagwati 2004). Globalization theorists, on the other hand, recognize the return of religion principally as a form of resistance to the homogenizing force of West-centred globalization. In the case of Islam, as noted, this problem is compounded in virtually all extant narratives by the durable presence of Orientalist structures of understanding (Said 1978), built upon the historical fault lines of relations between Christendom and Islam (Daniel 1960), or Western imperial encroachment into the Muslim heartland, notably in the nineteenth and twentieth centuries (Sayeed 1994). Indirectly, these historically textured understandings impinge upon not taking alternative conceptions of sovereignty, statecraft or governance as legitimate; they invariably appear as relativistic counterpoints to a universal meta-narrative. Specifically, the notions of overlapping sovereignties or concentric circles of obligation cannot seek materialization as viable alternatives.

The notion of overlapping sovereignties in several Islamic juridical texts recognizes not just the claims of God but those of Caesar as well, based on determinate principles. Although God's sovereignty is recognized as absolute, Islamic jurists have long made a distinction between the non-negotiable domain of faith and worldly affairs, including political matters. The idea of limited government in Islam remains an ideal, wholly violated by secular dispensations of national autocrats in all the ICZs. Similarly, the notion of concentric circles of obligations, drawn from Islamic thought, lays out different sets of principles to regulate alternative spheres of human activity: the family, the community, the state and the world community. In each sphere, different rights and obligations operate. This image challenges the misleading view that there is no appreciation for differentiated spheres in Islam.

Islamic discourses and the crisis of leadership

Islamic commentaries of all shades share the impression that the Islamic world is plagued by a perennial, multidimensional crisis of leadership. This crisis is visible on multiple registers, including the pervasiveness of authoritarian rule in the regions of Islamic culture, the absence of political legitimacy, diminished and declining state capacity and, most significantly, political corruption, reflected in the use of state apparatuses to advance private material interests. The state, on this view, does not represent the public interest; it serves only to help consolidate and promote vested interests without recourse to legal, judicial or political accountability. From the standpoint of Islamic political discourses, the fault lies in the nature of secular political authority divorced from Islamic norms and principles. The origins of this state of affairs lie in the collapse of the caliphate under colonial and imperial domination, the substitution of comprador secular élites for Islamic authority and the effacement of piety from governance. Produced over an extended historical period, especially during the fateful centuries of European colonization of Islamic lands, the crisis of leadership is intertwined with the character of the world order. Without the active sponsorship of hegemonic Western powers, Islamicists maintain, the Islamic predicament would be inconceivable.

However, disagreement exists whether the primary source of the crisis of leadership is internal to the Islamic political ethos, even to Islam itself (as hard Orientalists such as Daniel Pipes would suggest), or a derivative of the subordinate position of Islamic states within the world order (a view increasingly promoted by Islamicists). In either case, Muslim leadership is seen as the Achilles heel of Islamic civilization. Within this broader frame, complex questions arise linked to the evolution of political authority in the Islamic cultural zones: the persistent problem of political succession in Islamic history; the absence of a unified religious authority in Islam (unlike Catholicism), with the ever-present danger of dissension and instability; the excessive reliance of political rule on the military (Crone 1980), standing above society; and the endless cycle of 'barbarian' invasions threatening settled Islamic social life.

Political analysis and moral critique go hand in hand, often indistinguishable in popular Islamic consciousness (Davis and Robinson 2006). Moral critique provides sustenance and support for politics encoded in religious idiom. Politics presents the potential to realize moral values. A distinctive quality of political Islam is its readiness to collapse political and moral critique. Without recognizing this quality, the appeal of political Islam is unrecognizable. At the same time, Islamicists represent, perhaps, the *only* viable opposition to extant political regimes in most Muslim-majority countries. Bernard Lewis (1991: 7; emphasis added) sums up this historically produced sentiment:

For many, probably most, Muslims, Islam is still the most acceptable, *indeed in times of crisis the only acceptable*, basis for authority. Political domination can be maintained for a while by mere force, but not indefinitely, not over large areas or for long periods. For this there has to be some legitimacy in government, and for this purpose, for Muslims, is most effectively accomplished when the ruling authority derives its legitimacy from Islam rather than from merely nationalist, patriotic, or even dynastic claims – still less from such Western notions as national or popular sovereignty.

As noted, Islamic discourses provide both critique and alternatives to the existing social and political order. These discourses also offer meditations on the global order as a necessary complement of an engagement with the wider political field. Both are sustained by reference to the other. The distinguishing mark of political Islam is the seamless unity of critiques of internal political and social orders *and* critiques of the global order (one that buttresses the internal order). In this sense, current Islamic discourses conjoin (domestic) politics and international politics.

A wide variety of discourses paint the intellectual and political landscapes of the ICZs with diverse genealogies, commitments and aims. The historical contexts of the origins, constitution and maturation of each discourse are complex and multifaceted. Any attempt to render them into neat taxonomies, therefore, runs the risk of negating context and the salience of temporality. There is the other, all-important, aspect of an overlapping Islamic discursive field drawn from history, culture and belief. However, the effort to identify the principal currents presents the value of locating the *distinct* character of each discourse. Against that recognition and caveat, five separate discourses become identifiable, each centred on a key theme: redemption, rejection, reformation, revolution and reconciliation.

The discourse of *redemption* is embedded in the recognition of *internal* moral failing. Islamic decline after a millennium of civilizational glory is traceable in this instance to the inability of Muslim élites and subjects to adhere to the pure message of Islam. One part of this narrative finds fault with dissension, corruption and a generalized incapacity to reconcile Islam's moral message with conduct. In this discourse, the advance of Western modernity in the institutional straightjacket of colonial dispensation appears as a second-order cause of Islam's retrenchment. The theme of redemption feeds all discourses, moral and political. In essence, it seeks the rebuilding of the old Islamic city (a generic urban form prior to the 9th century that reflected and reinforced Islamic religious and social principles), or else erecting a new city over the ruins of the unsavoury political order found today in the ICZs. There is an obvious ambivalence in the politics of redemption, towards the West and modernity alike. To the degree that the diagnosis of decline lies *within*, the West serves the dual role of an unwelcome intruder, but it is also largely irrelevant to restoration from within. The relation between Islam and modernity in this discourse is more complex: the latter is instantiated in the ICZs only in its malevolent forms, but becomes unavoidable – a condition of possibility for Islamic alternatives. As with several other discourses, redemptive politics can also assume militant tendencies (Deep 1992).

Rejectionist currents in the ICZs take Islam to be self-subsistent, as a total system. These currents are premised on the assumption that all practical answers for ordering society, polities and human conduct are already well defined in the Islamic canon, notably in the Qur'an. No accommodation with things non-Islamic is necessary in order to build an Islamic community. As with the discourse of redemption, the rejectionist tendency can appear in both non-violent and violent forms. In the former instance, it assumes the form of Islamic *piety*: the regulation of human conduct, with an emphasis on the interior aspects of individual behaviour but also on social conduct. Pietism often presents itself as an apolitical social movement, divorced from the pressures of political agendas or juridical matters (*fiqh*). A notable example of such tendency is the Tablighi Jamaat (Society for Spreading Faith), a major global religious movement. However, rejectionist currents can also take dystopian forms, which are prominent in the directionless tendency towards violence, terror and nihilism (Pasha 2010). It is this tendency that appears to present the external face of Islamic politics in the global imaginary.

The theme of *reformation* departs radically from its Christian predecessor. Aspects of the latter are intrinsic to the modernity now engulfing the world, including Islam. Relations between piety and the work ethic or religious rationalization for the acquisition of wealth are found in all transcendental faiths, including Islam. However, to the degree that salvation escapes Islamic cosmology, playing virtually no role in structuring human conduct in the Islamic *Weltanschauung*, there are no fundamental contradictions in Islam between the pursuit of earthly happiness and rewards in the hereafter. Islam neither commands asceticism nor makes eternal life contingent upon earthly existence. It requires that, in *all* spheres of human activity, Muslims conduct their affairs in ways that live up to the ethical standards prescribed in the Qur'an, or the practice of the Prophet (Sunna) or the Islamic ethos of goodness and decency. The source of Islamic reformation currents lies in attempts to reconcile the Qur'an and the Sunna with the changing social reality facing Muslim society (Hashmi 2002). In the context of modernity, therefore, reformist movements have offered highly innovative schemata for interpreting the sacred texts in view of the radically altered conditions. These elaborate efforts are based on the assumption that continuity and change both constitute an essential part of projects to preserve and advance the Islamic faith (Voll 1982).

The most compelling case for the success of political Islam is offered by the triumph of the Islamic revolution in Iran, a predominantly Shi'a country, but an example for the entire Islamic community. It shows to millions of Muslims the possibility of establishing an Islamic state and society, through a very rapid revolutionary transformation – or 'war of manoeuvre', in the Gramscian sense. The *discourse of revolution* in Iran presents the most obvious synthesis of a moral and political critique of the ancien régime, on the one hand, and a critique of an 'imperialist' world order presided over by the 'Great Satan' (the United States) on the other. At the core of both aspects of the discourse is an unrelenting repudiation of the 'westoxification' of Iranian society and morals. Needless to say, the internal contradictions and ambivalences of embracing political power as the agent of transformation in the direction of a presumed Islamic future are becoming more pronounced as the regime faces new internal and external threats. What remains significant about the Iranian case, despite its Shi'a identity, is that Islamicists no longer see the establishment of an Islamic political and social order as an impossibility.

Ironically, the discourse of *reconciliation* originates from the same cultural zone that produced the first Islamic revolution in modern history: Iran. Perhaps the self-confidence generated by the Iranian Revolution allowed this to happen. A former president of the Islamic Republic of Iran, Mohammad Khatami, has articulated this discourse as a 'dialogue among civilizations' (Khatami 2000). Eschewing a 'clash of civilizations' (Huntington 1996), Khatami locates his proposal within an ethical perspective: 'The paradigm of dialogue among civilizations requires that we give up the will for power and instead appeal to the will of empathy and compassion.' Khatami (2000) outlines two principal ways to realize his proposal:

First, actual instances of the interaction and interpenetration of cultures and civilizations with each other, resulting from a variety of factors, present one mode in which this dialogue takes place. This mode is clearly involuntary and optional and occurs in an unpremeditated fashion, driven primarily by vagaries of social events, geographical situation and historical contingency.

Secondly, alternatively, dialogue among civilizations could also mean a deliberate dialogue among representative members of various civilizations such as scholars, artists and philosophers from disparate civilizational domains. In this latter sense, dialogue entails a deliberate act based upon premeditated indulgence and does not rise and fall at the mercy of historical and geographical contingency.

Repudiating 'the Cartesian–Faustian narrative of Western civilization', Khatami underlines the need to 'listen to other narratives proposed by other human cultural domains' with regard to the relation between humans and nature and among civilizations. The message of reconciliation embedded in Khatami's proposal offers a substantive blueprint to re-imagine the philosophical contours of a more humane world order. Combining Khatami's vision with an Islamic conception of global leadership can yield new intellectual resources to challenge the confining strictures of both Orientalism and global market fundamentalism. Ultimately, these resources are contingent upon a remapping of the philosophical design underpinning the existing order.

What are some of the more durable elements of an Islamic conception of political leadership? In its elemental form, leadership in Islam is viewed both as guardianship (*wilayah*), but also as trust between human beings, suggesting moral responsibility as a core value. According to the Qur'an, human beings are regarded as his representatives or vicegerents on earth (Al-An'am 6:165):

He has given you the earth for your heritage and exalted some of you in rank above others, so that He might prove you with His gifts. Swift is your Lord in retribution; yet is He forgiving and merciful.

Those in rank above others have a duty to abide by their moral obligation to create an environment in which Islamic piety can be fully realized. In exchange for their successful discharge of that foremost duty,
Muslims have an obligation to obey. There is a complex network of
rights and obligations binding the ruler and the ruled (Marlow 1997).
In no case is the ruler or the ruled granted absolute licence. Authority
and obedience are interwoven (Mottahedeh 2001). The ruler must have
qualifications to lead, and must enjoy the confidence of the community.
Any failure to produce the conditions that allow Muslims to meet their
primary obligations to God renders the ruler illegitimate. In situations
'when the individual's religious duty as a Muslim and his political duty as
a subject come into conflict, it is the individual's duty as a Muslim that
must prevail (Lewis 1991: 69).

Contrary to the expectation that the Islamic political ethos can generate
only autocratic or charismatic leadership, lacking the correlates of
modernity, two key elements of an Islamic conception militate against
received Orientalist wisdom: the notions of *shura* (consultation or deliberation) and *ihtisab* (accountability). Both notions underline the processual
nature of leadership. In the first instance, deliberation is essential in the
selection of leaders. In all vital affairs, leaders are expected to seek the
counsel and advice of the Islamic community, especially its intellectuals
and legal experts. The notion of accountability, in the second instance,
places severe checks on arbitrary or capricious rule. Limited government is
the essence of an Islamic conception of relations between rulers and ruled.
However, the difficulty that emerges in both instances is the potential for
abuse. To guard against this eventuality, the concept of *ad'l* (justice) plays
a pivotal role in the Islamic scheme. As Lewis (1991: 70) notes:

The notion of justice becomes central to Muslim discussions of the duties owed
by the ruler on the one hand to God, on the other to his subjects. While
definitions of justice vary from period to period, from country to country, from
school to school, even from jurist to jurist, the basic principle remains that justice
is the touchstone of the good ruler. It is the counterpart of obedience, the
converse of tyranny (*zulm*).

The main sources of the principles of Islamic leadership derive from the
Qur'an, from the sayings and conduct of the Prophet, the example of the
Rightly Guided Caliphs and other pious individuals in Islamic society.
However, it is the Qur'an that provides the original basis for leadership
principles. In Muslim belief, the Qur'an is an eternal text with universal
validity. It spans the totality of social and personal conduct, including
relations between the leaders and the led. Since the times of the Prophet
Muhammad, this view has offered the ideal type against which to evaluate

subsequent political performance. In the Shi'a tradition, in the absence of the Imam, leadership or guardianship belongs to selfless and righteous legal experts.

Concentrated on the notion of guardianship, the Islamic conception of leadership rests principally on the aspiration of establishing boundaries for permissive action. Human conduct, especially the conduct of those in authority, is circumscribed by ethical principles: respect for life and dignity in all its spiritual, biological and artistic forms. A second constraint emanates from the demand for respecting cultural and religious diversity. There is no compulsion in Islam, as the Qur'an enjoins. A third limit arises from the awareness that sovereignty belongs only to God. This makes absolute sovereignty, both of the state and of the individual, forms of *shirk* (heresy). Finally, within established boundaries, material pursuits such as wealth creation are fully endorsed, but they must all conform to the survival and sustainability of the human species. Material life cannot be its own end. The task of the leader is to ensure that these limits are observed. Self-observance is the first step in this regard. No leader is immune from the application of those vital principles. However, the gulf between received theory and current practice remains wide and unbridgeable. This is the major source of much of the perceived turmoil in the areas of Islamic culture.

The growing divergence between subaltern forces and dominant élites in the Islamic cultural zones rests principally on a crisis of legitimation engulfing state and society. To be certain, subalternity here is seen as a condition of *both* economic *and* cultural subordination in the face of West-centred globalization, neoliberal rationality and secular governance. Despite the rhetoric of Islamization, the vast majority of Muslim élites are largely alienated from the social temper of the multitude. Élites are drawn to the globalizing logic of neoliberal governance, ensuring their own longevity. Political repression is readily applied to address social and political protest.

Against the hegemonic current, the Islamic impulse becomes more explicable. Despite its heterodoxy, this impulse seeks alternatives to disciplinary neoliberalism in the form of ethical governance based on Islamic principles. A key element of ethical governance is the reconfiguration of notions of sovereignty and the liberal regime of rights. In the first instance, subordination to some higher authority places constraints on the power of the state, offering protection to citizens. The liberal regime of rights is seen as a frail substitute for social and political obligations to community. In terms of global governance, the implications of these principles are significant.

An Islamic receptivity to the question of global governance imposes strict limits on the drive towards self-seeking and institutions designed to realize self-seeking as an organizing principle of social existence. Global institutions cannot merely represent private authority; they need to balance societal needs with the compulsions of wealth creation. Equally salient is the balance between nature and society. Limits to self-aggrandizement can produce the conditions for such a balance. Secondly, an appreciation of the value of human diversity – including cultural diversity – is a repudiation of the drive towards homogenization. Multiple forms of life (as Khatami might suggest) require protection, not singularity.

Greater representation in global institutions from a variety of cultural zones is but an initial step towards a recognition of the diversity and multiplicity of political and social desires. A more critical element towards reshaping the contours of governance is an awareness of a civilizational crisis – a compound of multiple crises – demanding a paradigm shift. Islamic notions of permissive social action, self-regulation and cultural embeddedness offer one among many alternatives to rethink global governance. However, ultimately, alternatives emerge only in and through political struggles. Tragically, the forms some struggles have assumed in the Islamic cultural zones – often inspired by nihilistic violence or instrumental reason – not only are self-defeating but also have the potential to obviate other alternatives. The ethical content of reconstituting the world often recedes into the background. However, despite these challenges, the significance of the Islamic alternative cannot be negated, since it is inextricably tied to ordinary aspirations to build better lives in accordance with received principles and to reconcile very difficult life choices with faith.

Conclusion

The present conjuncture of global crises raises critical questions concerning the limits and possibilities of structural change and transformations in world order. These limits and possibilities are inextricably tied to the form of global leadership; the latter gives the world order the agency and mechanism to connect its different parts. The limits of the current global political constellation are marked by a growing tendency of both governance and surveillance to escape traditional patterns of political representation. The latent tension between politics and administration is augmented in the shift from a liberal form of representative governance to governance without either representation or accountability. It is also underlined by a widening gulf between the compulsions of managing the global political economy and the compulsions that reflect societal needs at local and national levels. In the second instance, the present conjuncture has brought to the surface wider concerns about the need for humane global governance, greater social justice and social/ ecological sustainability. New avenues to rethink the global political economy and its precarious reliance on neoliberal rationality are now urgently sought in multiple geographical and cultural sites. Nonetheless, there is also an apparent disjuncture between discourses on justice, equality and fairness in different cultural zones of the global South and the self-rationalizing claims to universal appeal of disciplinary neoliberalism.

The ideological predilection in reigning circles of the global political economy to silence alternatives to disciplinary neoliberalism has assumed two principal forms: depoliticization and delegitimation. Both are closely linked, as they mutually reinforce each other. Depoliticization typically rests on the strategy of marginalizing dissent through co-optation or repression. Delegitimation draws its sustenance from control over discursive fields of producing and circulating knowledge and information. Intellectual challenges to the hegemony of global neoliberalism are often presented as romantic utopias, as impractical or as merely unnatural. Hence, the ascendancy of liberal market fundamentalism is seen as the triumph of reason, materialized in the emergence of a 'flat world' (Friedman 2005), 'the end of history' (Fukuyama 1992) or West-centred globalization (Bhagwati 2004). On this view, alternative conceptions of world order lack the vitality of reason, practicality or intellectual merit to serve as viable paradigms. Not only is this sentiment prevalent in the upper tiers of global governance (the World Trade Organization, G8 or Davos) but it travels liberally among 'national' élites – those wedded to securing privilege and plenty through positive engagement with, or service to, the structures of global authority, both public and private (Cutler, Haufler and Porter 1999). Challenges to the hegemony of neoliberal discourse, therefore, are met with disdain and active opposition at local and global levels alike.

Aspects of the Islamic ethical vision briefly outlined in the preceding pages offer the kernel of an alternative template. Part of the success of neoliberal hegemony has been the foreclosure of different modes of thought, particularly those that originate in the global South. With the recent crisis of global neoliberalism, possibilities for entertaining alternative conceptions appear both real and attractive. However, the difficulty lies in aligning new philosophical schemes with political leadership committed to meaningful change. This edited collection offers important steps in that direction. Engagement with elements of thinking originating from the Islamic world may constitute part of the journey.

9   Public and insurgent reason: adjudicatory leadership in a hyper-globalizing world

Upendra Baxi

Summary

Although it is well known that apex or supreme court justices wield impressive, and at times awesome, interpretive powers and capacities for leadership and political and moral influence, this chapter specifically introduces the wider concept of *adjudicatory leadership* as a contribution to extending theories of global leadership. Adjudicatory leadership consists in the management and organization of the usual hierarchy of jurisdictions and court systems, and it also entails interpretive/hermeneutic leadership. This process now operates on a world scale. Indeed, courts and justices, rather than representative institutions, governments or political parties, have become, in many parts of the contemporary world, the mentors and mediators of the crisis of hegemony, particularly if they are understood as providing 'intellectual and moral leadership', to use Gramsci's phrase (Hoare and Nowell-Smith 1971: 57), as well as mediating and mentoring not just relationships between state and citizen but also social relations more generally. They are integral to the 'general activity of the law', which is 'wider than purely the State and governmental activity' and 'includes the activity involved in directing civil society, in those zones which the technicians of law call legally neutral – i.e. in morality and in custom generally', and thus to 'the entire juridical problem' (ibid.: 195). This 'problem' – as well as the crisis of hegemony – emerges in the contemporary moment as an aspect of the dialectic of constituted and insurgent power in the forging of public reason and progressive potentials of adjudicatory leadership.

Introduction: towards a theory of adjudicatory leadership

Adjudicatory leadership is as yet not a term of art, and its introduction into the discourse of constitutional, political and leadership theory may evoke contestation. Although pre-eminently an affair of national

161

societies, it now extends considerably across national boundaries. The proliferation of international courts, tribunals and related forums remains truly unprecedented. Supranational forums, such as the European Union and judicial systems in Africa and Latin America, have produced novel adjudicatory leadership; so has the multicultural composition and functioning of the International Court of Justice (ICJ). Although liable to critique as 'victor's justice', the Nuremberg and Tokyo trials provide justifications for ad hoc tribunals in former Yugoslavia, Rwanda and Sierra Leone, questioning international leadership patterns and forms of impunity that were able to thrive previously. The International Criminal Court (ICC) may finally now, besides having the jurisdiction to try war crimes and crimes against humanity, also tackle crimes of aggression, and may even address, in the remote future, the conduct of non-state actors, especially multinational corporations and allied entities for flagrant violations of human rights, human abuse, environmental degradation and ecological destruction. One may also add to this list the ongoing interpretive adjudicatory leadership, such as the United Nations human rights treaty bodies, the Office of the High Commissioner for Human Rights and the Human Rights Council, which have *often*, though not *always*, provided the space for counter-hegemonic contestation over the practices of the politics of cruelty, and much else as well, in terms of the amelioration of the lot of the worst off and rightless peoples.

In sum, the 'rights revolution' provides almost everywhere a remarkable potential for adjudicatory leadership to operate. This does not mean that it is always considered as 'legitimate' by governments, which are the bodies that usually appoint justices, or by scholars, who believe that justices ought to remain an inferior species compared with elected public officials, or by human rights and social movement activists, who are occasionally discomfited by adverse adjudicatory outcomes. Indeed, questions concerning the legitimacy of adjudicatory leadership may not gainsay its existence, nor may we reiterate old wisdoms distinguishing the tasks of the appellate/apex courts from those designated as trial or district courts. The latter have also begun to display some notable leadership traits, as, for example, outstandingly illustrated by Spanish investigative judge Balthasar Garzón, who triggered the initiation of the reversal of the logics of immunity and impunity of heads of state in the case of Augusto Pinochet, the Chilean general who seized power and ruled as that country's dictator from 1973 to 1990 (see Sugarman 2002). In the quarter-century-old Bhopal litigation, the district judiciary has done better in protecting the residuary human rights of the more than 200,000 people who were affected by the 1984 toxic gas disaster than has the Supreme Court of India (Baxi 2010). Increasingly, trial courts, otherwise tasked to find the facts and apply the law as it stands, have begun to assume the custodianship of the rule of law and human rights values, norms and standards. Indeed, the trial courts, in providing *injunctive relief* (the power of injunction) against developmental public projects such as large-scale irrigation or other infrastructure development projects contingent on a full hearing of those adversely affected, have created and sustained social and political space in which movements of resistance can more fully articulate themselves and marshal new sources of critical solidarities. Adjudicatory leadership theory errs egregiously if it confines its attention almost exclusively to the appellate/apex courts; other courts matter a great deal.

Moreover, apex or supreme court justices remain divided concerning the best possible points of arrival and departure for deliberative and reflexive judicial action and intervention in matters in which agencies of state and of public opinion remain sharply divided (e.g. in the use of their interpretive authority or judicial review powers). Some approaches urge restraint, relegating the formidable issues thus posed to the representative political institutions, no matter how great the human rights and the rule of law costs thus entailed for suffering and vulnerable people. Some other approaches remain imbued with conceptions of adjudicative power as forms of social trust and responsibility (i.e. fiduciary notions). Some justices eschew theories of adjudicative power altogether, privileging arguments from consequences (Posner 2010).

Moreover, many apex justices actually believe in and practise the virtue of judicial self-restraint, on the basis of notions of respect for other coordinate branches of governance. They believe in institutional deference and harmony. They do not believe that their oaths of office and constitutional obligation to protect basic rights should be interpreted so far as to lead to an enunciation of constitutional policies; for example, for a long time a majority of US Supreme Court justices declined, via the doctrine of 'political questions', to intervene in cases of slavery, race-based discrimination and electoral gerrymandering. 'Restraintivism' everywhere is associated with hands-off stances concerning excesses of domination – excesses co-produced by state and civil society, which then 'justify' forms of human and social suffering and rightlessness. Nonetheless, humans exposed to this awesome fate in the post-colonial, post-socialist or post-conflict global South insist that apex justices may no longer afford to entrust the custodianship of human rights and legality exclusively to political leadership.[1] This at least suggests that the virtue of judicial self-*restraint* may not go so far as to constitute judicial *abdication*.

'Judicial activism' marks a near-complete reversal of doctrines of judicial restraint. Activist justices everywhere do not merely elaborate political power as a form of social trust but also present high judicial power in fiduciary terms, and in the following respects.

(1) Judicial discretion concerning who, other than extravagantly paid private lawyers, may move and appear before the apex courts (the democratization of *locus standi*, or access to courts).
(2) What cases/controversies may be admitted to the adjudicative roster/docket (readdressing the problem of *justiciability*).
(3) How these may be argued (e.g. time limits, or more importantly, judicial compliance with internationally accepted human rights and humanitarian law in customary and treaty regimes).
(4) The contrast between writing judicial opinions as collegiate acts/performances of adjudicatory leadership and ways that allow for a plurality, even a multiplicity, of judicial decisions.
(5) Approaches leading to requests for advisory opinions (or for post-socialist apex courts for 'abstract' judicial review) on the future validity of legislation, and even proposed constitutional amendments.

In India, apex justices have explicitly subjected the power to amend the constitution to imply limitations based on the grounds of infringement of the basic structure and essential features of the constitution. This invention means that constitutional amendments duly passed by parliament may be held to be invalid; this doctrine has travelled well in south Asian jurisprudence as well. The idea of apex courts as 'constituent assemblies' in perpetuity, exercising adjudicative power as a form of conjoint constituent power, has also been put to use by the Indian Supreme Court, (1) to restore fundamental rights that the constitution makers had after due deliberation left out from the constitutional text; (2) to proclaim new (invented) human rights; (3) to treat socio-economic rights declared as judicially unenforceable under the rubric of the Directive Principles of State Policy as worthy of incorporation as additional fundamental rights; and (4) to enlarge the spheres of

---

[1] In saying this, one needs to acknowledge fully that, in traditions that valorize, for example, the principles of theocratic state formation, or neo-charismatic authority, hereditary forms of monarchical rule and forms of militarized and related dictatorships, the very idea of adjudicatory leadership may remain liable to the indictment of treason or sedition. *The question in almost all contexts is not the capacity of justices to lead but their legitimacy in so doing* (editor's emphasis added).

jurisdiction by the invention of epistolary jurisdiction (Baxi 1989, 2008a; Jacobshon 2003; Sathe 2001; Vandenhole 2002).[2]

A crucial question remains: how far can adjudicatory leadership 'theory' in non-theocratic constitutionalism engage with the fact that millions of humans, especially women, live under non-state law formations, either on the basis of charismatic law formations (the law as revealed by prophets) or under the patrimonial domination of customary law? A merely state-centric understanding of such leadership does not bring into view some crucial concerns about identity, difference, violence and justice as perceived and handled by forms of community- and religion-based adjudication. Further, how may adjudicatory leadership proceed to enable the communities of faith to develop respect for 'contemporary' and inclusive human rights values, standards and norms? Put another way, how may faith/cultural communities be enabled to perceive the difference between their 'law' and the 'law' of the state? For example, how far may state-centric adjudicatory leadership repudiate the distinction between fatwa-based cultures (or *decretal* legal cultures – i.e. those that involve the making of law by decree or fiat) and the law of the state? The *globalization of fatwa cultures* fostered by ongoing wars *of* and *on* 'terror' encourages the view that the fatwa cultures valorize non-public (secret) decision-making by decree, which is inherently non-participative, unaccountable and ethically irresponsible. Indeed, the 'wars' *of* and *on* terror both deploy, and proceed to justify, indiscriminate violence and the unreasonable and disproportionate use of force (Baxi 2009). How far may adjudicatory leadership address or redress the shrinking of the public sphere by such violent means, 'causing communities of fear and danger' and enormous hurt and harm that is unredressed? How may anyone urge before the courts the uncanny verisimilitude between the fatwas in the name of Osama bin Laden and those issued in the run-up to the 2003 invasion of Iraq, under the signature of the Bush and Blair regimes? How may *national* adjudicatory leadership best respond to this particular moment of crisis?

Put another way, the question is this: how may we today, engulfed by the crisis of global leadership, grasp what Gramsci understood as the 'general activity of law' within, and across, territorially organized nation states? The principal theoretical contestation concerns contrasts between a historical materialist understanding of late capitalism and a cultural pluralist understanding of 'inter-state relations' or global politics. Human-rights-oriented adjudicatory leadership has thus partly gone

[2] See Glossary for terms such as 'epistolary jurisdiction' and, later, 'fatwa' and '*lex mercatoria*'.

global, while sustaining tendencies towards pedagogies of 'civilizing' governance, in the sense Gramsci conferred on progressive leadership at all levels and all sites.

On the other hand, we should also note the new forms of global *lex mercatoria* that are now placed at the service of capital, though not with felicitous ease, as certain decisions of the WTO and other related bodies suggest (Eliason 2009; Shaffer 2008). The 'neoliberal penchant' for the privatization of dispute settlement transfers the potential for adjudicatory leadership as a public good to the maximization of the welfare of the cross-border trade and investment communities (Muchlinski, Ortino and Schreuer 2008; Schneiderman 2008). In the conjuncture of globalization, millions remain affected by the privatization of the form of modern law, allowing important investment and trade disputes to be decided by private commercial arbitration. This tends to minimize the role of the state as a political community as a seat and source of authority to define basic moral goods. As Michel Foucault (Davidson 2010: 121; emphasis added) puts it: '*One must govern for the market, rather than because of the market.*' If this description of neoliberal forms of law under conditions of hyper-globalization holds, we may ask: why is adjudicatory leadership so insufficiently recognized in either the conventional (e.g. much of the business literature) or critical approaches to 'global' leadership? May it also be the case that the dominant paradigm of international economic law now supervenes over elements of human rights law, and thus over more transformative forms of adjudicatory leadership?

In what follows I further outline aspects of the adjudicatory leadership concept as designating at least three sites of action or agency: (1) in repairing and innovating 'systems' of administration of justice; (2) as administrative or managerial leadership; and (3) as hermeneutic leadership.

Extra-curial adjudicatory leadership forms

It is clear (for most regions of the world) that justices are accorded the status of organic intellectuals with regard to reforms of systems of administration of civil and criminal justice. When incumbent or superannuated justices lead such reforms, what emerges is an important *extra-curial* dimension of adjudicatory leadership (i.e. forms of leadership, as it were, exercised outside the courts).

On the one hand, such leadership by justices raises important concerns, such as the danger of an appropriation by the political leadership of the symbols of judicial authority for its own, expedient, ends. On the other hand, the relation between high judicial power and extra-curial adjudicatory leadership becomes immensely complex when incumbent justices in an activist mode deploy their power to enunciate law reform. The Indian Supreme Court provides a leading example. It has interpreted constitutional provisions regarding appellate judicial appointments in a manner that has divested the supreme executive of its prerogative by investing such powers in a Collegium of Justices presided over by the Chief Justice of India; moreover, the Pakistan Supreme Court has recently followed this initiative. The Indian Supreme Court has also made binding judicial orders ameliorating the service conditions and salaries of the district judiciary. Furthermore, it has enacted mandatory legislative policies concerning, for example, sexual harassment in workplaces, campus violence (practices of bullying or ragging) and rights to dignity, shelter and livelihood. After some initial outcries, the executive and legislature have complied, thus establishing as unproblematic the explicit legislative role of the apex court in India.

Such developments raise some fundamental questions. Should law reform seek to maximize efficiency as a *non-moral* virtue, or as a virtue associated with the quest for justice in society? If the latter, how can Kafkaesque procedures and powers of state law be avoided? How far may it even seek to expand its potential to assist the silenced and disarticulated subjects of law? How can dominant models respond to human and social suffering and states of rightlessness, which are often produced by the very practices of judicial interpretation? All these, and related, concerns accentuate the need for comparative and cross-cultural research.

Adjudicatory leadership as a site of management practices

Law reform also raises issues regarding the organization and management of the legal system. The efficient management of courts as state institutions is a legitimate concern of all citizens, yet court reform has not been a high priority, even for 'transformative' and 'visionary' political leadership. Nor, as far as I know, have human rights and social movement activists in most parts of the Third World pursued court reform with any zeal. As a result, those who *go* to courts or are *taken* there often become 'victims' rather than 'beneficiaries' of the judicial system – at least, at the grass-roots-level courts. Here, in terms of court management, is an instance of 'leadership by default'.

However, the scenario for the Third World is changing rapidly, given the emergence of court reform as an aspect of conditionality for development assistance, and with it the unguarded solicitude towards the increased flow of direct foreign investment, and growing presence of multinational enterprises. Management gurus and digital experts who suggest various ways of e-judicial governance, 'paperless courts' or video conferencing, for the purposes of garnering witnesses and evidence, understandably remain concerned with maximizing the efficiency of court procedures and outputs. Presented as major breakthroughs in doing and achieving 'justice', such measures deepen the divide between the constitutional 'haves' and 'have-nots'. This rule by 'experts' regards organizational complexity as posing problems that require techno-fixes. Adjudicatory leadership thus becomes an appendage to ncoliberal development. The very notion of justices as chief executive officers (CEOs) and managers of public sector corporations is an integral part of the new agenda of 'judicial globalization'. However, judicial globalization means many things to different people. Technically, it means ways of maximizing judicial comity and cooperation so as to promote the handling of disputes or prosecutions that entail multi-state elements and reciprocal respect for other jurisdictions. Further, it signifies pooling knowledges (in the plural) concerning the management of complex relationships between many actors, be they justices, lawyers, administrative staff or, increasingly, the 24/7 media.

Such forms of judicial globalization often exceed their original intent by fostering tendencies towards homogenization via judicial training and related programmes to improve the skills and competences of adjudicative administrators. Even so, a global framework remains important for special situations of dependence, such as juvenile justice, or the residual rights of migrant workers, stateless persons, refugees and asylum seekers, and 'undocumented aliens'. A further implication lies in the persistent demands for court reforms so that courts become service-providers, as public sector corporations that must follow models of business management leadership theory. However, any consideration of social and cultural variables and power relations complicates understandings; juridically constituted publics thus always remain confronted by counter-publics. Revisiting Franz Kafka remains the best antidote for 'judicial-globalization'-led models for court reform.

Transformative/visionary conceptions of adjudicatory leadership

Here I make five points.

First, most post-colonial/post-socialist conceptions offer some new ways of imagining ideas of constitutionalism, signified by the dialectical relationships of four key conceptions: governance, rights, development and justice.

Second, many forms and styles of adjudicatory leadership in the global South (begun in India in the middle of the twentieth century, and further developed later in that century in South African constitutionalism) anticipate and privilege contemporary markers of the development of international human rights values, standards and norms (Baxi 2008b). The Indian constitution, coeval with the Universal Declaration of Human Rights, marked a radical departure from the liberal conceptions of rights and justice and inaugurated two kinds of human rights: those labelled as civil and political rights and made judicially enforceable and those named as the Directive Principles of State Policy (in sum, social and economic rights), proclaimed as constituting 'paramount' constitutional state obligations in the making of laws and policies. In a welcome contrast, the South African form seeks to promote a community of rights, specifically privileging the Constitutional Court with some burdens of judicial implementation, even when this is interpreted as inviting collaboration with parliament and the court. These forms remain transformative in different ways in India, Brazil and South Africa (Baxi 2008a; Feldman 2008; Schneiderman 2008).

Third, the 'transformative' moment varies: post-colonial constitutional forms were results of the subjugated people's ethical invention of their right to self-determination (Prashad 2007; Young 2001). The theory and practice of Latin American constitutionalisms remains overlaid with long and cruel histories of imperial predations (see Galeano 1997). Post-socialist constitutionalisms remain different, perhaps, since they occur mostly in an era of contemporary economic globalization, often labelled, curiously, as 'transitional' forms. The story is also different for 'post-conflict' societies emerging out of a politics of violence (e.g. the trauma of genocidal or ethnic cleansing, or after having been subject to the 'global' war on 'terror').

Fourth, new global South developments reconfigure the very idea of constitutionalism in what I term the 'four "Cs"'. The first 'C' refers to the constitutional text; the second 'C' refers to the executive and adjudicatory authoritative enunciation of constitutional law. The third 'C' is the power of citizen interpretation, which often iconically disrupts the second; examples include Martin Luther King, Nelson Mandela and Aung San Suu Kyi. I may further mention the various revolutions of colour in post-socialist/transitional societies. The fourth 'C' names the very idea of constitutionalism as the normative/ideological site that disrupts the unity of the liberal/libertarian narratives. This is where activist adjudicatory leadership and citizen practices often trump the dominant first and second 'Cs'. The power of social movement and human rights activisms, for example marching under the banner 'Women's rights are human rights', or the movements of indigenous peoples, the rights of religious and cultural minorities or the movement for liberation from 'despised sexualities', furnish crucial markers of new adjudicatory leadership formations, within and across nations.

Fifth, all these constitutional forms remain transformative, if only because they enunciate constitutionally desired conceptions of social order.[3] Such conceptions are transformative because they offer a comprehensive view not only of how legitimate authority may be constituted and sustained but also of how it may be constrained and challenged by those governed. The tasks of adjudicatory and political leadership thus entail a principled aspiration and respect for *pluri*-religious, -ethnic, -linguistic communities, even when they are located in theocratic constitutional forms (I scrupulously avoid here the conventional qualifier 'multi-'). As global-South-oriented comparative constitutional studies show, adjudicatory leadership emerges most significantly as a form of *deliberative* leadership often reinforcing political leadership but also pitted against the pathologies of some governance powers.

Public reason and insurgent reason

Interpretive adjudicatory leadership modes remain justified on the platforms of deliberative public reason. These vary immensely (Larmore 2003; Rawls 1996: 321–40, 2001). However, public reason as exemplified by adjudicatory leadership remains possible when (1) courts and justices are public forums, (2) deliberation is conducted by recourse to complex logics of legal and rhetorical argumentation, (3) relatively independent legal professions prevail, (4) courts and justices control their arbitrariness by giving reasons for their decisions/opinions subject to deliberative public scrutiny and (5) the reversibility of prior acts/performances of reasoned elaboration remains open.

Even so, what remains distinctive – to adapt John Rawls – is the fact that there is no social world without some loss; that is, no social world exists that does not exclude some ways of life that realize in special ways certain fundamental values. The inevitability of the loss of social worlds, or, put differently, 'some ways of life', is justifiable only when this loss is accepted as justified by those who actually experience it (Larmore 2003, 374–5). Note that justification does not mean simply providing 'good reasons' for the action of the dominant, nor does it consist in what Martha Nussbaum (2000) characterizes as 'adaptive preferences', by which the subalterns cope variously with the real-life experience of their subordination, even subjugation. Gramscians would recognize the latter

---

[3] See Baxi 1967 for a development of this notion with regard to India, and Baxi 2000 describing constitutionalisms as sites of state formative practices.

as the practices of hegemony, or even as dominance without hegemony (Guha 2007). The sovereign question then surely is: what may ever constitute good reasons for people to accept the loss of their social worlds?

Although Rawls' thought has been constantly evolving, it is clear that the idea of public reason constitutes a value in itself fostering the quest for the elements of a theory of a shared concept of justice. The Rawls of *Political Liberalism* (Rawls 2005) is explicit concerning justice as a *political* virtue, both as crystallizing 'the principles of justice for the basic structure' of society and as providing 'principles of reasoning and rules of evidence' enabling 'citizens to decide whether substantive principles properly apply and to identify laws and policies that best satisfy them' (Rawls 1996: 223–7). If the basic structure of a well-ordered society is to arrive at a shared understanding of the principles of justice as fairness (equal liberty for all and equality of opportunity, further supplemented by the 'difference principle' – solicitude for the worst-off people in society), the principles and procedures of public reason ought to be more securely in place. As Charles Larmore (2003: 177) suggests, the aim of 'a common point of view' concerning what justice may mean 'is to adjudicate disagreements by argument [for a] public life founded on what mutually acknowledged principles...of fairness entail'. Public reason allows scope for 'reasonable pluralisms' and 'overlapping consensus', based on the important distinction between the 'rational' and the 'reasonable'.

A rarely noted aspect of Rawls' notion of public reason is its *other*: the 'non-public' reason of social groups and collectivities. Rawls instances thus churches, universities, scientific associations and professional social groups; these hold non-public power 'with respect to political society and citizens generally'. Their acts of reasoning remain 'public with respect to their members', forming ways of 'reasoning as to what is to be done'. Furthermore, Rawls draws attention to the fact that voluntary exit from such associational forms of life remains possible if one is simply a member of a part of a wider political community; in contrast, exiting from the state remains far more onerous (Rawls 1996: 220–2).

The distinction between public and non-public reason surely remains important, if indeed not decisive, for Rawls' imagery of a well-ordered society. For one thing, autonomous forms of associational life are an aspect of liberty and, moreover, ought to be regarded as integral to the theory and practice of 'reasonable pluralism'. For another, associational forms shape a 'background culture' (ibid.: 220). Rawls is particularly sensitive to the importance of religion as providing comprehensive conceptions of the good life, whose forms of non-public reason public political institutions ought, as far as possible, to strive fully to respect. This poses several dilemmas of toleration for political institutions that ought to function as custodians of public reason. Without a sincere respect for the plurality of world views reflected in non-public religious power and reason, these custodians or guardians – be they legislators or justices – may not achieve the virtue of toleration as an aspect of the basic structure of political institutions or the burdens of judgement borne by adjudicatory leadership communities. Although the Rawls of *A Theory of Justice* here differs from the Rawls of *Political Liberalism*, how far the two may assist adjudicatory leadership tasks in the state regulation of hijab (headdresses and 'modesty' garments worn by Muslim women) and of building minarets in public spaces remains an open question. If one were to extend this framework to 'severely divided societies' across the global South (as Donald Horowitz (2003) names them), the tasks of adjudicatory leadership become even more formidable than those framed with the expedient and often hollow Euro-American prose of 'multiculturalisms'.

Equally at stake remain cross-border flows of the networked traffic in ideas, arrangements and institutions now represented by all our talk of globalization or 'neoliberalism'. Rawls refrains from addressing these forms of non-public reason – especially forms of corporate power: nevertheless, the first pages of *The Law of Peoples* (Rawls 2001) forcefully draw our attention to the fact that even laws may be bought and sold for a price in the US Congress (the reference being here to electoral campaign funding as an aspect of the sacrosanct rights of the first amendment). However, overall Rawls does not address the global networks of power and influence, especially those of the multinational enterprises, which even adjudicatory leadership may not fully escape (see Baxi 2010). As a resolutely non-cosmopolitan thinker, Rawls does not endorse calls for a theory of global justice.

Nonetheless, it remains not too far off the mark to say that performances of deliberative public reason, especially in the global South, remain fully confronted by the 'reason' of the non-public powers, increasingly constituted by the communities/networks of direct foreign investment, 'sovereign' funds, international and regional financial institutions, global corporations and multilateral-treaty-based trade agreements that stridently claim immunity and impunity from local 'constitutional essentials'. However, various forms of adjudicatory leadership have wrestled with the crisis of global public reason thus made manifest before them by such contemporary forms of neoliberalism. Accordingly, the Philippines Supreme Court and the Bombay High Court, both confronted with the need to adjudicate the constitutional legitimacy of their state's accession to the Dunkel (final) draft WTO agreements while granting *locus standi* (respecting the demands of procedural fairness), deferred adjudication to a future point of time when the adverse impacts on constitutional/human rights may be more fully demonstrated. By contrast, 'neoliberal' adjudicatory leadership constitutes the *time of* [human rights and constitutionalism] *that never will be*. It is this establishment of *null political time* (Agamben 2005) that constitutes the structures of 'engagement' and of 'postponement', as Gayatri Spivak names them. The emergent global economic 'new constitutionalism' (Gill 1992, 2003a; Grear 2010; Schneiderman 2008, 2010) illustrates the structures of engagement rather poignantly. Courts and justices increasingly accelerate the promotion and protection of the trade-related market-friendly human rights of multinational enterprises and related entities (Baxi 2008b) while at the same time disengaging themselves from the tasks of promoting and protecting the human rights of human beings, especially the worst off. The 'sacrifices' of 'an economic-corporate kind' that Gramsci thought will need, or ought, to be made by the hegemonic blocs are not writ large on the formations of neoliberal global economic law.

True, adjudicatory leadership and constitutional forms to sustain 'ethico-political' hegemony require that 'account be taken of the interests and tendencies of the groups over which hegemony is to be exercised' (Hoare and Nowell-Smith 1971: 161). However, what may 'taking account' historically signify in 'neoliberal' terms? Forms of adjudicatory leadership, even the most 'activist' ones, may take account of such interests and yet remain at the same moment inarticulate in terms of what Jacques Derrida (2002) famously names as the tasks not just of *responsibility* but of those constituted by the tasks of *response-ability*.

Taking account or judicial notice of proliferating human rightlessness and avoidable human and social suffering is one way of naming activist or progressive adjudicatory leadership. However, 'taking notice' is not equal to transforming what Gramsci names as 'the decisive nucleus of economic activity' (Hoare and Nowell-Smith 1971: 161). Indeed, as one privileged to assist the birth and growth of social action litigation in India, where, momentously, the Supreme Court *of* India became the Supreme Court *for* deprived, dispossessed and disadvantaged Indians, I now remain a more or less helpless witness to what must be named as the *structural adjustment* of the Indian adjudicatory leadership. I think that the situation is not dissimilar for Brazil and South Africa.

How, then, may one adapt Gramsci's reference to 'the interests and tendencies of the groups over which hegemony is to be exercised'? This requires us to go beyond Rawls' narratives of public reason. Thus,

I briefly make reference to the distinction between public reason and forms/grammars of *popular* and *insurgent* reason.

Popular reason speaks to us of the 'unreason' of human rights in the face of the 'reason' of hyper-globalization. This is a form of sentimental reason that contests the narratives of neoliberalism via forms of people's politics of civil disobedience and protest, at times inviting not just symbolic violence (forms of destruction/defacement of state and private property) but also the practices of violent protest, now terminally signi-fied in the figuration of the suicide bomber, in which the human body itself becomes a very destructive weapon. How may interpretive adjudi-catory leadership respond to such popular reason? This is a crucial comparative concern for all those who talk incessantly about counter-hegemony, if only because popular reason may not always be benign or progressively hegemonic – as, for example, we learn from the discourse of hate speech.

Insurgent reason has as its aim the reinvention of the *constituent* power of the people against the ensemble of the *constituted* powers of the dominant social formation (Negri 1999). Moreover, insurgent reason pressed to the end of an ethical project of revolutionary violence may not qualify as Rawlsian public reason, even when it prepares the ground for the organization of 'well-ordered' societies governed by public reason. Derrida's (2002) notions of *foundational* and *reiterative* violence, of the constitutions and the laws, also highlight this issue. However, insurgent reason may also aim at and lead to revolutionary transformations via relatively peaceful means. Two references must here suffice. The vari-ously coloured revolutions in post-socialist societies have brought into existence constitutional and political leadership forms without 'founda-tional violence'. So, in the most part, did a man called Mohandas Karamchand Gandhi, whose ethical project for emancipation and free-dom without foundational violence attracted at least a brief notice from Gramsci (rare in progressive Eurocentric texts) with reference to his concept of passive revolution (Hoare and Nowell-Smith 1971: 153; see also the discussion in Baxi 1993). Here we might ask: would any exten-sion of Gramsci to experiments in subaltern leadership, which Richard Falk has poignantly evoked in terms of 'citizen pilgrims' (e.g. Martin Luther King, the Dalai Lama, Aung San Suu Kyi), and to collective subaltern movements and projects of the indigenous, feminist, eco-logical, child rights, refuges and stateless persons, migrant workers and allied forms merely constitute moments of passive revolution? Put rather crudely, is non-violent popular reason always exhausted by the protean meanings of 'passive revolution' with and since Gramsci, or is revolution better thought of as a continuum of different forms and moments of revolt and transformation? Put counterfactually, how may the forms/modes of Gramscian adjudicatory leadership differ from the Gandhian? How may these institutional moral agents remain ever unaffected by what Lenin famously described as differing 'juridical world outlooks,' or the *Weltanschauung* (Baxi 1993)? More to the point, how may adjudicatory leadership practices encounter all that fond talk of constituting a smooth surface for the triumphant march of global capital?

Thus, how may activist adjudicatory leadership patterns, for example, arrest the untoward growth of flexible labour markets that cancel prior juridical histories that have given legal and ethical recognition to worker rights as more than mere factors of production? Pierre Bourdieu names 'neoliberalism' as a declaration of endless war against all forms of plurality (see Mitrović 2005). All that may be 'safely' and for the moment said is just this: transformative or visionary adjudicatory leadership presents a continuum. It may, and often does, proselytize new visions of public reason as related to insurgent and popular reason. However, its practices must speak to different tasks, such as shaping the variegated approaches towards the judicial/juridical capabilities and potentials to develop and promote the essentially contested notions of rights, justice and the rule of law.[4]

My discussion in this section reflects several of the tensions, even contradictions, between two complex spheres of norms: international economic law and human rights law and jurisprudence. The forms of cognitive dissonance thus produced permit no summary presentation. However, with regard to apex/summit national courts, adjudicatory leadership remains often confronted with a choice amid the imperatives of long-term economic development and the here-and-now demands of social justice. Nevertheless, a major perplexity is posed by the perpetual exile in international economic law formations of the 'J' word (justice), which seems no longer politically correct; what takes its place are contingent acts/feats of global social policy, such as those represented in the unfeeling and even soulless prose of Millennium Development Goals and Programmes of Action (Baxi 2008b; 2010).

Contemporary neoliberal economic globalization practices present a difficult and contested terrain for adjudicatory leadership. Although

---

[4] Once again, I name all this as *adjudicative* rather than *judicial* leadership, because the tasks of interpretive leadership may best occur *only to the extent that the overall integrity of adjudicative institutions is reasonably assured*. Further, these tasks also depend on the ways that justices at their work negotiate the privilege of their relative autonomy (from society, economy and polity) and respond as best they can to demands of social accountability for the exercise of their hermeneutic powers.

adjudicatory leadership always occurs in bounded societies, it is interpellated within networks of transnational judicial/juridical adjudication as a form of life that marks its presence everywhere (i.e. globalizing adjudicatory leadership and its different narratives). On the one hand are imageries advancing the values of international economic law, such as the EU and WTO judicial institutions, NAFTA and the international financial institutions networks (Braithwaite and Drahos 2000). On the other hand are imageries of the International Court of Justice, the International Criminal Court and the UN-related ad hoc tribunals directed towards genocide and crimes against humanity: the UN human rights treaty bodies and related specialized agencies such as the WHO, International Labour Organization (ILO), UNICEF, UNHCHR and UNDP (now heavily invested with the tasks of judicial reform as an integral aspect of 'good governance'). Further, one ought to note some remarkable accomplishments in terms of the African and Latin American arrangements directed towards the protection and promotion of internationally and regionally enunciated human rights values, norms and standards. Thus, contemporaneous manifestations of adjudicatory leadership comprise a seamless web. How may we ever grasp its infinite-looking yet finite forms? One way to rethink involves ways in which 'global public adjudicatory reason' may cohabit, or transgress, the virtue of constitutional and deliberative democracy by reinforcing notions of deliberative public reason. By contrast, hyper-globalizing narratives of progress affirm the virtues of public–private partnerships as the best possible mechanisms for serving the infrastructures of human rights values, norms and standards; in so doing, they trump the reason of contemporary human rights.

Adjudicatory leadership and political leadership

As noted in Chapter 2, by Nicola Short, Gramsci's formulation of political leadership as involving a 'mass element', a 'principal cohesive element' and an 'intermediate element' of leadership (Hoare and Nowell-Smith 1971: 152–3) frames a number of questions and issues for the development not only of transformative adjudicatory leadership but also of more general conceptions of global leadership.

First, how may adjudicatory leadership respond to the 'mass element' comprising 'ordinary, average men'? Put differently, what may be said to be wrong, and for what good reasons, with judicial responsiveness to the worst-off people?

Second, Gramsci insisted that the presence of the people matters but that they require 'somebody to centralize, organize, and discipline them'. In the absence of this cohesive force, 'they would scatter into an impotent diaspora and vanish into nothing' (ibid.: 152). If so, how ought adjudicatory leadership forms contribute to this task of cohesion?

Third, the force of 'cohesive, centralizing, disciplinary power' also speaks to the 'power of innovation' (ibid.). In what ways can the changing forms of adjudicatory leadership recombine/reconfigure these diverse elements, and with what innovations? Here, it matters not only 'what it actually does' but, equally, 'in what provision it makes for the eventuality of its own destruction' (ibid.: 153). Although Gramsci had the communist party specifically in view, I think his observations extend coequally to the courts.

Fourth, the aporia of leadership: it can be either progressive or regressive. Indeed, politics and law may either 'carry out [their] policing function to conserve an outward extrinsic order which is a fetter on the vital forces of history' or 'carry it out in the sense of tending to raise the people to a new level of civilization expressed programmatically in its political and legal order' (ibid.: 155). Gramsci's precious message remains extremely relevant to adjudicatory leadership, since it, like the communist party, and often with it, has to respond to the following considerations (ibid.: 156):

In fact, a law finds its lawbreaker...among the reactionary social elements that it has dispossessed, ...among the progressive forces that it holds back [and] among those elements which have not yet reached the level of civilization which it can be seen as representing... When the Party is progressive it functions democratically (democratic centralism); when the party is regressive it functions 'bureaucratically' (bureaucratic centralism). The Party in the second sense is a simple, unthinking executioner.

Fifth, Gramsci, much like Max Weber, had a relational conception of leadership and power. For Weber, it is clear that power was not a property of a person but always a social relation between the power wielders and the power yielders; Gramsci seemed to share this view of leadership, but with a different thrust, of course. Accordingly, Gramsci referred us to a '*continuous insertion* of elements thrown up from the rank and file into the *solid framework of the leadership* which ensures continuity and the *regular accumulation of experience*' (ibid.: 188; emphases added). These italicized expressions fully suggest that, although leaders may lead, they may often be led. However, what the second italicized phrase may mean is not entirely clear: if leadership is open to 'continuous insertion' by the led, how far may we say that the framework of leadership can remain 'solid'? Equally, how may we understand the last italicized term? Is it suggestive of the regular accumulation of governance/dominance or of a commonality of experiences between the leaders and those led? Moreover, since 'accumulation' is a temporal/ historical process, how shall we speak to the time, manner and circumstance of leadership?

A brief remark by Gramsci suggests that leadership in this way may be merely an affair of the immediately past and present generations. This suggests at least two 'components' for any insurgent theory of leadership: (1) a finite conception of political time and space; and (2) a certain sort of reflexivity that invites a return to spontaneity in terms of critical popular common sense, which, somewhat paradoxically, imperils, as well as reinforces, the '*solid framework of the leadership*'. Reflexivity entails the development of the capability to take *interest in our interests*, or what Rawls names the development of 'public reason'. For Gramsci, this signifies what he named (following Antonio Labriola) a 'philosophy of praxis'. If so, one may well ask how adjudicatory leadership can straddle the constantly shifting conceptions of 'hegemony', involving confluence as well as contradictions between 'social' and 'political' power formations.

Gramsci suggested that one version of 'hegemony' has as its goal the creation of a new intellectual and moral order and a new type of society, in which (ibid.: 181–2; emphases added):

Our own corporate interests, in their present and future development, transcend the corporate interests of the purely economic class, and can and must become the interests of the other subordinate groups too. This is the most political phase, and marks the decisive passage from the structure to the sphere of complex superstructures. . ., bringing about not only *a unison of economic and political aims* but also intellectual and moral *unity*, posing all the questions around which struggle rages not on a corporate but a 'universal' plane, and thus creating the hegemony of a fundamental social group. . .over a series of subordinate groups.

All this opens up a dialectical consideration of adjudicatory leadership as leadership of influence. As Weber reminds us constantly, tasks, or transformations, of leadership as social and economic enterprise begin only with the displacement of social relations embedded in charismatic or patrimonial relationships. This means at least the advent of complex and contradictory conceptions of 'legal-rational' domination. Put another way, this form is always crisis-ridden by the aporias of 'formal' as opposed to 'substantive' rationality. I read adjudicatory leadership as offering 'pedagogies for the oppressed': forms that afford dignity of articulation for the planet's worst-off *beings*, including sentient creatures and other objects in 'natural' nature and socially produced 'Nature'.

Part IV

Prospects for Alternative Forms of Global Leadership

10   Global democratization without hierarchy or leadership? The World Social Forum in the capitalist world

Teivo Teivainen

Summary

The globalization protest movements offer examples of the dilemmas that a search for democratic transnational political agency, and corresponding forms of leadership, are likely to encounter in coming years. Nevertheless, and despite their limitations, they have brought the question of democratic change onto the agenda of world politics, building on the alliances between transnational social movements that have existed for decades, or even centuries. It is now very difficult to ignore the social movements, non-governmental organizations, critical think tanks and other actors that are challenging the financial and cultural supremacy of transnational capitalism. Even if it is misleading to claim, as *The New York Times* did after the anti-war protests of February 2003, that they have become the world's 'second superpower', they form part of any comprehensive picture of the new world politics. What, though, is this new politics? This chapter reflects on this question without assuming that political change is necessarily tied to conquering the state. It uses the World Social Forum as a key example, as it symbolizes many questions of articulation between social movements, questions of leadership and the construction of a new common sense implicit in the new global politics.[1]

Introduction

The new global movements emerged in the eyes of the global media with the WTO meeting in Seattle in 1999. Since then the WSF has opened a window for contestations about the future of humanity. The deeper roots of these movements originate in the crises and contradictions of

---

[1] The WSF charter of principles, cited throughout this chapter, can be found at www.forumsocialmundial.org.br/main.php?id_menu=4&cd_language=2 (accessed 29 June 2010).

North–South relations, in particular in resistance to the policies used to download the effects of the Third World debt crises of the 1980s through neoliberal reforms. In these contestations, the various groups usually grouped together as 'global civil society' have increased in visibility and in agenda-setting capacity.

One of the novel features of many such movements is the global scope of their aims, in many cases intertwined with local and communal practices. This global focus also implies a search for less state-centred conceptions of political agency, and struggles against depoliticization and what I call 'economism': the effort to render key aspects of material life as non-political and outside political contestation – a key ideological legitimation of neoliberalism (Teivainen 2002). Another concern for some of the movements is how to democratize their own modes of action while aiming at a democratization of the world. The globalization of social movements and networks through initiatives such as the World Social Forum gives it new challenges. I use the WSF as a key example in this chapter because it raises questions of articulation between social movements, leadership and the remaking of world order.

As compared to previous transnational alliances seeking radical change of the world system, such as the early trade-union-based movements or communist-party-based internationals, many of today's movements seem to take more seriously the idea that democratic change needs to be generated through democratic forms of action. This is reflected, for example, in the emphasis on horizontal networks rather than hierarchical organization. One of its manifestations is the idea of an *open space* – a catchword of various social forums organized throughout the world since 2001. The open space idea has many democratic implications. One of them is that no single movement should be able to claim that its aims have intrinsic strategic priority over others. An example of the reasoning might go as follows: 'The class contradictions that your movement is facing should have no priority over the gender contradictions we confront. My sexual identity is no less important than your ethnicity. Therefore, none of us should have leadership over the others in our movement of movements.'

The democratic coexistence in the open spaces created by the movements has been refreshing and empowering. At the same time, its relativistic undertones can become frustrating in devising effective strategies to change the world. As frustrations have become more evident in and around the open spaces in the WSF and elsewhere, a new enthusiasm for explicit, and also hierarchical, forms of leadership has gained ground among some participants.

Prefigurative and strategic dimensions of leadership

Among today's activists, particularly within movements considered autonomist or anarchist, Mohandas Gandhi's call 'We must be the change we want to see in the world' has become an important source of inspiration. *Prefigurative* politics – trying to act today according to the principles one wants to establish in tomorrow's world – has challenged visions of social change that emphasize the need to establish strategic leadership through a party or state machinery. In the World Social Forum process, these contending visions have been expressed as differences about the articulations that the forum should seek, for example, with Hugo Chávez of Venezuela, or other 'traditionally political' leaders. Some of the activists have become frustrated with the civil-society-centredness of the WSF open space. They argue that, to become more effective, the forum needs to become more 'political' and therefore include progressive parties and state leaders, or at least consider them as strategic allies. Others claim that this would lead to destroying the civic virtues of the process and create new attempts to subordinate the civil society movements to 'politics as usual'.

I therefore argue that, in order to generate significant social change, forms of action need to be both *prefigurative* and *strategic*. Given the transnational and global spaces that social movements share, this means that many dilemmas have to be confronted. Some derive from the insufficient vocabulary available to discuss non-state-driven global political agency. In the state-centric mode of transformative action it used to be relatively easy to refer to the political parties as the key organizational form that could become – for better or for worse – the instrument of change beyond 'single-issue' movements. In the global context, global civil society or transnational corporations are often referred to as significant political *actors*, but there are more difficulties in talking about global political *agency*.

With friends and colleagues I have started discussing the concept of 'global political parties' (Patomäki and Teivainen 2007). Some advocate establishing (sooner rather than later) such political parties (e.g. in a 'Fifth International', as promoted by Samir Amin, and, more recently, by Chávez). Others, including me, place more emphasis on reflecting on the possibility of global parties as a way to rethink the dichotomy between depoliticized conceptions of civil society and traditional forms of political action expressed by parties. The world as a whole is not merely an enlarged copy of territorial states. To change that world beyond the territorial limits of states, we need to develop new ways of thinking politically about transformative agency.

For the new vocabulary of political agency, a country-specific example that can offer some new language is how Bolivian indigenous movements, coca growers' associations, trade unions and other civic actors created an alliance, the Movement Toward Socialism (MAS), that they called a 'political instrument' instead of a political party. Both the vocabulary and the praxis of this process offer insights into a new kind of relationship between social movements and political action. The leader of the movement, Evo Morales, has been president of Bolivia for over five years, and MAS, a novel movement of movements, increasingly resembles a relatively traditional party. When MAS was an oppositional force it was easier to remain committed to the bottom-up mode of democratic organizing, in which the movements challenged the state through coordinated communal action. Once in government, various forms of hierarchical practice have become more evident. Perhaps almost by definition, groups with radically democratic aims tend to make compromises with hierarchical structures of command once they conquer the government. At the very least, the Bolivian example can help us discuss political instruments and agency without falling back on the conceptual baggage of traditional political parties. The experience of MAS also shows us how difficult it is to create radical social change inside one country. This experience points to the question of transnational transformative processes.

In order to understand broader possibilities of global democratization, we also need to focus on the political implications of new contestations and new political instruments. Debates on the globalization protest movements have all too often relied on a dichotomous separation between depoliticized civic movements and state-centred understandings of the political. This is too simplistic. The lack of attention to the political articulations among the movements is reflected in how they have been considered as part of an emerging 'global civil society'. In much of the academic and activist literature, attributes such as 'horizontal' tend to characterize the spaces of civil society, and relations of power and hierarchies among the actors of these spaces are often simply assumed away. The tendency to project desired qualities in the analysed phenomena has been strong in much of this literature. According to David Chandler (2007), who has analysed this tendency critically, the idea of global civil society as a distinct space is also seen as an aspect of its moral distinctiveness. Accordingly, using the World Social Forum as an example, I explore civic-driven struggles not only as contestations entailing efforts to transform the unjust structures of the world but also as involving contradictions and new political articulations among organizations that constitute the globalization protest 'movement of movements'.

The World Social Forum and global democratization

The WSF had its first global meeting in Porto Alegre, Brazil, in January 2001. Thereafter it has been expanding through various mechanisms, including holding its main meetings in other continents, mushrooming into hundreds of local, national, regional and thematic forums around the world and increasing the diversity of the groups that participate. It by no means includes all the movements and networks that aim at democratic transformations. Its composition has various geographical, sectoral, ideological and civilizational limitations. However, its emergence was a key moment in the gradual shift in the aims of many of these movements. The reactive protest dimension has been partially replaced by a more proactive democratization dimension. A somewhat simplistic but illustrative way to locate this shift is to call the wave of activism that made one of its major public appearances during the World Trade Organization meeting in 1999 in Seattle 'globalization protest movements', and to use the term 'global democratization movements' to characterize the activism of the new millennium as symbolized by the WSF. In other words, the WSF has provided a channel through which many of the globalization protest movements of the 1990s have become global democratization movements of the twenty-first century.

What are these thousands of movements? As to their formal status, the World Social Forum charter of principles states that the WSF 'brings together and interlinks only organizations and movements of civil society from all the countries in the world'. The standard definition of civil society offered by the WSF charter states that it is 'a plural, diversified, non-confessional, non-governmental and non-party context'. Despite the oft-repeated lip service to the WSF as an open civil society space, it is not open to all kinds of social movements and NGOs. According to the relatively wide ideological orientation of the WSF charter of principles, the organizations that can participate in the forum are defined as 'groups and movements of civil society that are opposed to neoliberalism and to domination of the world by capital and any form of imperialism, and are committed to building a planetary society directed towards fruitful relationships among humankind and between it and the Earth'.

There is no ideological litmus test to screen the participants. One of the differences between the movements is the extent to which the desired change means building a 'social' counterpart to balance the 'economic' emphasis of the dominant institutions of the world, such as the initial symbolic adversary, the World Economic Forum at Davos. Even if the participating movements are, at least in principle, committed to the intrinsically political aim of structural and institutional changes to the world order, some have more limited 'social' aims, such as making the voices of their constituencies heard or alleviating the suffering of marginalized communities. Although these differences sometimes create tensions and suspicions about the level of radicalism of one or another, the WSF has been relatively successful in accommodating groups that in many other contexts have tended to accuse each of being excessively 'reformist' or 'revolutionary'. The overall WSF slogan, 'Another world is possible', has been sufficiently imprecise to allow for such coexistence.

The Brazilian educational theorist Paulo Freire (2000) has stated that, in order to change the world, it is first necessary to know that it is indeed possible to change it. This helps us understand one dimension of why, during its early years, the World Social Forum experienced such spectacular growth and provided so much inspiration for social movements and other actors engaged in processes of democratic transformation. The apparently simple WSF slogan, 'Another world is possible', generated enthusiasm precisely because it helped undermine the demobilizing influence of another simple slogan, generally attributed to Margaret Thatcher, according to which 'There is no alternative' to the existing capitalist order.

Following the repetition at forum after forum that another world is indeed possible, many WSF participants have become eager to know what that other world may look like and how people are supposed to get there. One of the main problems haunting the WSF is its perceived incapacity to provide adequate answers to these questions. Many of its participants and observers have become increasingly frustrated with the limitations of the open space method. Over the years the question of politicizing the WSF has thus become an increasingly controversial issue. One of the dimensions of this question is how to be politically meaningful without being traditionally political (traditional politics is generally understood as what parties and governments are engaged with).

The road from politicizing protests to transformative proposals is filled with dilemmas. The dilemmas become particularly thorny when the aim is to articulate the proposals of many movements into collective projects to create a radically different and more democratic world, as reflected in the World Social Forum charter of principles.

When speaking about 'globalization of solidarity as a new stage in world history', the charter says that it will rest on 'democratic international systems and institutions'. It also tells us that the WSF upholds respect for the practices of 'real democracy' and 'participatory democracy'. Various other parts of the charter can also be regarded as expressions of a radically democratic spirit. Even if democracy is not formally defined in the charter, my interpretation is that it refers to a world in which people have increased possibilities to participate in the decisions about the conditions of their lives, through participatory and representative mechanisms alike.

Various formulations of the charter express the prefigurative idea that democratic changes must be achieved through democratic means. In particular, it defines the WSF as an open meeting place for the 'democratic debate of ideas'. Especially during the first years of the process, there was relatively little attention to how democratically the space was, or should be, organized. Even if the forum asserts 'Another world is possible', it is embedded in the existing one, and many of its inequalities are reproduced in the internal mode of organization of the WSF. While speaking the language of a leaderless open space, the WSF cannot totally escape the hierarchies and command structures that exist in the capitalist world system.

Confronting economism outside and inside the World Social Forum

For the reproduction of the capitalist world system, one of its key ideological mechanisms has been the depoliticization of power relations, especially but not only those located in the socially constructed sphere of the 'economic'. The expansion of capitalism in the past few decades has expanded the boundaries of the economic institutions through economic crises, privatization processes and the strengthening of economic ministries, central banks and other private authority mechanisms vis-à-vis other state organs, such as the increased importance of credit-rating agencies. Among the most visible global vehicles of this expansion have been the WTO, the IMF and the World Bank. However, one of the ideological contradictions of the crisis-ridden contemporary expansion of capitalism is that, when the 'economic' institutions of governance become more powerful, their political nature becomes, at least potentially, more evident. In this sense, the expansion of capitalism has created possibilities for such responses to challenge the legitimation of neoliberal capitalism that stems from how economic institutions are represented as non-political, and therefore not subject to democratic contestation. This is a key form of 'economism'.

The political nature of economic institutions therefore does not become evident automatically, since, to use the Gramscian term, it has become part of the 'common sense' of disciplinary neoliberalism. Indeed, although the contradictions of capitalism create the conditions for critical responses, these responses are not generated without active social forces. The new transnational activism that emerged in the 1990s has made it more visible that the 'economy' is a political and historical construction. To the extent the movements can convincingly demonstrate that apparently economic institutions are in reality important sites of power, it becomes more difficult for the latter to be legitimately based on inherently non-democratic principles, such as 'One dollar, one vote'. The logic bears many similarities with the way that feminist movements have politicized patriarchal power by claiming 'The personal is political'. Their insistence that the patriarchal family is not a neutral space but consists of political relations that need to be brought under democratic control has been an important factor in creating legal and informal norms to regulate issues that range from childcare to domestic violence. Global civic-driven democratization projects should keep learning from this politicizing spirit of the feminists so as to legitimate the validity of democratic claims upon global institutions.

The doctrine of economic neutrality is most obvious in institutions such as the IMF, but it also manifests itself in the World Social Forum process. Especially during the first years of the process, questions of funding, labour relations and the provision of services within the WSF were considered mainly technical issues, handled through a depoliticized 'administration of things'. The fact that the WSF is organized inside a capitalist world is also evident in the disadvantaged structural position of participants from relatively poor organizations and countries.

To claim that the World Social Forum is an open space may sound like a joke in bad taste for those who do not have the material means to enter the space. In simple terms, to send representatives to faraway WSF events, an organization needs to have money or friends with money. There are examples of people compensating the lack of material resources with enthusiasm, such as the case of the dozens of young Peruvian activists who travelled for days in harsh conditions, including being held at gunpoint by robbers, with inexpensively organized bus caravans to the WSF events, where they held dance parties to collect money for the return trip. However, in general terms, the question of which organizations get to be represented by delegates in the WSF has been heavily conditioned by unequally distributed material resources. Furthermore, even if the organizers of the WSF have increasingly tried to apply the principles of a non-capitalist 'solidarity economy' in the forum itself, the apparently mundane issue of the logistics of accommodation has been greatly conditioned by local hotels heavily increasing their prices in order to make more profit from the events.

One example of the dilemmas that structural inequalities cause for the attempt to practise democracy inside the World Social Forum became evident in 2005. During the previous years there had been a debate on whether the organizing committees should single out certain key events in the programme. Various criticisms had been made of the undemocratic dimension of the organizers creating a hierarchy of events, based ultimately on political considerations. As a result, when the fifth forum was held in Porto Alegre in 2005, the printed programme was for the first time horizontal, in the sense that it did not designate any key panels. However, with this apparently democratic coexistence of events, the market mechanism became an important factor defining the relative importance of panels. Organizations with more resources to produce colourful posters and leaflets or distribute T-shirts and other paraphernalia became the visible ones. After that experience, organizers sought to give more equitable visibility to disadvantaged groups.

More generally, over the years there has been a learning process, and increasing attention is now being paid to the ways in which structural inequalities affect the process. Solidarity funds have been strengthened to help organizations from poor countries (and sometimes poor organizations from rich countries, such as the Poor People's Human Rights Campaign from the United States) to participate in the decision-making organs of the World Social Forum. The choice of the venue has become an object of debates about its ownership structure and labour conditions. The question of the funding for the process has also become more politicized, especially after there were various controversies related to the role of the Ford Foundation in the preparations for the forum held in Mumbai in 2004.

Enlightened tyranny of structurelessness

There are various depoliticizing elements of the World Social Forum charter of principles and other guidelines that have problematic consequences for democratic practice within the WSF. The dilemma is that these elements help avoid conflicts within the WSF and have therefore contributed to its success, but at the same time they make the WSF governance bodies vulnerable to accusations of reproducing undemocratic practices. The widely held idea that, in order to be an 'open space', the WSF cannot be considered an 'organization' or 'institution' also contributes to its internal depoliticization. To use an expression derived from the feminist movements of the early 1970s, the unwillingness to consider the WSF an organization politically, with rules and regulations, contributes to a 'tyranny of structurelessness'.

In civic-driven contexts based on principles of horizontality and a lack of élite leaders, there exists the danger that dominant cliques emerge without procedures to constrain their power. Jo Freeman (1972), who coined the concept of the tyranny of structurelessness, has analysed the proliferation of groups that claimed to be leaderless and structureless among the feminist movements of the late 1960s and early 1970s. However, the attempted structurelessness was impossible. For Freeman, to strive for a structureless group was 'as useful, and as deceptive, as to aim at an "objective" news story, "value-free" social science or a "free" economy'. In the WSF, the analogy with the illusions about a 'free economy' is evident in accounts that explicitly or implicitly consider the WSF an unregulated 'marketplace of ideas' – an example of which I have described above regarding the dilemmas of designating key panels in the programme.

For many feminists of the early 1970s, the attempts at structurelessness were a reaction against a society and particular political institutions and organizations that were perceived as over-structured. In the World Social Forum, the attempts to avoid a structured organizational form have various explicit and implicit references to the kinds of organizations that need to be avoided or excluded. The WSF was conceived as something that is not a political party, not a non-governmental organization and not even a social movement. All these presumed to rely on excessively hierarchical forms of leadership; at the beginning, the openness of the WSF was regarded as virtually synonymous with structurelessness, with similar dilemmas for democratic process.

When analysing the World Social Forum space, one needs to distinguish the WSF events as gathering places from the governance organs that make the decisions about organizing the events. Although the former have more of the attributes of an 'open space', in the case of the latter the open space discourse is more misleading. In the WSF governing organs, practices based on depoliticized understandings of an open space have had paradoxical consequences. On the one hand, it is sometimes argued that, because the WSF is an open space, its organs should have few explicit rules or procedures. On the other hand, if there are no procedures for including new members in its governing bodies, such as the International Council, they can become closed spaces by default. From 2002 to 2004 the International Council was unable to process membership applications because there were no rules on how they should be processed. The illusion of structurelessness contributed to the strengthening of organizational structures that prevented the inclusion of new members.

According to the WSF charter of principles, the forum 'does not constitute a locus of power to be disputed by the participants'. As an empirical description, this part of the charter is obviously erroneous, because various kinds of disputes of power have always existed within the WSF. As a statement of wish, it can also be considered problematic because it obstructs the possibilities to create procedures through which the disputes can be channelled in a transparent and democratic manner.

Some of the disputes inside the World Social Forum in general, and the International Council in particular, are more traditionally ideological, such as the perennial intra-left ones between 'social democrats', 'communists' and 'Trotskyites', reflecting the fact that WSF participants have various political affiliations. However, many, and perhaps most, disputes are difficult to classify along the traditional divides of the historical left. Nonetheless, the difference between the advocates of conquering state power, either through elections or other means, and those who emphasize more autonomist strategies is one of the main cleavages in the WSF as a whole.

According to Boaventura Sousa de Santos (2005), the multiple cleavages are one of the main strengths of the World Social Forum. For example, many of the radical activists of the WSF Youth Camp may agree with Francisco Whitaker, one of the original 'founding fathers' (sic) of the WSF, on the importance of keeping the WSF as horizontal as possible, even if they may disagree with him on various substantial issues about the future of the world. Although I find the general point of Santos correct, it would be a mistake to assume that it results in an overall harmony. Political disputes have existed, will exist and should exist in the organizational structure of the WSF. They sometimes take place in the plenary debates of the International Council or the organizing committees, but often they are waged in the corridors or through private e-mail exchanges, hidden from the public eye of the other WSF participants and observers.

As long as there are no clear procedures for resolving disputes within the governance bodies of the WSF, the workings of power will continue to take place mostly through mechanisms that have not been collectively agreed on. It is sometimes argued that this in itself is not a problem as long as the WSF process produces 'results' (e.g. enthusiasm, mobilizations or plans to democratize the world) that legitimate the way it functions. In other words, even if the WSF has elements of a tyranny of structurelessness in the sense described above, it should not matter as long as the tyranny is enlightened. This pragmatic argument, even if seldom stated in such explicit terms, has been reproduced from the beginning of the WSF organizing process. The depoliticized structurelessness was undoubtedly an important element in the initial enthusiasm about the novelty of the WSF. However, the WSF needs to take the political more seriously if it is to become an increasingly important platform for democratic transformations. This means recognizing relations of power in order to democratize them.

Moreover, the World Social Forum never had a 'democratic founding moment' that would have given it a clear democratic mandate. This paradox of democracy is common to most real-world processes in which a relatively democratic order has been established. Even if many national constitutions establish that the 'people have the power', the people were often absent at the moment of establishing the first constitution (Doucet 2005: 137–55). Similarly, it is logically impossible for a civic space such as the WSF ever to construct a totally democratic basis for its governance, but this paradox should not prevent it from constantly attempting to democratize its internal governance. In this issue, as in many others, there has certainly been a learning process, and questions of internal democracy are now taken more seriously than beforehand.

Can an open space generate action?

Apart from the depoliticization that hinders democratic practices within the World Social Forum, there exists another kind of depoliticization: that which consists of such rules and practices that reproduce the idea that the WSF is an open space, an arena that should have no attributes of a movement or a political actor (Whitaker 2002a, 2002b). The WSF provides a space for actors that may construct projects of democratic transformation in different contexts, both local and global. However, the WSF itself has avoided issuing declarations of support for any particular political processes, mobilizations or even responsibilities (Grzybowski 2003).

Relying on a more pronounced dichotomy between the forum as a space and the forum as a movement, Whitaker (2002a) has criticized the 'self-nominated social movements' seeking to serve their own mobilizing dynamics and objectives. Within the International Council, Whitaker has been the staunchest defender of maintaining the WSF as a space without ownership.

Among the World Social Forum activists, Walden Bello has challenged the open space method defended by Whitaker. In the International Council Bello represents Focus on the Global South, a Bangkok-based radical think tank. Like many who criticized the limitations of the open space method, Bello approves of Hugo Chávez's call to the 2006 forum in Caracas to enter 'spaces of power' at the local, national and regional levels. Pointing to the difficulties the open-space-oriented WSF has had in developing a strategy of counter-hegemony, Bello asks whether the new stage in the struggle of the global justice and peace movement means that the WSF should give way to new modes of global organization, resistance and social transformation (Bello 2007).

The pressures for more explicit political will formation are also expressed by and through the media. The press has tended to look at the World Social Forum as a (potential) political actor in itself, while many of the organizers have wanted to downplay this role and argue that they simply provide a space for different groups to interact. These different conceptions of the event have clashed, for example, when the press has asked for final declarations and considered the lack of any such document a proof of weakness in the organization. This perspective ignores the fact that the intention of most organizers has never been to produce any official final document that would pretend to represent the views of the thousands of other organizations that have participated.

This perspective is also sometimes expressed by arguing that the forum 'talks the talk' but does not 'walk the walk'. However, the example of the anti-war demonstrations of February 2003 reveals that it is at least partially misleading to call it a mere talking shop, even if it never made an official declaration against the US-led war in Iraq. Of course, the transnational anti-war demonstration of 15 February 2003 did not stop the war, but it was the largest civic-driven single-day mobilization in the history of humankind. Moreover, to a significant extent it was generated from within the social forum processes, especially the first European Social Forum, which took place in Florence in October 2002, and the Assemblies of Social Movements, which gather inside the WSF events without claiming to represent the WSF process as a whole.

The way the World Social Forum related to the anti-war demonstrations of 2003 turns the argument about it being a mere talking shop on its head. Was it not rather that the WSF did not talk the talk (i.e. pronounce anti-war statements with a unified voice through its governing bodies) but focused on walking the walk (i.e. helping to facilitate and organize the demonstrations and integrating the war theme visibly in its programme)? This example does not in itself invalidate the more general criticism about the WSF being of too little use for projects and movements of social transformation, but it shows that the real issue is not between 'talking' and 'doing'. It is between different conceptions of the WSF as a political process.

In the debates on the political usefulness of the WSF, there has been a tendency, on the one hand, to call for more traditional forms of political agency, such as making strategic alliances with progressive states and parties. On the other hand, those who have defended the open space orientation of the process have had difficulties in showing that the process has already been politically useful, and has indeed generated various kinds of action. One of the problems for the latter is the difficulty of establishing connections between what happens inside the forums and what happens outside. For example, we can speculate on the impact of the social forum process on the left turn in most South American elections since the first World Social Forum was held in 2001. To what extent have the enthusiasm and articulations generated by the WSF played a role in these concrete results? Some of the founding fathers of the WSF may emphasize its role in private conversations after a couple of drinks, but tend to avoid making such declarations publicly in order to avoid sounding arrogant or eager to assume leadership over people's campaigns. From an academic perspective, it is difficult, though not impossible, to show causal connections in this issue. The most concrete outcomes of the WSF consist of the dialogues, articulations and learning processes that take place in the workshops, panels, seminars, festivities and corridors of the events. I would argue that these encounters have helped generate political action, of which the above-mentioned anti-war demonstrations are one example.

New empirical research is needed to establish other connections. For example, to me it is obvious that the constantly intensifying articulations of the Andean indigenous movements, both between them across national boundaries and vis-à-vis other movements, have benefited from the social forums. The members of the different movements have been able to use the World Social Forum space to plan common action and to find various kinds of allies in other movements. They have also been able to strengthen their presence in the local and national politics of their own regions, either through participation in victorious electoral campaigns, as in the case of Ecuador and Bolivia, or through assuming an increasingly important role in protests against governments and corporate power, as in Peru. Some participant observers of the process, such as Immanuel Wallerstein and Vijay Pratap, have also claimed that organizing the WSF in India in 2004 played a significant role in the national elections later that year, in which the United Progressive Alliance defeated the ruling Bharatiya Janata Party. Be that as it may, the more general point here is that the WSF initiative has been able to generate politically relevant agency without relying significantly on traditionally political forms of organizing.

What about changing the whole world? The World Social Forum has been useful for articulating campaigns around world trade, as evidenced by the coordination of action around the WTO negotiations. The transnational peasant alliance Via Campesina has been an important actor in these campaigns, and also in the WSF process, even if in recent years it has often raised criticism of the limitations of the open space method. Other concrete examples could be mentioned, but here, towards the end of the chapter, I would like to take up the role of the

WSF in facilitating a debate and learning process on the institutional features of the possible futures of the world.

Towards possible worlds

The emergence of the globalization protest movements since the mid-1990s may imply a world-historical possibility for transnational democratic changes. Whereas in the early 1990s the belief in the non-political nature of the global economic institutions was still relatively strong, today, as the world economic crisis has globalized, articulated in a wider organic crisis, more people are likely to laugh at the claim that the IMF and World Bank are purely technical and non-political institutions. Apart from the politicizing efforts of the movements, several self-defeating actions, such as the scandals related to the nomination and sacking of Paul Wolfowitz as the president of the World Bank, have certainly contributed to this situation. As regards transnational corporations, the appearance of the corporate social responsibility talk is one of the defensive mechanisms that the rulers of these institutions resort to when their political nature becomes more evident.

In this context, the global democratization movements are facing an important window of opportunity. The doctrine of economic neutrality, or economism, has been a key ideological mechanism defending the undemocratic governance of global economic institutions. However, as Stephen Gill points out in Chapter 13, the so-called 'independent central banks' that have led many of the gigantic bailouts that have one-sidedly been in support of financial capitalism in 2008–10 are in fact not independent at all; they are controlled by the very same sets of private financial interests that generated the financial collapse – the very institutions that failed to regulate and adequately govern global finance. By showing that the actions of these constitutionally independent and apparently technical institutions are by no means neutral, non-political or beyond the realm of politics, the movements can in principle further open up the spaces constituted by their praxis for democratic demands.

This would leave the rulers of the undemocratic institutions of global governance with a dilemma. Either they would have to admit that they in fact favour authoritarian political rule to democracy, or, preferably, they would have to participate in the democratization of their institutions. By focusing on the inherently political nature of the transnational and global 'economic' spaces and by insisting on the thereby legitimated need to democratize them, the ideologically empowering banner of democracy may be taken out of the hands of neoliberals. It is, of course, open to debate as to the extent to which this shift of emphasis has happened in the global media, but the problems related to the global crisis of accumulation and undemocratic global governance are mentioned more often than previously. In addition, empirical findings, even before the current post-2008 crisis, have confirmed that the concerns expressed by the globalization protest movements 'are shared by a large majority of the national public opinions', at least in Europe (della Porta 2007). One of the often heard counterclaims is that globalization protest movements themselves are organized in a not too democratic fashion, which is one of the reasons why the question of internal democracy should be taken more seriously in spaces such as the World Social Forum. Another counterclaim is that, beyond repeating that another world is possible, the movements cannot offer any concrete alternatives for future institutional arrangements.

The political usefulness of formulating models of transnational, cosmopolitan or global democratic institutions of the future is not only that they can provide inspiration for those who might struggle for their realization. Such models are also important for the task of undermining the existing networks of power, because the legitimacy of the latter has been largely based on the 'There is no alternative' discourse. As analysed above, the movements participating in the World Social Forum have played a part in undermining the hegemony of this discourse. Among the events of the WSF, there have also been many debates on alternative institutional orders of the world.

One of the internal tensions of the WSF has been that those who organize panels on global democratic orders are often perceived as disconnected from concrete grass-roots struggles. One reason for this is the tendency of many analysts of alternative world orders to extrapolate the institutions of the existing territorial states to the global level. Especially, though not only, within the world federalist tradition, it is common to argue that we need to create a world parliament and the corresponding executive government and judiciary, just as in existing democratic states but on a larger scale, in order to democratize the world. A perceived problem in these kinds of global utopias is that they often seem to assume that the current institutional order of the 'liberal democratic' states is a sufficiently democratic model for future world orders. For those sectors of the movements that have radical critiques of the existing states, this assumption does not hold water. Apart from the desirability of this kind of world governance, the extent to which it is feasible is also questionable.

Even if another world is possible, not everything is. For example, it is not realistic to imagine that the World Bank, or in particular the narrower IMF, could be significantly democratized, especially in their current form. As stated above, it may still be useful to demand their democratization in order to delegitimate, sink or shrink them, but we should not have unwarranted illusions. The WTO, even now ultimately based on the possibility of using the 'one country, one vote' mechanism in its decision-making, is more ambiguous. Somewhat similar ambiguity exists in the United Nations, with its (somewhat democratic) General Assembly and (highly undemocratic) Security Council (Patomäki and Teivainen 2004).

One of the difficult questions is that, although the principle of the 'one country, one vote' mechanism is in theory the main decision-making method of these institutions, in practice it is often overruled by other mechanisms (more common in the UN) or not put into practice at all (as mostly happens in the WTO). The limited but real formal equality is not translated into democratic practice. Thus, it is tempting to conclude that formal equality does not matter in global affairs, and that therefore global civic-driven projects should discard attempts to democratize global institutions. However, it is important to understand why the moderately democratic international decision-making models such as the UN General Assembly are in such a bad shape. One of the main factors here is that the institutions themselves and their member states are both often subject to disciplinary mechanisms, especially related to their financial dependence.

It is not that formal equality would be unimportant; it is, rather, that the movements should pay particular attention to the various forms of conditionality and dependence that make the practice of democracy so difficult in international contexts. In other words, campaigns for global democratic institutions cannot have much hope unless there are successful campaigns to tackle issues such as foreign debt and the other forms of financial or commercial dependence that the members of these institutions face.

Global democratization movements, like all others, should undertake a realistic analysis of what is possible and what is not, and then make strategic prioritizations based on that analysis. This does not mean falling back to the 'old-left ideals' of focusing almost exclusively on some particular contradiction of the world, defined by a central committee, and leaving everything else to be resolved after the great transformation. Neither does it mean that everything about the internal organization of the process needs to be politicized all the time. At certain moments, such as the creation of the World Social Forum, an avoidance of explicitly political questions may be useful for establishing spaces of learning and articulation. Nevertheless, when these kinds of civic spaces expand across continents and civilizations, it becomes increasingly difficult to avoid explicitly political questions of leadership and future institutional orders.

11   After neoliberalism: left versus right projects of leadership in the global crisis

Ingar Solty

Summary

This chapter debates the future possibilities for global order and governance by mapping a political sociology of the current global crisis, and specifically the crisis of neoliberal capitalism. It looks at the political and class projects of the main leadership constellations in the Northern capitalist heartland and how these coalitions are preparing strategies for 'post-neoliberalization' – that is, for the period that will follow the present deep crisis of neoliberal rule and accumulation. The chapter considers the prospects for several sets of long-term ruling strategies (e.g. towards a 'post-neoliberal', 'green capitalist' or 'neo-neoliberal' period) as well as more populist, authoritarian and more barbaric tendencies for the world economic, social and political order. These are explored as they are actually being developed by the different right and left agencies of global leadership, especially in the United States and in Germany.

Introduction: capitalism and political sociology

The question of how political agency is shaped has little to say about global leadership if it merely looks at state and global/inter-state institutions, the affiliated actors and their ideas and is neither combined with nor starts from an understanding of the historically concrete sociological aspect of the question – in short, a theory of capitalist development and capitalist crisis. This shortcoming has been characteristic of many political analysts who have interpreted the electoral defeats of neoliberal parties in the past few years of the crisis of neoliberalism merely in terms of the need for better communicative strategies.[1] Furthermore, bracketing out capitalism results in theory that constructs either the institutions or the ideas underlying specific political leadership projects

---

[1] See, for example, the much-cited and noteworthy study of the Friedrich Ebert Foundation, *Politische Milieus in Deutschland* (Neugebauer 2007).

in a circular fashion. Leaders appear as self-reliant monads floating freely above and independent from social class structures. In other words, the political nature of ideas and actors thus becomes depoliticized, and the various ways are obscured in which these (successful) actors act as 'organic intellectuals' exercising, as Gramsci called it, 'moral and intellectual leadership'.

It is, of course, impossible even to perceive of capitalism without the state. The state has been present in the economic sphere from the beginning, and continues to be so even after primitive accumulation allowed the capitalist mode of production and commodity-equivalent exchange to dominate all other modes of production. The term 'state' must not be confined to the national state but, rather, extends to all forms of statehood that are being developed as coordinating institutions complementing the recent wave of transnationalization in terms of capitalist social relations and the global expansion of capitalism.

In other words, the question of global leadership implies a theory that conceptualizes the state in a wider, enlarged, sense as a 'condensation of a relationship of forces' (Poulantzas 2002; see also Hirsch 2005), while at the same time maintaining its integration with a theory of capitalist development, of the constant *making, unmaking* and *remaking* of class as a result of this dynamism, and of capitalist crisis and its management by and through the state. However, for the question of leadership, one cannot do without a theory of capitalist development and class formation, since the concrete form of the abstract logic of capitalism depends on many indeterminate factors, including the opposition to capitalism, which shapes how capital responds to labour (Silver 2003) and how oppositional classes are being co-opted and absorbed by the ruling class, thus helping to generate what Gramsci understood by hegemony: an alliance of non-antagonistic classes (Anderson 1976).

To sum up, therefore, developing a political sociology capable of bringing together the interrelations of capitalist economic development and the politics of capitalism in terms of hegemonic struggles around the political constitution of capitalism requires Gramsci's hegemony theory and a theory of the relation between social classes and politics (Gill 1990, 1993).[2]

---

[2] The complexity of class formation, political milieus and historically concrete cleavages sometimes inherited from pre-capitalist social formations, such as Protestant social democracy and (cross-class) Catholicism in Germany, can be seen in Marx's historical-political writings, such as *The 18th Brumaire* or *The Class Struggles in France*, and, for example, the processes forming the political subjectivity of the parcel farmers in France in the 1850s. In France, in contrast to much of Europe, landholdings and farms were not enclosed, and, as such, traditional patterns of landholding persisted until after World War I. On this, see Grantham (1980).

Social classes, hegemonic struggles and the
middle-class question

The intersections of class, gender and race – indeed, multiple interpellations of social stratification (including religion, 'post-material' 'cultural' orientations, etc.) – result in ultimately irreducible, non-identical 'individuals'. However, with regard to the question of (global) political leadership, this complexity is much reduced by the fact that political decisions are always made in terms of left and right. Although these decisions are always and necessarily rooted in the grand paradigms of modern political thought, and therefore they are never neutral and always contain political alternatives, the political behaviour of individuals and social groups, which is at the heart of political/sociological analysis, is often characterized by clear social patterns linked to analytical categories of social stratification such as social class. This does not mean, of course, that in capitalist societies the left–right distinction is identical to labour–capital antagonisms. Even during the early stages of capitalism the early forerunners of today's cross-class parties, as in Otto von Bismarck's Prussia in the 1870s, integrated parts of the (working-class) population based on other interpellations such as religion, thus developing trans-class doctrines to deal with the contradictions of capitalism.

It would therefore overstretch the concept of class if one were to assume that its impact could be reduced to the left–right distinction. Nonetheless, with the exception of the United States, for the global North the main issues for hegemonic struggles to define paths out of the current world economic crisis will concern (1) which political force will fill the vacuum left by traditional left parties among the working class clientele, (2) what kind of new political milieus are emerging from this vacuum and (3) how the various class factions of the middle classes, which for a long time provided hegemonic capacities to neoliberalism, are orienting themselves politically towards the future. This is because, in the history of capitalism in the West, hegemonic rule, through moral and intellectual leadership by organic intellectuals (i.e. rule based on consent rather than force), has become more or less the norm. Thus the multiple subjectivities developing (or sometimes failing to develop) upwards from the minimal category of 'class' – itself rooted in the dynamism of capitalism – can be described and analysed in terms of the left and right political coalitions across classes, in which the political orientation of the middle classes often becomes the decisive factor. This is simply because within capitalist societies, for a number of reasons, unlike capital and labour, they are located in what the

Marxist class theorist Erik Olin Wright has termed, subjectively, 'contradictory class locations' (Wright 1978). They are thus, in the long run, in a relationship that is antagonistic neither to capital nor to labour. This means that they are open for different political coalitions of (perceived) common interests that, if successfully generalized, appear as 'common sense' itself (see Anderson 1979 and Solty 2009).

Unfortunately, there is not enough space here to engage in a debate on what constitutes the middle classes. However, with regard to a political sociology of the crisis of neoliberalism and its implications for the future, the essential question seems to be the relationship to the welfare state or, in other words, the public sector. The main economic point of division and distinction appears to be the relationship between, on the one hand, the self-employed in the private sector and (highly specialized) small-scale businesses (often linked via outsourcing to forms of dependence on transnational corporations) and, on the other hand, the public sector employees who, as a result of their dependence on the state and the proximity to social reproduction, have tended to oppose or be more critical of neoliberal reforms.[3]

From neoliberal hegemony to the 'big' crisis

From a regulation theory standpoint, a discussion of the political sociology of the crisis of neoliberalism begins with the question of the nature of this 'crisis'. Here, regulation theorists have distinguished between 'big' crises and 'small' crises. Although small crises do not destabilize the regulatory arrangements that support a particular regime of accumulation, big crises are 'formation crises'. These big crises are characterized by the fact that they originate in one sphere but then spill over into the others. Mostly, the crisis originates in the economic sphere, and then affects or turns out to be also a political and an ideological crisis. However, it is also possible for it to occur the other way round. For the purpose here, which is to outline three possible hegemonic projects and paths of development emerging as a result of the current world economic crisis, it is assumed that the current crisis is, as Stephen Gill has characterized it in his contributions to this volume, an 'organic crisis' (see also Gill 2003a). Such a crisis is so structural and deep that the

---

[3] In Germany this division can be seen in differences between the Green Party and the Free Democrats, both of which are homogeneous middle-class parties. However, although the Green Party is characterized by a fairly high level of unionization, as a result of its anchorage in the public sector (teachers, professors, etc.), the Free Democrats are much more represented in the private sector.

solution, for the lack of a better term, must be called 'post-neoliberalism' (just as much as neoliberalism, for a long time, could be described only as 'post-Fordism'). An essential part of this crisis is the crisis in social reproduction (Bakker and Gill 2003). Further, the economic crisis is accompanied by a political crisis (a representation and legitimacy crisis) and a crisis of (neoliberal) ideology, both of which have increased the degree of force or coercion as means of political rule. This, for example, can be seen both in terms of the forceful realization and management of global capitalism as part of the so-called 'war on terror' and in the erosion of liberal forms of governance and government in the global North, where increasingly authoritarian forms of rule took hold. Indeed, the crisis has assumed the signs of a crisis of civilization – one that is also threatening the extinction of species and the destruction of ecosystems.

Based on these assumptions, the main task for a political sociology of the crisis is to carry out an analysis of the breakdown of the neoliberal coalitions, of the main capitalist states as well as of the neoliberal geopolitical order within the inter-state system. This is, of course, a difficult task to pursue. However, since hegemony is constructed from the bottom up and presupposes the existence of the state and forms of statehood, the original level of analysis must be the nation state. In this regard, I focus on some of the main issues I see at hand in terms of the hegemonic struggles around this crisis in the global North. Although some of the dividing lines and struggles do, in fact, occur in the global South as well, my remarks are restricted to the global North.

Regardless of geographical region, analytical interest lies in the new contradictions of the neoliberal accumulation regime insofar as we can identify how they may involve potentially new combinations of social forces and new historical blocs. Nonetheless, it is important to note that many critical and Marxist theorists have had difficulties accounting for the stability of neoliberalism. Nowhere is this as obvious as in Naomi Klein's erroneous thesis that neoliberalism could not come about through the ballot box (Klein 2008). Instead, even in some countries of the global South, such as in the Peru of Alberto Fujimori, neoliberalism could consistently appeal to the middle classes in ways that allowed for the re-election of neoliberal reformers.[4] Neoliberalism as it actually existed was not the realization of the wildest fantasies of the capitalist class but, rather, the specific historical product of, and a partial

---

[4] There are, of course, very different combinations of force and consent in neoliberalism in Rhineland capitalism compared with that in the Anglo-Saxon world. Margaret Thatcher and Ronald Reagan pursued a much more force-based approach, by slashing union resistance in the UK miners' and US air traffic controllers' strikes, respectively.

reflection of, the complex struggles between dominant and subaltern forces, some of which were absorbed and co-opted into a particular form of hegemony – that of neoliberal capitalism.

At the same time, there exist good reasons not to overstress the hegemonic appeal of neoliberalism. Neoliberal capitalism was, from the beginning, a 'two-thirds' society, inasmuch as it came about as a result of the distributional struggles resulting from the emergence of mass unemployment and the ensuing fiscal crisis of the state. In a sense, the social democratic era of neoliberalism in the global North, from Clinton's election in the United States in 1992 to the European social democratic electoral victories at the end of the 1990s, embodied a recognition of these new moments of 'exclusion', and strove to ameliorate social hardships that had occurred during the conservative era of neoliberalism while sticking to neoliberal economic philosophy (see Nachtwey 2009).

The social democratic era of neoliberal capitalism was characterized by a 'double movement'. On the one hand, it broadened the social base of neoliberal rule. This occurred, quite literally, through the absorption of the political personnel socialized by, and at times some of the protagonists of, the cultural revolution of the 1960s. This co-optation metaphorically beheaded the anti-neoliberal left and marginalized it; and it was clear that a renewed emancipation of the anti-neoliberal left from the co-opted social democratic left would take a very long time, just as much as the emancipation of the Fourth Estate as the proletariat took a good two decades following the hegemonic co-optation of the liberal bourgeois opposition to the feudal/monarchic regimes in the 1848 revolutions in Europe.[5]

At the same time, during the social democratic era of neoliberalism the limited hegemonic appeal of 1980s neoliberalism became even more limited, because the various national attempts to make flexible labour markets – from President Clinton's welfare reform to the German Agenda 2010 – not only led to increasing precariousness on the part of many blue-collar workers, but also could now be felt deeply in the middle classes. Accordingly, although the various theoretical conceptualizations of the 'new' information economy ('knowledge society', 'risk society', etc.) still reflected the notion of the two-thirds society, these moved noticeably further and further into the background as, more and more, the hegemonic appeal of neoliberalism started to vanish and

---

[5] The decision made by the new German Left Party to name itself simply 'die Linke' ('the Left') in 2007 was therefore a very powerful move, challenging the social democratic monopolization of what the left could be under neoliberalism.

different terms, which reflected the middle-class experience, filtered into public discourse and the media.

Regardless of the usefulness or lack thereof of the precariousness (in German *prekariat*) concept, its wider currency could be read as an indicator of an emerging hegemonic crisis of neoliberalism when, increasingly, the experience of the emancipative moments of flexibility began to be replaced by the experience of insecurity and limited freedoms. Thus, it can be argued that the social democratic era of neoliberalism was characterized, first, by a hegemonic generalization of neoliberalism through the absorption of the oppositional forces, and a corresponding weakening of the anti-neoliberal left, and then by an accelerated hegemonic evacuation when the impact of neo-social-democratic labour market reforms began to be felt more and more among the middle classes.

The immediate empirical fallout of the neoliberalization of social democracy was quite obvious. The consequences could be seen in the erosion of the middle classes, the shrinking of the public sector for skilled workers and the expansion of low-wage sectors, especially in countries such as Germany, which, as a result of the lack of a national minimum wage, low strike levels and the dependence of the average wage level on national bargaining coverage, as well as far-reaching employment security (*Kündigungsschutz*), were transformed into low-wage economies in very short periods of time. This all found its empirical reflection in the many studies that showed the growing social inequality within the global North and the rapid return of poverty, especially among single mothers and their children. However, these material developments were accompanied by the spread of a deep-seated sense of social insecurity, often independent of actual income levels, that had to result in political change.

Erosion of social democracy and conservatism and growing right-wing populism

Hegemonic theory is challenged by the fact that these social structural developments did not articulate themselves in an identical fashion, either among individuals or groups, despite the fact that the experiences were the same across countries. Nonetheless, a representation crisis was accelerated during the social democratic era of neoliberalism when it became clear that social democratic parties and conservative/Christian democratic parties alike had little to offer to the respective segments of the population that had been their traditional voters. This even included the United States, in which the Democratic Party had never been a class party in the European sense but, rather, had assumed quasi-social-democratic functions during the New Deal era while remaining to a large degree a classical liberal party. Thus, the trend towards voter abstention, or, to speak in terms of political sociology, the declining integrative potentials of political (cross-class) parties, was characterized by a clear class nature and a growing disenfranchising of the working-class segment of society, as well as of some parts of the eroding and less secure middle classes. This also meant that neoliberal attempts to portray abstention as a reflection not of people's dissatisfaction but, rather, of (passive) consent were doomed to fail.

However, this representation crisis was flanked by the rise of right-wing populism, both in terms of right-wing parties attracting protest votes from the radicalized middle classes and some parts of the alienated working class and in terms of deep-seated authoritarian reactions to the social restructuring under neoliberalism (Bischoff, Dörre and Gauthier 2004). Thus, not only did this right-wing populism form the backbone of any right-wing project, but it also poisoned the political situation in so far as, where it emerged, it shifted the political climate markedly to the right, and was partly responsible for new social democratic campaigns for workfare regimes and the increased flexibility of labour markets throughout the global North. It is absolutely correct to define right-wing populism as a petty bourgeois or (private sector) middle-class movement. The authoritarianism of the achiever ideology (*Leistungsideologie*) characteristic of right-wing populism (secular or religious) resonates among the radicalized middle classes. The middle classes experience capitalist competition in the most economically individualized manner; they feel squeezed between, on the one hand, the bourgeoisie and big business and, on the other, the working class. Many of them, such as members of the scientific and technical intelligentsia, as well as people in lower and middle management, are economically, culturally and socially oriented towards and aspire to the top of society.

Partly in response to their socialization and partly in response to the experience of struggles connected to the need to succeed amid conditions of cut-throat competition, they tend to develop a *habitus*, in Pierre Bourdieu's sense of the term, that seeks to distinguish – or is supposed to distinguish – themselves from the working class 'rabble'. Furthermore, often, and especially during economic crises, they display the particular type of authoritarianism that the Frankfurt School analysed so well (recall the *Studies in Prejudice* and Theodor Adorno's description of the dialectic of authoritarian submission, to the 'market' status quo, and authoritarian aggression, against those who cannot or do not want to keep pace in the market and are denounced as 'unproductive').

Although this lack of solidarity can also be focused towards 'parasitic' élites (financial speculators or politicians who support them), their anger is often – indeed, mostly – directed against groups at the social bottom. The form that this takes varies, but it is typically reflected in 'tax revolts'. Although the underlying sentiment is that those who are not as 'honest' and 'hard-working' should take the brunt of paying for the crisis (through higher taxation or lower social benefits or a combination of both), the targeting normally involves some form of ideological disenfranchisement. The unemployed working classes are targeted as 'lazy bums'. Also common are forms of racism, targeting minorities, asylum seekers, etc. As Chip Berlet and Matthew Lyons (2000) have argued in their classic text on US right-wing populism, such populism uses the 'ideology of the producer', which juxtaposes the 'hard-working', middle (or 'real') America and the objects of authoritarian aggression, whatever they may be.

In short, if right wing populism can be defined as the radicalization of economic liberalism propelled by (middle-class) authoritarianism mobilized during times of crisis, with its corresponding distributional struggles, the radicalized middle classes, in their fear of social decline, will turn the ideology of the producer against those groups that, according to them, should bear the costs of crisis, particularly those who have gained some social and economic protection from the state. Therefore, the aggression of the middle classes' core, such as the small-scale entrepreneurs, is usually directed against the bottom third or half of society, which is portrayed as 'parasitic' and used as a scapegoat. Moreover, it would be wrong to assume that the right-wing populist ideology could not become generalized across many other social strata, including the (unorganized) working class as well: economic position and (objective) class interest are important, but not determining, factors of political behaviour. Therefore, right-wing populism could hold hegemonic sway across some elements of the working class, especially in situations in which no alternative left forces exist or emerge, as a result of the shift towards neoliberalism on the part of traditional social democratic parties and the more or less thorough demise of communist parties throughout Europe since the late 1980s.

It should be noted, therefore, that the struggles to decide post-neoliberal pathways will be characterized by the struggle between two principles: the *right-wing populist achiever ideology*, with its middle-class social base, versus the (mostly working-class and public-sector-based) *social democratic/socialist ideology, focused on the solidarity principle*. The openness of the historic process is underlined by the fact that multiple constellations and social coalitions become thinkable – given that the divide between authoritarianism and cultural libertarianism runs vertical to the divide between horizontal collectivism and individualism, which is characteristic of the relationship of social forces vis-à-vis the economic sphere. Put another way, although the dominance of issues capable of mobilizing authoritarian sentiments among the precarious middle class and the class-unconscious working class – such as foreign threats, high crime rates or racial targets – can lead to the ascent of political right turns and more or less top–middle coalitions, the opposite is also possible if coalitions can be built between the culturally more left-/libertarian-minded middle classes and the collective-solidarity-oriented, but also more authoritarian, lower classes. This is particularly the case if the blocked wage-dependent middle classes, instead of turning against the bottom, form 'counter-élites' (Walter 2006) within 'middle–bottom coalitions' (Brie, Hildebrandt and Meuche-Mäker 2008) as a result of successful left hegemonic politics.

After the big crisis?

Based on what has been said before, it should be clear that the hegemonic crisis of neoliberal capitalism has widened the political vacuum left by traditional cross-class parties. It seems self-evident, therefore, that some force from the left or the right is necessarily going to absorb new political constituencies. Given the crisis of the wider left and the resulting rise of right-wing populist forces in the global North – either as powerful wings within the right-wing parties in two-party-systems, such as the United States, or independent formations – the chance of an upsurge in right-wing populism and strong anti-solidarity tendencies is tangible. Thus, the most pressing question today is how the current world economic crisis is going to unfold in political terms. This question is not only one of academic engagement. Given the political developments and disastrous results of the 'Age of Catastrophe' (Hobsbawm 1994) – fascism and inter-imperial war – the current crisis is a question of intellectual responsibility for the future for critical intellectuals. In a crisis this deep, it becomes impossible to stand on the sidelines of history.

What, therefore, are the implications of the world economic crisis for the hegemonic struggles under neoliberalism and which possible paths of post-neoliberalization within the global North seem likely as future scenarios? Clearly, as this question relates to the future and, although this future may be structured by the power relations and conditions of global capitalism, it is, nonetheless, an open process, any answer to this question can, as such, be no more than speculative. Thus, in what follows, only three general and interacting potential paths are sketched. The main goal here consists purely of developing a sense of the turning point that this current 'big crisis' may mark. I am convinced that the current world economic crisis is not a financial crisis that has spilled into the real economy. In regulation theory terms, it can be described as a 'big crisis' – a formation crisis simultaneously present at the economic, political and ideological levels. However, it is also more than just this, since some of its aspects run so deep that they go beyond a simple formation crisis and increasingly assume the features of a crisis of civilization, in which the basic survival, perhaps, of large parts of the human race is at stake.

These features are not new and have been endemic to neoliberal capitalism for a long time. The destruction of the developmental state, by means of the policies of the Washington Consensus and the emergence of the 'planet of slums' (Davis 2006), have long pedigrees. However, the important part is that the crisis has led both the global South and, in particular, the global North to a turning point, in which many things may be unclear but one thing is absolutely clear: The shape of the new economic, political and ideological order of the world is going to be different from the neoliberalism of the last decade. The sheer vastness of the (fictive) wealth destroyed and the guarantees given by the taxation state, using its political power as a means to stabilize the entitlements of the capitalist class, make a return to the status quo ante impossible.

The problem in conceptualizing the new has to do with the fact that history and the structures of society are always shaped by political agency; and it is particularly in times of historic transition and (hegemonic) crises that agency has the most leeway with regard to the structures. Just as it was true for Fordism (and neoliberalism), the 'owl of Minerva', to use Georg Hegel's famous metaphor from *The Philosophy of Right* (see Knox 1967), begins her flight only when an accumulation regime and a mode of regulation have reached their end and are making way for something new. We are currently observing the process of historical structures in the making, but, until we can be sure what the new regime of accumulation and mode of regulation will look like, we must initially rely on the prefix 'post', which indicates nothing more – but also nothing less – than that a historic social formation has come to an end. Not until this new formation has come to an end will it be possible for its real nature to be be identified.

Thus, it was only with the benefit of hindsight that the nature of the Fordist accumulation regime and mode of regulation could be thoroughly understood (Aglietta 2001; Hirsch and Roth 1986). In the same way, the emergence of a new transnational mode of production and a new way of life, which have been described as neoliberalism for a long time, can be discussed only in terms of the erosion of the old (Candeias 2009). The term used then was 'post-Fordism'; and both this term and the term 'neoliberalism' emerged only long after the crisis of Fordism and long after the main hegemonic struggle between economic democracy and neoliberalism had been determined. The recharged struggles over the use of different periodization terms – 'financial market capitalism', 'high-tech capitalism', 'post-Fordism', 'neoliberalism' – reflect how the crisis allows us to analyse the degree to which neoliberalism actually was hegemonic. The main argument here appears to be between the more economistic 'falling rate of profit' approaches, associated with such as Robert Brenner, and less economistic approaches, such as those of the German materialist state theory and the French regulation school. In all of this, it is important to separate oneself from Keynesian theorists, whose understanding of neoliberalism is that of a simple mode of regulation.

In what I have argued so far, it should have become clear that I follow those definitions that conceptualize neoliberalism as a capitalist social formation based on a computerized, high-tech capitalist mode of production with global value chains that, as a result, have fundamentally shifted the power relations of capital and labour in favour of capital. In this sense, the financialization that has occurred under neoliberalism is just as much a result of a disconnection between productivity increases and real wages – and, as a consequence, over-accumulation tendencies within capitalism – as it is an embodiment of the power shift between capital and labour through the subsumption of labour under finance (Panitch, Albo and Chibber 2011). In other words, it is a question of, in the last instance, the quite objective limits of capital accumulation as well as a question of the reconfiguration of the class struggle and class power realignment.

This means, quite simply, that neoliberalism is not yet over; it has not 'ended'. Merely to locate neoliberalism at the level of regulation would mean missing the irreversible and continued shifts in terms of the mode of production and ways of life that, together, constitute the social formation 'neoliberalism', with its specific forms of value: production, class composition, subjectivity, etc. However, there exist reasons to suggest that neoliberalism, at least as we know it, is *coming* to an end. This has to do with the fact that a return to the status quo ante is plainly impossible. To understand the depth of the hegemonic crisis of neoliberalism it is essential to understand hegemony, but not in its popularized sense – for example, in the way the term is used in much international relations theory. Hegemony is more than just the appeal of certain ideas or the combination of particular actors and interests. Hegemony is based on concrete material interests and the particular ways in which the surplus is appropriated and distributed. It is because the crisis has led to such an enormous destruction of productive capacities and because of the inevitability of fierce distributional struggles that the task at hand is to assess how the main question of the crisis – 'Who pays the bill?' – is going to be answered among the different state/civil society complexes and how it will impact the struggles between the specific social classes that have emerged under neoliberalism (on this question, see Foster and Magdoff 2009). In other words, the societies of the global North, depending on how and if they emerge from this crisis, will be very different.

Here I draw on Michael Brie's informative work (Brie, Hildebrandt and Meuche-Mäker 2008) to outline three possible political projects that might emerge from this crisis: (1) green capitalism, (2) democratic socialism and (3) barbarism. Each of these projects depends on the specific constellations that materialize during this crisis and the steps and measures each would take to recreate stable patterns of accumulation. A central moment in this constellation will be the question of how the middle classes respond to the precariousness of their livelihoods. The defeat of the economic democracy alternative to neoliberalism during the crisis of Fordism was the result of an alliance between the larger half of the middle class and the capitalist class or the top of society, whose privileges were at risk during the 1960s with the advance of left forces within both the global North and the global South. Obviously, there was also a world order dimension, as part of the unequal development of capitalism, which allows us to see the neoliberal counter-revolution also as a means to use financial and trade liberalization as a way of reinstalling US hegemony through a shift from production to financial power complemented by military power (Deppe and Solty 2004).

There is much to be said about the 'green capitalism' or 'green New Deal' alternative. Here, green capitalism is to be understood as a cipher for a path of development out of this crisis whose main characteristic features would be the emergence of a new accumulative base that could help shrink the causes of neoliberal financialization and financial bubbles, as a result of new investment opportunities in the green economy. In other words, therefore, green capitalism is a cipher for a solution for the over-accumulation problem of neoliberal capitalism and situations in which capital and labour surpluses can be brought together profitably again in the real economy. Furthermore, many see green capitalism as a possible alternative to the global economic instabilities and the (US) debt-driven accumulation process. One signal that this potential new phase of capitalism is likely would be if we were to see the use of the state both through tax incentives and other interventions, particularly in stimulus programmes, intended to restructure and 'green' the capitalist economies (of the global North).

In terms of political and global leadership, the emergence of a green capitalist alternative to neoliberalism depends on two major elements. First, it presupposes the existence of leadership capacities among the capitalist and ruling classes at all levels of statehood within global capitalism. Put another way, the institutional frameworks both of world order and of nation states must enable the state to assert itself as the ideal collective capitalist that can realize and defend a relative autonomy from the social forces outside the state institutions and ensure that the long-term interests of the capitalist class can prevail over the short-term interests of the capitalist class. This includes, for example, the relationship between the fiscal conservative/austerity instincts of individual capitalists and state interventionism. Second, inasmuch as the renewal of capitalism has always depended on the productive absorption of oppositional forces such as the labour movement during the New Deal era in the United States, the existence of such oppositional forces must be seen as complementary to, if not a *conditio sine qua non*, of a green capitalist turn. To assume that the capitalist classes wield enough political leverage and ideological foresight to allow the state to actively act for a prolonged period of time against the short-term interests of capital must be doubted. Just as much as with Fordism, as well as neoliberalism, the new phase of capitalism will necessarily be one in which oppositional forces inscribe themselves into the new order, and the outcome is an unintended one (see also, on this question, Chapter 4, by Tim Di Muzio, and Chapter 13, by Stephen Gill).

In terms of the political leadership capacities, it is striking that one of the most prominent proponents of a 'green New Deal', Thomas Friedman, has articulated his complaints about the lack of such capacities in his book wishing that the United States could be 'China for a day' (Friedman 2009). Similarly to David Harvey (2009), who notes that the political constellation within the United States, especially the strength of the capitalist class supported by authoritarian right-wing populism, would prevent the United States from using the power of its financial surplus to enact a green New Deal through heavy state intervention, Friedman thus reflects the lack of political autonomy of the US capitalist state, in particular preventing the state from creating a new accumulative base for capitalism. In other words, at least within the United States, the prospect of a green New Deal seems limited, especially because of the political constellation. The health care debate showed signs of a capitalist class that had 'won itself to death' (Solty 2009).

At the same time, the lack of political leadership capacities is nowhere more striking than in the context of the European Union, where the integration process itself, including the common currency, is at stake. The trend towards beggar-thy-neighbour policies within Europe and the apparent victory of the German conservatives and their austerity politics over their opponents, both in the United States and in Europe (and France in particular), appears to be a sign for such a development. Although it is unclear whether the deep and wide-ranging austerity programmes within the European Union might produce a double-dip recession, it is clear that these policies strangle both consumer and public demand and counteract the effects of the stimulus programmes similarly to the ways in which the fiscal conservatism of the US states counteracted the federal stimulus programme, thus increasing the trend towards a jobless recovery. However, what is more important is that the austerity programmes within Europe foster anti-solidarity tendencies within the global North. This includes the 'Who foots the bill?' question, evident within the European Union – as can be observed in the authoritarian and nationalist scapegoat reactions in the Greek crisis – as well as in the racist reactions, particularly on the part of some of the middle classes, across the global North.

Thus, the US health care debate and the right-wing populist resurgence as part of the Tea Party movement, which is increasingly colonizing the Republican Party, is closely associated with the rise of right-wing coalitions and right-wing populist forces in Europe as a consequence of this crisis. This can be seen, for example, in the rise of a neo-fascist/right-wing populist coalition government in Hungary, or the rise of Geert Wilders' right-wing Populist Party in the Netherlands. At the same time, the trend towards anti-solidarity within the global North is worsened by the fact that, with the exception of Italy, the severe austerity measures and efforts to force greater labour market flexibility in southern Europe have been partially enforced by the IMF and to a lesser degree the European Union, but are being implemented by centre–left governments, such as the social democracies in Spain, Portugal and Greece. Although in Greece and Portugal at least there exist parliamentary left alternatives and alternative patterns of social interpretation, this is not the case in Spain, which is undergoing not only economic distributional struggles but also cultural struggles revolving around the questions of fascism and Catholicism.

The alternative to a failure of utilizing this crisis for a renewal of capitalism and hegemony appears to be an increasing slide into some form of *barbarism*. Again, barbarism should also be understood as a cipher, inasmuch as it means an acceleration of trends already present within neoliberal capitalism. This includes the rise of authoritarian forms of rule as well as the forceful management of the growing contradictions of global capitalism through new imperial endeavours, motivated both by geo-economic and geopolitical considerations and the likely growth of 'blowbacks' and neoliberal 'boomerangs' from the global South. In other words, this development should be understood as a radicalization of the 'new imperialism' that emerged precisely in response to the crises produced by neoliberalism and particularly the attempt of the United States to use force as a means to avoid or deter hegemonic decline. The strengthening of elements of authoritarian capitalism would suggest growing inter-imperial rivalries, especially between the United States and China but possibly also between the United States and a German-led European Union. This scenario would also involve a potential fragmentation of the world market (e.g. through protectionism against German exports in the European Union, and possibly also in the United States, and against Chinese exports, especially in the United States but potentially also in Europe), a growing geo-economic conflict over the world's resources, particularly fossil fuels, and the necessary internal authoritarianism to complement and reinforce such inter-imperial rivalries.

Nonetheless, this historic moment is open, and a third alternative does exist. This can be seen partly in the emergence of the BRIC states (Brazil, Russia, India, China) and their attempts at developing not only growing economic, political and ideological independence from the global North but also social and political alternatives to the status quo. At the same time, these semi-peripheral big players are in ideological struggles with, for example, those states of the Latin American ALBA coalition (the Bolivarian Alliance for the People of Our America), which includes Venezuela and Bolivia, that seems to be moving more or less in the direction of an alternative to capitalism, or what it calls 'twenty-first-century socialism' – a move that is complemented by new regional military alliance structures. Similarly, also in the global North, the crisis of neoliberal hegemony has led not only to a vacuum filled by right-wing populist parties but, in some cases, most notably in Germany, the rise of political forces that, at least nominally, strive to replace capitalism with democratic socialism, understood as an economic system based on different forms of collective ownership.

It is clear that the German situation is an exception throughout the (leading states of the) global North. All the same, it does mean that alternative political projects exist that challenge green capitalist 'alternatives' to neoliberal capitalism. Of course, it might be exactly the emergence and growing strength of such projects, alongside a noticeable new militancy within labour movements across Europe, that fuels the re-establishment of a new form of capitalist hegemony under a green capitalist order. At the same time, the differences between green capitalism and authoritarian capitalism must under no circumstances be downplayed, since, as Karl Marx and Friedrich Engels noted in a clear non-teleological moment in probably their most historico-philosophical text, the *Manifesto of the Communist Party*, the history of class struggle may also end with the 'common demise of the struggling classes' (Marx and Engels 1974 [1848]).

12 Crises, social forces and the future of global governance: implications for progressive strategy

Adam Harmes

Summary

This chapter seeks to contribute to the development of progressive political strategy by examining the role of crises in progressive imaginaries and by comparing the views of liberal and progressive social forces on globalization and global governance. It argues for the need to focus less on the potential for a large-scale crisis to create the political conditions for alternatives to neoliberalism to emerge and, instead, to develop a strategy for promoting significant, but nevertheless incremental, issue-by-issue, change. This, I argue, will help expand the political 'limits of the possible' for progressive forces by incorporating those elements of the liberal camp who are ill at ease with 'disciplinary' neoliberalism and new constitutionalism.

Introduction

This chapter examines the role of crises in progressive imaginaries as well as the views of liberal and progressive social forces on globalization and global governance in order to assess their implications for progressive strategy. In doing so, three main arguments are made. The first is that, in contrast to the Great Depression, which, in the 1930s, brought an end to the nineteenth-century utopian vision of free market globalization, a crisis with similar *political* impact is less likely today. As a result, rather than focusing on the potential for a large-scale crisis to instigate similar large-scale political change, progressives need to develop a more concrete strategy for promoting significant, but nevertheless more incremental and issue-by-issue, change that works to increasingly expand the political limits of the possible. To develop such a strategy, it further argues that progressives need to follow the example of election campaign strategy by identifying other social forces that might support moving in, at least, a more progressive direction as well as a broad method for doing so. In the former case, the second section argues that a potential exists

216

for what I call the classical economic liberals to ally, perhaps in the short term, with progressive social forces. In the latter case, the third section argues that 'progressive multilateralism' is emerging as a broad method for expanding the political limits of the possible and that it may form a basis for common action among progressives and many classical liberals alike.

Neoliberal crises and progressive strategy

Crises occupy a special place in the progressive imaginary; so much so that, at times, they may have become a substitute for political strategy. In part, this is due to the legitimate differences between progressives over grand alternatives; if you do not agree on exactly where you are going, it is hard to agree on a strategy for getting there. It is also, arguably, due to the way that many progressives conceive the role that has been played by crisis in the last large-scale global movement away from a world order based on free market economic globalization. Important to framing this conception is the oft-cited work of Karl Polanyi (1944), and, in particular, his concepts of 'fictitious commodities' and the 'double movement'. Also important is the way that the crisis of the Great Depression has been constructed by some both as a seemingly inevitable outcome of the self-regulating market and as the historical turning point between the two stages of the double movement.

Polanyi's analysis of the nineteenth-century self-regulating market – seen by many as the original period of free market economic globalization – has been widely applied by progressives to the current period of neoliberal globalization. His basic argument is that the self-regulating market is politically unsustainable, owing to its reliance upon an intense commodification of land, labour and capital; that is, market forces seek to subject the natural environment, people and finance fully to the price mechanism and the laws of supply and demand. The problem, according to Polanyi, is that land, labour and capital are 'fictitious commodities' – that is, inputs of production rather than products produced for sale – and this means that prices and the laws of supply and demand cannot be applied to them in quite the same way. As Polanyi notes (ibid.: 76): 'To allow the market mechanism to be the sole director of the fate of human beings and their natural environment, indeed, even the amount and use of purchasing power, would result in the demolition of society.'

To illustrate this point concretely, we can consider a quick example. If the demand for apples were less than the supply, the market would clear when the producer allowed the price of apples to fall, sometimes drastically. For the classical liberals, the same logic could be applied to the factors of production. In the case of labour, if unemployment was high, the solution would be for the price of labour (in the form of wages and benefits) to fall. However, by separating the 'political' from the 'economic', the classical liberals ignored the fact that, unlike apples, people will not sit quietly by as their wages are cut. Instead, they will demand measures of social self-protection from governments. Governments, in turn, are forced to respond to these demands lest they face political instability, ranging from strikes to electoral pressures and, potentially, to violence. Measures of social self-protection, such as minimum wage policies and social welfare programmes, then serve to undermine the 'natural' working of the self-regulating market, by creating 'labour market rigidities' that prevent wages from adjusting to a fall in demand. This, in turn, means that the problem of high unemployment will fail to self-correct automatically as liberals predict. For Polanyi, this is the key reason why the self-regulating market is politically unsustainable. The commodification of land, labour and capital would work fine in theory, but, in reality, natural resources, people and finance simply do not behave in the passive manner predicted by liberal economic theory.

The concept of fictitious commodities explains why the nineteenth-century self-regulating market was politically unsustainable and why Polanyi believed that the growth of measures of social self-protection was inevitable. If this was *why* the self-regulating market inevitably led to the growth of market-inhibiting forms of government intervention, *how* it did so is found in Polanyi's concept of the 'double movement'. The first half of the double movement was the deliberate construction of a self-regulating market based on the commodification of land, labour and capital. The second half of the double movement began when the commodification of land, labour and capital produced dislocations for nature, people and the business and financial communities. These dislocations then led to the rise of counter-movements demanding protection in the form of government intervention. At first, this intervention responded to the business and financial communities and took the form of central banks and the gold standard system of fixed exchange rates, which were created to protect merchants and financiers from the exchange rate volatility that stemmed from the increasing commodification of capital. However, as the economists' 'impossible trinity' concept reminds us, the combination of capital mobility and fixed exchange rates had the effect of locking in a deflationary bias in monetary policy.[1] As a result, rather than eliminating volatility, the gold standard merely served

---

[1] See Glossary on the 'impossible trinity'.

to shift it from the merchants and financiers onto the workers. Currency volatility for the élites was replaced by increasing wage volatility for the poor.

Forced to bear the costs of economic adjustments, workers became increasingly subject to wage volatility and the ups and downs of market forces. 'In human terms,' notes Polanyi (ibid.: 176), 'such a postulate implied for the worker extreme instability of earnings, utter absence of professional standards, abject readiness to be shoved and pushed about indiscriminately, complete dependence on the whims of the market.' Thus, in a similar fashion to the merchants and financiers, counter-movements also developed among workers. They sought democracy and, through it, measures of social self-protection in the form of government intervention to protect wages and to stimulate employment. Eventually, it was these two forms of government intervention – the gold standard and measures to protect wages – that came into conflict during the Great Depression. To defend the gold standard in the face of various economic shocks, governments adopted policies to contract the economy, which, when combined with the 'labour market rigidities' of emerging social programmes and trade unionism, caused a dramatic rise in unemployment. The high unemployment and social hardships that emerged during the 1930s soon became politically unsustainable, and, in addition to discrediting economic liberalism among many élites and the broader public, they led to demands for greater government control over economic forces. In response, governments abandoned the gold standard so as to implement expansionary policies and other measures of social protection. Later they abandoned capital mobility in order to facilitate the growth of welfare nationalist (as well as fascist) forms of state.

Among progressives, Polanyi's concept of 'fictitious commodities' has generated much useful analysis of the contemporary neoliberal period in terms of the dislocations and hardships produced by a re-intensified commodification of land, labour and capital. At the same time, it can be argued that Polanyi's concept of the 'double movement', and the related construction of the Great Depression as both an inevitable outcome of the self-regulating market and the key turning point between the two stages of the double movement, have conditioned the way that many progressives conceive of how a second movement away from the self-regulating market may occur. First, there seems to be an implicit view among many (but clearly not all) progressives that change will come about in a 'revolutionary' way; that is, as a relatively 'big bang' shift away from neoliberalism in a way that corresponds to the second stage of the double movement. Thus, imagining alternatives to neoliberalism often seems to place a greater emphasis on grand alternatives or end states rather than on simply moving policy in a more progressive direction.

Second, there also seems to be an implicit view among many progressives that the second stage of a new double movement will, in a similar fashion to the Great Depression, be initiated by a large-scale crisis (whether financial, environmental or connected to social reproduction) that undermines consent for neoliberalism and creates an opportunity for grand alternatives. Accordingly, since the 1997 Asian (and partially global) financial crisis through the 'battle of Seattle' of 1999, the Enron/corporate scandals of the last two decades and the contemporary 'great recession', many progressives have framed these crises as the potential 'turning point' away from neoliberalism. As far back as 1998, for example, Robert Wade and Frank Veneroso spoke of a 'turning point' when they argued in *New Left Review* that the Asian crisis was producing a backlash against neoliberalism, and that 'this backlash may be the harbinger of the second stage of Karl Polanyi's "double movement"' (Wade and Veneroso 1998: 20). When the second stage of the double movement failed to materialize, many progressives seemed to turn their attention to the next potential crisis. (Some, more accurately, saw that crisis as providing a geopolitical opportunity for US-led neoliberalism to be extended further into the political economies of the east Asian region; see, for example, Gill 1999.)

In this sense, 'waiting for a crisis' seems to have, at times, become an implicit substitute for developing a concrete, step-by-step political strategy for achieving progressive change. Although large-scale crisis (of similar political significance to the Great Depression) and revolutionary change do remain possible, the rest of this section argues that they are probably unlikely, at least within the developed countries, and through them at the broad level of world order and global governance. If this is plausible, what is needed therefore is a concrete strategy for promoting significant, but nonetheless more incremental and issue-by-issue, change that works to increasingly expand the limits of the possible over time. The first reason for believing that a large-scale crisis of similar political significance to the 1930s is unlikely relates to how we define 'crisis'. Although most progressives would agree that the numerous dislocations and hardships produced by a re-intensified commodification of land, labour and capital – such as climate change and rising inequality – constitute environmental and human crises, it is important to recognize that they may not do so in more narrow political terms. Viewed in this more narrow political sense, a crisis is more compressed in time and is often linked to a specific 'event', which produces strongly amplified hardships and thus creates greater openness to more radical alternatives.

It may therefore be useful to distinguish 'crises', which occur sharply in the short term, from those 'dislocations and hardships' that occur in a relatively more incremental and long-term way.

The political significance of this distinction is found in the unpleasant allegory of the boiling frog, in which a frog placed in boiling water is said to jump out, while a frog placed in cool water that is then boiled stays in. The moral is that relatively slow change that takes place over time produces less of a reaction against it. In the contemporary context, this implies that issues such as climate change and ever-rising inequality, while constituting some of the 'big' dislocations of neoliberalism, are unlikely to produce a large-scale political 'crisis' of similar significance to the Great Depression of the 1930s. This is the case in that the hardships they have produced and will produce occur in a somewhat more incremental and long-term manner (rather than as a large-scale, singular event) and in ways unlikely to produce a 'big bang' revolutionary move away from neoliberalism. Instead, dislocations such as climate change and inequality are more likely to produce smaller and more numerous problems (i.e. melting polar ice caps, famines, etc.) that create opportunities for progressive change but on a more issue-specific basis. However, as argued later, an implicit focus on large-scale crisis and revolutionary change among many progressives has led to an insufficient political strategy for responding to these crises, and thus a number of missed opportunities.

Beyond the commodification of land and labour, it would seem that a large-scale financial crisis, at least one with similar political significance to the Great Depression, is also unlikely. Thus, although many progressives have framed the contemporary great recession as such a crisis and as a (yet another) 'turning point', Stephen Gill notes in Chapter 13 that '[d]espite the financial implosion on Wall Street that awakened the G8's somnambulant leaders, no coherent progressive alternative programme has, as yet, commanded sufficient political organization or popular support to mount a serious challenge and pose a credible leadership alternative'. As he notes, this was in part due to a lack of political organization among progressives. It was also arguably due to the fact that, as yet, the great recession has simply not produced the same level of hardship, particularly in the developed countries, as did the Great Depression. Moreover, although the crisis remains ongoing and some worrying possibilities do exist, it seems unlikely that it, or any future financial crisis, could take on the scale of that in the 1930s in a way that would provoke a similar degree of political change.

This is the case because of the seemingly historically unique conditions surrounding the Great Depression and the more strategic orientation of neoliberals today. Specifically, the Great Depression occurred in the 'impossible trinity' context of capital mobility and the gold standard system of fixed exchange rates, which precluded a Keynesian-style monetary stimulus. It also occurred at a time of pre-Keynesian economic knowledge, when even the notion that monetary and fiscal stimulus could be used to fight high unemployment was unknown. As Barry Eichengreen (1996: 6) argues, 'There was scant awareness that defense of the gold standard and the reduction of unemployment might be at odds.' Thus, when Britain finally abandoned the gold standard in 1931, Sidney Webb, a Labour Party MP and co-founder of the London School of Economics, illustrated the underdeveloped state of economic knowledge when he remarked 'Nobody told us we could do that' (cited in Eichengreen and Cairncross 1983: 5).

Therefore, although the contradictions between capital mobility, the gold standard and democracy made a collapse of the gold standard inevitable, the Great Depression itself was not an inevitable outcome of the hardships produced by the self-regulating market. As Krugman (1999: vii) argues:

Most economists, to the extent that they think about the subject at all, regard the Great Depression of the 1930s as a gratuitous, unnecessary tragedy. If only Herbert Hoover hadn't tried to balance the budget in the face of an economic slump; if only the Federal Reserve hadn't defended the gold standard at the expense of the domestic economy; if only officials had rushed cash to threatened banks, and thus calmed the bank panic that developed in 1930–31; then the stock market crash of 1929 would have only led to a garden variety recession soon forgotten.

Today, it seems that even neoliberal decision-makers have learned these lessons and have been strategic enough to implement them. Thus, in the context of the great recession that started in 2008, central banks lowered interest rates significantly and governments of all political stripes implemented fiscal expansions and, when necessary, financial sector bailouts. What this suggests is that a financial crisis with the political significance of the Great Depression is unlikely to be repeated. It further suggests the need for a progressive strategy emphasizing significant but incremental change designed to expand the limits of the possible by challenging the new constitutionalist and disciplinary aspects of neoliberalism. By emphasizing a progressive direction that creates space for a multiplicity of alternatives, rather than a specific end, such a strategy may have a better chance of uniting heterogeneous progressive social forces under a programme of common action.

What might such a progressive strategy look like, though? In an election campaign, political strategy is about determining *which* groups of voters you will get to support you in order to win, and, in broad strokes, *how* you will get them to support you. Central to strategy formulation is the notion of 'political triage', whereby voters are divided into base voters who will always support you, the opposition's base voters who will never support you and swing voters who might support you. For progressive social forces, whose current 'base' is not sufficiently broad to promote change, an immediate task is to identify those social forces that constitute the 'swing vote' of economic globalization: the social forces that might support at least some movement in a progressive direction. As argued below, a key potential here, particularly given the current strength of conservative populism among key segments of the working class, as outlined by Ingar Solty in Chapter 11, are those classical economic liberals rather than neoliberals. To understand this potential, it is necessary to achieve a better theorization of liberal views on globalization and, in particular, the differences between these two types of liberal thought and doctrine.

Theorizing liberal views on globalization

Among progressives, neoliberal social forces are often portrayed as a cohesive group that is uniformly in favour of the free market and globalization. One reason for this portrayal is that, when arguing in favour of free trade and capital mobility and against the arguments of so-called 'anti-globalization' activists, all economic liberals have employed an internationalist discourse emphasizing mutual gains and international peace. The result is that many progressives have viewed all liberals in a binary fashion as their political 'other'. At the same time, this view has been reinforced in the academic literature, which has tended to implicitly conflate the various political and economic strands of liberalism into a coherent and broadly pro-globalization whole. It has done so, in part, by viewing neoliberalism simply as a more recent revival of classical economic liberalism. However, to gain a better understanding of the potential for progressive alternatives it is necessary to disaggregate the different strands of liberalism and identify those aspects of globalization they actually support and why. In doing so, the argument of this section is that neoliberalism differs significantly from the other strands of liberalism, including classical economic liberalism, in that its support for internationalism is based on a different set of normative priorities.

Specifically, in contrast to neoliberalism, the other main strands of liberalism, including liberal internationalism, neoliberal institutionalism and classical economic liberalism, are all broadly internationalist, in that they support free trade and capital mobility as well as the expansion of many international regimes and institutions (Held and McGrew 2002; Helleiner 2002; Steans and Pettiford 2005). In terms of motivations, although each emphasizes different normative priorities, they all favour globalization for its stated ability to promote economic efficiency and mutual gains as well as interdependence, democratization and international peace. However, the same cannot be said for neoliberalism. In contrast to the other liberal strands, neoliberalism supports free trade and capital mobility, but is firmly opposed to the expansion of many international regimes and institutions. This is the case because, rather than emphasizing mutual gains or international peace, the normative priority of neoliberalism is individual freedom and, in particular, freedom from 'progressive' forms of government intervention designed to redistribute wealth and correct market failures.

To explain this opposition to government intervention and support for more laissez-faire markets, James Buchanan (1995: 20) exemplifies the neoliberal view by arguing:

The categorical difference between market and political interaction lies in the continuing presence of an effective exit option in market relationships and in its absence in politics. To the extent that the individual participant in market exchange has available effective alternatives that may be chosen at relatively low cost, any exchange is necessarily voluntary. In its stylized form, the market involves no coercion, no extraction of value from any participant without consent.

In neoliberal theory, therefore, government is viewed as a monopolistic rent-seeker whose intervention in the economy is unlikely to be either benevolent or effective. Thus, as Michael Howlett, Alex Netherton and M. Ramesh (1999: 27) observe, neoliberalism is distinguished by 'the supreme importance attributed to individuals and their freedom; they emphasize individual freedom even more than economic efficiency'. Taken together, this prioritization of individual freedom and more negative view of government lead to two key policy differences between neoliberalism and classical economic liberalism.

The first difference is that, rather than simply being a revival of classical economic liberalism, neoliberalism should be viewed as a much more orthodox version of the free market approach. Compared to classical economic liberalism, James Richardson (2001: 42) argues that 'contemporary neoliberal ideology...seeks to go further: it amounts to an attempt, far more thoroughgoing than its nineteenth-century predecessor, to subordinate the state to the market'. Specifically, in addition to viewing most wealth redistribution as a form of coercion, neoliberals also oppose the correction of many market failures, such as pollution and monopolies. On the one hand, they dispute the existence of many of the market failures identified by classical liberal and Keynesian welfare economics. On the other, they doubt that government intervention can effectively correct market failures, and, even if it could, they believe intervention should still be avoided in the interests of preserving individual freedom. Thus, even though many neoliberals trace their intellectual lineage to Adam Smith, a number of observers have argued that Smith was far less orthodox in his support for free markets (Richardson 2001; Stein 1994).

The second main difference between classical economic liberalism and neoliberalism stems from the latter's attempt to reconcile the desire for a strong state to promote property rights and markets with its more orthodox opposition to progressive policies. Illustrating this view, Barry Weingast (1995: 1) notes:

The fundamental political dilemma of an economic system is this: A government strong enough to protect property rights and enforce contracts is also strong enough to confiscate the wealth of its citizens. Thriving markets require not only the appropriate system of property rights and a law of contracts, but also a secure political foundation that limits the ability of the state to confiscate wealth.

To resolve this dilemma, and in contrast to classical economic liberalism, neoliberal theory places a much greater emphasis on creating 'a secure political foundation' for free markets through the use of constitutional and institutional mechanisms to 'lock in' free market policies – an element of neoliberalism that Gill (1998a) has termed the 'new constitutionalism'. This focus in neoliberalism on locking in free market policies is evident in both the 'constitutional economics' developed by Hayek and Buchanan and the 'market-preserving federalism' (and internationalism) developed by Hayek, Buchanan and Weingast. In the former case, the aim of neoliberal constitutionalism is to limit progressive forms of intervention through the use of legal and juridical mechanisms, such as having balanced budget amendments and protection for property rights included in national bills of rights (Buchanan 1989; Gill 1998a). In addition to these legal/juridical constraints, neoliberals also argue for the locking in of free market policies through the use of 'market-preserving' forms of federalism and internationalism – what international relations scholars call the 'structural power' of capital mobility (Gill and Law 1993). The idea is to create an 'exit option' in the realm of politics whereby individuals and firms can move their assets across borders in a way that forces governments to compete for them by providing the most desirable policies.

Intellectually, this method for limiting government intervention originated with the neoliberal approach to federalism that, in the context of the limits on trade and capital mobility since World War II, sought to create an exit option within the context of individual countries (Harmes 2006). First outlined by Hayek (1960) and Friedman (1962), the neo-liberal approach to federalism includes two broad principles for deter-mining which policy capabilities should be assigned to which levels of government. The first principle is to centralize those policy capabilities that relate to protecting property rights, enforcing contracts and creating markets. Of particular importance here is the belief that subnational governments should not have the ability to limit the right to exit (or enter) their jurisdictions. This ensures a national economy based on internal free trade and capital mobility, and, in turn, that individuals and firms have the ability to move their assets across subnational juris-dictions. The second principle is to decentralize the policy capabilities that neoliberals do not support, including those that relate to wealth redistribution and the correction of many market failures. Ideally, this includes the assignment of redistributive taxing powers to the sub-national level, along with jurisdiction over redistributive social programmes such as public education, health care and social security. It also includes a similar decentralization of regulatory powers related to, for example, environmental and labour policy. In each case, the intent is to prevent national policies on these issues and to confine as many of the undesired tax and regulatory powers as possible to the subnational level, at which they will be constrained by the need of governments to compete for mobile citizens and firms.

Seeking to formalize this approach, Weingast has developed the notion of 'market-preserving federalism', which starts with the standard view that federal systems have two main characteristics: (F1) a hierarchy of governments – that is, at least 'two levels of government rule the same land and people' – each with a delineated scope of authority, so that each level of government is autonomous in its own, well-defined sphere of political authority; and (F2) the autonomy of each government is institutionalized in a manner that makes federalism's restrictions self-enforcing. In addition to these general characteristics, Weingast (1995: 4) argues:

A federal system is market-preserving if it has three additional characteristics: (F3) subnational governments have primary regulatory responsibility over the economy; (F4) a common market is ensured, preventing the lower governments from using their regulatory authority to erect trade barriers against the goods and services from other political units; and (F5) the lower governments face a hard budget constraint, that is, they have neither the ability to print money nor access to unlimited credit. This condition is not met if the central government bails out the lower one whenever the latter faces fiscal problems.

Emphasized in Weingast's version, therefore, is the need to have the private economy, in the form of free trade and capital mobility, operate at a level above that of tax and regulatory capabilities related to wealth redistribution and the correction of market failures. This, he believes, will have the effect of constraining the ability of governments to implement more progressive policies. Moreover, demonstrating the consistency of neoliberal thought in this area is a similar approach to federalism – what he calls 'competitive federalism' – from Buchanan and its adoption by the American Enterprise Institute's Federalism Project. As project director Michael Greve (2000) notes, competitive federalism 'does not seek to empower states; rather, it seeks to discipline governments by forcing them to compete for citizens' business'.

It is this consistency in the neoliberal approach to federalism that brings us to, and helps to explain, the neoliberal case for internationalism. Specifically, whereas classical economic liberals support free trade and international capital mobility for reasons of mutual gains and international peace, neoliberals support them primarily for their ability to promote individual freedom through the creation of an exit option and policy competition. Therefore, whether implemented at the regional or global level, the neoliberal case for internationalism is based on the same logic as that of market-preserving federalism. As Buchanan (1995: 27) argues,

The relationship between federalism, as an organizing principle for political structure, and the freedom of trade across political boundaries must be noted. An inclusive political territory, say, the United States or Western Europe, necessarily places limits on its own ability to interfere politically with its own internal market structure to the extent that this structure is, itself, opened up to the free workings of international trade, including the movement of capital.

Thus, it is apparent that neoliberalism differs significantly from the other strands of liberalism, including classical economic liberalism, in that its support for internationalism is based on a fundamentally different set of normative priorities. Moreover, it is these different priorities that create the potential for a split in the liberal coalition and, thus, an opportunity for progressive social forces. To understand this opportunity, the next section argues that, despite the seeming heterogeneity among progressives, a progressive alternative to neoliberal global governance, in terms of direction rather than in terms of final strategic goals, has begun to emerge, and that it is sufficiently flexible so as to provide a basis for common action, including with some classical liberals.

Theorizing progressive views on globalization

In contrast to liberal social forces, progressive views on globalization are often portrayed as strongly heterogeneous, with divisions seen between, for example, localists, anarchists, social democrats and socialists, between North and South NGOs, between NGOs prioritizing different single-issue agendas and between those who advocate anti-globalization and those who are in favour of more progressive forms of global governance. Testimony to this seeming heterogeneity, as outlined by Teivo Teivainen in Chapter 10, is the 'open space' and anti-hierarchical nature of the World Social Forum and its resulting unwillingness to advocate specific alternatives to neoliberalism or strategies for promoting them.

However, despite this seeming heterogeneity, the argument of this section is that a progressive alternative to neoliberalism, in terms of direction rather than ends, has begun to emerge, and that it is sufficiently flexible as to provide a basis for common action, even with some classical liberals.

At the heart of this progressive alternative is a focus on the mechanisms that neoliberals have employed to create a 'secure political foundation' to 'lock in' free market policies against any 'tyranny of the majority'. Thus, for all the reasons that neoliberals support policy competition, progressives oppose it. Empirically, they agree with neoliberals that policy competition constrains governments in their ability to implement progressive policies. However, normatively, they view policy competition as limiting the ability of governments to levy the taxes they deem necessary for funding redistributive social programmes and to introduce the regulations they believe are required to improve labour, environmental and other social standards. In fact, many progressive social forces decry policy competition for creating a 'race to the bottom' in terms of these programmes and standards (Barlow and Clarke 2001).

Based on this opposition to policy competition, many progressive social forces have opposed the implementation of various trade and investment agreements at both the regional and global levels. The result is that many commentators have described these groups as being inherently 'anti-globalization'. However, it should be apparent that the label 'anti-globalization' is not an accurate term. As Michael Hardt and Antonio Negri (2001: A21) argue, 'Anti-globalization is not an adequate characterization of the protestors... The protestors are indeed united against the present form of capitalist globalization, but the vast majority of them are not against globalizing currents and forces as such; they are not isolationist, separatist or even nationalists.' Thus, rather than being anti-globalization (or anti-regionalization, in the case of NAFTA or the Single European Act – SEA), many labour and social activists are opposed to having the economy, in the form of free trade and capital mobility, operate at a level above that of the tax and regulatory capabilities related to wealth redistribution and the correction of market failures.

Accordingly, progressive social forces have sought to have these tax and regulatory capabilities operate at the same level as capital mobility, in order to limit the constraints imposed by policy competition. However, it is important to note that, in the present context of neoliberal globalization and regionalization, this goal can be realized in two different ways. The first is by 'bringing the economy back down' to the level of national democratic control, through economic nationalism and an end to free trade and capital mobility. The second is by 'bringing democratic control up' to the level of the global or regional economy, through the harmonization of the tax and regulatory policies related to wealth redistribution and the correction of market failures – key components of what has been termed 'social democratic' or 'progressive' multilateralism (Held 2004; Held and McGrew 2002).

In fact, each of these approaches has been advocated by different social forces in both the global protest movement (Green and Griffith 2002) and the European Union (Hooghe and Marks 1997), and it has been the growing shift towards progressive multilateralism that may form the basis for a progressive strategy. Specifically, when faced with policies of economic globalization or regionalization, many progressive social forces initially responded by advocating economic nationalism to bring the economy back down to the level of national democratic control. This was evident in the opposition of unions, social activists and many left of centre political parties to free trade agreements such as the European Common Market, the SEA, NAFTA and the various negotiations that led up to the creation of the WTO. To counter these efforts, economic liberals and neoliberals responded with an internationalist discourse emphasizing mutual gains and peaceful internationalism. However, when free trade and capital mobility became more entrenched, many progressive social forces increasingly shifted from a strategy of economic nationalism to one of progressive multilateralism (Held and McGrew 2002). In other words, because it was proving more difficult to 'bring the economy back down' because of the entrenchment of free trade and capital mobility, many progressives sought to 'bring democratic control up' as an alternative strategy for limiting policy competition. Applied practically, this strategy has involved the promotion of various multilateral agreements (such as the OECD Initiative on

Harmful Tax Competition, the Kyoto Protocol and a variety of 'global' taxes) and side agreements (such as the EU Social Charter and the labour and environmental side accords to NAFTA) designed to upwardly harmonize various taxes, regulations and social standards and thus limit the constraints imposed by policy competition.

Methodologically, this shift in strategy among progressives is difficult to demonstrate, given the sheer number and heterogeneous nature of the different groups within the global protest movement and the national politics of various countries. However, certain proxies do provide some initial evidence. One early example occurred when the British Trades Union Congress (TUC) and Labour Party abandoned their long-standing opposition to the European Community and its more recent extension into the European Union through the SEA. They did so at least partially in response to Jacques Delors' announcement that the SEA would have a social dimension in the form of the Social Charter. The Social Charter was designed to harmonize various labour and social standards in order to prevent the policy competition and 'social dumping' that it was believed would accompany the SEA. Thus, while progressive social forces in Britain retained their key goal of preventing policy competition by having the economy operate at the same level as that of democratic control, they now saw a different way to pursue it. Specifically, rather than 'bringing the economy back down' to the level of national democratic control through economic nationalism, the TUC and the Labour Party began to advocate 'bringing democratic control up' to the level of the regional economy through the Social Charter and broader support for the European Union. As one study notes (Addison and Siebert 1991: 618), 'The enthusiastic reception given to the Charter by trade unions suggests that it will assist them. It is noteworthy, in this connection, that the...TUC...abruptly changed its anti-Community stance in 1988 in response to the advantages it perceived as emanating from the establishment of a Community-wide plinth of social rights.'

At the more 'global' level, another representative example of the shift among progressives has been the publication of various blueprints for a more progressive form of globalization. Among activists, the International Forum on Globalization (IFG), an international coalition of high-profile intellectuals and activists who together claim some of the 'leadership' of the global protest movements, produced one of the most prominent blueprints for the progressive governance of globalization. In 2002 the IFG published a report entitled *Alternatives to Economic Globalization (A Better World Is Possible)*. As the *Financial Times* reported, this document 'set out an alternative agenda calling for new institutions of global governance under a reformed United Nations', and provided 'a sense of what is becoming the unifying theme of an inchoate movement: the creation of democratic institutions of global governance' (Harding 2002). Taken together, these examples provide some initial support for the view that a shift has occurred in the approach of many progressives away from economic nationalism and towards a broad strategy of progressive multilateralism.

Two points are important for understanding the potential of progressive multilateralism as an initial alternative to neoliberalism. First, although many social democrats may regard progressive multilateralism as an end in itself, perhaps in the form of a more globalized form of Keynesianism or embedded liberalism, this need not be the case. Specifically, to the extent that progressive multilateralism seeks to challenge policy competition and thus the 'secure political foundation' of neoliberalism, it is more about expanding the political limits of the possible to a broader range of alternatives than it is about promoting a single and predetermined end. In this sense, progressive multilateralism is an international counterpart to more meaningful democratization at the domestic level, in that it is compatible with a broad range of progressive projects and thus consistent with the democratic aims of the World Social Forum.

Second, many of the specific policies associated with progressive multilateralism can also appeal to the broad internationalism of classical liberals, and, to return to the election campaign metaphor, have already become a key 'wedge issue' dividing classical liberals from neoliberals. As evidence of this potential split, one need only point to the greater support among classical liberals (such as many Democrats in the United States, 'third way' Labour Party supporters in the United Kingdom and those promoting notions of 'global public goods' at the United Nations Development Programme) for policy initiatives such as the Kyoto Protocol, various 'global' taxes and the stronger attempts to re-regulate international finance. To the extent that such policies undermine the disciplinary effects of policy competition, the views of classical liberals stand in stark opposition to those of neoliberals. Illustrating this difference, Roger Bate (2004) of the American Enterprise Institute illustrates the neoliberal view when he argues:

There has been a slow and now accelerating push for global governance, and away from the sovereignty of nation-states... The global governance institutions that pressure groups, bureaucrats and politicians promote include international treaties on numerous issues such as climate change, chemicals, and tobacco. There are also proposals pushed by powerful and respected international bodies for agreements on labour standards, environmental protection, and tax harmonization. These entail an entirely different form of globalization – one that is beginning to have a significant, and deleterious, effect.

Thus, although most classical liberals would clearly not support more radical progressive alternatives, they do provide a potential ally for at least expanding some of the limits of the possible in ways that should enhance the ability of progressives to build support for such alternatives over the longer term.

Conclusion: from global strategy to national tactics

Although a large-scale crisis of similar political significance to the Great Depression is unlikely (in terms of ushering in 'revolutionary' change at the level of world order), crises are nevertheless endemic to neoliberalism and do create opportunities for progressive social forces. However, as Gill has argued earlier in the case of the current great recession, progressives have often missed such opportunities owing to a lack of political organization. Arguably, this is at least partially due to the implicit focus on large-scale crisis and 'revolutionary' change. From this perspective, many progressives (albeit with numerous exceptions) act as if crises are objective events that will automatically create support for alternatives to neoliberalism, rather than as events whose popular understanding is the outcome of subjective framing by competing social forces. Thus, although progressives have strong critiques of the specific neoliberal policies that lead to crises as well as fairly concrete proposals for alternatives, they have failed to develop a sufficiently robust infrastructure for promoting these ideas among national politicians and the broader public.

As Nicola Short highlights in Chapter 2, neoliberal lobby groups, think tanks and political consultants have been adept at promoting their ideas and providing a 'rapid response', thereby framing crises through political marketing techniques such as the quick production of detailed and issue-specific policy briefs, as well as the use of communications 'war rooms' and political advertising. Such an approach – which uses crises to promote issue-by-issue incremental reform through engagement with both the 'traditional politics' of individual countries and global governance – stands in stark contrast to the focus of many within the WSF on grand alternatives, and also to the 'tyranny of structurelessness' outlined by Teivo Teivainen in Chapter 10. Although it is open to question which approach may prevail in the future, progressives may want to consider which approach has prevailed in the past.

13 Organic crisis, global leadership and progressive alternatives

Stephen Gill

Summary

Many global struggles over the future of global leadership and global governance are connected to the question of rights, redistribution and recognition of the dignity and equality of peoples. Indeed, such struggles are grounded in responses to changing conditions of existence constituted, in part, by the crises, contradictions and consequences of the acceleration of both intensive and extensive aspects of global capitalism. This chapter identifies three such processes and contradictions. It argues that political responses to such contradictions on the part of dominant and subaltern forces will shape global development and the making of the emerging world order.

(1) A renewal of what Marx called the original or 'primitive' accumulation of capital, which involves the dispossession of communities and producers of their basic means of subsistence and livelihood.[1]
(2) Increases in the turnover time of capital associated with the greater global scope and intensity of the exploitation of human beings and nature.

I thank Isabella Bakker, Teivo Teivainen, Tim Di Muzio, Adrienne Roberts, Ingar Solty and Kaarlo Metsäranta for their helpful comments.
[1] Such dispossession is long-standing but ongoing; processes of original accumulation have also begun to accelerate since the 1960s. Reflected in the privatization of common resources and lands, public enterprises and public space, it has led to further enclosure of the social commons and the expropriation of the basic means of livelihood, such as water, energy and land. Global resources are increasingly privately owned (e.g. the concentration of ownership and control by oligopolies and monopolies over global food production and distribution; for detailed evidence on different forms of concentration in agribusiness, see Wilkinson 2009, and on the use of contracts and vertical integration by large transnational corporations to control local producers, see UNCTAD 2009). A result is that the provision of basic necessities, such as food and water, is increasingly governed by corporations and market forces, mediated by world market prices.

(3) A profound restructuring of the institutions of and conditions for social reproduction.[2]

These contradictions are related to relatively unprecedented global problems, such as rapid population growth, degradation of the biosphere, climate change, highly developed powers of production and destruction, surveillance and control, and the militarization of space. These constitute some of the 'morbid symptoms' of an increasingly contradictory world order characterized by extreme global inequality and social polarization.[3] Put differently, global struggles are connected to intersecting economic, social, ecological and political crises, which I have referred to as a 'global organic crisis' – a historical situation in which much of the 'old' order seems to have largely exhausted its potentials and in which 'new' forces are still struggling to emerge in a politically coherent manner. In this context, the task of the progressive lefts (in the plural) is to combine politically and seek to construct new constitutions, new governance mechanisms and new policies for attaining social justice, equality, human security, human rights and human development; in short, a new type of world order.

Introduction: capitalism, crisis and leadership

Twenty-first-century political struggles over global leadership and world order will be related to the crises, contradictions and consequences of global capitalism, and, more broadly, by an intensifying global organic crisis.[4] In this crisis, at least so far, the primary mechanisms of governance, particularly in the global South, have been manifested in coercion – rather than by a politics of consent premised on ethical forms of political leadership. In the key neoliberal countries, such as the United States and the United Kingdom, over the past thirty years there has been a notable increase in incarceration rates, and, since 9/11, an intensified use of surveillance of populations (panopticism), justified as being

---

[2] Social reproduction refers to the biological reproduction of the species (and, indeed, its ecological framework) and the ongoing reproduction of the commodity of labour power. Social reproduction involves many institutions, processes and social relations associated with the creation and maintenance of communities, upon which, indeed, all production and exchange ultimately rests. For an extensive review of the concept, see Bakker (2007); see also Glossary.

[3] The scale of these processes accelerated massively after 1950; virtually all human-induced ecological change has occurred since then, with uneven regional effects.

[4] The term 'world order' is used in an analytical rather than a normative sense, to capture the actual nature of world orders. It refers to the configurations of power and authority, relations between rulers and ruled, leaders and led, and the problématiques of war and peace, and of socio-economic development in particular epochs.

necessary because of a state of emergency. During this period there has been a fusion of the growing public and private security apparatuses so as to secure private property and sustain public order, not least to police the perimeters of the gated communities of the affluent. There is also growing intolerance and criminalization of displays of dissent by neoliberal leaderships, most obviously reflected in the paramilitary policing strategies and mass arrests that have occurred at recent WTO and IMF meetings or at G8 and G20 summits, most recently in 'lockdown' Toronto in June 2010, when emergency law was invoked and the security bill topped C$1 billion (for detailed accounts of some of these practices, see Gill 2000, 2003a, 2003b, 2003c).

Undeniably, we find ourselves in a specific conjuncture in which a now global capitalism has experienced its deepest crisis of accumulation since the Great Depression of the 1930s. Paradoxically, whereas the 1930s saw the breakdown of liberal capitalism and innumerable defaults on sovereign debts, as well as the rise of fascism and Nazism, and the Stalinist consolidation of the Soviet alternative, today disciplinary neoliberalism and capitalist globalization remain powerful, and apparently supreme, on the stage of world history. Despite the financial implosion on Wall Street that awakened the G8's somnambulant political leaders, no coherent progressive alternative programme has, as yet, commanded sufficient political organization or popular support to mount a serious challenge and pose a credible leadership alternative. Indeed, one of the themes of this volume is how, over the last decade, not only has disciplinary neoliberalism been extended but also it has been deepened, through crises and the declaration of de facto states of emergency, particularly since 9/11.

Nevertheless, it is very important that progressive forces (by which I mean the multiple, non-authoritarian lefts in both the global North and the global South) emphasize that the economic/emergency measures of the G8 and G20 governments and central banks from 2007 to 2010 occurred only when vital financial interests were jeopardized or, indeed, when the capitalist market system as a whole was threatened – not in order to deal with urgent social needs, the sustainability of the biosphere or the plight of poor countries in the wake of financial and natural disasters.

In this context, progressive forces need to demystify the mechanisms of global finance and come up with credible measures for its control and regulation. In fact, the evidence seems to be that financial crises have far more negative effects on overall economic activity than those caused mainly by shortfalls in aggregate demand (or what radical economists refer to as crises of over-accumulation/over-production and/or under-consumption). The liberalization of finance worldwide since the early 1980s has been accompanied by financial crises of increasing severity (Brittan 2009, citing IMF 2009):

There is widespread agreement [among economists] that the damage done in a recession associated with a financial crisis tends to be twice as severe as one that is not. More important is the finding that much of the loss of output in a severe recession is permanent and that the economy never gets back to its old trend line.

The IMF now estimates that recessions caused by financial crises cut long-term output growth potential by some 10 per cent, as activity drops below its previous medium-term trend. This scenario affects about two-thirds of global activity, since in 2009 the IMF estimated that countries with severe banking crises accounted for roughly $40,000 billion ($40 trillion) of world GDP. World total output was $60,109 billion ($60 trillion) at market exchange rates in 2008. Thus, the financial crisis has now permanently lowered global GDP by approximately $4 trillion each year; if we project forward, in each future year the global output forgone will be roughly equal to annual Chinese GDP, which in 2008 was $4.327 trillion. Therefore, if we imagine a world with economic activity reduced by an amount equivalent to that produced by over 1 billion Chinese, including its exports to supply global consumer markets, we can get some idea of the losses of output involved (IMF 2008: 241, tab. A1, 2009).

However, this macroeconomic view of the crisis and, indeed, the G8/G20 bailout overlooks several very important points. First, it does not question the qualitative aspects of output measured by GDP figures. Much of what is produced, including that in China, feeds patterns of consumerism and waste and is linked to the irrational use of non-renewable resources; such output may not be socially desirable or connected to the health of the population as a whole, or to the sustainability of ecological structures that support life itself. Second, opportunity costs need not simply be measured in terms of output forgone, but also in terms of the alternative uses of public expenditure. Much of the massive bailout and stabilization expenditures – involving perhaps as much as $17 trillion in low-cost loans, subsidies or outright nationalizations, mainly of financial corporations – could have been used to improve health, education, public transport, energy efficiency and the environment. This would also have served to maintain employment levels and allowed resources to be used for redistribution with a qualitative component (e.g. to provide healthier nutrition and basic medical care in the global South).

It is also worth mentioning that many problems in the debt crises of the 1980s were caused by reckless lending by the very commercial banks at the heart of the recent meltdown in the global financial markets. Then, as now, corporate losses were socialized. The Third World debt crises of the 1980s were used to initiate or to deepen neoliberal reforms and restructuring by the US Treasury, the World Bank and the IMF. Indeed, debt cancellations had never been on offer from the creditor governments to the global South – at least, until the global outcry following the Haiti earthquake in early 2010 appeared to force the hand of the G8. The way such crisis situations were conceptualized by the neoliberals is reflected in the following quotation from one of its patron saints. In 1982 Milton Friedman wrote (cited in Klein 2008: 140; and quoted in Haar 2011: 13):

Only a crisis – actual or perceived – produces real change. When that crisis occurs, the actions that are taken depend on the ideas that are lying around. That, I believe, is our basic function: to develop alternatives to existing policies, to keep them alive and available until the politically impossible becomes politically inevitable.

How, then, can the lefts, for example in situations of crisis, make what is currently considered politically impossible – progressive global governance – more politically plausible, if not inevitable? In my view, this requires sober analysis of global realities, their contradictions and potentials and the creative fostering of forms of political organization that can overcome sectarianism (and the regressive myth of vanguard leadership) and credible policies that win broad popular support and, ultimately, state power. As Gramsci put it during the 1930s, framing the basic problem facing the creation of 'The modern prince': 'The crisis consists precisely in the fact that the old is dying and the new cannot be born; in this interregnum a great variety of morbid symptoms appear' (Hoare and Nowell-Smith 1971: 276). Today, while it is doubtful whether the present period constitutes an interregnum between two different types of world order, it might be more accurate to characterize the current moment in world order as reflecting an *impasse* shaped by the degenerative structures and processes associated with disciplinary neoliberalism, with no clear or generalized progressive solution yet in sight, and, indeed, with the potential for authoritarianism to prevail in the context of intensifying global competition for resources and food and the emerging politics of austerity. However, one of the key stumbling blocks to a solution is the way that most of the prevailing responses to the crisis are being couched in terms of an underlying liberal assumption – one that is, sadly, shared by many on the left – that material progress can continue regardless of ecological and environmental constraints; for example, none of the G20 political leaders have acknowledged the constraints of peak oil (see Chapter 4, by Tim Di Muzio; see also Mulligan 2010).

Morbid symptoms and original accumulation

A swift review of our present predicament reveals many 'morbid symptoms' that are truly global and experienced unequally across classes and nations in the North and South. The recent catastrophic experiences in Haiti – the effects of hurricanes and a devastating earthquake against the backdrop of decades of debt imperialism and foreign intervention – underline the vast disparities in life chances in the western hemisphere. We live in a world characterized by the intensified exploitation of human beings and nature by capital, whose power is continuing to be concentrated in ever fewer giant corporations. Nonetheless, myriad forms of contestation are emerging to rethink lifestyles and sustainability and to challenge the hyper-consumerism, mass advertising, ecological myopia and waste associated with the affluent development patterns of market civilization. Deadlock over climate change and food and health security is linked to political struggles over growing corporate domination and private control of world agriculture, food production and distribution, life sciences, medicine and the pharmaceutical industries (on the relation between the crisis of accumulation and the deterioration in global public health, see Benatar, Gill and Bakker 2011). This situation involves global inequality in patterns of malnutrition: 25 per cent of the world is obese or overweight; 25 per cent is starving (Albritton 2009).[5]

Related to the above is the accelerated privatization of water, land, natural resources and public goods such as education and health systems, at the very moment when public opinion supports universal access to public education and, especially, to health care.[6] The global

---

[5] Poor nutrition impairs mental development, particularly for the young, and weakens the immune system. Some 70 per cent of those living in absolute poverty globally are women; more than 60 per cent of those suffering malnutrition are women, living mainly in the Third World.

[6] For example, a 2009 survey carried out by the Employee Benefit Research Institute (EBRI) showed very strong popular support for public health insurance systems in the United States, with only 14 per cent of the population opposed. EBRI is a conservative organization funded by big US corporations, including AT&T, Bank of America, Boeing, General Dynamics, General Mills, IBM, JPMorgan Chase, Morgan Stanley, Northrop Grumman and Wal-Mart, and the large private insurers Blue Cross, Blue Shield, CIGNA, Hartford, Kaiser Permanente, Massachusetts Mutual, Metropolitan Life, Union Labor Life and UnitedHealth. See www.ebri.org/publications/ib/index.cfm?fa=ibDisp&content_id=4293.

organic crisis is exacerbated by these new enclosures and the expropriation of the social commons. Indeed, in an earlier work co-authored with Isabella Bakker, I note that original accumulation is reflected not only in the privatization of state assets, a trend that increased massively throughout the 1990s, but also in the 'privatization of parts of the state form itself'. Both the 'privatization of previously socialized institutions associated with provisioning for social reproduction' and the 'alienation or enclosure of common social property', we argue, can be seen as 'part of a new global enclosure movement'. We note that 'these changes tend to grant more power to capital, while simultaneously undermining socialized forms of collective provisioning and human security' (Bakker and Gill 2003: 18–19).

Such dispossession is paralleled by the wholesale defunding of the development potentials of many of the poorest countries in the world – as well as a number in the richer North – as they struggle to pay their accumulated debts, typically to the very foreign bankers who made the reckless, highly leveraged and risky investments, largely with other people's money, that were central features of the global financial meltdown of 2008–10. These bankers and associated 'experts' have subsequently preserved the so-called financial innovations, such as complex and risky derivatives that were at the heart of the crash, as well as more or less preserving the very systems of regulation that amplified the financial meltdown in the United States and Europe.[7]

The policy responses to debt and fiscal crises typically demanded by the major players in the financial markets (private bankers and other investors in government bonds and notes) include higher interest rates ('coupons') on new bond issues; fiscal austerity measures (e.g. regressive tax increases, cuts in public sector wages, expenditure reductions in public services, reductions in public pensions) and, to raise extra revenue, the privatization of public assets and lands, thus enlarging the new enclosures and shrinking the social commons. These measures in effect dispossess the majority in order to socialize the losses of the large financial and automobile firms (and protect the jobs of their workers and suppliers).

Thus, it is not only in the Third World that we find the general dispossession of populations by capital in ways that Marx characterized as original accumulation – a process he associated with earlier forms of

---

[7] See Chapter 1, by Stephen Gill, and Chapter 3, by Claire Cutler, on how such 'experts' were able to cast the debate after the crash in terms of better prudential management of financial capitalism, avoiding questions of its legitimacy and social efficiency.

colonization. Indeed, the scale of such dispossession is proportionately much greater in the Third World. It has been estimated that many of the poorest countries, such as Haiti, pay up to 20 per cent of their annual fiscal revenues in foreign debt servicing, often in the repayment of debts whose principal has already been repaid several times over, and in many cases substantial parts of the original loans may have been siphoned off to fill the coffers of the powerful in offshore bank accounts. These 'public' debt obligations are overseen by consortiums of private banks and public institutions such as the IMF and World Bank, along with the governments of wealthier countries. In the case of Haiti, for example, many of these debts were incurred by the notorious Duvalier regime, a veritable kleptocracy of thugs and gangsters that terrorized the population for decades, with support from the United States and its allies justified on the grounds that the Duvaliers were on the 'right' side of the Cold War struggle.[8]

The broader point is that this exploitation of much of the global South has come with huge opportunity costs of development possibilities forgone. The trillions of dollars paid by the global South for the debt servicing since at least the early 1980s has come at the expense of social programmes that affect most of the population, most of all poor women and children, who are deprived of adequate food, education and primary health care, including reproductive health care, that they otherwise might receive. Recurring financial and debt crises, with their devastating social and economic effects, are not new in the global South, even though, until recently, they have been largely avoided in much of the global North.

Thus, the present global situation involves far more than a crisis of financial markets. Its resolution therefore cannot simply involve macro-economic stabilization. Long before the G20 summit in Toronto in June 2010 announced an era of fiscal austerity in order to pay for the massive bailouts, many governments had already begun to indicate that they would seek to download the burden of payment on the backs of the unprotected and least represented working people, with wage cuts, especially for public sector employees, reductions in social benefits and health expenditures, and the privatization of education and public assets and lands: a return to fiscal and social austerity.

---

[8] The Duvaliers ruled Haiti from 1957 until 1986. 'Papa Doc' came to power using his private militia, the Tontons Macoutes. On his death, 'Baby Doc', his nineteen-year-old son, was named president-for-life. The Duvaliers plundered billions of dollars from the people of the poorest nation in the western hemisphere, spiriting much of it away in offshore (e.g. Swiss) banks. See also Di Muzio (2008).

These measures – unless effectively opposed by workers and unions (and, indeed, some economists and elements of capital concerned at the prospect of a global depression) – will confiscate workers' bargaining, pension and other rights, erode public goods and privatize the social commons. Across Europe there have been demonstrations and strikes opposing public sector cuts; the mass demonstrations in Egypt were preceded by extensive organized resistance from workers; in the United States in February 2011, in the state of Wisconsin, the ruling Republicans sought to eliminate collective bargaining rights and reduce pensions (though, as elsewhere, this attempt was met with strong resistance and mass protests from public sector unionized workers, in a confrontation that is widely seen as being of national significance). The resemblance to the very types of ongoing surplus extraction premised on the prioritization of debt servicing that have characterized Third World development for much of the past three decades is, therefore, no coincidence. The debt crisis and its political ramifications are as a result becoming global.

Neoliberal strategy on this question seems relatively consistent across the main ruling parties of the OECD, and was reflected in a speech by former IMF chief Dominique Strauss-Kahn.[9] He predicted that public debt in the OECD nations would rise by about 35 per cent on average, to the equivalent of about 110 per cent of GDP, by 2014, and thus, 'for the next decade or two, cyclical upswings should be used to reduce public debt, rather than finance expenditure increases or tax cuts' (emphasis added). Although his speech was disrupted by Cambridge University protesters with a banner that read 'The IMF is part of the problem, not the solution', Strauss-Kahn made it clear that the IMF has a solution: the huge bailouts should be paid for by ten to twenty years of fiscal austerity, so as to guarantee holders of government bonds that they will continue to receive their interest payments in full and on time (*Financial Times* 2010b).

Indeed, the IMF's stance on fiscal austerity is premised on the emergence of legally and politically 'independent' central banks since the early 1980s – a key feature of new constitutionalism. In 2008 this gave central banks substantial latitude to massively bail out and socialize the losses of private banking interests (as 'lender of last resort'). Although central banks are independent of governments (and insulated from the influence of broader political forces), their governors are drawn largely

---

[9] DSK, as he is known to the media, resigned from his IMF position on 19 May 2011. He had been arrested and jailed on charges of sexual assault in New York earlier that week. Up to that point DSK had been the leading Socialist Party candidate for the French presidency.

from private financial interests – not from trade unions or the multitudes of very able progressive political economists. This pattern of representation allows capital to dominate economic policy and provides further opportunities for neoliberal forces to deepen disciplinary neoliberalism, and 'lock in' deeper new constitutionalist measures. Perhaps the clearest example of this is provided by the European Union, where in 2010–11 member states sought to shore up the euro system, accelerate the competitiveness agenda of the large corporations and make other neoliberal reforms to centralize inter-state economic power in the unelected European Commission – all of which was presented as an apparently technocratic and apolitical 'economic governance' framework. One entirely new aspect of the economic governance initiative is intended to redress 'macroeconomic imbalances between member states'. It will confer the right on the European Union to make key decisions on fundamentally important questions such as wage levels and social services budgets for member states, significantly deepening the new constitutionalist measures that originated in the Maastricht agreement of 1992. At that time I noted how the emerging framework of European economic governance was characterized by the 'construction of legal or constitutional devices to remove or insulate substantially the new economic institutions from public scrutiny or democratic accountability' (Gill 1992: 165). Reflecting the lack of significant public awareness of the changes at issue, European Commission president José Barroso, in a speech at the European University Institute in June 2010, described the new measures as 'a silent revolution in terms of stronger economic governance by small steps'.[10] One expert claimed at the time that the effects, if fully adopted, would 'have the regulatory effect on fiscal policy comparable to the effect on security policy of the nuclear bomb'.[11]

Nonetheless, despite the recent recovery in stock market prices and output, unemployment is still high and rising in much of the world, and much higher than official statistics suggest (although it is very unevenly distributed across countries); world hunger is growing; and serious social dislocations have already emerged, not only in the global South but also increasingly in various locations throughout the North, not least as a result of further cuts in public provisions, health care and wages (recent examples in Europe are Greece, Spain, Ireland and Romania, and in an extreme form in Britain, which is intending to cut 500,000 public sector

[10] Speech by José Manuel Barroso at the European University Institute, Florence, 18 June 2010; cited by Kenneth Haar (2011: 3).
[11] Professor Peder Nedergaard, quoted in *Politiken*, 7 September 2010; cited by Haar (2011: 3).

jobs, 350,000 of which are held by women). These cuts tend to further depress economic activity by lowering the multiplier effects of government expenditures and constraining aggregate demand, while undercutting the tax base, as people have less income to spend. Indeed, this type of fiscal strategy runs the risk of stagnation, since creating pools of money for future bailouts may radically reduce purchasing power in the economy. Thus, battles over 'macroeconomic imbalances' and future fiscal stringencies to pay for the gigantic bailouts can be anticipated to generate potent political struggles. Up to now the code word for these battles has been 'exit strategies' – again, a term that implies a technical, apolitical exercise rather than one that is deeply political and involves the distribution and use of immense economic resources.

Nevertheless, following the 'near-death experience' of global capitalism as markets crashed, the globalizing élites who lead neoliberal global capitalism and who congregate annually at the World Economic Forum in Davos (and in the more secretive Trilateral Commission) have begun to regain their political self-confidence and to focus on the reform of global governance.[12] At the Davos 2010 conference an initiative was launched to 'rethink, redesign and rebuild' the world 'after a crisis that has shaken faith in many of its core institutions and ideas' (*Financial Times* 2010a). This does not mean that the globalizing élites are united: they seek out a minimal consensus on governing that can permit the existing social and class relations to be sustained. This could mean some concessions where the strength of political opposition demands it, as well as some weaning of the financial world away from its deep addiction to making risky investments with other people's life savings.[13] However,

---

[12] Davos and the Trilateral Commission now include business, political and civil society leaders from old and new poles of capital accumulation alike, and incorporate many of the global plutocracy of billionaires. The Trilateral Commission has members from Mexico, eastern Europe, South Korea, Australia, New Zealand, the Association of South-East Asian Nation countries, China and India. See www.trilateral.org/memb. htm (accessed 11 April 2010).

[13] Following the crash of the 1930s, banks were largely required to maintain reserve requirements at ratios of approximately 1:10 or 1:12 as measures of prudence (the size of the capital base relative to the loans issued). However, regulations introduced mainly during the administration of Bill Clinton allowed 'financial innovation' and massive leverage previously prohibited, resulting in financial firms borrowing against their capital base at a ratio of 1:30, or even greater. We now know that systemic risk (once thought by the IMF and US leaders to have been reduced) was actually greatly amplified, by a combination of explosive growth in derivatives and cheap credit (see Chapter 3, by Claire Cutler, for details). The absence of effective regulation since the crash is now prompting fears of a second financial meltdown, as excess savings from China, Japan and Germany seek higher yield overseas. 'With [the] Federal Reserve... keeping policy interest rates at rock bottom, investors are being driven into riskier assets such as junk bonds and leveraged loans' (Plender 2011).

this structure is unlikely to be redesigned and rebuilt, as the world's
biggest players (and speculators) in the global financial markets are not
just banks but also pension funds, insurers and hedge funds, which
compete to increase their post-tax rate of return, ensure fund growth
and attract more customers/savers, and these firms demand regulations
that allow them to use leverage in order to remain competitive. This
structure is the one defended by the bulk of the globalizing élites of
Davos. If they remain in control of policy, the best that can therefore be
expected are marginal reforms.[14] However, as the June 2010 G8/G20
meetings in 'lockdown' Toronto suggest, global agreement on these
issues has so far proved impossible to achieve, though there were signs
of a consensus in favour of the implementation of austerity programmes,
particularly in the European Union.[15]

Green capitalism?

Several chapters in this book – particularly those by Tim Di Muzio,
Richard Falk and Ingar Solty – have raised the issue of the economic and
ecological sustainability of fossil-fuel-intensive capitalism, directly or
indirectly posing the question: what will constitute the future relationship between capital and nature? Indeed, the question of 'green
capitalism' was increasingly raised before the crash of 2008, in effect
shifting the terrain of the debate in ruling circles away from President
George H. Bush's earlier intransigent defence of market civilization and
American-style lifestyles. That position seems to be echoed publicly only
in the stance of the US Tea Party, which defends drilling for oil almost
anywhere regardless of the environmental impact, and stands for the civil
right of Americans to continue driving huge sports utility vehicles, to live
in mcmansions and to otherwise continue with their energy-intensive
way of life in spite of the ecological and health consequences of their
actions. Nevertheless, the financial and economic crash has slowed down

[14] For example, such reforms could include some global coordination of macroeconomic
policies and in systems of regulation, such as separating banks from hedge funds,
introducing quantitative controls on excessive leverage, enforcing more transparency
on bank balance sheets and clamping down on the use of derivatives and other exotic
financial instruments to camouflage profits, losses and levels and forms of risk.
[15] In a sign of the times, Canadian paramilitary police patrolled a 3-metre-high, 3.5-
kilometre-long concrete and metal fence enclosing the G20 summit in downtown
Toronto. The nearby subways, railway station, banks and CN Tower were all closed.
Despite preaching fiscal austerity, the federal government spent over C$1 billion on the
summit, 90 per cent of which was for security, including the purchase of sound cannons.
Almost 1,000 people, even including bystanders, were detained in the largest mass
arrests in Canadian history.

rates of global energy consumption and pollution, allowing a breathing space for serious reconsideration of the green capitalist option.

Therefore, assuming that some political consensus is possible following the crash, does green capitalism offer the possibility for a revitalized neoliberal hegemony to co-opt those forces of political opposition that do not oppose capitalism as a system per se – but that remain deeply concerned at the narrow materialism and ecological myopia of hyper-consumerist forms of capitalism? That many elements of society wish to see the 'greening of development' and, indeed, the rise of 'green' consciousness is an optimistic sign for world society. However, the question is not only whether 'green capitalism' is a meaningful political option for dominant forces but, more fundamentally, whether it can offer a meaningful solution to economic and ecological problems. By contrast, what would a progressive stance look like on the ecological question? These are big issues for the future, and here only a few brief observations must suffice.

'Green capitalism' or a 'green New Deal' as a potential hegemonic strategy would involve a compromise not only between dominant and subaltern political forces but also between those elements of capital that profit and gain competitive advantage from green technologies and production and those placed at a disadvantage (e.g. transportation, packaging, oil and heavy industries, much of industrialized agribusiness). Is that consensus possible? Although it clearly remains elusive, it has been variously addressed at Davos, the Trilateral Commission and the Clinton Global Initiative, and smaller groups such as the Elders Project.[16] All these initiatives seek to initiate and direct strategic concepts of global leadership that are largely consistent with the prevailing global order, albeit with different degrees of emphasis on questions of redistribution and human rights. Of these, CGI is particularly keen on a 'greener capitalism' that it sees as both environmentally friendly and as extending opportunities for capital accumulation.[17] Its approach is an extension of the market-related solutions (e.g. carbon

---

[16] The latter involves Kofi Annan, Fernando H. Cardoso, Jimmy Carter, Mary Robinson, Desmond Tutu, Nelson Mandela, Aung San Suu Kyi, Richard Branson and Peter Gabriel. This as yet modest initiative seeks to provide a more ethical and legitimate face for questions of leadership and global capitalism. See www.theelders.org.

[17] President Obama's Secretary of State, Hillary Clinton, was the first female board member of Wal-Mart when her husband Bill was governor of Arkansas, where Wal-Mart has its headquarters. Wal-Mart 'partnered' with CGI to explore ways to use its purchasing power to lower prices on 'environmentally friendly' technologies and to create new markets while reducing US dependence on foreign oil. See Environmental News Network (2007). Wal-Mart, the world's largest retailer, has no unions, and much of its merchandise is produced in China.

emissions trading and other related regulatory measures associated with the Kyoto Protocol) that have characterized global accords; however, such measures have thus far proved to be ineffective in addressing climate change.

Of course, it is desirable for capital to be constrained from the completely reckless exploitation of global resources and forced to use energy more efficiently. However, 'green capitalism' seems compatible with prevailing forms of growth, even if reconciled with somewhat lower levels of fossil fuels and chemical fertilisers allied to the promotion of more renewable sources of energy. It can also go with the wider use of genetically modified seeds and new technologies of control over life forms, such as bigger feedlots and the expanded use of hormones for beef, pork and poultry production – allowing agribusiness to be more 'energy-efficient' and reap economies of scale and to increase the turnover time of agrarian capital (cattle are fattened much more quickly). This is all to feed the meat-based diets of affluent consumers. Nevertheless, two-thirds of Americans are obese or overweight, mainly as a result of eating processed foods that contain additives, sugar and salt. Mexico is second only to the United States in obesity rates and in the per capita consumption of soft drinks. This over-consumption of unhealthy foods has been linked to all manner of diseases and chronic conditions, such as type 2 diabetes, which exact their toll on hard-pressed public health systems (Albritton 2009: 106–7).

On the other hand, many of the current problems of global starvation are linked to the diversion of food production away from food grains to massively subsidized biofuels.[18] Biofuels have contributed to the colossal rise in world food prices: many of the world's poor cannot afford to buy food. Indeed, malnutrition is greatly exacerbated in situations of economic crisis; in 2008, for example, the G8 gave $5 billion to the UN World Food Programme in an effort to avert a worsening of the food crisis; in 2009 these sums were cut and food aid reached its lowest level in twenty years. This was despite the fact that food prices, already at record levels in 2008, were, in many parts of the world, even higher in 2009–11. The longer-term trend is even more alarming, and, in the absence of massive economic redistribution and a transformation of the conditions of livelihood for the poor, it is unlikely to be significantly

---

[18] US ethanol production rose rapidly after 2001 and is projected to increase massively; by 2008 approximately 33 per cent of all US corn production went to ethanol production, receiving an astonishing $7.14 in government subsidies for the energy equivalent of one gallon of gasoline. The United States tried to make the World Bank suppress a report that indicated that biofuels accounted for as much as 75 per cent of the global rise in food prices. The report was leaked to the press in July 2008 (Albritton 2009: 152).

reversed by 'green capitalism' (United Nations World Food Programme [UNWFP] 2009: emphasis added):

[From 1995] [t]he number of chronically hungry in developing countries started to increase at a rate of almost four million per year. By 2001–2003, the total number of undernourished people worldwide had risen to 854 million and the latest figure is 1.02 billion. Today, *almost one person in six does not get enough food to be healthy and lead an active life, making hunger and malnutrition the number one risk to health worldwide* – greater than AIDS, malaria and tuberculosis combined.

Returning to the question of energy production, it is often argued that biofuels – like nuclear power – are less polluting, 'greener' and more 'sustainable' than fossil fuels. However, evidence indicates that corn, the main crop that is used for ethanol, consumes more chemical fertilisers and pesticides than any other crop in the United States, where most ethanol refineries are powered by coal, which produces toxic emissions and greenhouse gases. Biofuel production in Brazil has been linked to deforestation (Albritton 2009: 151–2). Nonetheless, most G20 political leaders, including President Obama, are in favour of expanded nuclear power as the centrepiece of a 'cleaner' approach to energy supply – a strategy that not only risks the wider proliferation of nuclear weapons but also mortgages the welfare and security of future generations, who will be forced to secure and decommission reactors.[19] A worldwide surge in the building of new reactors also has deep implications for intensified internal policing, surveillance and authoritarianism.

More fundamentally, it needs to be asked whether capitalism, even in a 'greener' form, is ultimately compatible with ecological sustainability. Capital and ecology are ontologically distinct and governed by very different dynamics, rhythms and temporalities. As noted, capitalism is concerned with acceleration in the turnover time of capital so as to produce greater profit – a dynamic that involves control over and exploitation of human beings, animals and nature in general – in order to capture value and profits. In turn, this requires creating globally commensurable values exchangeable for money; accordingly, labour and land, which are, respectively, parts of human life and of nature, become saleable commodities subject to futures markets, securitization, derivatives and other extended forms of capital accumulation.

---

[19] The priorities of the Obama administration were reflected in its proposed 2011 budget: $8 billion for research on clean energy (wind, solar, advanced batteries); $36 billion in loan guarantees to finance new nuclear plants (similar to its 2010 request); and the permanent removal of $3.6 billion in oil, gas and coal subsidies; the above was coupled with an estimated 13 per cent reduction in the Environmental Protection Agency's 2012 budget. See the *Guardian* (2011).

Capital thus performs a continuous and often violent extraction of value from the complex, differentiated, uneven, incommensurable values associated with ecosystems, societies and cultures. To do this, capital reduces and simplifies qualitatively different aspects of life into commensurable, saleable and quantifiable items, called commodities; the fabrics of human life and nature are reduced to their most profitable elements, which become objects of accumulation. In this sense, capital accumulation is largely indifferent to the complexity and continuity of ecological and social structures, and how they may be governed by different rhythms, seasons and social relations from those associated with the capitalist market system.

This problem is further compounded by the normative and ideological form of market civilization, which promotes possessive individualism and militates against community-based, collective responses to regulate the relations between human communities and the biosphere in a consistent, equitable and sustainable manner. In short, green capitalism not only fails to address the structural nature of the ecological problem but also, in important ways, makes it more intractable, by subordinating ecological considerations to exploitation, the profit motive and 'shareholder value'.

In evaluating green capitalism, therefore, progressive forces might consider the following points. First, proposals for 'green capitalism' should be judged as to whether they address not only environmental challenges but also the general crisis of social reproduction and livelihood, which compounds the ecological problem.

Second, one of the reasons capitalism is in contradiction with ecology and sustainability is the private enclosure of the social commons, whereby private profit supervenes over social needs and rights, and private property rights hold monopolistic private control over life forms, knowledge, technologies and 'natural resources'. Private corporations hold intellectual property rights over many of the environmental resources and technologies needed to solve ecological issues and to generate more sustainable livelihoods; the corporations want significant rents for using these technologies, which poorer farmers and countries can ill afford. This helps explain the North–South impasse in the climate change negotiations. Progressives should press for such technologies to be global public goods – not controlled by private corporations or the most powerful states (e.g. the United States and the European Union). Currently these technologies are protected by new constitutional organizations, such as the WTO, which has gained global jurisdiction over intellectual property rights, redefining them as tradable commodities.

Third, green capitalism does very little to address the extreme inequality and insecurity of a majority of people; it is still premised on allowing the over-consumption of global resources by the affluent. Thus, if it is viewed as a part of the global organic crisis, we can see clear limits to the capacity of green capitalism to co-opt most of the world's potential forces of political opposition. Indeed, there is widespread scepticism as to whether this accumulation strategy is all that different from neoliberalism (see, for example, Heartfield 2008; Luke 2008; Mueller and Passadakis 2009; Sullivan 2009; Wallis 2009).

A return to normalcy?

In most north Atlantic countries about 70 per cent of workers are in services, many in public services are now threatened with dismissal, and such services may undergo further privatization to repay the huge government debts racked up during the bailouts. However, in some parts of western Europe, especially in Germany, where unemployment has been kept surprisingly low, many remain sympathetic to the argument that G8/G20 leaders have cooperated successfully and can continue to resolve the crisis and return to 'normalcy'. Indeed, many 'protected' workers in trade unions have been shielded from some of the worst effects of the crisis (partly as a result of Keynesian automatic stabilizers, such as unemployment insurance), whereas insecurity is increasing for the vast majority of workers worldwide; such workers are 'unprotected' and may not be eligible for state assistance.

However, the general fiscal situation for many governments (local, regional and federal) is worsening as pressures constrain their ability to tax and borrow to refinance their debts, pressures on the latter arising from investors in the sovereign bond and foreign exchange markets. In Europe's single currency system, countries are denied the option of depreciating their currencies – a move that would lower their relative price levels and make their exports more competitive, which, in turn, would tend to increase domestic production, raise revenues and help service debts. Without the policy option of depreciation, 'adjustment would have to come exclusively through a fall in wages and brutal fiscal austerity'. This is exactly the type of adjustment that could be anticipated under the European Union's 'economic governance' plans, discussed earlier in this chapter, to attempt to obviate a situation in which '[t]he threat of a [sovereign debt] default is transmitted automatically from the first to the next vulnerable country' (Münchau 2010).

More generally, the idea of an early return to 'normalcy' seems delusional in light of the global financial and fiscal situation, which appears far worse than EU, G8 and G20 leaders can admit publicly: global leaders seem unable to even achieve stabilization of the existing order. Moreover, the 'normal' of the past few decades meant not only a deep crisis of social reproduction but also relentless environmental destruction, obscene and ever-increasing levels of inequality and, not least, global economic stagnation. The question of 'normalcy' is therefore a global question, and, if its return involves austerity coupled to regressive fiscal policies that service the primitive accumulation of the global sovereign debt regime, this will deepen the global organic crisis. We can therefore expect global political conflict to begin to increase; the question is: how do we channel this for progressive ends?

What is to be done? Progressive leadership and the organic crisis

I noted in Chapter 1 that progressive forces – with some exceptions, such as those in Latin America and in Germany – have been relatively quiescent in responding to the crisis. Indeed, it has been claimed that this reflects the political weakness, immaturity and lack of organization of the global lefts. One might have expected that the World Social Forum would mobilize millions, as it did in response to the invasion of Iraq in 2003. Have the global lefts perhaps missed a critical moment to respond?

Whether this is true or not, such is the severity of the organic crisis that progressive forces have no alternative but to continue to organize and combine and to present credible policy and institutional alternatives in a concrete way. This is because neoliberal capitalism, if it maintains its power, will further intensify a crisis of social reproduction and destroy many of the basic institutions of welfare, care and livelihood – with fundamental implications for democracy, equality, justice, solidarity, ecological sustainability and public health.

To garner support, progressives could begin by emphasizing that the present economic emergency measures could have been, and could still be, targeted in less costly and more socially productive and efficient ways (e.g. by strengthening public goods for the social, health and educational commons). They should stress that one of the means for this is public and democratic control over the commanding heights of the economy, to make economic activity less risky, more stable and more sustainable. Concrete steps would include much more progressive and fair taxation (e.g. particularly for the top 20 per cent of wealthy people), a crackdown on tax evasion and offshore centres (both of which would alleviate fiscal problems) and the promotion of tax regimes and pricing strategies designed to channel production towards more socially and ecologically useful ends.[20] This would provide a clear alternative to the regressive indirect tax increases and cutbacks in public education, pensions, health and social provisions that are now being imposed.

Nevertheless, it is clear that all this will be far from easy. It requires greater political organization, led by millions of organic intellectuals worldwide, not only to critique the existing order but also to creatively promote new forms of global solidarity and policies so as to move the world onto a saner path. It is a project that involves shared ideas, institutions and power potentials in order to create coherent mechanisms for change, both within existing institutional complexes, including the state, and in new institutions and potentials. For example, many scientists, technicians, teachers, professors, judges, lawyers, carpenters, factory workers, doctors and nurses, as well as many businesspeople and workers in the global North, are repelled by an order that generates such inequalities, waste and other morbid symptoms, and many of them would work as organic intellectuals to promote change within the institutions they work in. Capitalist states need to be transformed and made more democratically accountable and socially responsive, which is a necessary first step in achieving progressive strategic objectives and, in so doing, creating the groundwork for a new kind of state and collective capacity. This mandates strategies for national and global redistribution, via democratic control of public institutions and resources, and systems of representation based upon both formal and substantive equality between all human beings.

Indeed, this type of strategy is already taking concrete form in the global South, as in the new coalitions being developed in Latin America, where new forms of state and new forms of progressive politics may be emerging from the womb of the old, despite the ongoing and long-term fiscal austerity caused by sovereign debt problems that has lasted for decades. This may also prove to be the case in some of the Arab world, as monarchs, dictators and kleptocracies more generally are overthrown by popular uprisings. Since, it seems, Third World economic conditions will soon surface more extensively in much of the global North, the present situation may also be pregnant with new possibilities. Indeed, if this occurs, we must keep alive the memory not just of present-day but also of earlier democratic struggles for political representation – for

---

[20] There may be growing evidence that an increase in progressive taxation – especially on the super-rich and on corporations – is gaining widespread support from the public, as evidenced in proposals to increase taxes in thirty-three US states and in popular surveys of Canada, along with support for using such taxation to pay for social services, health care and education. For evidence on the United States, see www.progressivestates.org/node/24497 and Campbell (2010).

rights, equality and recognition. These include the struggles of generations against colonization and imperialism, for 'the right to have rights' and representation, which have so often been denied to indigenous peoples, as well as to the Arab masses currently in revolt. In this regard, despite Pentagon threats that it will produce 'shock' and 'awe' in the minds of its adversaries, left-wing populism, state capitalism and a range of progressive political forces have emerged in Latin America. There, the 'Bolivarian Revolution' in Venezuela and the Movement Toward Socialism in Bolivia have openly repudiated new constitutionalism and US leadership.[21] MAS was created in the mid-1990s by indigenous peasant grass-roots organizations to build their own political organization. More broadly, throughout the world – in Asia, Africa and Latin America – various workers' and peasant movements, feminists, environmentalists and others have combined to construct their own power resources and institutions, as well as sharing relatively common frameworks of analysis of the problems associated with the organic crisis. Some are forging real and practical 'eco-agricultural' methods and social relations of production and alternatives to the rule of capital.

Many of these new forces are more radical than orthodox leftist parties, and they have engaged in new practices and discourses of politics. Indeed, perhaps the most radical stronghold for left-wing resurgence in Latin America is the landless peasantry – which has formed a large, strong, dynamic, innovative and effective social and political movement in Brazil. In Bolivia, Paraguay and Mexico, peasant movements have been prominent in reshaping and redefining the terrain of politics, often in combination with traditional civic and union movements. What often unites these movements is how disciplinary neoliberal capitalism and predatory state forms have gone with primitive accumulation and the expropriation of small producers of their means of livelihood. Of course, these forces of resistance are diverse. Some form a 'silent revolution', aimed principally at relative self-sufficiency (Cheru 1997). Others resist in defence of their minimum needs for survival, whereas others seek to maintain 'traditional' social relations in ways that are not necessarily

---

[21] Almost two-thirds of Bolivians supported the MAS government's concept of grass-roots participatory democracy and expansion of the rights and 'key demands' of indigenous and peasant organizations, including the nationalization of gas reserves. MAS also involved widespread popular participation in making a new constitution 'that dramatically expands indigenous rights,. . . stimulating an increased sense of pride and dignity among the long-oppressed indigenous majority'. However, in the April 2010 regional elections, support for MAS fell to 51 per cent, because, it seems, MAS made ill-judged electoral alliances with some former reactionary figures and backed away from its earlier grass-roots approach. See Fuentes (2010).

progressive (Harvey 2005: 162ff). However, much of the resistance of peasants to dispossession is also a resistance to capital, even if some of the terms of resistance reaffirm pre-modern social and political forms.

Thus, these new forces engage questions of livelihood, racism and the relationship between men and women. Perhaps, therefore, the potential and concept of a progressive party and of global leadership need to be rethought to reflect the new combinations of social forces and historical conditions of our epoch. Let us, in conclusion, imagine a 'party of a new type' that embodies a novel conception of global political leadership. This party – which is coming into being and is already asserting itself in action in some locations and thus takes a concrete form in what I have called the postmodern prince – is a political movement and a social and pedagogical process (Gill 2000, 2008). It promotes the realistic development of imagined alternatives. It does not necessarily provide a unified response to all problems, nor is it combined organizationally in a traditional political party with restrictive membership requirements. It encompasses largely subaltern but progressive political forces. It is to be understood as diverse movement(s) whose unity is still in formation but is nonetheless premised on a relatively shared recognition of common problems and principles of collective action. It is a 'party', of both North and South, that does not simply focus on industrial workers as its 'vanguard'; its leadership encompasses peasants, other workers, feminists, ecologists, anarchists, indigenous peoples and a wide range of forces, including churches and experts with scientific and technological expertise. Its leaders are millions of organic intellectuals, locally and globally interlinked through powerful modes of communication and as radical media outlets. Such outlets – when secured from censorship – lay bare and place practices of dominant power under scrutiny, with critiques and evidence of unethical and illegitimate practices that can be instantaneously communicated worldwide: what I call 'democratic surveillance' (Gill 1995b, 1997).

In sum, a key task of these organic intellectuals as a collective leadership element is to move forward to foster a new 'common sense' and principles and practices of unity, in order to make the postmodern prince more effective in creating a new culture, a new form of state and a new global society. In so doing, a new global common sense will involve more sustainable relations between human beings and the biosphere.

Finally, implicit throughout this book has been the imperative to construct a new political science – or, more precisely, a new set of knowledge and institutional forms in the social sciences, humanities and the sciences – that recognizes the legitimacy of a vision of the progressive, subaltern movements. This vision would be ultimately designed to abolish the 'primordial' distinction between rulers and ruled and replace it with a true democracy based on collective principles of political self-determination. It would, in sum, be grounded in new understandings of power, production and social reproduction, and, therefore, allow for the universal flourishing of creative human potentials.

Glossary

Alterity: 'otherness', or the construction of political or cultural 'others'; e.g. the concept of Orientalism.

Apex courts: supreme or constitutional courts that are at the summit (apex) of a legal system.

Aporia: an impasse; a doubt or state of puzzlement.

Adjudicatory leadership: the power of judges to manage and organize the institutions of a legal system, as well as to use their knowledge and powers of interpretive reason to constitute, define and determine the juridical field and, by extension, political possibilities.

Billion: 1,000,000,000, or one thousand million.

Collateralized debt obligation (CDO): a financial asset that provides a flow of payments that are funded by underlying combinations of bonds, mortgages or other forms of debt. Senior tranche holders are paid first. If defaults occur in the underlying payment assets (e.g. mortgage defaults), junior holders of lower-ranked tranches therefore suffer the initial losses.

Condottiere: in Europe during the fourteenth to the sixteenth centuries, and specifically in Renaissance Italy, mercenary military leaders, known as *condottiere*, were paid to lead the armies of powerful houses, such as the Medici, Sforza and Colleoni.

Disciplinary neoliberalism: a term used to describe the socio-economic project of transnational capital to expand the scope and increase the power of market-based structures and forces so that governments and other economic agents are disciplined by market mechanisms.

Epistolary jurisdiction: a procedure that allows any citizen or social group to approach a court for redress on behalf of the oppressed or subaltern classes; the attention of the court can even be drawn by writing a letter.

Extra-curial: extra-judicial, or exercised outside the courts.

Fatwa: a religious opinion delivered by a scholar on a matter of Islamic law.

Global governance: a contested term, often used to describe how patterns of rule and authority operate on a global scale to regulate forms of human interdependence across political jurisdictions.

Governmentality: a concept used to emphasize the union between governmental practices and mentalities of rule. It directs our attention to (1) the politico-strategic rationalities underlying the exercise of political rule and authority; (2) the tactics, techniques and mechanisms that are deployed by those who seek to govern others; and (3) the utopian ends for which these practices of government are carried out.

Impossible trinity: the 'impossible trinity', or, more properly, the Mundell–Fleming thesis. This widely accepted economic concept asserts that governments can pursue no more than two of the following three policy options at the same time: capital mobility, a fixed exchange rate and an independent monetary policy. For example, if a government had capital mobility and a fixed exchange rate, it would be unable to stimulate its economy through an expansionary monetary policy. Doing so would cause capital to leave the country and the value of the currency to drop out of its fixed-rate band. If the government wanted to pursue a monetary stimulus and maintain a fixed exchange rate, it would have to implement capital controls to prevent capital from leaving the country.

Insurgent reason: a mode of reason that aims to reinvent the *constituent* power of the people against the ensemble of the *constituted* powers that rule or dominate them. Such a mode of reason could promote either violent or peaceful strategies for change.

Italian Risorgimento: the political and social upheavals of the nineteenth century that unified Italy into a modern nation state.

Leverage: when investors or banks use money they have borrowed to make multiple loans and thus greater returns on an investment. Historically, banks have been subject to capital controls that limit the degree to which they can use leverage, but such restrictions have gradually been lifted over recent decades, and they do not apply to all investors.

Lex mercatoria: a Latin term for private trading principles governed by customary commercial law that have been used in Europe since the Middle Ages. Literally 'merchant law', it was enforced by the merchants themselves, in their own courts along the major trade routes. Its goals were to protect freedom of contract and private property and expand trade, and, in doing so, to increase local tax revenues for states and principalities. Self-regulation by merchants has grown in the modern world, with private international courts of arbitration for commercial disputes across jurisdictions.

Market civilization: a social order in which the allocation of goods, services, everyday life and culture is mediated and arbitrated by capitalist market mechanisms, market forces and market values.

New constitutionalism: the politico-juridical project associated with disciplinary neoliberalism and market civilization that seeks to lock in the power of capital through a series of pre-commitment mechanisms, such as multilateral trade agreements and Structural Adjustment Programs. These mechanisms serve to constitute the limits of political possibility and inspire the confidence of investors by increasing the role and scope of market values and disciplines.

Organic intellectual: either (1) an intellectual who is linked to the preservation of the existing mode of production and relation between rulers and ruled and, if possible, committed to fostering ruling-class hegemony or (2) a counter-hegemonic intellectual who is linked to subaltern forces, for example to workers' organizations and to struggles for rights and livelihood, and who seeks to transform the existing order.

Public reason: a mode of thought and deliberation for solving public problems. Rooted in Kant, the term has been used by Rawls to describe a mode of reason applied to an entire society rather than a particular element of it. It imagines there can be a shared common reason among individuals with different interests and backgrounds.

Social reproduction: the ways in which any society produces, consumes and reproduces, and how it conceptualizes and understands these and justifies its particular pattern of historical development. Feminists note that it involves crucial gender dimensions that concern biological reproduction, the reproduction of the labour force, household divisions of labour and caring institutions for education, health and welfare.

Structural power: a form of power embedded in historical structures and/ or institutions that set the parameters for the limits and conditions of possibility for action in any given age.

Transformative agency: a form of collective action aimed at transforming relations of power, privilege and authority while seeking to constitute a new social order with a different set of political possibilities and relations of power.

Trillion: 1,000,000,000,000, or one million million.

Weltanschauung: a world view or a philosophy of life.

Bibliography

Abd al-Rahman ibn, M., and Issawi, C. P. (eds.). 1950. *An Arab Philosophy of History: Selections from the Prolegomena of Ibn Khaldun of Tunis (1332–1406)*. London: John Murray.

Abramovitz, Mimi. 2006. 'Welfare reform in the United States: gender, race and class matter'. *Critical Social Policy* **26** (2), 336–64.

Abu-Lughod, Janet. 1991. *Before European Hegemony: The World System AD 1250–1350*. Oxford University Press.

Acheson, Dean. 1969. *Present at the Creation: My Years at the State Department*. New York: W. W. Norton.

Addison, John T., and Siebert, W. Stanley. 1991. 'The Social Charter of the European Community: evolution and controversies'. *Industrial and Labour Relations Review* **44** (4), 597–625.

Agamben, Giorgio. 2005. *The Time that Remains: A Commentary on the Letter to the Romans*. Stanford University Press.

Aglietta, Michel. 2001. *A Theory of Capitalist Regulation*. London: Verso Books.

Ahmad, Aijaz. 2011. 'Autumn of the patriarchs'. *Frontline* **28** (4), www.frontlineonnet.com/stories/20110225280401400.htm (accessed 21 February 2011).

Albo, Greg, Gindin, Sam, and Panitch, Leo. 2010. *In and Out of Crisis: The Global Financial Crisis and Left Alternatives*. London: Merlin Press.

Albritton, Robert. 2009. *Let Them Eat Junk: How Capitalism Creates Hunger and Obesity*. London: Pluto Press.

Anderson, Perry. 1976. 'The antinomies of Antonio Gramsci'. *New Left Review* **100**, 5–78.

Araghi, Farshad. 2000. 'The great global enclosure of our times'. In Magdoff, Fred, Foster, John Bellamy, and Buttel, Frederick H. (eds.), *Hungry for Profit: The Agribusiness Threat to Farmers, Food, and the Environment*. New York: Monthly Review Press, 145–60.

Arrighi, Giovanni. 1982. 'A crisis of hegemony'. In Amin, Samir, Arrighi, Giovanni, Frank, Andre Gunder, and Wallerstein, Immanuel (eds.), *Dynamics of Global Crisis*. New York: Monthly Review Press, 55–108.

1994. *The Long Twentieth Century: Money, Power, and the Origins of Our Times*. London: Verso Books.

Ashman, Sam. 2009. 'Editorial introduction to the symposium on the global financial crisis'. *Historical Materialism* **17** (2), 103–8.

Assadourian, Erik. 2010. 'The rise and fall of consumer cultures'. In Worldwatch Institute, *State of the World 2010: Transforming Cultures: From Consumerism to Sustainability.* New York: W. W. Norton, 3–20.

Avant, Deborah. 2005. *The Market for Force: The Consequences for Privatizing Security.* Cambridge University Press.

Bakker, Isabella. 2007. 'Social reproduction and the constitution of a gendered political economy'. *New Political Economy* **12** (4), 541–56.

Bakker, Isabella, and Gill, Stephen (eds.). 2003. *Power, Production and Social Reproduction: Human In/security in the Global Political Economy.* Basingstoke: Palgrave Macmillan.

  2011. 'Towards a new common sense: the need for new paradigms for global health'. In Benatar, Solomon R., and Brock, Gillian (eds.), *Global Health and Global Health Ethics.* Cambridge University Press, 329–32.

Barber, Benjamin R. 1996. *Jihad vs. McWorld: How Globalism and Tribalism Are Reshaping the World.* New York: Ballantine Books.

Barker, Debbie. 2007. *The Rise and Predictable Fall of Globalized Industrial Agriculture.* San Francisco: IFG; available at www.ifg.org/pdf/ag%20report.pdf (accessed 29 June 2010).

Barlow, Maude, and Clarke, Tony. 2001. *Global Showdown: How the New Activists Are Fighting Global Corporate Rule.* Toronto: Stoddart.

  2003. *Blue Gold: The Battle against Corporate Theft of the World's Water.* Toronto: McClelland & Stewart.

Bassiouni, M. Cherif. 2008. 'Evolving approaches to jihad: from self-defense to revolutionary and regime change political violence'. *Journal of Islamic Law and Culture* **10** (1), 61–83.

Bate, Roger. 2004. 'Taxing times: the fight for national sovereignty in Europe'. National Review Online, 6 May, www.aei.org/article/20466 (accessed 23 February 2011).

Baxi, Upendra. 1967. '"The little done, the vast undone": reflections on reading Granville Austin's *The Indian Constitution'. Journal of Indian Law Institute* **9** (3), 323–430.

  1989. 'Taking suffering seriously: social action litigation before the Supreme Court of India'. In Baxi, Upendra, *Law and Poverty: Critical Essays.* Bombay: N. M. Tripathi, 367–415.

  1993. *Marx, Law, and Justice: Indian Perspectives.* Bombay: N. M. Tripathi.

  2000. 'Constitutionalism as a site of state formative practices'. *Cardozo Law Review* **21** (4), 1183–210.

  2008a. 'Preliminary notes on transformative constitutionalism'. Paper presented at the second Brazil, India, South Africa conference 'Courting justice', New Delhi, 29 April.

  2008b. *The Future of Human Rights,* 3rd edn. New Delhi: Oxford University Press.

  2009. The globalization of fatwas amidst the terror wars'. In Benda-Beckmann, Franz von, Benda-Beckmann, Keebet von, and Griffiths, Anne (eds.), *The Power of Law in a Transnational World: Anthropological Enquiries.* Edinburgh: Berghahn Books, 96–114.

2010. 'Writing about impunity and environment: the "silver jubilee" of the Bhopal catastrophe'. *Journal of Human Rights and the Environment* **1** (1), 23–44.

Bayne, Nicholas. 2000. *Hanging In There: The G7 and G8 Summit in Maturity and Renewal*. Brookfield, VT: Ashgate.

2005. *Staying Together: The G8 Confronts the Twenty-First Century*. Aldershot: Ashgate.

Beck, Ulrich. 2000. *World Risk Society: Towards a New Modernity*. London: Sage.

Bello, Walden. 2002. *Prospects for Good Global Governance: A View from the South*. Bangkok: Chulalongkorn University; available at focusweb.org/publications/Research%20and%20Policy%20papers/2001/prospects%20for%20global%20governanace.pdf (accessed 25 July 2010).

2007. 'The Forum at the Crossroads'. Foreign Policy in Focus, 5 May; www.fpif.org/fpiftxt/4196 (accessed 30 June 2010).

Benatar, David. 2007. 'The chickens come home to roost'. *American Journal of Public Health* **97** (9), 1546–7.

Benatar, Solomon R. 1997a. 'Streams of global change'. In Bankowski, Zbigniew, Bryant, John H., and Gallagher, James (eds.), *Ethics, Equity and Health for All: Proceedings of the 29th CIOMS Conference*. Geneva: Council for International Organizations of Medical Sciences, 75–85.

1997b. 'Towards social justice in the new South Africa'. *Medicine Conflict and Survival* **13** (3), 229–39.

1998. 'Global disparities in health and human rights'. *American Journal of Public Health* **88** (2), 295–300.

2005. 'The HIV/AIDS pandemic: a sign of instability in a complex global system'. In van Niekerk, A. A., and Kopelman, L. (eds.), *Ethics and AIDS in Africa: The Challenge to Our Thinking*. Cape Town: David Philip, 71–83.

2009. 'Global health: where to now?' *Global Health Governance* **2** (2), 1–11.

Benatar, Solomon R., and Brock, Gillian (eds.), 2011. *Global Health and Global Health Ethics*. Cambridge University Press.

Benatar, Solomon R., Daar, Abdallah S., and Singer, Peter A. 2003. 'Global health ethics: the rationale for mutual caring'. *International Affairs* **79** (1), 107–38.

Benatar, Solomon R., and Doyal, Len. 2009. 'Human rights abuses: toward balancing two perspectives'. *International Journal of Health Services* **39** (1), 219–23.

Benatar, Solomon R., Gill, Stephen, and Bakker, Isabella. 2009. 'Making progress in global health: the need for new paradigms'. *International Affairs* **85** (2), 347–72.

2011. 'Global health and the global economic crisis'. *American Journal of Public Health* **101** (4), 646–53.

Benatar, Solomon R., Lister, Graham, and Thacker, Strom C. 2010. 'Values in global health governance'. *Global Public Health* **5** (2), 143–53

Bensimon, Cécile M., and Benatar, Solomon R. 2006. 'Developing sustainability: a new metaphor for progress'. *Theoretical Medicine and Bioethics* **27** (1), 59–79.

Berlet, Chip, and Lyons, Matthew N. 2000, *Right-Wing Populism in America: Too Close for Comfort*. New York: Guilford Press.

Bernstein, Steve. 2002. 'Liberal environmentalism and global environmental governance'. *Global Environmental Politics* **2** (3), 1–16.

Beyer, Peter. 1994. *Religion and Globalization*. London: Sage.

Bhagwati, Jagdish N. 2004. *In Defense of Globalization*. New York: Oxford University Press.

Bichler, Shimshon, and Nitzan, Jonathan. 2010. 'Notes on the state of capital', bnarchives.yorku.ca/282/03/20100300_bn_notes_on_the_state_of_capital. pdf (accessed 25 May 2010).

Bieling, Hans-Jürgen. 2006, 'Europäische Staatlichkeit'. In Bretthauer, Lars, Gallas, Alexander, Kannankulam, John, and Stützle, Ingo (eds.), *Poulantzas lessen: Zur Aktualität marxisticher Staatstheorie*. Hamburg: VSA, 223–39.

Binder, Leonard. 1988. *Islamic Liberalism: A Critique of Development Ideologies*. University of Chicago Press.

Birn, Anne-Emanuelle. 2005. 'Gates's grandest challenge: transcending technology as public health ideology'. *The Lancet* **366**, 514–19.

Birn, Anne-Emanuelle, Pillay, Yogan, and Holtz, Timothy H. 2009. 'The political economy of health and development'. In Birn, Anne-Emanuelle, Pillay, Yogan, and Holtz, Timothy H., *Textbook of International Health: Global Health in a Dynamic World*, 3rd edn. Oxford University Press, 132–91.

Bischoff, Joachim. 2009. *Jahrhundertkrise des Kapitalismus: Abstieg in die Depression oder Übergang in eine andere Ökonomie*. Hamburg: VSA.

Bischoff, Joachim, Dörre, Klaus, and Gauthier, Elisabeth (eds.). 2004. *Moderner Rechtspopulismus: Ursachen, Wirkungen, Gegenstrategien*. Hamburg: VSA.

Biswas, Asit K. 2008. 'From Mar del Plata to Kyoto: an analysis of global water policy dialogue'. *Global Environmental Change* **14** (Supplement 1), 81–8.

Bodansky, Daniel. 1999. 'The legitimacy of international governance: a coming challenge for international environmental law?' *American Journal of International Law* **93** (3), 596–624.

Boltanski, Luc, and Chiapello, Eve. 2006. *Der neue Geist des Kapitalismus*. Konstanz: UVK.

Bond, Patrick. 2004. 'South Africa's frustrating decade of freedom: from racial to class apartheid'. *Monthly Review* **55** (10), 45–59; www.monthlyreview. org/0304bond.htm (accessed 21 July 2010).
    2008. 'The state of the global carbon trade debate'. *Capitalism Nature Socialism* **19** (4), 89–106.

Booth, Ken. 2007. *Theory of World Security*. Cambridge University Press.

Borren, Sylvia, Lubbers, Ruud, and Vanenburg, Sayida. 2009. 'Negotiations will not save the planet'. *Trouw*, 30 November.

Braithwaite, John, and Drahos, Peter. 2000. *Global Business Regulation*. Cambridge University Press.

Braudel, Fernand. 1980. *On History* (Matthews, Sarah, trans.). University of Chicago Press.
    1981. *Civilization and Capitalism: 15th–18th Century*, vol. I, *The Structures of Everyday Life: The Limits of the Possible* (Reynolds, Siân, trans.). London: Collins.

1982. *Civilization and Capitalism: 15th–18th Century*, vol. III, *The Perspective of the World* (Reynolds, Siân, trans.). London: Collins.

1995. *A History of Civilizations* (Mayne, Richard, trans.). London: Penguin Books.

Brecher, Jeremy, Costello, Tim, and Smith, Brendan. 2000. *Globalization from Below: The Power of Solidarity.* Cambridge, MA: South End Press.

Brie, Michael, Hildebrandt, Cornelia, and Meuche-Mäker, Meinhard (eds.). 2008. *Die Linke: Wohin verändert sie die Republik?* Berlin: Dietz Verlag.

Brittan, Samuel. 2009. 'Goodbye to the pre-crisis trend line'. *Financial Times*, 29 October.

Brock, Gillian. 2009. *Global Justice: A Cosmopolitan Account.* Oxford University Press.

Brzezinski, Zbigniew. 2004. *The Choice: Global Domination or Global Leadership.* New York: Basic Books.

2008. *Second Chance: Three Presidents and the Crisis of American Superpower.* New York: Basic Books.

Buchanan, Allen. 1995. 'Privatization and just healthcare'. *Bioethics* 9 (3/4), 220–39.

Buchanan, James. 1989. *Explorations into Constitutional Economics.* College Station: Texas A&M University Press.

1991. *The Economics and Ethics of Constitutional Order.* Ann Arbor: Michigan University Press.

1995. 'Federalism as an ideal political order and an object for constitutional reform'. *Publius: The Journal of Federalism* 25 (2), 1–9.

Bull, Hedley. 1977. *The Anarchical Society: A Study of Order in International Politics.* London: Macmillan.

Burchell, Graham, Gordon, Colin, and Miller, Peter. 1991. *The Foucault Effect: Studies in Governmentality.* Toronto: Harvester Wheatsheaf.

Burrows, Gideon. 2003. *The No-Nonsense Guide to the Arms Trade.* Oxford: New Internationalist.

Butterwegge, Christoph. 2006. 'Globalisierung, Neoliberalismus und Rechtsextremismus'. In Bathke, Peter, and Spindler, Susanne (eds.), *Neoliberalismus und Rechtsextremismus in Europa.* Berlin: Dietz Verlag, 5–33.

Buttigieg, Joseph (ed., trans.). 1991. *Antonio Gramsci: Prison Notebooks*, vol. I. New York: Columbia University Press.

1996. *Antonio Gramsci: Prison Notebooks*, vol. II. New York: Columbia University Press.

2007. *Antonio Gramsci: Prison Notebooks*, vol. III. New York: Columbia University Press.

Callinicos, Alex. 2009. *Imperialism and Global Political Economy.* Cambridge: Polity Press.

Campbell, Bruce. 2010. 'Canadians no longer see red over prospect of higher taxes'. *Toronto Star*, 7 April.

Candeias, Mario. 2009. *Neoliberalismus, Hochtechnologie, Hegemonie: Grundrisse einer transnationalen kapitalistischen Produktions- und Lebensweise Eine Kritik*, 2nd edn. Hamburg: Argument.

Carr, Edward Hallett. 1946. *The Twenty Years' Crisis 1919–1939: An Introduction to the Study of International Relations*, 2nd edn. London: Macmillan.

Carson, Rachel. 1964. *Silent Spring*. New York: Fawcett Crest.

Cashore, Benjamin, Auld, Graeme, and Newsom, Deanna. 2003. *Governing through Markets: Forest Certification and the Emergence of Non-State Authority*. New Haven, CT: Yale University Press.

Castel, Robert, and Dörre, Klaus (eds.). 2009. *Prekarität, Abstieg, Ausgrenzung: Die soziale Frage am Beginn des 21. Jahrhunderts*. Frankfurt: Campus.

Castree, Noel. 2008. 'Neoliberalizing nature: the logics of deregulation and reregulation'. *Environment and Planning A* **40** (1), 131–52.

Center for Women's Global Leadership, Rutgers University, Economic Policy and Human Rights Initiative of the International Network for Economic, Social and Cultural Rights and Political Economy Research Institute, University of Massachusetts. 2010. *Towards a Human Rights-Centered Macroeconomic and Financial Policy in the US*. New Brunswick, NJ: Rutgers University.

Chandler, David. 2007. 'Deriving norms from "global space": the limits of communicative approaches to global civil society theorising'. *Globalizations* **(4)** 2, 283–98.

Chang, Ha-Joon. 2000. 'The hazard of moral hazard: untangling the Asian crisis'. *World Development* **28** (4), 775–88.

Chang, Ha-Joon, and Grabel, Ilene. 2004. 'Reclaiming development from the Washington Consensus'. *Journal of Post Keynesian Economics* **27** (2), 273–91.

Chapman, Audrey R. (ed.). 1994. *Health Care Reform: A Human Rights Approach*. Washington, DC: Georgetown University Press.

Cheru, Fantu. 1997. 'The silent revolution and the weapons of the weak: transformation and innovation from below'. In Gill, Stephen, and Mittelman, James (eds.), *Innovation and Transformation in International Studies*. Cambridge University Press, 153–69.

Chesterman, Simon, and Lehnardt, Chia (eds.). 2007. *From Mercenaries to Market: The Rise and Regulation of Private Military Companies*. Oxford University Press.

Cheung, Fanny, and Halpern, Diane. 2010. 'Women at the top: powerful leaders define success as work plus family in a culture of gender'. *American Psychologist* **65** (3), 182–93.

Chorev, Nitsan. 2007. *Remaking U.S. Trade Policy: From Protectionism to Globalization*. Ithaca, NY: Cornell University Press.

Clapp, Jennifer, and Fuchs, Dorothy (eds.). 2009. *Corporate Power in Global Agrifood Governance*. Cambridge, MA: MIT Press.

Clark, Ian. 2009. 'Bringing hegemony back in: the United States and international order'. *International Affairs* **85** (1), 23–36.

Cohen, Edward S. 2007. 'The harmonization of private commercial law: the case of secured finance'. In Brütsch, C., and Lehmkuhl, D. (eds.), *Law and Legalization in Transnational Relations*. New York: Routledge, 58–80.

Conca, Ken. 2000. 'The WTO and the undermining of global environmental governance'. *Review of International Political Economy* **7** (3), 484–94.

Cooney, Rosie, and Lang, Andrew. 2007. 'Taking uncertainty seriously: adaptive governance and international trade'. *European Journal of International Law* **18** (3), 523–51.

Cox, Robert W. 1987. *Production, Power, and World Order: Social Forces in the Making of History.* New York: Columbia University Press.

Crone, Patricia. 1980. *Slaves on Horses: The Evolution of the Islamic Polity.* New York: Cambridge University Press.

Cutler, A. Claire. 1995. 'Global capitalism and liberal myths: dispute settlement in private international trade relations'. *Millennium: Journal of International Studies* **24** (3), 377–95.

  1997. 'Artifice, ideology, and paradox: the public/private distinction in international law'. *Review of International Political Economy* **4** (2), 261–85.

  2003. *Private Power and Global Authority: Transnational Merchant Law in the Global Political Economy.* Cambridge University Press.

  2005. 'Critical globalization studies and international law under conditions of postmodernity and late capitalism'. In Appelbaum, Richard, and Robinson, William I. (eds.), *Critical Globalization Studies.* New York: Routledge, 197–206.

  2008a. 'Transnational law and privatized governance'. In Pauly, Louis, and Coleman, William (eds.), *Institutions, Governance, and Global Ordering.* Vancouver: University of British Columbia Press, 144–65.

  2008b. 'Problematizing corporate social responsibility under conditions of late capitalism and postmodernity'. In Nettesheim, Martin, and Rittberger, Volker (eds.), *Authority in the Global Political Economy.* Basingstoke: Palgrave Macmillan, 189–216.

  2009. 'Constituting capitalism: corporations, law, and private transnational governance'. *St Antony's International Review* **5** (1), 99–115.

  2010. 'The legitimacy of private transnational governance: experts and the transnational market for force'. *Socio-Economic Review* **8** (1), 157–85.

Cutler, A. Claire, Haufler, Virginia, and Porter, Tony (eds.). 1999. *Private Authority and International Affairs.* Albany: State University of New York Press.

Daniel, Norman. 1960. *Islam and the West: The Making of an Image.* Edinburgh University Press.

Davidson, Arnold I. (ed.). 2010. *Michel Foucault: The Government of Self and Others: Lectures at the Collège de France 1982–83* (Burchell, Graham, trans.). Basingstoke: Palgrave Macmillan.

Davis, Mike. 2006. *Planet of Slums.* New York: Verso Books.

Davis, Nancy J., and Robinson, Robert V. 2006. 'The egalitarian face of Islamic orthodoxy: support for Islamic law and economic justice in seven Muslim-majority nations'. *American Sociological Review* **71** (2), 167–90.

Dawson, Angus, and Verweij, Marcell (eds.). 2007. *Ethics, Prevention and Public Health.* New York: Oxford University Press.

Day, Richard. 2005. *Gramsci is Dead: Anarchist Currents in the Newest Social Movements.* London: Pluto Press.

De Angelis, Massimo. 2001. 'Marx and primitive accumulation: the continuous character of capital's "enclosures"'. *The Commoner 2*, www.commoner.org. uk/02deangelis.pdf (accessed 21 June 2011).

2004. 'Separating the doing and the deed: capital and the continuous character of enclosures'. *Historical Materialism* 12 (2), 57–87.

2007. *The Beginning of History: Value Struggles and Global Capital*. London: Pluto Press.

Deep, Mary-Jane. 1992. 'Militant Islam and the politics of redemption'. *Annals of the American Academy of Political and Social Science* 524 (1), 52–65.

Della Porta, Donatella. 2007. 'The global justice movement in context'. In della Porta, Donatella (ed.), *The Global Justice Movement: Cross-National and Transnational Perspectives*. Boulder, CO: Paradigm, 232–51.

Deppe, Frank, and Solty, Ingar. 2004. *Der neue Imperialismus*. Heilbronn: Distel.

Derrida, Jacques. 2002. *Acts of Religion*. London: Routledge.

Dezalay, Yves, and Garth, Bryant G. 1996. *Dealing in Virtue: International Commercial Arbitration and the Construction of a Transnational Legal Order*. University of Chicago Press.

2010. 'Marketing and selling transnational "judges" and global "experts": building the credibility of (quasi)judicial regulation'. *Socio-Economic Review* 8 (1), 113–30.

Di Muzio, Tim. 2007. 'The "art" of colonisation: capitalising sovereign power and the ongoing nature of primitive accumulation'. *New Political Economy* 12 (4), 517–29.

2008. 'Silencing the sovereignty of the poor in Haiti'. In Shilliam, Robbie, and Bhambra, Gurminder K. (eds.), *Silencing Human Rights: Critical Engagements with a Contested Project*. Basingstoke: Palgrave Macmillan, 205–22.

Diamond, Jared. 2005. *Collapse: How Societies Choose to Fail or Succeed*. New York: Viking.

Djelic, Marie-Laure. 2006. 'Marketization: from intellectual agenda to global policy-making'. In Djelic, Marie-Laure, and Sahlin-Andersson, Kerstin (eds.), *Transnational Governance: Institutional Dynamics of Regulation*. Cambridge University Press, 53–73.

Djelic, Marie-Laure, and Kleiner, Thibaut. 2006. 'The international competition network: moving towards transnational governance'. In Djelic, Marie-Laure, and Sahlin-Andersson, Kerstin (eds.), *Transnational Governance: Institutional Dynamics of Regulation*. Cambridge University Press, 287–307.

Djelic, Marie-Laure, and Sahlin-Andersson, Kerstin (eds.). 2006. *Transnational Governance: Institutional Dynamics of Regulation*. Cambridge University Press.

Domhoff, G. William. 1996. *State Autonomy or Class Dominance? Case Studies on Policy Making in America*. New York: Aldine de Gruyter.

Dörre, Klaus. 2010. 'Landnahme und soziale Klasse: zur Relevanz sekundärer Ausbeutung'. In Thien, Hans-Günter (ed.), *Klassen im Postfordismus*. Münster: Damfboot, 113–51.

Dörre, Klaus, Lessenich, Stephan, and Rosa, Hartmut. 2009. *Soziologie, Kapitalismus, Kritik: Eine Debatte*. Frankfurt: Suhrkamp.

Doucet, Mark G. 2005. 'The democratic paradox and cosmopolitan democracy'. *Millennium: Journal of International Studies* **34** (1), 137–55.

Doyal, Len, and Gough, Ian. 1991. *A Theory of Human Need*. London: Macmillan.

Doyle, Leonard. 2008. 'Starving Haitians riot as food prices soar'. *Independent*, 10 April.

Duménil, Gérard, and Lévy, Dominique. 2004. *Capital Resurgent: Roots of the Neoliberal Revolution*. Cambridge, MA: Harvard University Press.

Dwivedi, Gaurav. 2010. *Public–Private Partnerships in Water Sector: Partnerships or Privatization?* Badwani, India: Manthan Adhyayan Kendra.

Eagleton, Terry. 1988. 'The ideology of the aesthetic'. *Poetics Today* **9** (2), 327–38.

Eichengreen, Barry. 1996. *Golden Fetters: The Gold Standard and the Great Depression, 1919–1939*. Oxford University Press.

Eichengreen, Barry, and Cairncross, Alec. 1983. *Sterling in Decline: The Devaluations of 1931, 1947, 1967*. Oxford: Blackwell.

Elhefnawy, Nader. 2008. 'The impending oil shock'. *Survival* **50** (2), 37–66.

Eliason, Antonia. 2009. 'Science versus law in WTO jurisprudence: the (mis)-interpretation of the scientific process and the (in)sufficiency of scientific evidence in EC-Biotech'. *New York University Journal of International Law and Politics* **41** (2), 341 406.

Elson, Diane. 1995. 'Gender awareness in modeling structural adjustment'. *World Development* **23** (11), 1851–68.

Elver, Hilal. 2008. 'New mechanisms: water as a fundamental human right'. In Falk, Richard A., Elver, Hilal, and Hajjar, Lisa (eds.), *Human Rights*. London: Routledge, 395–423.

Environmental News Network. 2007. 'Wal-Mart, Clinton climate initiative in partnership'. Environmental News Network, www.enn.com/business/article/24212 (accessed 6 November 2007).

Escobar, Arturo. 2004. 'Beyond the Third World: imperial globality, global coloniality and antiglobalization social movements'. *Third World Quarterly* **24** (1), 207–30.

European Commission. 2010. 'Energy strategy for Europe: Europe 2020 initiatives'. European Commission, Brussels; ec.europa.eu/energy/index_en.htm (accessed 25 June 2010).

Falk, Richard A. 1972. *This Endangered Planet: Prospects and Proposals for Human Survival*. New York: Random House.

  1995. *On Humane Global Governance: Toward a New Global Politics*. University Park: Pennsylvania State University Press.

  1999. *Predatory Globalization: A Critique*. Cambridge: Polity Press.

  2009. 'The second cycle of ecological urgency: an environmental justice perspective'. In Ebbesson, Jonas, and Okowa, Phoebe (eds.), *Environmental Law and Justice in Context*. Cambridge University Press, 39–54.

Falk, Richard A., and Strauss, Andrew. 2001. 'Toward global parliament'. *Foreign Affairs* **80** (1), 212–20.

Farmer, Paul. 2003. *Pathologies of Power: Health, Human Rights, and the New War on the Poor*. Berkeley: University of California Press.

Feinberg, Richard E. 1988. 'The changing relationship between the World Bank and the International Monetary Fund'. *International Organization* **43** (3), 545–60.

Fidler, David. 2009. 'After the revolution: global health politics in a time of economic crisis and threatening future trends'. *Global Health Governance* **2** (2), 1–21.

Fillippini, Michele. 2009. 'Direzione'. In Liguori, Guido, and Voza, Pasquale (eds.), *Dizionario Gramsciano 1926–1937*. Rome: Carocci Editore.

Financial Times. 2010a. Special report: 'Long-term survival strategies'. *Financial Times*, 25 January.
  2010b. 'IMF warns high public debt "tremendous" challenge'. *Financial Times*, 11 April.

Finger, Matthias, and Allouche, Jeremy. 2002. *Water Privatization: Trans-national Corporations and the Re-regulation of the Water Industry*. London: Spoon Press.

Finlayson, Alan. 2002. 'Elements of the Blairite image of leadership'. *Parliamentary Affairs* **55** (3), 586–99.

Flathman, R. E. 1980. *The Practice of Political Authority*. University of Chicago Press.

Flecker, Karl, and Clarke, Tony. 2005. 'Turning off the taps on the GATS'. In McDonald, David, and Ruiters, Greg (eds.), *The Age of Commodity: Water Privatization in Southern Africa*. London: Earthscan, 76–96.

Food & Water Watch. 2009. *Dried Up, Sold Out: How the World Bank's Push for Private Water Harms the Poor*. Washington, DC: Food & Water Watch; available at www.foodandwaterwatch.org/water/pubs/reports/dried-up-sold-out (accessed 30 June 2010).

Foster, John Bellamy, and Magdoff, Harry. 2009. 'Implosion des finanzmarkts und stagnation'. *Zeitschrift Sozialismus* 2/2009, Supplement.

Fraser, Nancy. 1997. 'From redistribution to recognition? Dilemmas of justice in a "poststructuralist" age'. *New Left Review* **212**, 68–93.

Frau-Meigs, Divina. 2008. 'Les médias et l'information dans l'Amérique de George W. Bush'. *Vingtième Siècle: Revue d'histoire* **97** (1), 143–57.

Freeman, Jo. 1972. 'The tyranny of structurelessness'. *Berkeley Journal of Sociology* **17**, 151–65.

Freire, Paulo. 2000. *Pedagogia da indignação: Cartas pedagógicas e outros escritos*. São Paulo: Universidade Estadual Paulista.

Friedman, Milton. 1962. *Capitalism and Freedom*. University of Chicago Press.

Friedman, Thomas L. 2005. *The World Is Flat: A Brief History of the Globalized World in the Twenty-First Century*. London: Allen Lane.
  2009. *Hot, Flat, and Crowded: Why We Need a Green Revolution – and How It Can Renew America*, 2nd edn. New York: Picador.

Friel, Howard. 2010. *The Lomborg Deception: Setting the Record Straight about Global Warming*. New Haven, CT: Yale University Press.

Fuentes, Federico. 2010. 'Bolivia: bittersweet victory highlights obstacles for process of change'. The Bullet, e-bulletin no. 338, www.socialistproject. ca/bullet/338.php#continue (accessed 10 April 2010).

Fukuyama, Francis. 1992. *The End of History and the Last Man*. London: Penguin Books.

Galaz, Victor. 2004. 'Stealing from the poor? Game theory and the politics of water markets in Chile'. *Environmental Politics* 13 (2), 414–37.

Galbraith, John K. 1992. *The Culture of Contentment*. New York: Houghton Mifflin.

Galeano, Eduardo. 1997. *Open Veins of Latin America*. New York: Monthly Review Press.

García-Salmones, Mónica. 2009. 'Taking uncertainty seriously: adaptive governance and international trade: a reply to Rosie Cooney and Andrew Lang'. *European Journal of International Law* 20 (1), 167–86.

Garrett, Laurie. 1994. *The Coming Plague: Newly Emerging Diseases in a World out of Balance*. New York: Farrar, Straus and Giroux.

Garvey, James. 2008. *The Ethics of Climate Change: Right and Wrong in a Warming World*. London: Continuum.

Giddens, Anthony. 1991. *Modernity and Self-Identity: Self and Society in the Late Modern Age*. Stanford University Press.

2009. *The Politics of Climate Change*. Cambridge: Polity Press.

Gill, Stephen. 1990. *American Hegemony and the Trilateral Commission*. Cambridge University Press.

1992. 'The emerging world order and European change: the political economy of European Union.' In Miliband, Ralph, and Panitch, Leo (eds.), *The New World Order: Socialist Register 1992*. London: Merlin Press, 157–96.

(ed.) 1993. *Gramsci, Historical Materialism and International Relations*. Cambridge University Press.

1995a. 'Globalization, market civilization, and disciplinary neoliberalism'. *Millennium* 23 (3), 399–423.

1995b. 'The global panopticon: the neoliberal state, economic life, and democratic surveillance'. *Alternatives* 20 (1), 1–49.

1997. 'Finance, production and panopticism: inequality, risk and resistance in an era of disciplinary neo-liberalism'. In Gill, Stephen (ed.), *Globalization, Democratization and Multilateralism*. New York: Macmillan, 51–76.

1998a. 'New constitutionalism, democratization and global political economy'. *Pacifica Review* 10 (1), 23–38.

1998b. 'European governance and new constitutionalism: EMU and alternatives to disciplinary neo-liberalism in Europe'. *New Political Economy* 3 (1), 5–26.

1999. 'The geopolitics of the Asian crisis'. *Monthly Review* 50 (10), 1–10.

2000. 'Toward a postmodern prince? The battle in Seattle as a moment in the new politics of globalisation'. *Millennium* 29 (1), 131–40.

2003a. *Power and Resistance in the New World Order*. Basingstoke: Palgrave Macmillan.

2003b. 'Social reproduction of affluence and human in/security'. In Bakker, Isabella, and Gill, Stephen (eds.), *Power, Production and Social*

Reproduction: Human In/security in the Global Political Economy. Basingstoke: Palgrave Macmillan, 190–207.

2003c. 'National in/security on a universal scale'. In Bakker, Isabella, and Gill, Stephen (eds.), *Power, Production and Social Reproduction: Human In/security in the Global Political Economy.* Basingstoke: Palgrave Macmillan, 208–23.

2008. *Power and Resistance in the New World Order,* 2nd edn. Basingstoke: Palgrave Macmillan.

2009. 'Kritische Intellektuelle im 21. Jahrhundert'. *Das Argument – Zeitschrift für Philosophie und Sozialwissenschaften* **51**, 135–43.

2010. 'The global organic crisis: paradoxes, dangers, and opportunities'. *Monthly Review, MRZine* **61** (9), http://mrzine.monthlyreview.org/2010/gill150210.html (accessed 5 July 2011).

Gill, Stephen, and Bakker, Isabella. 2011. 'The global political economy and global health'. In Benatar, Solomon R., and Brock, Gillian (eds.), *Global Health and Global Health Ethics.* Cambridge University Press, 221–38.

Gill, Stephen, and Law, David. 1993. 'Global hegemony and the structural power of capital'. In Gill, Stephen (ed.), *Gramsci, Historical Materialism and International Relations.* Cambridge University Press, 93–124.

Gills, Barry K. (ed.) 2010. 'Financial crisis special issue: globalization and crisis'. *Globalizations* **7** (1/2).

Global Health Watch. 2008. *An Alternative World Health Report.* London: Zed Books.

Global Water Intelligence. 2010. *Global Water Market 2011: Meeting the World's Water and Wastewater Needs until 2016.* Oxford: Media Analytics; available at globalwaterintel.com.

Gong, Geritt W. 1984. *The Standard of 'Civilization' in International Society.* Oxford: Clarendon Press.

Gowan, Peter. 1999. *The Global Gamble: Washington's Faustian Bid for World Dominance.* London: Verso Books.

2010. *A Calculus of Power: Grand Strategy in the Twenty-First Century.* London: Verso Books.

Grande, Edgar, and Pauly, Louis (eds.). 2005. *Complex Sovereignty: Reconstituting Political Authority in the Twenty-First Century.* University of Toronto Press.

Grantham, George W. 1980. 'The persistence of open-field farming in nineteenth-century France'. *Journal of Economic History* **40** (3), 515–31.

Graz, Jean-Christophe, and Nölke, Andreas (eds.). 2008. *Transnational Private Governance and Its Limits.* London: Routledge.

Grear, Anna. 2010. *Redirecting Human Rights: Facing the Challenge of Corporate Legal Humanity.* New York: Palgrave Macmillan.

Green, Duncan, and Griffith, Matthew. 2002. 'Globalization and its discontents'. *International Affairs* **78** (1), 49–68.

Green, Maurice B. 1978. *Eating Oil: Energy Use in Food Production.* Boulder, CO: Westview Press.

Greve, Michael. 2000. 'The AEI Federalism Project'. *Federalist Outlook* no. 1, July/August; available at www.federalismproject.org (accessed 1 June 2010).

Grzybowski, Cândido. 2003: 'Fórum Social Mundial: a construção de uma utopia'. *TerraViva*, 24 January.

2004. 'Challenges, limits and possibilities of the World Social Forum'. *TerraViva*, 20 January; www.ipsnews.net/focus/tv_mumbai/viewstory.asp?idn=244 (accessed 23 March 2004).

Guardian. 2011. 'Barack Obama 2012 budget provides $8bn for clean energy'. *Guardian*, 14 February.

Guha, Ranajit. 2007. *Dominance without Hegemony: History and Power in Colonial India*. Cambridge, MA: Harvard University Press.

Haar, Kenneth. 2011. *Corporate EUtopia: How New Economic Governance Measures Challenge Democracy*. Brussels: Corporate Europe Observatory; available at www.corporateeurope.org/lobbycracy/content/2011/01/corporate-eutopia (accessed 28 January 2011).

Hall, Rodney Bruce, and Biersteker, Thomas J. (eds.). 2002. *The Emergence of Private Authority in Global Governance*. Cambridge University Press.

Hall, Stuart. 1996. 'Gramsci's relevance for the study of race and ethnicity'. In Morley, David, and Chen, Kuan-Hsing (eds.), *Stuart Hall: Critical Dialogues in Cultural Studies*. London: Routledge, 411–40.

Halperin, Morton H., Laurenti, Jeffrey, Rundlet, Peter, and Boyer, Spencer P. (eds.). 2007. *Power and Superpower: Global Leadership and Exceptionalism in the 21st Century*. New York: New Century Foundation Press.

Hamilton, Clive. 2004. *Growth Fetish*. London: Pluto Press.

Hamilton, James D. 2009. 'Oil prices and the economic downturn', testimony prepared for the Joint Economic Committee of the US Congress, 20 May; www.house.gov/jec/news/2009/Hamilton_testimony.pdf (accessed 15 June 2010).

Hansen, James. 2009. *Storms of My Grandchildren: The Truth about the Coming Climate Catastrophe and Our Last Chance to Save Humanity*. New York: Bloomsbury.

Hardin, Garrett. 1968. 'The tragedy of the commons'. *Science* **162** (December), 1243–8.

Harding, James. 2002. 'Capitalism's critics urge new global institutions'. *Financial Times*, 2 February.

Hardt, Michael, and Negri, Antonio. 2001. 'What the protestors in Genoa want'. *New York Times*, 20 July.

Harmes, Adam. 2006. 'Neoliberalism and multilevel governance'. *Review of International Political Economy* **13** (5), 725–49.

Hartsock, Nancy. 1983. *Money, Sex, and Power: Toward a Feminist Historical Materialism*. Boston: Northeastern University Press.

Harvey, David. 2005. *The New Imperialism*. Oxford University Press.

2006. *The Limits to Capital*, 2nd edn. London: Verso Books.

2007. *A Brief History of Neoliberalism*. Oxford University Press.

2009. 'Why the US stimulus package is bound to fail', http://davidharvey.org/2009/02/why-the-us-stimulus-package-is-bound-to-fail (accessed 30 June 2010).

Harvey, Fiona. 2010. 'Study finds banks cool on green ideas'. *Financial Times*, 28 January.

Hashmi, Sohail H. (ed.). 2002. *Islamic Political Ethics: Civil Society, Pluralism, and Conflict*. Princeton University Press.

Haufler, Virginia. 1997. *Dangerous Commerce: Insurance and the Management of International Risk*. Ithaca, NY: Cornell University Press.

    2001. *A Public Role for the Private Sector: Industry Self-Regulation in a Global Economy*. Washington, DC: Carnegie Endowment for International Peace.

Hawken, Paul, Lovins, Amory L., and Lovins, Hunter. 2008. *Natural Capital: Creating the Next Industrial Revolution*. Boston: Back Bay Books.

Hay, Douglas, Thompson, Edward, and Linebaugh, Peter (eds.). 1975. *Albion's Fatal Tree: Crime and Society in Eighteenth-Century England*. London: Allen Lane.

Hayek, Friedrich A. von. 1960. *The Constitution of Liberty*. University of Chicago Press.

Heartfield, John. 2008. *Green Capitalism: Manufacturing Scarcity in an Age of Abundance*. London: Openmute.

Heilbroner, Robert. 1993. *21st Century Capitalism*. New York: W. W. Norton.

Heinberg, Richard. 2005. 'Threats of peak oil to the global food supply'. Paper presented at the conference 'What will we eat as the oil runs out? Food security in an energy-scarce world', Dublin, 25 June 2005; available at www.energybulletin.net/node/7088 (accessed 30 June 2010).

Held, David. 2004. *Global Covenant: The Social Democratic Alternative to the Washington Consensus*. Cambridge: Polity Press.

Held, David, and McGrew, Anthony. 2002. *Globalization/Anti-Globalization*. Cambridge: Polity Press.

Helleiner, Eric. 2002. 'Economic nationalism as a challenge to economic liberalism? Lessons from the 19th century'. *International Studies Quarterly* **46** (3), 307–29.

Henderson, Peter. 2010. 'Coal fuels much of internet "cloud", Greenpeace says'. Reuters, 30 March; www.reuters.com/article/2010/03/30/us-climate-internet-idUSTRE62T0MK20100330 (accessed 5 July 2011).

Heynen, Nik, and Robbins, Paul. 2005. 'The neoliberalization of nature: governance, privatization, enclosure and valuation'. *Capitalism Nature Socialism* **16** (1), 5–8.

Hille, Kathrin. 2011. 'Love you and leave you'. *Financial Times*, 4 February.

Hinsliff, Gaby. 2006. 'The PM, the mogul and the secret agenda'. *Observer*, 23 July.

Hira, A. 2007. 'Should economists rule the world? Trends and implications of leadership patterns in the developing world, 1960–2005'. *International Political Science Review* **28** (3), 325–60.

Hirsch, Joachim. 2001. 'Internationalisierung des Staates: Anmerkungen zu einigen aktuellen Fragen der Staatstheorie'. In Hirsch, Joachim, Jessop, Bob, and Poulantzas, Nicos (eds.), *Die Zukunft des Staates: Denationalisierung, Internationalisierung, Renationalisierung*. Hamburg: VSA, 101–38

    2005. *Materialistische Staatstheorie: Transformationsprozesse des kapitalistischen Staatensystems*. Hamburg: VSA.

Hirsch, Joachim, and Roth, Roland. 1986. *Das neue Gesicht des Kapitalismus: Vom Fordismus zum Post-Fordismus.* Hamburg: VSA.

Hoare, Quintin (ed., trans.). 1977. *Antonio Gramsci: Selections from Political Writings 1910–1920.* London: Lawrence & Wishart.

Hoare, Quintin, and Nowell-Smith, Geoffrey (eds., trans.). 1971. *Selections from the Prison Notebooks: Antonio Gramsci.* New York: International Publishers.
  1991. *Selections from the Prison Notebooks: Antonio Gramsci*, 2nd edn. London: Lawrence & Wishart.

Hobsbawm, Eric. 1994. *The Age of Extremes: A History of the World 1914–1991.* New York: Pantheon Books.

Hodges, Michael J. 1999. 'The G8 and the new political economy'. In Hodges, Michael J. (ed.), *The G8's Role in the New Millennium.* Aldershot: Ashgate, 69–74.

Hodgson, Marshall G. S. 1974. *The Venture of Islam.* University of Chicago Press.

Hooghe, Liesbet, and Marks, Gary. 1997. 'The making of a polity: the struggle over European integration'. *European Integration Online Papers* 1 (4), 1–26.

Horn, Norbert, and Schmitthoff, Clive (eds.). 1982. *The Transnational Law of International Commercial Transactions.* Deventer, Netherlands: Kluwer.

Horowitz, Donald L. 2003. *Ethnic Groups in Conflict.* Berkeley: University of California Press.

Howlett, Michael, Netherton, Alex, and Ramesh, M. 1999. *The Political Economy of Canada: An Introduction.* Oxford University Press.

Huisch, Robert, and Speigel, Jerry M. 2008. 'Integrating health and human security into foreign policy: Cuba's surprising success'. *International Journal of Cuban Studies* 1 (1), 1–13.

Huntington, Samuel P. 1996. *The Clash of Civilizations and the Making of the World Order.* New York: Simon & Schuster.

Hurd, Elizabeth Shakman. 2007. *The Politics of Secularism in International Relations.* Princeton University Press.

IEA. 2007. *World Energy Outlook 2007: China and India Insights.* Paris: IEA (available at www.iea.org/textbase/nppdf/free/2007/weo_2007.pdf; accessed 30 June 2010).
  2008. *World Energy Outlook 2008.* Paris: IEA.
  2009. *Key Energy Statistics 2009.* Paris: IEA.

IFG. 2002. *Alternatives to Economic Globalization (A Better World Is Possible).* San Francisco: Berrett-Koehler.

Ikenberry, G. John, and Slaughter, Anne-Marie. 2006. *Forging a World of Liberty under Law: US National Security in the 21st Century.* Princeton, NJ: Woodrow Wilson School of Public and International Affairs, Princeton University.

IMF. 2006. *Global Financial Stability Report: Market Developments and Issues.* Washington, DC: IMF.
  2008. *World Economic Outlook April 2008: Housing and the Business Cycle.* Washington, DC: IMF; available at www.imf.org/external/pubs/ft/weo/2008/01/pdf.
  2009. *World Economic Outlook October 2009: Sustaining the Recovery.* Washington, DC: IMF; available at www.imf.org/external/pubs/cat/longres.cfm?sk=22576.0.

International Consortium of Investigative Journalists. 2003. *The Water Barons: How a Few Powerful Companies are Privatizing Your Water.* Washington, DC: Public Integrity Books.

IPCC. 2007. *Climate Change 2007: Synthesis Report.* New York: IPCC; available at www.ipcc.ch/pdf/assessment-report/ar4/syr/ar4_syr.pdf (accessed 22 June 2010).

Jacobshon, Garry. 2003. *The Wheel of Law: Indian Secularism in a Comparative Context.* New Delhi: Oxford University Press.

Jowit, Juliette. 2010. 'Economic and corporate powers call for hike in global water price'. *Guardian*, 28 April.

Kamat, Sangeeta. 2004. 'The privatization of public interest: theorizing NGO discourse in a neoliberal era'. *Review of International Political Economy* 11 (1), 155–76.

Kantz, C. 2007. 'The power of socialization: engaging the diamond industry in the Kimberley process'. *Business and Politics* 9 (3), article 2; www.bepress.com/bap/vol9/iss3/art2 (accessed 20 November 2008).

Kapoor, Ilan. 2004. 'Deliberative democracy and the WTO'. *Review of International Political Economy* 11 (3), 522–41.

Kassirer, Jerome P. 1995. 'Managed care and the morality of the market place'. *New England Journal of Medicine* 333 (1), 50–2.

Kaul, Inge, Grunberg, Isabelle, and Stern, Marc. 1999. *Global Public Goods: International Cooperation in the 21st Century.* New York: Oxford University Press.

Kennedy, David. 2005. 'Challenging expert rule: the politics of global governance'. *Sydney Law Review* 27 (1), 5–28.

Keohane, Robert. 1984. *After Hegemony: Cooperation and Discord in the World Political Economy.* Princeton University Press.

Khatami, Mohammad. 2000. *'Dialogue among civilizations'* [provisional verbatim transcription]. Round table, New York, 5 September; unesco.org/dialogue/en/khatami.htm (accessed 9 April 2010).

Kindelberger, Charles P. (1973). *The World in Depression, 1929–1939.* London: Allen Lane.

2005. *Manias, Panics and Crashes: A History of Financial Crises.* London: Wiley.

Klare, Michael. 2009. *Rising Powers, Shrinking Planet: The New Geopolitics of Energy.* New York: Holt.

Klein, Naomi. 2008. *The Shock Doctrine: The Rise of Disaster Capitalism.* Toronto: Vintage Canada.

Knill, C., and Lehmkuhl, D. 2002. 'Private actors and the state: internationalization and changing patterns of governance'. *Governance: An International Journal of Policy, Administration and Institutions* 15 (1), 41–63.

Knox, T. M. (ed., trans.). 1967. *Hegel's Philosophy of Right.* New York: Oxford University Press.

Koskenniemi, Martti. 2007. 'The fate of public international law: between technique and politics'. *Modern Law Review* 70 (1), 1–30.

Kotz, David. 2009. 'The financial and economic crisis of 2008: a systemic crisis of neoliberal capitalism'. *Review of Radical Political Economics* 41 (3), 305–17.

Kraemer, Klaus. 2009. 'Prekarisierung: jenseits von Stand und Klasse?' In Castel, Robert, and Dörre, Klaus (eds.), *Prekarität, Abstieg, Ausgrenzung: Die soziale Frage am Beginn des 21. Jahrhunderts*. Frankfurt: Campus, 241–53.

Krahmann, Elke. 2008. 'Security: collective good or commodity?' *European Journal of International Relations* **14** (3), 379–404.

Krugman, Paul. 1999. *The Return of Depression Economics*. New York: W. W. Norton.

   2009a. *The Conscience of a Liberal: Reclaiming America from the Right*. London: W. W. Norton.

   2009b. 'How did economists get it so wrong?' *New York Times Magazine*, 6 September.

   2010. 'Green economics: how we can afford to tackle climate change'. *New York Times Magazine*, 11 April.

Labonte, Ronald, Schrecker, Ted, Sanders, David, and Meeus, Wilma. 2004. *Fatal Indifference: The G8, Africa and Global Health*. University of Cape Town Press.

Larmore, Charles. 2003. 'Public reason'. In Freeman, Samuel (ed.), *Cambridge Companion to Rawls*. Cambridge University Press, 368–93.

Latham, Andrew. 2002. 'Warfare transformed: a Braudelian perspective on the revolution in military affairs'. *European Journal of International Relations* **8** (2), 231–66.

Leander, Anna. 2005. 'The power to construct international security: on the significance of private military companies'. *Millennium* **33** (3), 803–26.

Levy, David L., and Newell, Peter J. 2002. 'Business strategy and international environmental governance: toward a neo-Gramscian synthesis'. *Global Environmental Politics* **2** (4), 84–101.

Lewis, Bernard. 1991. *The Political Language of Islam*. University of Chicago Press.

   2003. *The Crisis of Islam: Holy War and Unholy Terror*. London: Weidenfeld & Nicolson.

Liguori, Guido, and Voza, Pasquale (eds.). 2009. *Dizionario Gramsciano 1926–1937*. Rome: Carocci Editore.

Lipschutz, Ronnie D. 2009. *The Constitution of Imperium*. Boulder, CO: Paradigm.

Lipschutz, Ronnie D., and Fogel, Cathleen. 2002. 'Regulation for the rest of us? Global civil society and the privatization of transnational regulation'. In Hall, Rodney, and Biersteker, Thomas (eds.), *The Emergence of Private Authority in Global Governance*. Cambridge University Press, 115–40.

Luke, Timothy. 2008. 'The politics of true convenience or inconvenient truth: struggles over how to sustain capitalism, democracy, and ecology in the 21st century'. *Environment and Planning A* **40** (8), 1811–24.

Machiavelli, Niccolò. 1975 [1513]. *The Prince*. Harmondsworth: Penguin Books.

Mair, Peter. 2000. 'Partyless democracy: solving the paradox of New Labour?' *New Left Review* **2**, 21–35.

   2006. 'Ruling the void? The hollowing of Western democracy'. *New Left Review* **42**, 25–51.

Mansfield, Becky. 2004. 'Neoliberalism in the oceans: "rationalization", property rights and the commons question'. *Geoforum* **35** (3), 313–26.

Markon, Jerry. 2010. 'Wall Street cases lag despite anti-fraud effort'. *Washington Post*, 18 June.

Marlow, Louise. 1997. *Hierarchy and Egalitarianism in Islamic Thought.* Cambridge University Press.

Marx, Karl. 1976 [1867]. *Capital: A Critique of Political Economy*, vol. I (Fowkes, Ben, trans.). New York: Penguin Books.

  1978 [1867]. 'Crisis theory'. In Tucker, Robert C. (ed.), *The Marx–Engels Reader.* New York: W. W. Norton, 443–68.

Marx, Karl, and Engels, Friedrich. 1974 [1848]. 'Manifest der Kommunistischen Partei'. In *Karl Marx und Friedrich Engels: Werke*, vol. IV. Berlin: Dietz Verlag, 459–93.

Matthew, Richard A. 2007. 'Climate change and human security'. In DiMento, Joseph F. C., and Doughman, Pamela (eds.), *Climate Change: What It Means for Us, Our Children, and Our Grandchildren.* Cambridge, MA: MIT Press, 161–80.

Matthew, Richard A., Barnett, Jon, McDonald, Bryan, and O'Brien, Karen L. (eds.). 2010. *Global Environmental Change and Human Security.* Cambridge, MA: MIT Press.

Mbeki, Moeletsi. 2009. *Architects of Poverty.* Johannesburg: Picador Africa.

McCaffrey, Stephen. 1992. 'Human right to water: domestic and international implications'. *Georgetown International Environmental Law Review* **5** (1), 1–24.

McCarthy, James, and Prudham, Scott. 2004. 'Neoliberal nature and the nature of neoliberalism'. *Geoforum* **35** (3), 275–83.

McChesney, Robert W. 2001. 'Global media, neoliberalism, and imperialism'. *Monthly Review* **52** (10), 1–19.

MccGwire, Michael. 2001. 'The paradigm that lost its way'. *International Affairs* **77** (4), 777–803.

  2003. 'Shifting the paradigm'. *International Affairs* **78** (1), 1–28.

McKibben, Bill. 2010. *Earth: Making a Life on a Tough New Planet.* New York: Times Books.

McNally, David. 2009. 'From financial crisis to world slump: accumulation, financialisation and the global slowdown'. *Historical Materialism* **17** (2), 35–83.

  2011. *Global Slump: The Economics and Politics of Crisis and Resistance.* Oakland, CA: PM Press.

McNicol, J. 2006. 'Transnational NGO certification programs as new regulatory forms: lessons from the forestry sector'. In Djelic, Marie-Laure, and Sahlin-Andersson, Kerstin (eds.), *Transnational Governance: Institutional Dynamics of Regulation.* Cambridge University Press, 349–74.

Meadows, Donella H., Meadows, Dennis L., Randers, Jørgen, and Behrens, William W. 1972. *The Limits to Growth.* New York: Universe Books.

Meidinger, E. 2006. 'Beyond Westphalia: competitive legalization in emerging transnational regulatory systems', Legal Studies Research Paper no. 2006–019. Baldy Center for Law and Social Policy, Buffalo, NY.

Mitchell, Timothy. 1988. *Colonizing Egypt*. Cambridge University Press.
Mitrović, Ljubiša. 2005. 'Bourdieu's criticism of the neoliberal philosophy of development, the myth of mondialization and the new Europe'. *FACTA UNIVERSITATIS Philosophy, Sociology and Psychology* 4 (1), 37–49.
Mittelman, James. 2000. *The Globalization Syndrome: Transformation and Resistance*. Princeton University Press.
  2010. *Hyperconflict: Globalization and Insecurity*. Stanford University Press.
Moaddel, Mansoor, and Talattof, Kamran (eds.). 2000. *Modernist and Fundamentalist Debates in Islam*. New York: Palgrave Macmillan.
Morgan, Glenn. 2006. 'Transnational actors, transnational institutions, transnational spaces: the role of law firms in the internationalization of competition regulation'. In Djelic, Marie-Laure, and Sahlin-Andersson, Kerstin (eds.), *Transnational Governance: Institutional Dynamics of Regulation*. Cambridge University Press, 139–60.
  2010. 'Legitimacy in financial markets: credit default swaps in the current crisis'. *Socio-Economic Review* 8 (1), 17–45.
Morgen, Sandra, and Maskovsky, Jeff. 2003. 'The anthropology of welfare "reform": new perspectives on US urban poverty in the post-welfare era'. *Annual Review of Anthropology* 32, 315–38.
Morton, Adam. 2007. *Unravelling Gramsci: Hegemony and Passive Revolution in the Global Political Economy*. London: Pluto Press.
Mottahedeh, Roy P. 2001. *Loyalty and Leadership in an Early Islamic Society*. London: I. B. Tauris.
Muchlinski, Peter, Ortino, Frederico, and Schreuer, Christophe (eds.). 2008. *The Oxford Handbook of International Investment Law*. New York: Oxford University Press.
Mueller, Tadzio, and Passadakis, Alexis. 2009. 'Green capitalism and the climate: it's economic growth, stupid!' *Critical Currents* 6, 54–61.
Mulhall, Stephen, and Swift, Adam. 1992. *Liberals and Communitarians*. Oxford: Blackwell.
Mulligan, S. 2010. 'Energy, environment, and security: critical links in a post-peak world'. *Global Environmental Politics* 10 (4), 79–100.
Münchau, Wolfgang. 2010. 'Europe needs to show it has a crisis endgame'. *Financial Times*, 7 February.
Munck, Ronaldo. 2003. 'Neoliberalism, necessitarianism and alternatives in Latin America: there is no alternative (TINA)?' *Third World Quarterly* 24 (3), 495–511.
Murphy, Craig N. 2010. 'Lessons of a "good" crisis: learning in, and from the Third World'. *Globalizations* 7 (1/2), 203–15.
Nachtwey, Oliver. 2009. *Marktsozialdemokratie: Die Transformation von SPD und Labour Party*. Wiesbaden: VS Verlag für Sozialwissenschaften.
Navarro, Vincent. 2007. *Neoliberalism, Globalization and Inequalities: Consequences for Health and Quality of Life*. Amityville, NY: Baywood.
Negri, Antonio. 1999. *Insurgencies: Constituent Power and the Modern State* (Boscagli, Muarizia, trans.). Minneapolis: University of Minnesota Press.
Neugebauer, Gero. 2007. *Politische Milieus in Deutschland: Die Studie der Friedrich-Ebert-Stiftung*. Berlin: Dietz Verlag.

Neumann, Franz. L. 1942. *Behemoth: The Structure and Practice of National Socialism*. London: Victor Gollancz.

Newell, Peter, and Paterson, Matthew. 1998. 'A climate for business: global warming, the state and capital'. *Review of International Political Economy* 5 (4), 679–703.

Nitzan, Jonathan, and Bichler, Shinshon. 2009. *Capital as Power: A Study of Order and Creorder*. London: Routledge.

Nixon, Stephanie, Upshur, Ross E., Robertson, Ann, Benatar, Solomon R., Thompson, Alison, and Daar, Abdallah S. 2008. 'Public health ethics'. In Bailey, Tracey M., Caulfield, Timothy, and Ries, Nola M. (eds.), *Public Health and Law Policy in Canada*, 2nd edn. Markham, Ontario: LexisNexis, 37–59.

Nölke, Andreas, and Perry, James. 2007. 'The power of transnational private governance: financialization and the IASB'. *Business and Politics* 9 (3), article 4; www.bepress.com/bap/vol9/iss3/art4.

Nordmann, Jürgen. 2005. *Der lange Marsch zum Neoliberalismus*. Hamburg: VSA.

Nussbaum, Martha C. 2000. *Women and Human Development: The Capabilities Approach*. Cambridge University Press.

OECD. 2009. *Private Sector Participation in Water Infrastructure: OECD Checklist for Public Action*. Paris: OECD; available at www.oecd.org/dataoecd/36/13/42362893.pdf (accessed 30 June 2010).

Olivera, O., and Lewis, T. 2004. *Cochabamba! Water War in Bolivia*. Cambridge, MA: South End Press.

Oreskes, Naomi, and Conway, Erik M. 2010. *Merchants of Doubt: How a Handful of Scientists Obscured the Truth on Issues from Tobacco Smoke to Global Warming*. New York: Bloomsbury.

Orford, Anne. 2003. *Reading Humanitarian Intervention: Human Rights and the Use of Force in International Law*. Cambridge University Press.

Orr, David. 2009. *Down to the Wire: Confronting Climate Collapse*. New York: Oxford University Press.

Ougaard, Morten. 2006. 'Instituting the power to do good?' In May, Christopher (ed.), *Global Corporate Power: International Political Economy Yearbook 15*. Boulder, CO: Lynne Rienner, 227–48.

Pachauri, Rajendra K. 2010. 'Despite attacks from critics, climate science will prevail'. Yale Environment 360, http://e360.yale.edu/feature/despite_attacks_from_criticsclimate_science_will_prevail/2264 (accessed 22 April 2010).

Panitch, Leo, Albo, Greg, and Chibber, Vivek (eds.). 2011. *The Crisis This Time: Socialist Register 2011*. London: Merlin Press.

Panitch, Leo, and Konings, Martijn (eds.). 2008. *American Empire and the Political Economy of Global Finance*. Basingstoke: Palgrave Macmillan.

Pasha, Mustapha Kamal. 1997. 'Ibn Khaldun and world order'. In Gill, Stephen, and Mittelman, James (eds.), *Innovation and Transformation in International Studies*. Cambridge University Press, 56–74.

    2009. 'Global exception and Islamic exceptionalism'. *International Politics* 46 (5), 527–49.

2010. 'In the shadows of globalization: civilizational crisis, the "global modern" and "Islamic nihilism"'. *Globalizations* 7 (1/2), 167–79.

Patel, Raj. 2008. *Stuffed and Starved: From Farm to Fork, the Hidden Battle for the World Food System*. London: Portobello Books.

Patomäki, Heikki, and Teivainen, Teivo. 2004. *A Possible World: Democratic Transformation of Global Institutions*. London: Zed Books.

2007. 'Conclusion: beyond the political party/civil society dichotomy'. In Sehm-Patomäki, Katarina, and Ulvila, Marko (eds.), *Democratic Politics Globally: Elements for a Dialogue on Global Political Party Formations*. London: Zed Books, 151–8.

Perelman, Michael. 2000. *The Invention of Capitalism: Classical Political Economy and the Secret History of Primitive Accumulation*. Durham, NC: Duke University Press.

Perkins, John. 2004. *Confessions of an Economic Hit Man*. New York: Penguin Books.

Pfeiffer, Dale Allen. 2006. *Eating Fossil Fuels: Oil, Food and the Coming Crisis in Agriculture*. Gabriola Island, British Columbia: New Society.

Pijl, K. van der. 1984. *The Making of an Atlantic Ruling Class*. London: Verso Books.

1998. *Transnational Classes and International Relations*. London: Routledge.

Pipes, Daniel. 1983. *In the Path of God: Islam and Political Power*. New York: Basic Books.

Plender, John. 2011. 'Bad habits of credit bubble make comeback'. *Financial Times*, 22 February.

Pogge, Thomas. 2002. *World Poverty and Human Rights*. Cambridge: Polity Press.

Polanyi, Karl. 1944. *The Great Transformation: The Political and Economic Origins of Our Time*. Boston: Beacon Press.

1957. *The Great Transformation: The Political and Economic Origins of Our Time*, 2nd edn. Boston: Beacon Press.

Porter, Tony. 1999. 'Hegemony and the private governance of international industries'. In Cutler, A. Claire, Haufler, Virginia, and Porter, Tony (eds.), *Private Authority and International Affairs*. Albany: State University of New York Press, 257–82.

2005. *Globalization and Finance*. Cambridge: Polity Press.

Posner, Richard A. 2010. *The Crisis of Capitalist Democracy*. Cambridge, MA: Harvard University Press.

Poulantzas, Nicos. 2002. *Staatstheorie: Politischer Überbau, Ideologie, autoritärer Etatismus*. Hamburg: VSA.

Pow, Choon-Piew. 2009. 'Neoliberalism and the aestheticization of new middle-class landscapes'. *Antipode* **41** (2), 371–90.

Powers, Madison, and Faden, Ruth. 2006. *Social Justice: The Moral Foundations of Public Health and Health Policy*. New York: Oxford University Press.

Prashad, Vijay. 2007. *The Darker Nations: A Biography of the Short-Lived Third World*. New Delhi: Leftword Books.

Quack, Sigrid. 2007. 'Legal professions and transnational law-making: a case of distributed agency'. *Organization* **14** (5), 643–66.

2010. 'Law, expertise and legitimacy in transnational economic governance: an introduction'. *Socio-Economic Review* **8** (1), 3–16.

Rawls, John. 1996. *A Theory of Justice*. Cambridge, MA: Belknap Press.

2001. *The Law of Peoples, with 'The Idea of Public Reason Revisited'*. Cambridge, MA: Harvard University Press.

2005. *Political Liberalism*. New York: Columbia University Press.

Rehmann, Jan. 2008. *Einführung in die Ideologietheorie*. Hamburg: Argument.

REN21. 2009. *Renewables Global Status Report: 2009 Update*. Paris: REN21.

Rich, Frank. 2010. 'It's a bird, it's a plane, it's Obama!' *New York Times*, 4 April.

Richardson, James. 2001. *Contending Liberalisms in World Politics: Ideology and Power*. Boulder, CO: Lynne Reinner.

Rist, Gilbert. 1997. *The History of Development: From Western Origins to Global Faith*. London: Zed Books.

Robinson, William I. 2004. *A Theory of Global Capitalism: Production, Class, and State in a Transnational World*. Baltimore: Johns Hopkins University Press.

Roht-Ariazza, Naomi. 1995. 'Shifting the point of regulation: the International Organization for Standardization and global lawmaking on trade and the environment'. *Ecology Law Quarterly* **22** (3), 479–539.

Roth, Daniel. 2010. 'Radical pragmatist: energy secretary Steven Chu wants to change the way people think about global warming'. *Wired* **18** (5), 104–10.

Rowden, Rick. 2009. *The Deadly Ideas of Neoliberalism: How the IMF Has Undermined Public Health and the Fight against AIDS*. London: Zed Books.

Roy, Olivier. 2004. *Globalized Islam: The Search for a New Ummah*. New York: Columbia University Press.

Royal Danish Ministry for Foreign Affairs. 2000. *Building a Global Community: Globalization and the Common Good*. Copenhagen: Royal Danish Ministry for Foreign Affairs.

Ruggie, John. 1982. 'International regimes, transactions, and change: embedded liberalism in the postwar economic order'. *International Organization* **36** (2), 379–415.

Runge, C. Ford, and Senauer, Benjamin. 2007. 'How biofuels could starve the poor'. *Foreign Affairs* **86** (3), 41–54.

Saad-Filho, Alfredo, and Johnston, Deborah (eds.). 2005. *Neoliberalism: A Critical Reader*. London: Pluto Press.

Said, Edward W. 1978. *Orientalism*. New York: Vintage Books.

Salter, Liora. 1999. 'The standards regimes for communication and information technologies'. In Cutler, A. Claire, Haufler, Virginia, and Porter, Tony (eds.), *Private Authority and International Affairs*. Albany: State University of New York Press, 97–128.

Sandbrook, Richard. 2000. 'Globalization and the limits of neoliberal development doctrine'. *Third World Quarterly* **21** (6), 1071–80.

Santos, Boaventura de Sousa. 2002. *Toward a New Legal Common Sense: Law, Globalization, and Emancipation*, 2nd edn. London: Butterworths.

2005. 'The World Social Forum: towards a counter-hegemonic globalization'.
In Polet, François, and CETRI [Centre Tricontinental] (eds.), *Globalizing Resistance: The State of Struggle*. London: Pluto Press, 165–87.

Sathe, S. P. 2001. *Judicial Activism in India*. New Delhi: Oxford University Press.

Sayeed, Khalid B. 1994. *Western Dominance and Political Islam: Challenge and Response*. Albany: State University of New York Press.

Schaper, Marcus. 2007. 'Leveraging green power: environmental rules for project finance'. *Business and Politics* **9** (1), article 3; www.bepress.com/bap/vol9/iss3/art3 (accessed 21 June 2011).

Scharlemann, Jörn P. W., and Laurance, William F. 2008. 'How green are biofuels?' *Science* **319** (January), 43–4.

Scharpf, Fritz. 1999. *Governing in Europe: Effective and Democratic?* Oxford University Press.

2009. 'Legitimacy in the multilevel European polity', Working Paper no. 09/01. Max Planck Institute for the Study of Societies, Cologne.

Schelsky, Helmut. 1965. 'Die Bedeutung des Schichtungsbegriffs für die Analyse der gegenwärtigen deutschen Gesellschaft'. In Schelsky, Helmut, *Auf der Suche nach der Wirklichkeit*. Düsseldorf: Eugen Diederichs, 331–6.

Schneiderman, David. 2006. 'Transnational legality and the immobilization of local agency'. *Annual Review of Law and Social Science* **2**, 387–408.

2008. *Constitutionalizing Economic Globalization: Investment Rules and Democracy's Promise*. Cambridge University Press.

2010. 'Movement, countermovement, and investment rules'. Paper presented at the annual meeting of the Law and Society Association, Chicago, 27 May.

Schui, Herbert. 2006, 'Rechtsextremismus und totaler Markt: Auf der Suche nach gesellschaftlicher Klebmasse für den entfesselten Kapitalismus'. In Bathke, Peter, and Spindler, Susanne (eds.), *Neoliberalismus und Rechtsextremismus in Europa*. Berlin: Dietz Verlag, 48–59.

Seabrook, Jeremy. 2010. 'The spectre of laissez-faire stalks Britain'. *Guardian*, 20 June.

Segerfeldt, F. 2005. *Water for Sale: How Businesses and the Market Can Resolve the World's Water Crisis*. Washington, DC: Cato Institute.

Sell, Susan. 2003. *Private Power, Public Law: The Globalization of Intellectual Property Law*. Cambridge University Press.

Shaffer, Gregory. 2004. 'Recognizing public goods in WTO dispute settlement: who participates? Who decides? The case of TRIPS and pharmaceutical protection'. *Journal of International Economic Law* **7** (2), 459–82.

2008. 'A structural theory of WTO dispute settlement: why institutional choice lies at the center of the GMO case'. *Journal of International Law and Politics* **41** (1), 1–101.

Shiller, R. 2008. *The Subprime Solution: How Today's Global Financial Crisis Happened, and What to Do about It*. Princeton University Press.

Shultz, J. 2009. 'The Cochabamba water revolt and its aftermath'. In Shultz, J., and Draper, M. C. (eds.), *Dignity and Defiance: Stories from Bolivia's Challenge to Globalization*. Berkeley: University of California Press, 9–44.

Sidel, Victor. 1995. 'The international arms trade and its impact on health'. *British Medical Journal* **311**, 1677–80.

Silver, Beverly. 2003. *Forces of Labour: Workers' Movements and Globalization since 1870*. Cambridge University Press.

Sinclair, Timothy. 2004. *The New Masters of Capital: American Bond Rating Agencies and the Global Economy*. Ithaca, NY: Cornell University Press.

Singer, Peter A. 2002. *One World: The Ethics of Globalization*. New Haven, CT: Yale University Press.

Sklair, Leslie. 2000. *The Transnational Capitalist Class*. Oxford: Blackwell.

Slaughter, Anne-Marie. 2004. 'Disaggregated sovereignty: towards the public accountability of global governance networks'. *Government and Opposition* **39** (2), 159–90.

Smil, Vaclav. 1994. *Energy in World History*. Boulder, CO: Westview Press.
    2007. 'The two prime movers of globalization: history and the impact of diesel engines and gas turbines'. *Journal of Global History* **2** (3), 373–94.

Smith, Adam. 1998 [1776]. *Wealth of Nations*. Oxford University Press.

Smythe, Elizabeth. 2003. 'Just say no! The negotiation of investment rules at the WTO'. *International Journal of Political Economy* **33** (4), 60–83.

Snitow, Alan, Kaifman, Deborah, and Fox, Michael (eds.). 2007. *Thirst: Fighting the Corporate Theft of Our Water*. San Francisco: Jossey-Bass.

Solty, Ingar. 2009. 'Kämpfe um Hegemonie: Scheitert die Gesundheitsreform in den USA?' *Luxemburg* 2/2009, 27–38.

Spanogle, John A. 1991. 'The arrival of private law'. *George Washington Journal of International Law and Economics* **25** (2), 477–522.

Spivak, Gayatri. 2003. *Death of a Discipline*. New York: Columbia University Press.

Steans, Jill, and Pettiford, Lloyd. 2005. *International Relations: Perspectives and Themes*, 2nd edn. Harlow, UK: Pearson.

Stein, Herbert. 1994. 'Adam Smith did not wear an Adam Smith necktie'. *Wall Street Journal*, 6 April.

Steinert, Heinz. 2010. 'Das Prekariat: Begriffspolitik und Klassenpolitik'. In Thien, Hans-Günter (ed.), *Klassen im Postfordismus*. Münster: Dampfboot, 174–201.

Steinhardt, Ralph G. 1991. 'The privatization of public international law'. *George Washington Journal of International Law and Economics* **25** (2), 523–53.

Stern, Nicholas. 2007. *The Economics of Climate Change: The Stern Review*. Cambridge University Press.

Stiglitz, Joseph. 2010. *Freefall: America, Free Markets, and the Sinking of the World Economy*. New York: W. W. Norton.

Streeck, Wolfgang, and Schmitter, Philippe (eds.). 1985. *Private Interest Government: Beyond Market and State*. London: Sage.

Stuckler, David, and McKee, Martin. 2008. 'Five metaphors for global health'. *The Lancet* **372**, 95–7.

Sugarman, David. 2002. 'From unimaginable to possible: Spain, Pinochet and the judicialization of power'. *Journal of Spanish Cultural Studies* **3** (1), 107–24.

Sullivan, Sian. 2009. 'Green capitalism, and the cultural poverty of constructing nature as service provider'. *Radical Anthropology* **3** 2009/10, 18–27.

Sussman, Gerald, and Galizio, Lawrence. 2003. 'The global reproduction of American politics'. *Political Communication* **20** (3), 309–28.

Teeple, Gary. 2000. *Globalization and the Decline of Social Reform: Into the Twenty-First Century.* Aurora, Ontario: Garamond Press.

Teivainen, Teivo. 2002. *Enter Economism, Exit Politics: Experts, Economic Policy and the Damage to Democracy.* London: Zed Books.

Teubner, Guenther. 2002. 'Breaking frames: economic globalization and the emergence of *lex mercatoria*'. *European Journal of Social Theory* **5** (2), 199–217.

Tibi, Bassam. 1998. *The Challenge of Fundamentalism: Political Islam and the New World Disorder.* Berkeley: University of California Press.

Trubek, David M., Dezalay, Yves, Buchanan, Ruth, and Davis, John R. 1994. 'Global restructuring and the law: studies in the internationalization of the legal fields and transnational arenas'. *Case Western Law Review* **44** (2), 407–98.

Tucker, Robert C. (ed.). 1978. *The Marx–Engels Reader.* New York: W. W. Norton.

Turk, Elisabeth, and Krajewski, Markus. 2003. 'The right to water and trade in services: assessing the impact of GATS negotiations on water regulations'. Paper presented at the CAT+E conference, Berlin, 31 October.

UN. 1992. 'Rio Declaration on Environment and Development'. UN, New York; available at www.un.org/documents/ga/conf151/aconf15126-1annex1.htm.

2011. *Report of the Working Group on the Universal Periodic Review: United States of America.* New York: UN; available at http://daccess-dds-ny.un.org/doc/UNDOC/GEN/G11/100/69/PDF/G1110069.pdf?OpenElement (accessed 28 April 2011).

UN-Habitat. 2003. *The Challenge of Slums: Global Report on Human Settlements 2003.* London: Earthscan.

2010. Press kit for *State of the World's Cities 2010/2011: Bridging the Urban Divide.* London: Earthscan; available at www.unhabitat.org/documents/SOWC10/R4.pdf (accessed 13 June 2010).

UNCTAD. 2009. *World Investment Report: Transnational Corporations, Agricultural Production and Development.* Geneva: UNCTAD; available at unctad.org/en/docs/wir2009_en.pdf (accessed 18 February 2011).

UNDP. 2000. *World Energy Assessment: Energy and the Challenge of Sustainability.* New York: UNDP; available at www.undp.org/energy/activities/wea/drafts-frame.html.

2007. *Human Development Report 2007/2008: Fighting Climate Change: Human Solidarity in a Divided World.* Basingstoke: Palgrave Macmillan.

2009. *Human Development Report 2009: Overcoming Barriers: Human Barriers and Development.* Basingstoke: Palgrave Macmillan.

UNEP. 1972. 'Declaration of the United Nations Conference on the Human Environment'. UNEP, Nairobi; available at www.unep.org/Documents.Multilingual/Default.asp?DocumentID=97&ArticleID=1503&l=en.

2009. *The Environmental Food Crisis: The Environment's Role in Averting Future Food Crises.* Birkeland, Norway: Birkeland Trykkeri.

UNHCHR. 2002. *Economic, Social and Cultural Rights: Liberalization of Trade in Services and Human Rights*, E/CN.4/Sub.2/2002/9. Geneva: UNHCHR; available at www.unhchr.ch/Huridocda/Huridoca.nsf/0/32f8a4ad6cc5f9b9c1256c05002a87f8/$FILE/G0214114.pdf.

UNWFP. 2009. 'What is hunger?' UNWFP, Rome; www.wfp.org/hunger/what-is (accessed 14 November 2009).

Van Harten, Gus. 2005. 'Private authority and transnational governance: the contours of the international system of investment protection'. *Review of International Political Economy* **12** (4), 600–23.

Vandenhole, Wouter. 2002. 'Human rights law, development and social action litigation in India'. *Asia-Pacific Journal on Human Rights and the Law* **3** (2), 136–210.

Venkatraman, Amritha. 2007. 'Religious basis for Islamic terrorism: the Quran and its interpretations'. *Studies in Conflict and Terrorism* **30** (3), 229–48.

Vidal, John. 2006. 'Sweden plans to be world's first oil-free economy'. *Guardian*, 8 February.

2009. 'Health risks of shipping pollution have been underestimated'. *Guardian*, 9 April.

2010. 'UN report: world's biggest cities merging into "mega-regions"'. *Guardian*, 23 March.

Vogel, Berthold. 2009. 'Das Prekariat: eine neue soziale Lage?' In Castel, Robert, and Dörre, Klaus (eds.), *Prekarität, Abstieg, Ausgrenzung: Die soziale Frage am Beginn des 21. Jahrhunderts*. Frankfurt: Campus, 197–208.

Voll, John. 1982. *Islam: Continuity and Change in the Modern World*. Boulder, CO: Westview Press.

Vulliamy, Ed. 2005. 'Blair's relationships with Berlusconi, Bush and Murdoch have defined his premiership. Now Merkel is to join the trio'. *Guardian*, 27 October.

Wade, Robert, and Veneroso, Frank. 1998. 'The gathering world slump and the battle over capital controls'. *New Left Review* **231** (5), 13–42.

Wai, Robert. 2001. 'Transnational liftoff and juridical touchdown: the regulatory function of private international law in an era of globalization'. *Columbia Journal of Transnational Law* **40** (2), 209–74.

Wallerstein, Immanuel. 1999. *The End of the World as We Know It: Social Science for the Twenty-First Century*. Minneapolis: University of Minnesota Press.

Wallis, Victor. 2009. 'Beyond green capitalism'. *Monthly Review* **61** (9), 32–48.

Walpen, Bernhard. 2005. *Die offenen Feinde und ihre Gesellschaft*. Hamburg: VSA.

Walter, Franz. 2006. *Die ziellose Republik: Gezeitenwechsel in Gesellschaft und Politik*. Cologne: Kiepenheuer and Witsch.

Waltz, Kenneth. 1979. *Theory of International Politics*. New York: McGraw-Hill.

Warf, Barney. 2003. 'Mergers and acquisitions in the telecommunications industry'. *Growth and Change* **34** (3), 321–44.

Weigt, Jill. 2006. 'Compromises to carework: the social organization of mothers' experiences in the low-wage labor market after welfare reform'. *Social Problems* **53** (3), 332–51.

Weingast, Barry. 1995. 'The economic role of political institutions: market-preserving federalism and economic development'. *Journal of Law, Economics, and Organization* **11** (1), 1–31.

Weisbrot, Mark. 2010. 'Recovery takes political courage'. *Guardian*, 11 June.

Whitaker, Francisco. 2002a. 'O FSM como método de ação política'. In Loureiro, Isabel Maria, Cevasco, Maria Luisa, and Leite, José Corrêa (eds.), *O Espírito de Porto Alegre*. São Paulo: Paz e Terra, 237–44.

  2002b. 'Fórum Social Mundial: origins e objetivos', www. forumsocialmundial.org.br/por/qorigen.asp (accessed 12 April 2010).

  2003. 'O que o Fórum Social Mundial traz de novo como modo de atuação política?' *Democracia Viva* **14** (January), 20–4.

White House. 2010. 'Energy and environment', policy statement, www.whitehouse.gov/issues/energy-and-environment (accessed 23 June 2010).

Whitehorn, Will, and Leggett, Jeremy. 2009. 'Do not discount the threat of peak oil'. *Financial Times*, 9 August.

WHO. 2008. *Social Determinants of Health*. Geneva: WHO; available at www. who.int/social_determinants/en (accessed 28 April 2009).

WHO and UNICEF. 2010. *Progress on Sanitation and Drinking-Water: 2010 Update*. Geneva: WHO.

Wilkinson, John. 2009. 'The globalization of agribusiness and developing world food systems'. *Monthly Review* **61** (4), 38–50; www.monthlyreview. org/090907wilkinson.php (accessed 18 February 2011).

Williams, J. W. 2006. 'Private legal orders: professional markets and the commodification of financial governance'. *Social Legal Studies* **15** (2), 209–35.

  2008. 'Conceptualizing business corporations as norm-entrepreneurs'. Draft on file with A. Claire Cutler.

Wolf, Klaus Dieter. 2006. 'Private actors and the legitimacy of governance beyond the state: conceptual outlines and empirical explorations'. In Benz, Arthur, and Papadopoulos, Yannis (eds.), *Governance and Democracy: Comparing National, European and International Experiences*. New York: Routledge, 200–27.

Wolf, Klaus Dieter, Deitelhoff, Nicole, and Engert, Stefan. 2007. 'Corporate security responsibility: towards a conceptual framework for a comparative research agenda'. *Cooperation and Conflict* **42** (3), 294–319.

Wolf, Martin. 2009. *Fixing Global Finance: How to Curb Financial Crises in the 21st Century*. New Haven, CT: Yale University Press.

Wolff, Jonathan. 2011. 'The human right to health'. In Benatar, Solomon R., and Brock, Gillian (eds.), *Global Health and Global Health Ethics*. Cambridge University Press, 108–18.

Wolff, Richard D. 2009. 'Economic crisis from a socialist perspective'. *Socialism and Democracy* **23** (2), 3–20.

Wood, Ellen Meiksins. 1998. *The Retreat from Class*. London: Verso Books.
2002. *The Origin of Capitalism: A Longer View*. London: Verso Books.

Worldwatch Institute. 2004. *State of the World 2004: Special Focus: The Consumer Society*. New York: W. W. Norton; available at www.worldwatch.org (accessed 23 June 2010).

Wright, Erik Olin. 1978. *Class, Crisis, and the State*. London: New Left Books.
1985. *Classes*. London: Verso Books.

WWC. 2009. *Global Water Framework: Outcomes of the 5th World Water Forum*. Marseilles: WWC.

Young, Robert. 2001. *Postcolonialism: An Introduction*. Oxford University Press.

Žižek, Slavoj. 2009. *First as Tragedy, Then as Farce*. London: Verso Books.

Index

regulation
  financial, 4
  liberal, 25
Renewable Energy Policy Network, 86
resistance, 2, 15, 137, 145, 149, 151, 163,
    182, 192, 203, 241, 252
  movements, 115
responsibility to protect, 93
Rich, Frank, 54
Richardson, James, 224
rightlessness, 163, 167, 173
Rio de Janeiro, Brazil, 116
Rio Declaration on Environment and
    Development, 100, 121
Rio 'Earth Summit', 95, 110
risk, 31, 57, 61
  business, 58
  ecological, 99
  management, 59, 61, 62, 65, 66
risk society, 62
Risorgimento, 42
'road to serfdom', 137
Roberts, Adrienne, 233
Robinson, Mary, 245
Robinson, William, 49
rule of law, 163, 175
Russia, 53, 94
  climate change, 93
  Strategic Arms Reduction Treaty, 96
Rwanda, 162
RWE-AG, 113

scenario planning, 13
Schneiderman, David, 60
Seattle, Washington, 181, 185, 220, 269
securitization, 49
security
  international, 59
  privatized, 50
Shell, 13
Shinawatra, Thaksin, 53
Short, Nicola, 26, 28, 176, 232
shura, 157
Sierra Leone, 162
Single European Act, 229
Siyassat Nameh, 9
Sklair, Leslie, 13
Slaughter, Anne-Marie, 12
slavery, 139
Smith, Adam, 225
social change
  progressive, 40
social democracy, 205
social forces, 4
  dominant, 13, 233

progressive, 216, 217, 222, 227, 228,
    229, 230, 232, 235, 250
  ruling, 28
  subaltern, 6, 19, 34, 36, 46, 158, 233
social justice, 5, 33, 37, 129, 133, 137, 140,
    160, 175, 234
social movements, 182, 184, 186
  democratization of, 185
  transnational
    See social forces
social reproduction, ix, 18, 25, 34, 35, 36,
    50, 73, 75, 76, 77, 78, 79, 80, 85, 87,
    128, 202, 203, 220, 234, 239, 248,
    250, 254
  crisis of, 1, 7
  definition of, 75
  and energy, 73, 74, 75
  general crisis of, 74, 85
  post-carbon, 83, 88
  pre-fossil-fuel, 76, 81
  primitive, 250
social security, 226
social welfare
  in China, 7
socialism, 15, 136, 214
Socialist Register, 12
solidarity, 5, 33, 37, 97, 127, 133, 135,
    136, 137, 138, 139, 142, 186, 188,
    207, 208, 213, 251
Solty, Ingar, 41, 44, 46, 54
Sorel, Georges, 42
Sousa de Santos, Boaventura, 191
South Africa, 34, 94, 114, 115, 173
  apartheid, 138
  constitution, 119, 169
  Treatment Action Campaign, 132
South America, 114
  left turn, 194
Spain, 10, 213
Spivak, Gayatri, 173
Sri Lanka, 50
Stalinism, 235
staphylococcus, 128
state of emergency, 235
state of exception, 23, 27
Stiglitz, Joseph, 4
'Stockholm Declaration', 99, 119, 121
Stockholm Water Symposium, 117
Strategic Arms Reduction Treaty
  negotiations, 96
Strauss-Kahn, Dominique, 241
Structural Adjustment Programs, 48, 142
sub-Saharan Africa, 136
suburbanization, 82
Suez, 113, 114